TAKING SIDES
against ethnic cleansing in Bosnia

The story of the Workers Aid for Bosnia convoys

Cover Photo: Part of the first Workers Aid convoy to
reach Tuzla, on the outward journey, March, 1994

Published by Workers Aid for Bosnia
35, Hilton Road, Leeds LS8 4HA
Tel/Fax 44 113 2622705
e.mail: JohnGDav@aol.com

Design and Typeset by Graphic Works 01274 308424

Printed by Trade Union Printing Services, Newcastle upon Tyne

ISBN: 0-9531826-0-6

Contents

MAPS

Editors' note

This book is not an 'official' history of Workers Aid for Bosnia. Like the Workers Aid campaign itself, it is the work of many people. Our campaign drew together people with different views and this is reflected in the contributions to this book. But the selection and editing of this varied material reflects the outlook of the three editors. Other members of Workers Aid might well have produced a very different book.

We have included additional material concerning both the Whitehall 24-hour picket and the continuing activities of the Bosnia Solidarity Campaign since many Workers Aid members were involved in that work and there was overlap. There were, of course, many others, not members of Workers Aid, who made major contributions to Bosnia Solidarity Campaign.

It should also be said that for every person mentioned in the book, there are ten who have been missed out. The solidarity campaign with Bosnia involved many hundreds of people without whose contribution none of our work would have been possible. The book focuses on our work with the Bosnian mining town of Tuzla. The resistance to ethnic division, however, was to be found across all of Bosnia, not just in Tuzla.

Besides those pieces which are credited within the book, we would like to thank Charlie Pottins, Ed Vulliamy and Attila Hoare for permission to use their written work. Individual photographs are not credited, but we would like to thank the following photographers for work which appears in the book: Naseem Akhtar, Lisa Beckmann, Alan Clark, John Davies, Seth Drysdale, Rex Dunn, Phil Edwards, John Enright, Sean Hefferan, Paul Henderson, Ken Hennigan, Hilary Horrocks, Faruk Ibrahimovic, Rhian Jenkins, Bozena Langley, Dave Lawrence, Paul Maddox, Paddy McCloy, Dave McKenzie, Pete Morrissey, Tony Myers, Bob Myers, Maggie Nichol, Geoff Pilling, Charlie Pottins, Billy Pye, Christine Simm, Ian Simpson, Dan Tuffs, Jackie Vance and Kim Ward.

We would also like to thank Faruk Ibrahimovic and Azra and Zelko Marosevic for their help with translation, Peter Fryer, Steve Drury and Hilary Horrocks for their proofreading and general advice, Becky Husband, Norman Harding and Davie Eyre for typing and Dave Temple at TUPS. All the uncredited newspaper articles are by Workers Aid member Charlie Pottins, writing in a weekly newspaper, Workers Press. Finally, a big thankyou to Graham Tansley for his patience with the design of the book.

Prices are given in Deutschmarks. For a quick conversion, £1 = 2 1/2 DM.

Geoff Robinson
Bob Myers
John Davies

Terminology and abbreviations

Throughout the war in Bosnia the media in Britain reported it as a civil war, an ethnic conflict. This was untrue and led to many distortions. Throughout this book the following terms are used:

Bosnian – all people who saw themselves first and foremost as Bosnian and only secondarily, if at all, as Serb, Croat or Muslim.

Bosnian Government – the multi-cultural government that throughout the war stood by the 1992 referendum for an undivided, independent country with equal rights for all citizens. It should properly be called the government of Bosnia and Herzegovina, the full name of the country, but for reasons of space it is here shortened to Bosnia. This does not imply support for the Croatian regime's attempts to annex Herzegovina from Bosnia. Bosnia-Herzegovina is often shortened to BiH.

Bosnian Army (BiH Army) – the multi-cultural army comprising Muslims, Serbs, Croats, Jews and others, created by Bosnians to defend themselves following the Serb nationalist attack on Bosnia.

JNA – the Yugoslav People's Army

Bosnian Serb – Bosnian people from Orthodox Christian background. They fought on both sides of the war.

Republika Srpska – the state, occupying about 50 per cent of Bosnia's territory, set up by Serb nationalists after a campaign of 'ethnic cleansing'.

Serbian Nationalists – Serbs, from Serbia and Bosnia and elsewhere who fought for an ethnically pure, Greater Serbia through the annexation of territory in Bosnia, Croatia, Kosova etc.

Chetniks – a term for Serbian nationalists dating from World War II.

Croat Nationalists – Croats supporting the Croatian regime's attempt to seize part of Bosnia.

Herceg-Bosna – the state set up by Croat nationalists in Herzegovina after a campaign of 'ethnic cleansing'.

Ustashe – World War II term for Croatian nationalists.

HVO, Hrvatsko Vijece Obrane – the military force established among some Bosnian Croats. The HVO was influenced by Croatian nationalism but the local HVO forces varied. There were those, like the Croat villages in the Tuzla region, who fought alongside the Bosnian army throughout the war, and there were those in Herzegovina – under Zagreb control – who fought against Bosnia to establish their own small Croat state, Herceg-Bosna.

Slobodan Milosevic – the President of Serbia, who encouraged Serb nationalism; architect for a Greater Serbia.

Radovan Karadzic – the President of Republika Srpska and instigator of 'ethnic cleansing' in Bosnia.

Ratko Mladic – a former officer in the JNA who became the leader of the Serb nationalist army. Responsible for organising mass murder.

Introduction

by Bob Myers

Early on a June morning in 1993 I set off to attend a meeting called to discuss the war in Bosnia. I was going with a certain reluctance. For several years I had followed the newspaper version of events from Yugoslavia. First the wrangling of nationalist politicians, the suppression of the Albanian population in Kosova, the invasions of Slovenia and Croatia and the outbreak of full-scale violence. Then the first signs of the nightmare to come: the Croatian town of Vukovar, whose inhabitants had voted against all the nationalist politicians, was pounded by Serbian artillery and everyone driven from their homes or killed.

Fleeing Vukovar

Ethnic cleansing of Muslims

Finally came the invasion of Bosnia-Herzegovina. While leaders of France, Britain and the US prepared to commemorate D Day and victory over the Nazis, in Yugoslavia fascist gangs were encircling village after village, and driving out their 'ethnic undesirables'. A couple of journalists revealed the existence of concentration camps.

My reluctance to go to the meeting in London was not indifference to events in Bosnia. It was the opposite – the paralysing feeling of powerlessness to do anything about inhumanity on such a scale. In the past I had joined demonstrations against the war in Vietnam, against apartheid in South Africa, against the persecution of the Palestinians. But now only silence greeted the news from Bosnia. The pictures of traumatised women and children pushed on to trucks and driven from their homes, the gaunt faces of men staring out from behind barbed wire, provoked no protests, no organised outrage. Just millions of people, like myself, who watched with horror. I talked with an old friend, another lifelong socialist, and we shook our heads in despair. What could be done except weep and hope that somehow people would learn a lesson from this orgy of killing?

But some people had tried to do something. In London a handful of people had held protests outside the old Yugoslav Embassy. They then called a demonstration to be followed next day by the meeting I was now setting out for. Thirty people had turned up for the demonstration and fifteen of them had gone home when they saw how few people there were. The other fifteen had marched through the streets.

About sixty people came to the meeting and for the first time I heard Bosnian people, mostly refugees, talking about the war. One Bosnian woman in particular started to make me think. She explained that from 1984-85, when the British miners had been on strike, the Tuzla miners, themselves desperately poor, had given a day's pay every month for their comrades in Britain. She described the way they had followed the strike, hoping for a victory over Margaret Thatcher. Now Tuzla was cut-off, its multi-cultural population being driven into starvation by the combined forces of Serbian and Croatian ethnic cleansers, assisted by the 'great powers' and the UN, who supported the division of Bosnia. This report really struck me, as I was involved at that time in the campaign to stop the closure of Parkside Colliery, the last mine in the Lancashire coalfield.

Another speaker, a trade unionist from Fords in Dagenham, added to the report. He read out a letter from a friend of his in Serbia, an opponent of the nationalist regime there. This letter also spoke about Tuzla, about its multi-ethnic mining community that had formed armed brigades to try to stop the town falling to the ethnic cleansers. The letter was addressed to British trade unionists and working people. It asked them to remember the solidarity shown by the Tuzla miners in 1985. Now Tuzla miners and their families were starving. Couldn't the British miners, or other workers, try to take food to Tuzla? Without solidarity the Bosnian miners' resistance to 'ethnic cleansing' would surely collapse.

The meeting voted to set up an organisation called Workers Aid for Bosnia . We agreed a set of founding principles and decided that our first action would be to try to take food to the Tuzla miners. We all left the meeting without a clue how this was going to be done, without any money, vehicles, drivers or food – but we were determined to try to make it happen. We were determined to get to Tuzla.

The following Saturday members of the Miners' Support Group I was in set up our regular campaign table in the shopping precinct in Leigh, an old mining town on the outskirts of Manchester. This time, instead of collecting for the local Parkside campaign, we put up a poster saying, 'Don't let Bosnian miners starve'. We had people queuing up to put money in our collecting tins. We collected about £30 that morning – double what we usually collected. Clearly we were not the only people to care about events in Bosnia. Looking back, I laugh at our surprise at this collection. Within a few days, when our campaign for the Tuzla convoy really got going, we would be collecting hundreds of pounds a day. But that Saturday that £30 made me feel we could do it. We would get to Tuzla.

This book is a record of the next four years' work. It is not a full picture of the break-up of Yugoslavia or the war, nor does it try to detail the political intrigues and disgusting diplomacy of the 'great powers'. What it tries to do is to tell the story of some of the people outside Bosnia who could not stand by and do nothing as multi-cultural society was destroyed. It tries to tell how we 'took sides'.

Workers Aid soon became an international campaign. This account is based mainly on the work in Britain. But we could not have done what we did without collaboration with friends in many countries, especially Spain, and above all in Bosnia itself. If people there had not stood up against this new rise of fascistic violence, against the barbaric notion of ethnically pure states, then we would all be facing a new millennium with a bleak message that nothing can be done to stop Europe descending into ethnic ghettos.

Today Bosnia is divided. Sixty thousand NATO troops stand guard over the lines of division. The architects of 'ethnic cleansing' and their western backers are counting up their spoils of war. For the moment they seem to have won. But the resistance is still alive. People suffered four years of hell because they refused to give up the vision of a society where people could live together. And they are still there, still resisting. We have played a small part in supporting this resistance.

Original Aims of Workers Aid for Bosnia

WORKERS AID FOR BOSNIA seeks to mobilise working class organisations and the anti-racist movement in support of refugees from Bosnia, with the following aims:

- To campaign for the opening of the asylum doors to all victims of 'ethnic cleansing' and those facing political persecution.

- To help provide material assistance to refugees in Britain: housing, jobs, unemployment benefit, food, clothing, welfare advice etc. To take direct action to stop threatened deportations.

- To expose the hypocrisy of the present Conservative government in their relation to refugees, and show how western governments are supporting right-wing nationalists (and even fascist) forces in ex-Yugoslavia.

- To forge links with left-wing and trade union organisations in ex-Yugoslavia to assist in our aims. To support democratic forces genuinely fighting for democratic rights against dictatorial rule and imperialist intervention and to oppose the European Community policy of partition in Bosnia.

- To build links throughout Europe with those of a similar outlook with a view towards co-ordinated action with an international Workers Aid.

- To support other campaigns to open asylum doors, stop deportations and to oppose racism and fascism.

- To campaign for the immediate lifting of the British-backed United Nations arms embargo on Bosnia and for the withdrawal of UN troops.

June 6th, 1993

Where did modern Yugoslavia come from?

Modern Yugoslavia was born in the carnage of World War II. For centuries the Balkans formed the dividing lines between great empires which fought out their battles on Balkan soil, leaving behind their cultural and religious diifferences. During 1939-45, Nazi Germany became the driving force for an orgy of killing and 'ethnic cleansing' between the various people.

But for the first time in Balkan history there emerged a united opposition against the invader. The Partisan Army brought together people from across the region. In the mountains, forests and villages they fought back against the local and foreign fascists. The Tuzla mining region of Bosnia became the largest liberated zone in Nazi occupied Europe. In 1943, the Partisans defeated the occupation forces and also swept away the local regimes that had sided with the fascists and ethnic cleansers. The Partisan victory established federal Yugoslavia, consisting of six republics: Bosnia-Herzegovina, Croatia, Macedonia, Montenegro, Serbia, and Slovenia. There were also two autonomous provinces: Vojvodina, with a large Hungarian population, and Kosova, with a mainly Albanian population.

The separate republics and the provinces had their own parliaments and also sent representatives to the Federal Yugoslav Parliament.

This new Yugoslavia contained people from many national and ethnic backgrounds. Within each republic there were large minority populations. The most culturally mixed region was Bosnia-Herzegovina. Hundreds of years ago Bosnia was the dividing line between the Catholic empires to the west and the Orthodox to the east. In the 15th century, the Turkish empire also expanded into the region. The influence of these empires left Bosnia with three main religious communities. Some shared the Catholic religion of their Croat neighbours, some the Orthodox religion of their Serb neighbours, while a majority had become Muslim under Turkish influence – Bosnian Croats, Bosnian Serbs, and Bosnian Muslims.

The Partisan resistance to fascism and the freeing of the whole region from imperialist rule laid the basis for transcending all the old ethnic categories. As post-war industrialisation developed, urban populations grew up with all ethnic groups living inter-mixed and often inter-marrying. Thirty per cent of marriages in Bosnia before the recent war were across ethnic lines. In the census, in which people could state their nationality, many people simply declared themselves to be 'Yugoslav'. Those defining themselves in this way were largely those for whom religion (Orthodox Christianity, Catholicism, Islam, Judaism) or nationality (Croat, Serb, Muslim) were now less important than a sense of Yugoslav identity, an identity above all based on a unity of these national and religious differences. The Bosnian city of Tuzla had the highest percentage of people registering simply as Yugoslav in all of Yugoslavia.

This process was uneven. Many rural areas remained predominantly Serb, Croat or Muslim. Towns like Mostar had a mainly Croat side and a mainly Muslim side. But everywhere the influence of religion declined. In Bosnia, the categories 'Muslim', 'Serb' and 'Croat', were clearly identifiable in many people's family names, reflecting ancestry more than religious beliefs. In a similar way any British city school register might reveal Scottish, Irish, English, Welsh, Caribbean or Asian names. The children may or may not be religious. They are all British.

SOCIALIST FEDERAL REPUBLIC OF YUGOSLAVIA

(showing republics and autonomous provinces)

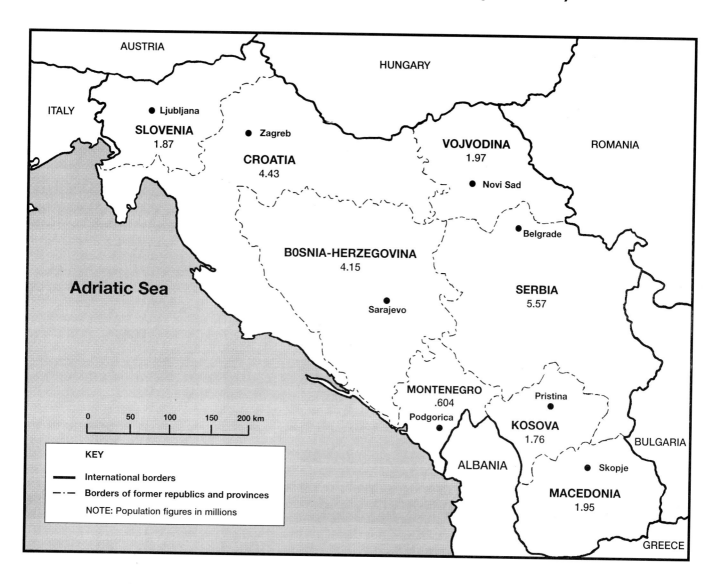

War looms: the Yugoslav Peoples' Army on the Slovenian border, July 1991.

Chapter 1

APRIL 1993	Fighting breaks out on new fronts in Bosnia between BiH Army and Croat nationalists.
AUGUST 1993	Owen-Stoltenberg plan proposes three-way partition of Bosnia.

The beginning of Workers Aid

At the founding meeting of Workers Aid we had voted to organise a convoy to take food to Tuzla miners. We were not the first people to try to take aid to Bosnia. Far from it. As the war escalated during 1992 there were many actions to try and help the suffering people.

From Britain and other countries, people drove to Croatia or Bosnia in cars, buses and ambulances to bring the survivors of 'ethnic cleansing' to safety. Others took food to the refugee camps springing up throughout the region.

Big aid organisations put appeals in the papers and cash poured in. Huge convoys of food tried to reach refugees trapped in starving towns. Some reached their targets, others were held up for week after week or simply looted.

The scale of this effort to take aid was matched by the scale of confusion about what was going on in Bosnia. The humanitarian agencies made no distinction between aggressor and victim. For them, there were simply soldiers fighting each other, and suffering civilians. But Bosnians, both soldiers and civilians, were starving for a reason. They were refugees for a reason and they were fighting for a reason. They were victims of a planned military operation to divide Bosnia and its people between Serbia and Croatia, creating two 'ethnically cleansed' states, with no place left on earth for Bosnia's two million Muslims. The humanitarian organisations didn't want to take sides in the war, only to provide humanitarian help. But what future would there be for the Muslims, or for humanity as a whole, if 'ethnic cleansing' was not stopped from the areas they seized. Their actions

Demonstration in Leeds, April 1993

3.1.90

Terror in Kosovo

Serb police are carrying out a reign of terror in the mainly Albanian Kosovo region, attacking teachers and school students.

Last month police entered a building in Kosovska-Mitrovica where pupils of the Architect Sinani Secondary School were having lessons. They ordered the pupils to leave. They then reportedly beat teacher Rexhep Ahmeti, and forced him to burn a sociology textbook by Croatian author Rudi Supek.

The police also beat another teacher Bujar Naxhiu, and forced English teacher Luljeta Sefaja to burn an English language textbook.

The following day the police entered a house where pupils of the Trepca technical school were being taught, attacking the pupils as they attempted to flee.

11.5.93

How long for Bosnia?

"How long before Bosnia becomes another Palestine, another Kashmir?"

This was one of many angry questions raised at a rally in Leeds last Friday. The rally outside the civic hall was the culmination of a march through the city attended by all sections of the Islamic community, including a large contingent of vocal youth, as well as a sprinkling of trade unionists.

The contrast between the United Nations' swift action over Kuwait and its tacit acceptance of Serbian 'ethnic cleansing' in Bosnia was highlighted by Mohammmed Shakil of the Leeds Islamic Centre: "How long did it take the UN to act over Kuwait? To bomb Baghdad? And now, when our mothers and sisters are being raped in Bosnia, where are your principles now?"

When John Gunnell, Labour MP for Leeds South and Morley, said that everything should be left to the UN, a section of the crowd became understandably very angry. One irate youth had to be prevented from attacking the shaken Gunnell. It must have been very clear, even to him, that faith in the UN amongst the Muslim community is extremely low. One of the marchers, Imtiaz Khan, said: "Why do we have to keep listening to all this stuff about needing to go through the UN? Why this Labour collaboration with the Tories? They tell us that it's because any other action will make the situation worse. But there are concentration camps already!"

encouraged Croatian nationalists to do the same. The UN and European Governments supported this carve-up of Bosnia. David Owen, the EU (European Union) chief negotiator, produced map after map in which he drew and redrew borders through the heart of mixed communities. Bosnians soon lost count of the number of peace plans, truces and international conferences organised by the EU, the UN and the USA and, while diplomats politely swapped plans for a negotiated division of Bosnia, the 'ethnic cleansers' got on with the bloody business of actually implementing these plans. Gorazde, Zepa, Srebrenica, Bihac, Sarajevo – the hangman's noose closed round town after town.

In April, the UN voted to send troops into Bosnia but only to help convoys get through to refugees in the besieged towns, not to liberate them. Instead, it declared these towns were 'safe havens'. The townsfolk and their defenders, and the hundreds of thousands of refugees who had poured in from 'ethnically cleansed' areas, were to be fed just enough to keep some of them alive – and disarmed. But their encircling tormentors were to be in left in place, pouring in shells from their hilltop artillery positions. In the history of the meaningless phrase, 'safe haven' must take first prize.

This tearing apart of society could be stopped, but only if a force stronger than the 'ethnic cleansers' and their international backers appeared. It needed mass protests on the streets of every European city demanding an end to government support for ethnic division, demanding the lifting of the arms embargo, so the Bosnians could defend themselves. It needed trade unions to send trainloads and shiploads of food and weapons to the unarmed defenders of a united Bosnia. It needed anti-fascist and women's organisations to raise a hurricane of protests over the rape and killing of Muslims.

It needed all this to stop the nightmare, but there was virtually nothing, silence. The aid businesses set up their warehouses and offices outside the borders of Bosnia and helped to hide western governments' support for division behind a humanitarian camouflage. Lies were reported as truths, without contradiction. A war involving invasion and occupation became a 'civil war.' A multi-cultural government and army became 'Muslim'. Miners and other workers trying to stop the division of Tuzla became one of the 'warring factions' and the European TUC, with sixty million members, said not a word.

So what could the sixty people at the founding meeting of Workers Aid do? There was no doubting the scale of public outrage over the war, but it remained unorganised and unfocused. Yet across Europe people belonged to organisations, like trade unions and political parties, that had been born in struggles for democratic rights and justice, organisations that had changed the course of history. Could they be made to take sides on Bosnia?

We called ourselves Workers Aid because we knew that European governments would never interfere with the 'ethnic cleansers'', plans, but that they could only be stopped by the mass of people of Europe if a spirit of international solidarity could be rekindled. We had to find a way to begin to rebuild a movement of workers' internationalism.

The proposal for the convoy was put forward at the founding meeting with just this in mind. The Tuzla miners were defending their united communities and faced being starved into submission. A basic act of solidarity would be to take them food. Trade unions were the obvious organisations to do this. They had the resources and organising skills. The original proposal from Serbia asked British miners to organise a convoy, but they had just suffered the destruction of their industry at the hands of the Tories, and their spirit was all but gone.

So how could we move the unions, or any other mass organisations? Send them letters? Pass resolutions? Organise meetings? We started to do all these things but we felt that actually to get a workers' convoy on the road would show what could be done, and would inspire others. Sixty people could not themselves change the situation, unless what they did acted as a catalyst for wider action.

We left the London meeting and set the ball rolling. We wrote to unions, to Labour MPs and Labour Party branches, to antifascist groups, to mosques. We set up stalls in high streets and carnivals, collected money, gave out publicity and spoke at meetings.

The stamp beside Radovan Karadzic's signature in the background below contains the Chetnic four Cs symbol: Samo Sloga Srbina Spasava (Only Unity Saves Serbs)

THE METHODS OF FASCISM
Concentration Camps

KERATERM: They were locked along with 200-300 men into a single room of about eighty sq. metres. The temperature was stifling. On July 24th soldiers opened fire with machine guns...an estimated 150 were killed or wounded.

OMARSKA: Two Serbian brothers were let into the camp....the brothers forced Alic to drink a glass of motor oil and then to drink urine. Alic was then beaten until he was unconscious...Alic was forced to take his pants off, and the brothers then forced Emir to bite off his testicle. Alic died of his wounds that night.

LUKA-BRCKO: About 3,000 men, women and children were killed during May and June at this camp. One example was an individual who had his ears cut off. As he grabbed for his ears in pain, a young woman cut off his genitals with an instrument called a 'spoon'. As he fell forward and lay on the ground he was shot in the head by a guard. In June, some 50-60 men had their genitalia removed....shooting occurred on a daily basis....the trucks carrying bodies drove into a building that had three industrial-sized cooking vats with furnaces used ordinarily to make animal feed...the bodies were dumped into the furnaces.

ZVORNIK: Serb soldiers moved through the paediatric centre breaking the necks and bones of the twenty seven remaining Muslim children. The oldest were about five.

Summary excerpts from the Third U.S. State Dept Report on Atrocities in Bosnia-Herzegovina

The first defenders

" I bring greetings from Bosnia-Herzegovina and I thank you for the chance to say something about my town. Tuzla is the biggest mining community in Bosnia-Herzegovina. In 1992, the number of people working in the mining industry was 11,000, which together with their families makes 45,000. Throughout the whole world miners from Tuzla are famous for their solidarity. In every strike which has been held by miners around the world miners from Tuzla gave their support.

Tuzla miners were always first in the struggle for a better life and a brighter future. Through World War II miners from Tuzla gave their lives in the fight against fascism. Unfortunately at the end of the 20th century in the heart of Europe the rage of war is going on. The attack on Tuzla began on May 15th, 1992. The first defenders of Tuzla were the miners.

Instead of doing their jobs they were forced to fight and defend the little bit of property which they were building throughout the years, doing their very hard and dangerous job. After one year the inhabitants of Tuzla are facing destruction. People are suffering from all different kinds of diseases which have been caused by the shortage of medicine and food. The citizens of Tuzla are hoping that somebody is going to help them and stop this terrible aggression.

Please, I ask you to help the Workers Aid convoy for the Tuzla miners that starts on August 7th from Scotland. "

A Tuzla miner's son speaking at a demonstration in July, 1993 against the closure of Parkside Colliery, the last pit in Lancashire.

Members of the convoy team with strikers at the Timex factory, Dundee, from where the convoy set off on August 9th, 1993

26.6.93
Gorazde

An amateur radio operator in the town of Gorazde, where 91 people were killed and 152 wounded in one day of fierce fighting last week, reported that parts of human bodies were dangling from trees and telephone lines.

"If anyone survives here," he declared, "all they will need will be a pair of crutches or a wheelchair."

As many as 70,000 residents and refugees were thought to be jammed in the Gorazde area, where they have been cut-off for months and pounded by Serb guns for three weeks.

As the convoy campaign gathered strength problems which seemed insurmountable were overcome and support grew. A timetable was worked out. After discussions with the Timex workers' Strike Committee, it was agreed that the convoy would set off on August 9th from the gates of their factory in Dundee, where they were holding mass pickets as part of a long and bitter campaign for reinstatement. The convoy would then make its way down through Britain, campaigning for support along the way.

No one involved in the campaign so far had any experience of transport, aid or convoys and no clear idea what we actually meant by 'convoy'. At first we talked about a couple of cars, then a couple of transit vans. Money began to be raised and as the word spread, new people joined in the work.

In Manchester, for example, four people met in June and agreed to fly-post for a public meeting. Thirty people turned up, including a refugee from Tuzla who had seen the poster. At the next meeting sixty people came, including many refugees. The following week Branka Magas, the Croatian historian, addressed a crowd of over 100 people. Between these meetings teams of people got together every day to organise street collections and to visit shopkeepers, churches and mosques. Groups of refugees and trade unionists visited factories and got donations from union committees. Various people volunteered to go with the convoy to Bosnia. And so it was in many different towns.

Convinced that this response would grow, the campaign took out a bank loan and bought our first 7.5ton lorry at auction. Some Bosnian refugees painted 'Workers Aid Convoy to Bosnia' on the side.

We met the Muslim Solidarity Campaign to discuss the convoy. We explained we were for a society where all nationalities and religions could live together and that we believed the fascists in Bosnia could only be defeated by the workers' movement. They had no hesitation in backing the convoy and donated £5,000, to put another lorry on the road. Information was also circulated through the mosques.

Outside the Timex plant in Dundee

I have regained my strength

❝ I come from Tuzla and once, not a long time ago, it was easy to go to that town or to get out and go to any part of the world. Now, when Tuzla is the aim of this workers' project, it seems to me to be so far and almost unreachable. I have a feeling that only those with a very strong will can defeat all the obstacles that may appear on the way to Tuzla.

I have been in Britain for almost ten months and I have been happy that my children are safe and secure. But all this time I have been thinking that I could be doing something to help my people.

My husband stayed in Tuzla because he felt the town needed him and at that time I only had a mother's instinct and wanted to save my children. In Britain they are surrounded by friends and teachers and have become much more confident, but it seems that I was losing my confidence.

When I heard about the Workers Aid convoy it uplifted me. Now that I am aware that there are people who have such a strong will as to organise this movement, I have regained my strength. I want to help and now I have the chance to do so.

Tuzla is an industrial town made up mainly of miners, workers and students. Because of this no national factions have been established. Even now, despite the butchery, Tuzla remains a unified oasis within a lost nation. ❞

AZRA MAROSEVIC, Bosnian refugee, speaking at the first Manchester meeting of Workers Aid.

❝ We are perfecting the art of killing with a rusty shoehorn, so that it will be impossible to determine whether the victim was butchered or died of tetanus. ❞

VOJISLAV SESELJ, Serbian MP and leader of the Radical Party

Safeta (53) and Mesud Karabasic (64) are from Prijedor, in north-west Bosnia. They now live in a small council flat in east London.

The war was intensifying more and more when the SDS (Serbian Democratic Party), the political side of Serbian aggression, occupied the major buildings in Prijedor and seized power on April 29th and 30th. The Yugoslav army had been ethnically mixed but all Muslims and Croats had to give their weapons back. The only ones left with weapons were Serbs.

When we got up on the morning of April 30th, we could see all the flags with the Serbian insignia. Then almost all the Muslim and Croat population who were working were sacked from their jobs.

I was already retired from my job as a mechanical engineer on the railway, but I was a consultant. My wife was an accountant for a paper factory. There were only two Muslim directors in Prijedor. The Serbs had dominated the most prominent positions before the war. The Communist Party had been mostly run by Serbs. The police were controlled by Serbs.

After bombing the surrounding villages came Prijedor itself. It started early in the morning of June 1st. Explosions and fighting erupted at 5.30am. We got up, and could see through the window that there were Serbian snipers on the buildings high up. We drew the curtains, but they were old and split, and we could see through them. But you couldn't go near the window for fear of a bullet.

In the morning there was chaos – sporadic fighting and explosions. I saw some soldiers in camouflage uniforms, hitting other soldiers, but I think they were all Serbs.

Later in the day the Serbs drove tanks over to the old town, which was 100 per cent Muslim. They went from house to house, and shelled them. You could hear people screaming. They destroyed the ancient mosque. The intellectuals were murdered – lawyers, doctors, engineers – maybe 60-70 per cent of them, killed on the spot.

One of my son's friends was taken from his house. He said: "Let me just put my shoes on." They told him: "Well for that, you'll never have time," and just boom, they shot him.

Then they came to our flat, saying that someone was shooting from our building, and asked, "Do you know anything?" They held a gun to my head as they questioned me. Two soldiers took my wife into the other room. They threatened her, and one wanted to rape her. Some other guy – luckily there is always one better than the others – came into the room and told them to leave, that there was nothing there. He probably recognised me from my firm. They were all wearing balaclavas.

When the Croatian and Muslim flats had been checked out, we had to put white cloths on the windows, to show that they were clean – there were no weapons.

The Chetniks went around the villages one by one, after Prijedor. In these villages, one half were killed, one quarter escaped and one quarter ended up in the camps.

After the killing started to cool down, they went to all the people who still had flats or houses, and pressured them to sign papers saying they were giving the flat away.

For any non-Serb it was possible to be picked up on the street, imprisoned or killed. If a Serb had a grudge against you from five years ago, now was the time to settle it. I didn't go out for three months. We had no money because we were not working, and when I went to my old firm to get my pension they refused to give it to me – after thirty-five years of work. We had no heating, no electricity, nothing to eat. It wasn't only Omarska that was a camp, the whole of Prijedor was a camp. It was extreme in Omarska, but people were being tortured in their flats in Prijedor.

We were waiting for the UN officials to turn up, and they never came. They were there in the beginning and then they just disappeared. Then we went through the Red Cross, and eventually after a long and painful journey we got to Britain.

Before the war there were 5,000 Muslims out of a population of 65,000 in Prijedor. Now there are hardly any. None of our family is left. They are scattered all around Europe, in Sweden, in Norway, in Germany and in Holland.

We are homesick for Prijedor. But there is nothing to see there now. Anything to do with Muslims or Croats has been destroyed. We miss Prijedor as we knew it, but not Prijedor as it is now. We will never go back.

Campaign supporters were now working in towns across the country. A second lorry was bought and the lorries and a convoy team of a dozen people were given a rousing send-off by the Timex strikers.

In towns along the route contacts were made. Places were found each night to accommodate and feed the growing team of people accompanying the lorries. Trade unions in bus garages and council depots gave mechanical assistance and refuelled vehicles. Unemployed centres, mosques, local trade union organisations, Bosnian refugee groups and many others collected food and clothes to put on the lorries as they passed. Everywhere people were enthusiastic that they could do something, not just to help starving people, but to defend Bosnia and multi-culturalism.

Public meetings were held along the route and more money was raised, more people joined the convoy. Some volunteered after seeing the telephone number on the lorries as they drove past.

At some meetings Bosnian refugees anxiously asked how the lorries were going to reach Tuzla. These people understood the nature of the siege around the town, but for us the main problem was still to get the convoy on the road. Only later were we to appreciate the full meaning of the Bosnians' question.

26.6.93
EC Carve-Up

European Community leaders were poised at the beginning of this week to accept a 'settlement' of the war in Bosnia which would leave Serbs and Croats in possession of most of the land they have seized.

They told Bosnian President Alija Izetbegovic that in their opinion even a "bad peace settlement" – their phrase for the proposed carve-up – is better than none at all.

But, though EC ministers reaf-firmed their commitment to the territorial integrity of Bosnia-Herzegovina, Owen admitted that the Serbs could not now be compelled to give up all the land they had grabbed.

"The Serb roll-back will be less than we hoped," he said. "That is a sad fact of life and I do not like it." After what was described as, "an extremely tense meeting," one minister was heard to say: "I hope we are not preparing a new Wannsee conference" – a reference to the Nazi decision on the final extermination of the Jews during World War II.

My first day on the convoy

" When I decided to travel up to Edinburgh to visit my sister, I never imagined that I would be joining an international convoy taking aid to the people of Tuzla.

However, while wandering around Edinburgh one sunny afternoon, I came across the brightly painted trucks of Workers Aid and met someone I now know as Tall Nigel. He told me all about the aims of the convoy, and that evening I went to a public meeting. The next day I found myself on the road to Glasgow!

I was so overwhelmed by the sense of purpose and commitment of the people I met that I felt compelled to join up, even if only for a few days. Since making that decision I have come to realise the incredible significance of this event, not only in humanitarian terms but as a political statement. After months of government apathy and inaction, here is a chance for us to help the workers who are suffering and dying at this moment.

Although I joined the convoy out of the need to 'do something', I think that humanitarian aid is ultimately pointless without political pressure to stop the conflict. The humanitarian aims cannot be separated from the political, and this convoy is a political statement by people who are sick of government inactivity and cynicism.

On a personal level, taking part in this convoy has given me a chance to get to grips with the issues revolving around Bosnia. It is an opportunity to develop my own ideas and listen to new ones which I had never even considered!

What's more, it's the chance to work as part of a team in an atmosphere of enthusiasm, friendship, internationalism and openness which make this event unique in my experience. There is a feeling of being a part of something which is getting bigger by the day. **"**

June, 1993

MOYA KNEAFSEY is a 22-year-old student in History and Irish studies, soon to start work on her PhD at Liverpool University.

We had four lorries by this time. The convoy 'team' was mostly unemployed youngsters plus a few seasoned union and political organisers, but none of them knew much about the job in hand. Knowing how to chair a meeting was one thing, repairing a lorry was another. Everyone had different ideas of what we should be doing. Even before leaving Britain, keeping the team together was no easy job. Some of the political activists, familiar with union meetings and political debates, were not so good at working with the unemployed, the ex-squaddies and the ex-cons – the kind of people who were free enough and mad enough to volunteer to drive into a war.

We were deluged with 'advice' from people who had already taken lorries of aid. Their advice was generally that no-one but themselves could get aid to Bosnia. You could never get straight answers to simple technical questions about customs and vehicles. Some said our public support for an undivided Bosnia would make it harder for us to get through front lines. The trade union leaders shared this attitude. We held a meeting with the International Committee of UNISON, Britain's biggest union, with over a million members, asking them to help us get the food to the Tuzla miners. They declined to support their fellow trade unionists in Bosnia. Instead they urged their members to support 'humanitarian' charities, like Feed the Children, because their neutrality in the war would enable them to get food through.

26.6.93
C18 sides with Chetniks

Britain's notorious neo-Nazi thug outfit, Combat 18, which boasts of its' part in violence against left-wing opponents, has had no trouble deciding who to support in Bosnia.

C18 is supporting the Serb nationalist Chetniks, whose 'ethnic cleansing' presumably comes closest to what it wants everywhere.

In the past the anti-fascist magazine *Searchlight* has exposed neo-Nazi and right-wing mercenaries serving with the Croat militias. But in its April issue, Ray Hill, who knows the British Nazi milieu from the inside, wrote:

"The hard men of C18 hold an entirely different position on the war in former Yugoslavia. They steadfastly support the Serbs and their Slavonic ultra-nationalist supporters and claim that the alliance between Croatia and the Bosnian Muslims is a blow to the future of an all-white Europe."

A young Bosnian collecting at the Cardiff U2 concert

Counting the £4,000 collected at the Leeds U2 concert

GREAT MYTHS OF THE WAR

- ## The war in Bosnia was an ethnic, civil war based on old 'tribal hatreds'

Contrary to many statements made by journalists and politicians in the West, Bosnia has a tradition of mutual tolerance among its different ethnic groups that goes back centuries.

Fact: Until the 20th century, there was not a SINGLE incident of large-scale violence by members of one group against the members of another.

Fact: In all of Bosnia's cities, members of all three groups lived side by side, co-existing peacefully. One-third of marriages within BiH were between members of different groups.

It is not difficult to understand why the myth of civil war was believed within Serbia; the state controlled media provided 'news' to support it. It became a myth internationally when it was found to be a convenient explanation by the western superpowers, intent on pursuing their own interests by dividing Bosnia. There was a massive military disparity between the attacking Yugoslav People's Army (JNA), now in the hands of the Serb nationalists, and the poorly armed multi-ethnic Bosnian defenders. This disparity was frozen by the West's 'impartial' imposition of an arms embargo. The justification for the embargo was largely dependent on the fables of 'ancient tribal hatreds', and 'civil war'.

The myth was even encouraged by sections of the so-called left. The following letter, published without comment in the pro-Milosevic journal *Living Marxism*, echoes the superior, racist tone of most western government explanations of the conflict:

Do we have to wait until the twenty-fourth century to learn the wisdom of Star Trek's 'prime directive', i.e. non-intervention? By providing humanitarian assistance which has kept the society functioning well enough to allow those involved in the violence to focus on fighting rather than earning a living, the UN has prolonged the Bosnian war. Neither UN nor US intervention will resolve this 200-year-old conflict or stop its' tit-for-tat genocide. Let 'em fight it out. The only long-term consequences will be fewer stupid genes.

The leaders of most British trade unions were informed of the convoy. They neither supported it nor made alternative proposals how their members could support fellow trade unionists in Bosnia. In the face of a war directed against workers, they just stayed silent. Where people supporting the convoy managed to speak directly to the union membership, however, they did get a warm response.

At the GPMU (Printworkers) annual conference a delegate, a woman originally from Poland, who was already involved in the convoy, was allowed to move an emergency resolution on Bosnia and the plight of the Tuzla miners. She reported the build-up of the convoy and asked the union to back it. The vote was unanimous, and another delegate commented that if there was one thing that had lifted the conference from its normal dull routine it was this response to the war which was on everyone's mind, but was never discussed in the union movement.

Sponsorship came in from many local Trades Councils, union branches, local Labour Party wards, especially from those along the route of the convoy, who met the team and collected money and aid.

With great help from thousands of members of trade unions, the Labour Party and Muslim organisations, as well as from students and others up and down the country, and with no help from the leaders of the labour movement or most of the socialist organisations, the convoy made its way down to London.

I have been waiting for two years

The people of Bosnia-Herzegovina are faced today with the destruction of their state. What is happening is not only mass murder of an innocent civilian population, and the destruction of their cities and villages, not only occupation by foreign armies, but its total destruction. Nothing like this has happened in Europe since World War II. The destruction of Bosnia-Herzegovina is a tragedy for all its peoples: Serbs, Croats and Muslims. It is the Muslim nation, however, which is and will be the chief victim since it has no other state but Bosnia-Herzegovina.

We are witnessing today a 'final solution' directed this time not against Jews but against the Muslims of Bosnia. The war against Bosnia is fought in the name of the reactionary ideology of blood and soil, one that argues that certain territories must become the exclusive property of one ethnic group and that different nationalities cannot co-exist within the borders of the same state. This ideology leads directly to so-called ethnic cleansing.

A year into the war, the estimated number of killed or missing persons amounts to 200,000 and 750,000 wounded. A quarter of them are children under the age of twelve. Out of the 4 million total Bosnian population, million have been displaced by the war and over 1 million have left the country. Some 1.6 million are now dependent on UN aid.

The chief blame for the tragedy lies with the so-called international community and with the British government in particular. They are now doing all they can to force the Bosnian government, one that was from the start multi-national and has remained so to this day, to sign their so-called peace plan, which amounts to a death warrant for Bosnia.

The UN have continued to maintain the arms embargo against Bosnia, preventing it from defending itself. One needs only to read the newspapers to know what this means for places like Srebrenica, Gorazde or Sarajevo. Today the press reports an attack by a Serb tank division on Mount Igman overlooking Sarajevo. The Bosnian army has never had the weapons to match the power of the invaders. For example, at the start of the war in May 1992, the Serbian army in Bosnia had 300 tanks, 330 armoured vehicles, 48 aircraft, 4 ballistic missile launchers, 300 pieces of artillery of high calibre, and 5,120, 120mm mortars. The Bosnian army began with 5 tanks and 6 howitzers. Bear these figures in mind when you hear Owen praising Milosevic as a peace-maker, when you see the Western politicians shaking hands with Milosevic and Karadzic.

The imperialists are very used to carving up other people's countries. The peace that they are now pushing is not in the interests of the people who live in Bosnia. It is an imperialist peace.

British people in all walks of life, the workers of this country, must denounce the policy of their government towards Bosnia. Workers Aid for Bosnia is an example of solidarity in action. It is an action by workers and for workers, an act of workers' internationalism in practice. This is why it is most welcome.

I have been waiting for this moment for the last two years, for workers in this country, for the left in this country, to take up the case of the victims of this war. I feel extremely pleased to be here and welcome you.

BRANKA MAGAS, author of the book, **The Destruction of Yugoslavia,** *speaking at a meeting welcoming the convoy to London, August, 1993.*

KHAN CHAUDRY, of Leeds Islamic Centre, welcomes the convoy to Leeds

Warring parties

Any idea that by leaving the claustrophobic environment of a city under siege I would have an opportunity to define the meaning of Sarajevo's suffering now appears meaningless. The simple reason is that from Sarajevo I can see Europe better than Europe sees Sarajevo. The world's repeated definition of the crime against Bosnia-Herzegovina as a 'conflict among warring parties' – which freezes my blood – tells increasingly of a mass lobotomisation of public understanding.

Fascism, now in its most terrible and tangible form, is rampant in Bosnia-Herzegovina, from ethnic cleansing of the Muslim people to concentration camps for all those who think differently – the recognition of fascism as fascism is being sidelined.

In Sarajevo, humanity still takes priority over nationality. This Sarajevan stubbornness is a defence of the principle of co-existence.

The shells that have fallen on Sarajevo have also killed some of the 70,000 Serbs in the city who long ago denied Radovan Karadzic, so called 'Bosnian Serb leader', the right to represent them, and we shall choose to continue living in Sarajevo as Bosnians, as Europeans and as anti-fascists.

GORAN SIMIC, a Bosnian Serb and one of former Yugoslavia's leading poets (from Casablanca, *London)*

Marching to Trafalgar Square

On Sunday, September 5th a large crowd of people joined the lorries and marched to Trafalgar Square behind the Murton Colliery Brass Band to demonstrate their support for the convoy and its message of solidarity with multi-cultural Bosnia. Although the convoy had not yet left Britain, it had already travelled thousands of miles in three weeks and visited seventeen British cities. We now had twelve lorries.

In Trafalgar Square, the police arrested one man for holding up a placard saying that Foreign Secretary 'Hurd is a Turd'. A Bosnian woman addressing the crowd, repeated this claim, adding that it was Major, Clinton and Mitterand who were murdering Bosnia. (She spoke in Bosnian. The police couldn't understand.) The speeches

In Brighton outside the TUC conference

from Nelson's column went on for hours. Michael Foot, former Labour Party leader, made an impassioned condemnation of this new rise of fascism. So many people who had helped the convoy wanted to speak, as well as a few who had not.

The following day, two of the convoy lorries parked outside the Trades Union Congress (TUC) annual conference in Brighton and we held a lunchtime meeting calling upon the unions to help the Bosnian miners. A lot of money was dropped into our buckets during the day, but the war in Bosnia was not discussed at the 1993 TUC Conference, nor would it be at its' next three conferences, during which time nationalist killers continued to divide the workers of former Yugoslavia.

It was no wonder, given the silence of the trade union leaders, that the Bosnian people and the various organisations concerned about the war directed their appeals to the mighty governments. NATO had thousands of tanks and planes that could halt the killing. People lobbied, begged and petitioned these great powers to 'do something'. No-one looked to the other Europe, the Europe of ordinary people, to intervene. No one saw them as a power.

If a Bosnian soldier, from his or her hell, could see the TUC conference, how could they see a possible ally in that apparently indifferent gathering which supposedly represented working people?

Our campaign had found a response amongst many people. We now had twelve lorries but, cut off from all the skills and resources of the existing workers' movement, the convoy had grown too large for us to organise it properly. Despite frenzied last-minute preparations, we assembled in the ferry queue in some chaos. We did not know, for exam-ple, how many people were travelling with us. We did not know if there were enough seats or who one of the drivers was. We were swept along both by the momentum of events and by the overwhelming response we were getting; we could not organise many of the things which the aid 'professionals' would consider indispensable. The past month had been a maelstrom of activity as we tried, with absolutely no experience, to respond to a terrible situation. Mistakes were numerous and inevitable.

As we drove up the ramp the twelve lorries looked very impressive, stretching out in a line with their freshly painted Bosnian, French and English slogans. The convoy was on its way, leaving behind a network of people across the country, working to stop the division of Bosnia. We had come a long way from the fifteen people who had marched through London on June 6th. We had taken a first faltering step.

Where did the idea of the convoys to Tuzla come from?

by RADOSLAV PAVLOVIC, Serbian carpenter

"On May 31st, 1992 I was on the road for France to find work. I still had my Yugoslav passport, but after the destruction of Vukovar I no longer had a country. I did not know if I was going to be able to re-join my family in Serbia. 'Ethnic cleansing' in Bosnia was in full spate. Since hearing Radovan Karadzic on Serbian TV in January, I understood that having razed Vukovar in Croatia, Serb nationalists were going to ravage Bosnia. But nobody could imagine the extent of the horror which unfolded in so short a time. In Paris, I could hear nothing but the bombs which fell on Bosnia's towns, the fall of Prijedor, Drvar, and Jajce, then the cries of Muslim women and children fleeing on the road from Travnik, their columns bombed by Serb planes.

I could not hide my tears of anger – fascism was assassinating Yugoslavia, my country. Since World War II we were first and foremost Yugoslavs, only afterwards, for administrative matters, Serbs, Croats, Slovenes, Macedonians. My brother lived for four years in Bosnia, in Travnik, the most beautiful years of his life because there was that wonderful understanding among the mixed population, which we, Serbs from Serbia, found hard to imagine.

What was to be done? To defend Bosnia against the fascist war was for every honest Serb or Croat the defence of his own country. When the fascists who volunteered to fight in Bosnia returned home to Serbia and Croatia could anyone expect them to lay down their arms and swear to live in an honest manner from then on?

In Paris I joined the 'Sarajevo Association'. It was honest and democratic but there was no work for the mass of members like myself. A few well-known members gave interviews, explained the war, defended the idea of a united, multi-ethnic Bosnia, wrote day and night to French politicians on the left and the right; everywhere they found warm agreement that something must be done for this unhappy country, but they did nothing to challenge the coldly calculated French government policy of non-intervention.

I tried to combat these illusions, but in vain. The naivete and impotence of the democratic intellectuals convinced me of the necessity of a workers mobilisation, capable of becoming a mass movement and in which there is work for everybody.

Many intellectuals had the air of being defeated in advance, of not believing that they could influence the outcome of the war, the only force behind their fight being their moral conscience.

We needed the deep links, common vision, the widely and democratically discussed political progamme necessary to turn the strength of the masses into lasting action. Fascism did not conceal its anti-working class aims – the destruction of Yugoslavia, which had come out of the partisan revolution, which itself was born in Bosnia with its multi-cultural fraternisation. In the same way our fight could be none other than to strengthen the Bosnian workers, morally, politically and materially, without any distinction of nationality. But how to start?

The experience of the 'Sarajevo Association', together with efforts to make my own political organisation, *Workers' International,* understand the Bosnian war in class terms, rose to fever pitch for me when the Serb conquest reached the end of its first terrifying stage. Eastern Bosnia – Visegrad, Foca, Bratunac, Zvornik, Bijeljina – emptied of the Muslim population, who were then surrounded in three small enclaves: Zepa, Srebrenica and Gorazde. Sarajevo was being bombed daily in an attempt to force its capitulation. Mostar and Western Herzegovina were abandoned to the Ustashe (Croatian fascists). The Prijedor region was ferociously 'cleansed'. Mladic bombed the region in order to maintain the fear and terror.

But in February 1993 we did not know the real strengths of forces or the exact political and military calculations of Karadzic and Mladic. What we did see was the awful weakness of one side and the barbarous and crushing advance on the other. We shouted out the urgent need for solidarity from the international working class. Tuzla was a workers' centre, a miners' centre, a cultural centre and regional capital, crossroads of the major routes, with a mixed population which rejected nationalism, and Tuzla defined itself as the first target of international working-class solidarity.

When I say 'we', I mean a handful of people in France with no material resources. But no-one had made any call to the working class; both the Communist and Socialist Parties kept away from the fight by putting all the warring sides in Bosnia in the same bag. We made our appeal to the working people of Europe – "take food to Tuzla – do not let the miners be starved into division." We did not know if workers would listen or respond to us. Our analysis was clear, but the means at our disposal were derisory. Workers in Britain were the first to respond to our proposal."

ENCLAVE IN BOSNIA REPORTED TO FALL AFTER U.S. AIRDROP

SERBS SAID TO SEIZE TOWN

American Provisions May Have Missed the Target Zone — Rebuff for Clinton Seen

By JOHN F. BURNS
Special to The New York Times

GORAZDE, Bosnia and Herzegovina, March 2 — The latest American airdrop of relief supplies appears to have come too late for the besieged Muslim community of Cerska in eastern Bosnia, which was reported today to have fallen to Serbian nationalist forces only hours after United States military aircraft dropped supplies to the town.

The report of Cerska's fall came from the radio station of the Bosnian Government, whose forces had defended Cerska since the outbreak of war in Bosnia and Herzegovina last April. The report could not be independently verified, but senior Bosnian military officers had been saying for weeks that Cerska's defenders, mainly reservists with light weapons, were likely to be overwhelmed by the superior Serbian forces.

By overrunning Cerska, and stepping up military pressures on other isolated Muslim communities, the Serbian nationalist leaders in Bosnia appeared in effect to be offering a direct rebuff to President Clinton.

Airdrop Snag Reported

Mr. Clinton ordered the airdrops to besieged Muslim communities in eastern Bosnia last week, as well as to Serbian and Croatian communities, in an effort to help the Muslims sustain themselves against attempts by Serbian nationalist forces to starve them out.

The United States airdrop to Cerska appeared not only to come too late, but to have also gone seriously awry. Radio Sarajevo said that the food and medicines dropped by the C-130 transport planes flying from the Rhein-Main Air Base in Germany fell well outside the main settlement at Cerska, in an area that lay under Serbian guns. According to the radio, several people from the town were killed by Serbian sniper fire as they tried to reach the supplies.

The New York Times, March 3rd, 1993

Dear Mr Major

**From
Dr Anadi Begic,
Department of Plastic and
Reconstructive Surgery,
Kosevo Hospital,
Sarajevo.**

"I AM a 32-year-old Bosnian doctor. Though still young, I am now head of the plastic surgery department at Kosevo Hospital. Since the start of the siege of Sarajevo, all the qualified plastic surgeons have fled. Our clinic is now run by me and student surgeons.

I am separated from my wife and two children who are refugees abroad. I have not seen my wife or six-year-old son since the start of the war. I have never met my 11-month-old daughter.

At the plastic surgery department we often help out with the work of the trauma unit — which treats many, many civilian casualties — children wounded by shells, old men shot through the head by snipers.

The work places a heavy burden on our young staff. But we have no time now for nightmares — perhaps they will come later.

When we are lucky enough to find some power we do plastic surgery operations. But in the last two months we have had almost no energy. We have only been able to do a handful of operations and the waiting list is growing longer every day.

Life in Sarajevo is hell. We live without the things you take for granted in England — electricity, running water, gas, fruit, vegetables and meat. People are becoming more and more desperate. I can't tell you of their despair when they find out that operations to restore their faces, limbs or internal functions have to be postponed from week to week.

We can't tell them why. Can you?

Yesterday you evacuated 21 people, including seven children. It is a drop in the ocean. I am afraid that it is not enough to improve our opinion of your goodwill or your conscience.

As a doctor, working to save lives, I can't ask for military intervention. But I can beg you to do something more to save Bosnian people — who are dying together in Sarajevo regardless of their ethnic origin.

Our clinic used to be famous throughout Europe. We were capable of doing very sophisticated operations. But now our hands are tied behind our backs because we have nothing to work with.

It would be much better if you sent us the tools to do our jobs properly than for you to make a big show of a few token evacuations. After all this publicity is over, will you forget us?

I haven't lost my faith in the British people but I must say I have lost all faith in you and in your government."

The Guardian,

The Times, February 10th, 1993

Starvation drives out Muslims

FROM TIM JUDAH IN BELGRADE

THOUSANDS of Muslim refugees have been fleeing by night through the woods of eastern Bosnia. Officials of the United Nations High Commissioner for Refugees said yesterday they feared that up to 50,000 more people were about to run for their lives.

The UN officials said the Muslims were travelling along "humanitarian corridors" opened by the Serbs. However, the officials believed that the corridors were in fact funnels through which enclaves resisting Serb rule were being emptied. "They are being starved and shelled out by Serb irregulars who do not want us to deliver food or assistance," said Sylvana Foa, the refugee agency's spokeswoman in Geneva.

More than 300 refugees are fleeing from the enclaves of Kamenica and Cerska every day and others are joining them from the Serb-controlled town of Zvornik. In the past ten days 5,000 refugees have arrived in Tuzla. Many are reported to be suffering from scabies, malnutrition, lice, and frostbite.

In Belgrade, the refugee agency said that on January 30 the Serbs in eastern Bosnia told the Muslims in the enclaves that as a "humanitarian gesture" they could leave for Muslim territory. One official said the Muslims left after food ran out. Judith Kumin, the head of the agency in Belgrade, said: "This is 'ethnic cleansing' by another name."

In Belgrade, officials from the Serb-held enclave of Krajina in Croatia insist that Croat forces killed 830 civilians as they stormed over the ceasefire line last month, though the Red Cross says about 200 people are "unaccounted for". In Benkovac refugee camp, three witnesses told of the death of a Serb woman in the village of Islam Grcki. "Olga wanted to find her husband," said one. "She ran towards her house but five Croat soldiers were already on the terrace. They told her to stop, but she turned to run and they mowed her down." Another witness said he saw Croats cut the throats of a married couple.

□ **Zagreb:** Relief flights to Sarajevo will resume from here today after a three-day halt and will use a safer route over Slovenia, UN officials said. Flights were suspended on Saturday after a German plane was hit by Serb anti-artillery fire over a Serb-held area of Croatia. *(Reuter)*

Chapter 2

SEPTEMBER 1993	BiH Army takes offensive against former Croat allies, HVO.
SEPTEMBER 1993	UN threatens air strikes, Karadzic threatens retaliation; no air strikes.
OCTOBER 1993	Danish aid driver killed. UNHCR suspends convoys.

The first convoy

As the convoy campaigned through Britain, we had also been thinking about the journey across Europe. Could we get the trade union movement there to help fuel and feed the convoy? Would they add lorries? These questions were soon answered as we dealt with a flood of requests for the convoy to visit this or that town – in Belgium, France, Germany, Switzerland, the Czech Republic and Italy. Again, the campaign was acquiring its own momentum. We said yes to every invitation, with little idea of how we would keep these appointments.

A chaotic meeting in a Calais car park at four in the morning agreed that the convoy would split up into sections. Eight lorries went to Paris, to be welcomed by the Mayor of Montreuil, the rest to Belgium. The convoy later split into smaller and smaller sections to enable us to visit seventeen cities, including Besancon, site of Dundee's sister Timex factory.

The Paris ring-road

" Waiting for Bob Milne, who had gone back for his maps, parked on a huge, cobbled roundabout and watching the endless traffic jam on the Paris Périphérique below us. A crash course on basic maintenance while we wait. Terry and Olly take us around the vehicles, showing us oil sticks (is that the technical term?), air tanks etc. Bob returns and leads us onto the Périphérique. He leaves at the first exit and loses Paddy, in the next truck, who swings off at what he thinks is the next exit but which turns out to be a slip road to a garage. The vehicle behind, the large pull and drag with Terry and Olly, is too high for the garage entrance and has to park on the inside lane of the motorway. The rest of our vehicles back up behind it and soon block the preceding slip road from which we have just joined the Périphérique. A thousand French motorists start honking their horns. Clement scrambles up the bank and succeeds in finding Bob, tells him to wait and then spots a way for us to get out of the garage area and back onto the Périphérique. But when we get there, the pull and drag and the other vehicles have disappeared. We are now in three bits. Paddy and I drive around for about 15 minutes with my blood pressure slowly rising, until we get back to the original roundabout to find all the trucks, like migrating geese, regrouped. Seven drivers jump out of their trucks and start shouting. "

JOHN DAVIES, Sept 13th, 1993

Coverage of the convoy in the French press

With Belgian trade unionists

In many of the towns en-route campaigns were already underway to help the convoy, but many organisational problems arose which meant some difficult decisions. For example, we found we simply could not afford to continue with such a large team. Some people – who had all worked hard for many weeks – had to return to Britain. Everyone agreed to put the convoy first.

News came of developments elsewhere. A trade union in Sweden and Denmark (SAP) had raised enough money to send two lorries. Mineworkers' unions in Hungary and Slovakia announced they would be adding two lorries. Trade unionists in Belgium and Italy also promised vehicles. Resolutions of support came from Spain and South America.

On September 20th the last section of the convoy arrived at Jesenice in Slovenia. Twelve British lorries joined vehicles from Sweden, Denmark, Italy and Belgium. The convoy team now comprised over fifty people from fifteen countries.

At the Brandenberg Gate, Berlin

In Nancy, France, with local organisers after receiving a cheque from the mayor

At the European Parliament

" A beautiful drive from Nancy through the blue-green Vosges. Maize fields. We meet Jean Pierre, A Socialist Party member (mais, à gauche!). He has arranged for us to enter the European Parliament to meet the Socialist Group of MEPs. Unfortunately, the group had only heard about our arrival at the last minute and we try to collar MEPs as they go in and out of the Willy Brand room. I bump into Mike MacGowan, our Leeds MEP, who spoke at the convoy meeting there. Apparently they are expecting our convoy to be made up of Scottish miners! Where these crossed wires originated is beside the point – our Strasbourg hosts are concerned that we don't upset the apple cart. "You must pretend!" For a milli-second I toy with this ludicrous idea, but one look at our Scottish miners delegation shows we could never get away it: Julian, a dreadlocked Namibian student; Robin a very tall and skinny cockney; Musa, who speaks impenetrable Mancunian Somali and myself, a middle-class actor. We are ushered into the visitors' gallery before there is time to resolve our quandary and at that moment the arrival of the Scottish miners' delegation is announced. A hundred Socialist MEPs rise from their seats, look up to us, and applaud thunderously. Sphincters contract. "

JOHN DAVIES, Sept 15th, 1993

Italy

" We set off at six as planned, after five hours sleep. We get to the border about two miles out of Geneva very quickly, but I realise that I still have the other truck's customs papers. We can't return as the motorway is closed to trucks on Sundays. I arrange for the Swiss guard to hand over the papers when the other truck arrives on Tuesday. We then leave for Chamonix as dawn breaks, the Mont Blanc massif coming out of the indigo dark. A sleepy Musa behind the wheel makes the descent hairy, but after a long drive we arrive in Brescia, a stunning mediaeval city. Our lorry scrapes through the very narrow streets to an exquisite square with a columned hall at one end and, catching the afternoon sun in an ochre glow, a giant Renaissance clock. There is a small crowd.

The local organiser, Ros-Angela, is very concerned that I might say something against the UN – the welcome has been organised in a coalition with one wing of the former Communist Party who are neutral over the war and definitely pro-UN. They are influential in the trades unions and Ros-Angela is worried that I might scupper their alliance. She has even prepared a speech for me! I make my own speech, and save the arguments for the public meeting in the evening.

We park next to a display about the war and load forty boxes of aid which the Italian comrades have collected. The display includes a placard commemorating an Italian aid worker who had been shot near Mostar, by bandits apparently.

Our speeches require lengthy translations; English-Italian-Bosnian. There is a sizeable group of Bosnian refugees, nearly all women, and one speaks. She is diplomatic about the UN. The others listen with sad, serious faces. "

JOHN DAVIES, Sept 19th, 1993

THE METHODS OF FASCISM
Atrocities

Alan Brown, a former British soldier, fought with the Croatian army against the Chetniks in 1991. He was a driver on the first Workers Aid convoy.

At first I was put to work alongside other international volunteers on burial parties. The people we were burying were Croats and some Muslims. There were men and women of all ages, from the youngest infant to the very old. Most had been shot or bayonetted. Some had died in bomb blasts.

One of the things the Chetniks did was to cut the hearts out of old men and women and then leave the corpse in a sitting position with their hearts in their hands. What this was supposed to signify was lost on me.

At the end of September 1991 I moved to Osijek and then to Vukovar. Serb gunners had completely devastated Vukovar. When we left we had to run for our lives as if the devil was after us – in a sense this was so. On the way out we 'internationals' stopped to help an old man take what was his grandson down off a door. The Serbs had crucified him. He was about eight years old. His crime was that he was not a Serb.

I last saw that old man sitting on the ground holding the dead boy, crying and rocking him. I think the old man had gone completely mad.

After the defeat we reorganised at Vinkovici. We got new men to replace our dead and wounded – we had left many good friends behind. Soon we began to fight back and we pushed them out of some villages. In one we found horrors that left our minds numb. We found a pile of twenty-two babies – none older than infants. The top ones were white from loss of blood. The bottom ones were reddish brown from the children above. All had the left sides of their necks cut. Their little eyes cried out at you for an explanation.

It had been done systematically, like a production line in a factory.

In and around the houses we found pregnant women. They had been bayonetted through their stomachs. We found no men.

We internationals photographed and documented all these crimes and they were posted to a higher level, to headquarters. Nothing has been done.

People in Britain and elsewhere will find this shocking and hard to take in. Some misguided people will even deny that these atrocities ever took place – just like the fascists do when talking about the holocaust.

Not only did these things happen, but I witnessed the aftermath and helped to bury the victims.

In Slovenia, formerly part of Yugoslavia, we finally had to confront the question asked by the refugees in Britain – how could we reach Tuzla?

The Chetniks first attacked Tuzla from the east, west and north. Territory remained open to the south, stretching down to the border, near Split. Much of this area was mountainous. In places the only route was along newly made dirt tracks but supplies for Tuzla trickled in. This lifeline was cut in April, 1993. Croatian nationalists joined the Chetnik attack on Bosnia. In Herzegovina, at the southern end of the Tuzla route, they launched their own campaign of genocide. The people of the predominantly Muslim side of the old city of Mostar, who had shrunk in terror under a hail of Chetnik shells from the east, were now bombarded from the west. On November 9th, Stari Most, the famous mediaeval bridge linking the different communities either side of the River Neretva, finally collapsed under a barrage of shells.

1st Convoy Factfile

DATE:
December 1993

LORRIES: 18
– 12 from Britain, 2 from Denmark and Sweden, 1 from Italy, 1 from Belgium, 2 from Hungary and Slovakia

WEIGHT: 60 tons of mixed aid

RECIPIENTS:
Savudrija Refugee camp and the Selce and Rijeka orphanages in Croatia. Three lorries to Tuzla miners, the rest left in storage for later convoy

PEOPLE: 70

Red Cross aid convoy after attack by Serbian nationalists in Bosnia

For many, the collapse of Mostar's Stari Most symbol-ised the collapse of multi-cultural Bosnia.

Aid convoys were now caught up in the chaos of war, banditry and village to village fighting. A Tuzla bound convoy of eighty-five lorries was looted by the HVO and many of its Bosnian drivers killed. Tuzla and northern Bosnia were cut off. For six months only UN helicopters had been able to get in or out.

Most of our convoy team spent nine frustrating days at an off-season Slovenian skiing lodge as we tried to find a way to Tuzla. The Slovenian metal workers' union lent us the use of their Jesenice office.

Some people went by car to Split to check out the situ-ation in the south. They reported that fighting made that route very dangerous. Through another channel a British ex-army officer working for Edinburgh Direct Aid offered to try and deliver our aid under UN protection. One or two people, frustrated at the delays, thought we should accept this offer. The majority rejected the idea of handing over our workers' aid to a go-between who might get some food to hungry people but would cer-tainly not deliver the message of workers' solidarity. After such a long, hard journey the desire to deliver some aid, somewhere, was very great. A little of our aid was taken to refugee camps and this helped let off steam and keep the team focused on reaching Tuzla.

The Swedish lorry, Jesenice customs warehouse, Slovenia

GREAT MYTHS OF THE WAR

• Milosevic and the Yugoslav People's Army (JNA) was neutral in the Bosnian war

Edited extract from an article by Ed Vulliamy which originally appeared in *The Guardian.*

Djordje Djukic, the Serbian general being held in The Hague by war crimes investigators, is a general in the army of Yugoslavia proper, and not an officer in the Bosnian Serb army.

The Guardian has exclusively obtained Gen Djukic's identity documents, which show him serving in the Yugoslav army. Leaked military correspondence also shows that the General Staff in the Serbian capital secretly organised the Serbian campaign in Bosnia.

In August 1994, Mr Milosevic promised "military and political sanctions" against the Bosnian Serbs. The UN Security Council duly suspended sanctions against Serbia/Yugoslavia on September 23rd. But Mr Milosevic's 'blockade' of the Bosnian Serbs was a sieve.

Reports submitted by international monitors reveal constant traffic across the border from Yugoslavia into Bosnia. Gen Djukic is head of logistics for their army. The flood of men and weapons escalated before the bloody offensives against Bihac and Srebrenica. As head of logistics, Gen Djukic would have been pivotal.

The JNA told the world that it would pull out of Bosnia in May, 1992. But an extraordinary internal correspondence between Belgrade and Bosnia shows how the Yugoslav army was stitched into the war, directing the Bosnian Serb military.

Entwined with Bosnia's war, the JNA stayed long after its declared May depar-ture date. Muslims from the eastern towns of Visegrad, Zvornik and Foca were driven out by units brought in from garrisons at Uzice, Novi Sad and Nis – all within Serbia.

A leaked memo talks not about the withdrawal of the Yugoslav army, but of its "transformation". It reads: "All units and institutions of the Second Military District were informed about the transformation of the JNA ... Informal meetings were held by all units of the Second Military District."

Financially, Belgrade paid the salaries of officers in the Bosnian Serb army above the rank of major.

Although it agreed to suspend sanctions, the UN knew Belgrade was lying. In the year up to July 1995, UN monitors logged vast quantities of equipment, munitions and fuel crossing from Serbia. The flow accelerated before the Bihac offensive of 1994 and the debacle at Srebrenica last year.

In Banja Luka last week *The Guardian* was told by Gen Mladic's adjutant that Gen Djukic's role in the Bosnian war was to "distribute bread and potatoes".

Another reconnaissance team went up to Zagreb, the Croatian capital. Here we made our first real contact with Tuzla – albeit an outpost. Several towns in Bosnia had established Logistic Centres in Zagreb to try and get food through. The separate existence of these Centres showed how unprepared Bosnia had been for war – the resistance had been organised town by town.

The Tuzla Logistic Centre staff showed us the importance of the northern route: Zagreb – Zupanja – Orasje – Tuzla. Pre-war, this was the main road, most of it along the Zagreb-Belgrade motorway – a four hour drive. Only 15km of the route, inside Bosnia, was under the control of the Chetniks. The Bosnians explained that it was the only route capable of carrying the quantities of aid required. Despite classifying it as a 'blue' aid route the UN, whose role in Bosnia was supposedly to deliver aid convoys, had never attempted to use it. The route was northern Bosnia's main link with the world. Its closure meant slow starvation and defeat for the Bosnian forces in the region, removing an obstacle to the UN's planned division of the country. The 15km under Chetnik control connected their occupied territories in western Bosnia with Pale, their main base in the east. If the Chetniks lost control of that 15km they would be unable to supply a large part of their occupied territory.

The northern route was not simply a question of the best way to get aid to Tuzla – the route was of strategic military importance to both sides. The UN's failure to use it was a refusal to challenge the Chetniks' control and strangulation of Bosnia.

The Tuzla Logistic Centre people asked us to attempt the northern route. This meant we had to get permission from the Croatian government to exit Croatia at Zupanja and push the UN to escort us.

At the lobby of the British TUC we had met a delegate from the Union of Autonomous Trade Unions of Croatia. Now we visited his office in Zagreb and were introduced to the head of the union's international department, Jasna Petrovic. She supported the fight for an undivided BiH and welcomed our initiative. The union gave us logistical support which proved invaluable and issued a statement in support of the convoy calling on other unions in Europe to help stop the division of Bosnia.

Jasna organised a meeting with the Croatian Foreign Ministry. They said they would welcome the opening of the northern route but our passage would depend upon getting UN assistance.

We had already applied to the UN High Commission for Refugees (UNHCR) for help to get to Tuzla. They refused, on the grounds that our aims did not come within their mandate – which was only to help refugees, not citizens in Tuzla. The UNHCR referred us to the UN Protection Force (UNPROFOR) – the military force sent to protect aid convoys. They passed us on to the civil department, which passed us back to the UNHCR. We were on a merry-go-round.

We contacted supporters in other countries asking them to get trade unions and politicians to fax the UN demanding they help the convoy use the northern route.

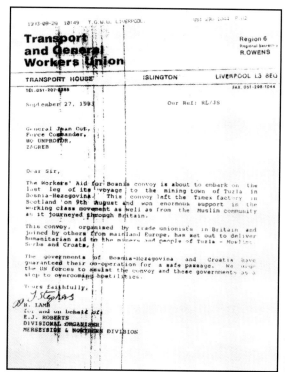

One of the many faxes to General Jean Cot, demanding that the convoy be allowed to use the northern route

In Britain a team went to the Labour Party conference and a number of MPs and union general secretaries were persuaded to send faxes to General Cot, UNPROFOR commander. Faxes poured in from all over the world, including from the leaders of the Confederation General du Travail (CGT) in France, but the the UN still refused to help.

For nine days, while these talks were going on in Zagreb, the rest of the convoy had been waiting in the Slovenian ski lodge. Large convoy meetings, conducted in three or four languages, were lengthy and exhausting. It was not always possible to communicate with the team in Zagreb and frustrations were threatening to get out of hand. A few convoy members had quarrelled and one had stabbed another, but luckily the injury turned out to be not too serious.

Why I'm joining the convoy

" I didn't want to get involved simply in humanitarian activity but from a working class angle. I thought with my experience of driving I would be an ideal person and as a shop steward I will be able to deal with problems as they arise on the route.

In my own way I'm repaying my debts from 1984-85 when the miners of Tuzla came to the aid of the British miners. With my Welsh background this affects me greatly. "

VAUGHAN THOMAS, bus driver, Wood Green Garage, London

To the Victor, the Spoils

Wife of the Serb nationalist war criminal Arkan and patriotic pop singer Ceca Velickovic is seldom off Belgrade television. She appeared in a phone-in programme one day when a woman called to compliment her on her elegance. "You have a beautiful necklace", the caller added, "but it seems there is a stone missing."

Ceca confirmed this was true. "Madame you are very sharp-sighted," the presenter commented.

The caller continued, suggesting that if they examined the back of the necklace they would find a number. They did. "Madame, are you a clairvoyant?" asked the presenter.

"No," the woman said, speaking slowly and carefully. "It is the necklace of my daughter, who was murdered at....on..." and she gave the date. At this point the screen faded, and the programme did not resume.

THE METHODS OF FASCISM
Rape

They came to my village, Kelosevici, on 3rd January. When they came into my house, my six year old sister, Amela, clung to me crying with fear, as one of them started beating our mother.

When we were taken outside I saw that Amela had wet herself in terror. We saw a score of bodies lying in the streets. Many houses were on fire.

After about five hours of marching through a forest they brought us to a clearing where there was already a large group of women, children and older men surrounded by barbed wire. They separated me and other young girls from the rest of the group. That was the last time I saw my mother and my little sister. I doubt that they are alive.

They took us to a compound where they raped us every night, all young women and girls. I can't describe all the things they did to us during these rape sessions. Their minds invented the most perverted acts. Afterwards we had to cook their food and serve them naked.

All the rapes took place in front of everybody. Those who resisted had their throats cut or their limbs severed. The whole place became permanently covered in blood. More girls were brought in, and there were finally about one thousand. I spent about four months in the camp.

One night twelve of us tried to escape. We were helped by my cousin, a Serb. They caught two immediately. The rest of us ran through the forest, hiding for days, walking at night, carefully choosing paths. If it hadn't been for my cousin and his help I would have killed myself – death seemed easier than what we had been through.

I feel that I can't live with my memories. I wonder if I shall be able to find a way that will not lead me to a psychiatric asylum.

From the Croatian monthly, ARENA, January, 1993

A double puncture on the way to Zagreb

Above: At a meeting at the offices of the Autonomous Trade Unions of Croatia in Zagreb, the convoy team decides to blockade UNPROFOR headquarters (below and opposite)

The advance team recommended bringing the whole convoy up to Zagreb and this was done the next day. It was a difficult journey with numerous breakdowns, one of which was irreparable. However our arrival in Zagreb coincided with that of the Hungarian miners and the meeting of trades unionists from east and west raised everyone's spirits. After its lengthy stay in Slovenia, the large team was now champing at the bit. The advance team had reached a dead-end with the UN after days of fruitless negotiations. The convoy members decided on some direct action. On October 1st, we took our lorries and blocked the UNPROFOR HQ entrance. We sounded our horns continually. There was pandemonium. Two members of the convoy team went inside the compound demanding to see General Cot. A letter was handed in protesting that we had received no reply to our requests for protection to take aid to Tuzla. Crowds of local people going home from work gathered outside. Our worries about the response to our presence in Zagreb were unfounded. The Croatian Government was intent on its carve-up of Bosnia but in the large urban population of Zagreb, with its big workers' movement, there was a very different feeling. Many people couldn't understand Croatia's involvement in the Bosnia carve-up when large parts of Croatia were occupied by Chetniks. It was clear that the UN were far from popular in Zagreb. Local citizens had built a low brick wall right round the perimeter of the UN compound. Each brick was inscribed with the name of someone killed during the destruction of the Croatian city of Vukovar. They blamed the UN for doing nothing and joined our protest, some calling out, "Remember Vukovar!" Croatian policemen arrived outside, but decided it was none of their business.

Inside UN officials pleaded with our two representatives to move the lorries. "We have a difficult enough situation here as it is," they said. "The people don't like us. You're making matters worse. Somebody will come and speak to you if you move the lorries."

We told the officials it must be the other way round. Let the General come and talk first.

They took our people to see Brigadier General Jehan Geccaldi. He told them that UNPROFOR's mandate was only to escort UNHCR convoys and only to travel along routes for which they have permission from the forces controlling them.

"So the workers and fighting people of BiH are left to die?"our people asked. He shrugged. "Tell the politicians. They are the ones controlling the situation. All I can suggest is you go and see the UNHCR."

While this was going on someone noticed sand around the oil cap of the front lorry parked just inside the

UNPROFOR barracks. A UN soldier had put sand in it. If we moved, the engine would be damaged. We had been there four and half hours. Now we refused to move until the UN repaired the lorry.

We sat there all night. At 6am the road was blocked off by armed soldiers and UN towing trucks brought in. Our drivers sat behind our lorries and blocked them.

Suddenly Brigadier General Geccaldi appeared. "We will mend your truck." The convoy team demanded this promise in writing. He sent a soldier to get paper and in front of local TV cameras signed a pledge.

The truck was repaired and we moved.

We had blocked the entrance for fourteen hours, but still had no UN assistance. As we moved off a local man said to us, "What kind of a world is it that can bring the army to stop an aid convoy?"

Our protests were shown on Croatian TV. The headline in the Zagreb morning paper was 'Demand protection from Zupanja to Tuzla'.

VJESNIK

HRVATSKI POLITICKI DNEVNIK

U Tuzlu i bez Unprofora!

ZAGREB – U subotu je u Zagrebu Međunarodna radnička pomoć održala konferenciju za novinstvo, objašnjavajući razloge svojoj blokadi zgrade Unprofora u Zagrebu, započeto u petak u 1655 sati i okončano u subotu ujutro u 7.00 sati. Ova humanitarna akcija dopreme devet kamiona s humanitarnom pomoći u hrani i lijekovima radnicima Tuzle inicirana je od strane rudara iz Velike Britanije, a podržali su je svi rudarski i drugi sindikati Europe, kao i druge humanitarne organizacije. Međutim, kada je konvoj u pratnji 25 predstavnika radnika i sindikata iz više europskih država stigao u Zagreb, Unprofor nikako nije htio dopustiti da u Tuzlu krenu preko Hrvatske, već je inzistirao da idu preko Srbije. Odbijajući u svojim lecima, pismima i javnim istupima takvu rutu »jer ne žele ništa od Miloševićeve vlade i Karadžićeve bande«, glasno-

govornici Međunarodne radničke pomoći inzistirali su da im Unprofor pruži zaštitu na putu Virovitica – Županja – Orašje – Srebrenik – Tuzla. Nakon 14-satno blokade zgrade Unprofora sa svojih pet kamiona i izraženog solidariziranja sa zahtjevima prognanika i obitelji poginulih u domovinskom ratu, a koji već više dana prosvjeduju pred istom zgradom, u nedjelju ujutro snago Unprofora su sa dva oklopna vozila i naoružanjem krenuli protiv humanitaraca, jer je hrvatska policija odbila uključiti se u nasilno odvođenje kamiona.

Na današnjoj press-konferenciji Dot Gibson, voditeljica konvoja, te predstavnici Radničke pomoći iz Belgije i Italije, kao i iz drugih europskih zemalja, oštro su osudili ponašanje Unprofora, pitajući se otvoreno »koja je svrha Unprofora na ovom području, kad hrvatski prognanici nisu vraćeni u svoje domove, kad se ne otvaraju putovi humanitarne pomoći za srednju Bosnu, kad je jasno da Unprofor samo nadzire rad ili čak omogućava četnicima da ostvare svoje ciljeve«. (pcs)

Forging friendship

" I worked in a bank in Tuzla for twenty years as senior officer in the foreign exchange department. The salary was not so bad. We did not have a car but we managed to travel a lot. My last trip was to Germany in March 1992, when the situation seemed to be stabilising. On the way back I saw many destroyed houses in Croatia. There were many JNA soldiers along the River Sava giving the impression of defending Bosnia and Herzegovina from an outside enemy. But.....

Soon after came Bijeljina, Zvornik, Konjevic Polje. The refugees flooded into Tuzla. It seemed so far away and I thought somebody would stop these aggressors and defend unarmed people. The JNA barracks was close to my flat. In the darkness of the night empty, long vehicles with covered registration plates went to the barracks and the next night they went back heavily loaded.

Until May 15th, 1992 I thought it was just a bad dream. On that day there was a heavy fight at the crossroads when people ambushed a JNA column. In the night, the first shells were fired at Tuzla. It was difficult to predict what our lives would be like in a couple of days, months....We

Bosnian refugees, spring 1992

could not receive mail and very soon telephone communication with the outside world was cut off.

On the way to work I used to read the new death notices stuck on tree trunks and buildings. I joined Radio Tuzla to translate and read news in English. A few months later I moved to the press centre in the Town Hall.

I am very active in the Photographic Association of BiH. When BiH was recognised by the UN, we photographers decided to apply for membership of the FIAP (International Association of Art Photography). Our membership was accepted, but the Congress – scheduled for May, 1993 in Holland – had to ratify it. The situation in Central Bosnia was very tense. It was very risky to travel and the trip was very long. The only way out was to the south and up the Adriatic coast via the island of Pag to Zagreb. The Mayor of Tuzla helped me with the money and I left. On the way the bus and its passengers were imprisoned twice, but after several long hours of questioning we were released.

I got to the Congress a day late because of visa problems, but I met many people there – some of them had sympathy with Bosnia, some did not understand the situation at all.

My life was turned upside down when I returned to Zagreb: it was not possible to proceed to Tuzla since the only road was blocked by Croats. I did not have much money on me and had to look for cheap accommodation. It was difficult as Croatia was at war and the prices were high.

I started to work in the Tuzla Logistic

Office in Zagreb although nobody could tell me whether I would be paid or not. Many delegations came to the office asking for information about the situation in Tuzla. Some of them went to Tuzla in UNPROFOR helicopters, but local people could not. These people travelling to Tuzla became a channel for letters, money and medicine and for me to receive back information on their way home. Autumn was coming and I asked one of the travellers to bring me some warm shirts from home. Astonished, she asked why I couldn't buy them in Zagreb.

In July we got a message from a Bosnian in Britain that people were campaigning in support of Bosnia and they were preparing a convoy with miners – they would try to reach Tuzla. This idea seemed completely crazy. Towns under the Bosnian government were blockaded and only a few UN convoys were let through. Nevertheless, in Zagreb we all looked forward to meeting these brave people.

One day a group of four or five – an advance team – came to our office. They were in white t-shirts with a logo. They were dirty, which was in total collision with the image we had from UN convoys. A couple of them said they were Trotskyists. We did not know much about Trotsky. He had betrayed the Soviet Communist Party and left the country with the help of the Soviet Union's enemies from the West. Now we had his followers in front of us! And they campaign for Bosnia and they support Bosnia? To me, none of this made sense.

The first issue they wanted to clarify was the route to Tuzla and we had long discussions about this and the importance of the route across the Posavina pass in the north – the northern route. In the meantime the convoy arrived and we prepared a welcome dinner party. Accommodation was a problem for so many people. There was a Bosnian who had started to construct a motel and he offered a big, unfurnished room and a cellar. "

FARUK IBRAHIMOVIC

"UNPROFOR – Why do you want Tuzla to die? Let the convoy through!" Behind the placard is the Vukovar wall of remembrance.

Despite the blockade of the UNPROFOR HQ, we were still in Zagreb and every day was costing us a further £200 as drivers had to be fed and boarded. We were in debt from the long delay in Jesenice. We could wait no longer and headed off to Zupanja. On the way police stopped the convoy in Bjelovar and everyone taken to a local police station. We demanded to know under what law we were being detained. There was no answer. They told us they were waiting for documents from the Croatian Foreign Ministry.

A day later we were still being held, so we decided to test out the nature of this arrest. Everyone got in their lorries in the compound and started sounding their horns non-stop. We managed to open the compound gates and drove out.

An angry convoy member confronts a US military policeman

We arrived in Zupanja and across the River Sava could see Bosnia for the first time. All the bridges over the Sava had been blown up. Traffic had to use a large motorised raft to reach Orasje, a Bosnian town under HVO control but surrounded by Chetniks. The police refused to let us on the ferry and showed us a document signed by the Croatian Foreign Secretary, saying we were only allowed to exit Croatia via Lipovice, that is into Serbia.

We demanded to know what law prevented us from leaving via Zupanja and into Bosnia. There was no answer.

The Tuzla Logistic Centre had telephoned the Mayor of Orasje and the local HVO commander and made arrangements for our accommodation there. They also told us that they had contacts that might make it possible for us to negotiate with the Serb soldiers on the front line, just outside Orasje. But we could not just cross the river in the same way we had driven out of the police station. The river crossing point was bristling with troops and guns. The sound of shelling and gunfire from across the river was constant.

We waited in our trucks by the river, plagued by mosquitoes. After two nights the chief of police told us we could cross, but by now UNPROFOR had sent out a message warning all regional authorities not to help us. When we telephoned the HVO authorities on the other side of the river in Orasje, they would no longer let us in. We had reached an impasse.

For three weeks we had been trying to push forward, testing the relations between the Croat government, the UN and the Chetniks. The campaign in Britain, France, Spain and elsewhere had been giving political support to the convoy, but it was not yet strong enough to be decisive.

Zupanja

" It was the UN who were to be the biggest obstacle to our journey. We had no illusions about the UN, and they were fully aware of who we were. When we demanded UNPROFOR protection to pass 15km of nationalist held territory, their role as a pro-nationalist, pro-partition force in Bosnia was made clear. They said Workers Aid would not get protection and that we should leave our aid in warehouses for possible delivery by the UNHCR at some future date.

We moved on and arrived in darkness at Zupanja. Come morning it was a shock to realise that we had finally arrived in the war zone. Each building had its windows protected by huge planks of wood or uncut logs and the doors had pallets of bricks in front to guard against shrapnel.

In Zupanja

We were waiting for confirmation that we could cross the river into Bosnia on the ferry, but each day brought new disappointments. The Croatian Government claimed it was reluctant to put our lives at risk by authorising passage without UN protection. The Mayor of Orasje, a mainly Bosnian Croat enclave on the opposite bank completely surrounded by Chetniks, didn't want to offend the Croatians upon whom his town had relied for all its supplies. So we produced leaflets for the locals asking for their support and we parked our lorries outside the border post.

As previously on our journey, we turned to the organised working class in Europe and asked for messages of support for the convoy to be sent to the Croatian Government. The response was immediate, with faxes arriving from union branches and officers, including my union General Secretary, Bill Morris, as well as from many Labour MPs.

We camped there on the river bank for two days and nights, our conversation punctuated by the sound of mortars and gun fire and the sound of Moslem prayers from the mosque on the opposite bank. But it was impossible for us to cross the river. We had to take the bitter decision to turn back. "

VAUGHAN THOMAS, London bus driver

Until now every apparent stalemate had been broken by a forward movement. Now a difficult decision had to be made. A tense meeting of tired, frustrated people took place – people mostly unknown to each other a few weeks earlier. On the road friendships, alliances and antagonisms had grown up. A proposal was made to return home to campaign for the opening of the northern route. Everyone was bitterly disappointed at not reaching Tuzla, to be so near and yet so far. Most of the team had never experienced the kind of campaign now being proposed. The convoy, they could understand. It was something definite. But to return to launch a campaign? It was hard to see this as anything but defeat.

Some drivers wanted to try the southern route from Split. Others argued that the whole purpose of the convoy was to build a movement across Europe. If that wasn't done, getting to Tuzla or not getting to Tuzla made little difference. If lorries went down the southern route there was a chance that someone would get killed. Many drivers were willing to take the personal risk, but imagine what the death of a convoy member would mean for the further development of solidarity in Britain or elsewhere. The convoy had received support across Europe but its base was still very small. Many people, union leaders, politicians etc, opposed the convoy's clear support for one side in the war. Even before we left we were accused of being irresponsible towards our young volunteers. Our opponents would use a death to blow our embryonic campaign out of the water.

The meeting swayed to and fro, with most of the arguing being done by members of different political groups. Then one of the young people, who had joined the convoy en-route in Britain, backed the proposal to go home and fight for the northern route. He carried most of the 'non-aligned' people with him. The following resolution was passed: *The international Workers Aid convoy cannot reach the workers of Tuzla on this occasion. It has been forced to turn back only seventy-five kilometres from the town by UNPROFOR and those who speak and act for the UN in the region.*

It was the Chetniks' guns which pointed at Tuzla. But we had been prevented from even getting to talk to them. The UN formed a protective ring around the Chetniks.

On October 17th the lorries returned to Zagreb, distributing some of the aid in refugee camps and putting some of it in store, ready to go to Tuzla whenever the possibility arose.

The difficult decision taken in Zupanja continued to be discussed and disputed. Five people announced they were taking three lorries down to Split. Workers Aid had started only a few weeks earlier. It did not have the kind of democracy that could have said a majority decision was binding.

They painted out the Workers Aid logos on their lorries, registered with the UNHCR as a humanitarian charity and got permission to cross into Bosnia via Split.

They negotiated their way through the Croat nationalists lines and after many weeks they reached Tuzla. They were received with great joy by the miners' union leaders and other people leading the multi-cultural resistance in Tuzla. The drivers told them of the campaign for international workers' solidarity and it made a big impact. When they left Tuzla, snow was falling and the tracks were treacherous. Two of the lorries, including one costing £11,000, were abandoned and never recovered.

The progress of the convoy right through Europe had been closely followed in Britain, particularly by the Bosnian community and a convoy report back meeting was organised for October 30th, in Manchester. Some 400-500 people attended the meeting in the Town Hall, including a number of people from

Convoy organiser, Dot Gibson, reporting back to the Manchester meeting

Europe and two guests from the Tuzla Logistic Centre in Zagreb.

Reports were given on all the experiences of the first convoy. Two resolutions were tabled. One proposed a large convoy to go down the northern route in March, 1994. The other, following the example of the people who had broken away from the convoy, was to try to take small convoys in via Split.

All day people from both sides of the argument spoke. The differences were not just about convoy tactics. The northern route campaign involved a confrontation with the UN who were strangling multi-cultural Bosnia. This meant building the biggest mass movement possible. The people backing the other perspective spoke of the UN's role being contradictory. They put more emphasis on the 'aid' aspect of the campaign rather than mobilising the workers' movement. There were also differences about the campaign's structures. The northern route supporters wanted a committee open to anyone, while the other grouping wanted to establish a more formal, delegate system.

The Logistic Centre representative spoke in favour of the campaign for the northern route and late in the afternoon the

Counting the vote at manchester

resolutions were put to the vote. The northern route campaign was carried nearly two to one, with all the Bosnian refugees present and most of the convoy members voting for it.

Hungarian representatives at the Manchester meeting

The group which had ended up in the minority had organised a meeting for the following day. They said that the previous day's vote only held for people in Britain and that this meeting was for all international supporters to decide what to do. A Hungarian convoy member, a leading participant in the 1956 Hungarian uprising, asked if the meeting was to discuss implementing the previous day's decision. The chairman said no, whereupon the Hungarian, the Spanish, the Tuzla representatives and several others left the meeting.

The remaining people set up their own organisation, called International Workers Aid, based mainly in Scandinavia. They planned their programme of aid for Tuzla but deleted opposition to the UN from their campaign's aims.

We started our campaign for a big convoy to open the northern route.

Resolution passed at Manchester Conference

Our convoy revealed the United Nations' conspiracy to starve the people of Bosnia into submission, to accept the Vance-Owen plan to strangle their country and create ghettos in line with 'ethnic cleansing'.

We therefore call upon European trades unions, workers, young people, and those who defend democratic rights to build an international Workers Aid convoy to Bosnia at the end of February to open the northern corridor to Tuzla.

To co-ordinate the work of the local Workers Aid Committees, a steering committee should be set up of all those who want to take a lead in this work. The first meeting should elect a chairperson, secretary and treasurer.

Experience shows that, together with the fund-raising and political campaign of the local committees, the organisation of a convoy requires a core team of people to deal with trucks, route, customs and the permits to travel etc. We therefore propose that such a team be comprised of members of the first convoy team.

October 30th, 1993

It takes all sorts

Hilary, editor
Dave, community worker
Naseem, teacher
Terry, lecturer
Zejlko, telecom engineer, refugee
Pete, council worker
Steve, mature student
Norman, pensioner
Kano, car sprayer, refugee
Polly, teacher
Jeremy, administrator
Sue, lecturer
Shirley, nurse
Max and Jacob, school-children
Dave, microbiologist
Jill, teacher
Arthur, unemployed
Oz, student
Alma, school pupil, refugee
Elma, school pupil, refugee
Rabija, housewife, refugee
David, unemployed
Faruk, translator, refugee
Shamina, student
Paul, lecturer
Susanna, student
Tom, unemployed
Charlie, unemployed
Jorde, student
John, lecturer
Edna, cleaner
Margaret, community worker
Josephine, librarian
Sean, taxi driver
Paddy, student
Jasmina, school pupil, refugee
Barbara, community worker
Jean, writer
Tony, community worker
Bozena, print worker
Jim, maintenance engineer
Phil, teacher
Azra, teacher, refugee
Bob, unemployed
Sue, lorry driver
Patrick, criminologist
Damir, student
Dave, restaurant worker
Vanessa, public relations
Geoff, sports officer
Nippon, translator
John, actor
Greg, media worker
Adam, unemployed
Martin, lecturer

A small cross-section of Workers Aid volunteers

Behind the war - a view from Serbia

The Bosnian war was only inter-ethnic in appearance. In reality, it was a war against working people imported from outside. Following Tito's death the Yugoslav Government and the whole bureaucracy was threatened with popular anger because of the country's debt; unemployment was growing, prices were spiralling.

Five hundred million dinars: inflation in Serbia, 1993

Far from being able to build 'self-managed' socialism in a single country, the bureaucracy was unable to solve a single problem facing people and split along national lines, relying more and more on nationalism to deflect popular protests.

The bureaucracy was weak and unable to confront the united Yugoslav working class head on. It had to be divided. The bureaucrats, nearly all members of the Communist Party, encouraged nationalism to become a dominant force among all the different people of Yugoslavia, but its significance was not the same everywhere.

The national movement of the Albanians of Kosova deserves support. It is the response of a small and oppressed people. Serbian nationalism, however, is completely reactionary, arrogant and aggressive, flirting openly with fascism. Without Milosevic in Serbia there would be no Tudjman in Croatia. It was in response to the Serb nationalists' growing arrogance that nationalist bureaucrats in the other republics could draw 'their' people to their side.

Nationalist hysteria was unleashed in Serbia by the bureaucrats, led by Milosevic, because their positions of privilege in Serbia were the most threatened. The Serbian workers would have finished off this regime several years ago if Milosevic had not succeeded in creating permanent political tension, whipping up an infernal spiral of hate, first in Kosova, then Slovenia, Croatia, Bosnia.

Milosevic sowed this poison of nationalism to save the ruling bureaucracy from a workers' revolution. Every time there was the threat of a strike or major protest, it was thwarted by some spectacular coup amongst the bureaucracy.

There was a direct relationship between the escalation of conflicts in Kosova, Croatia and Bosnia and the threat of workers' uprisings in Serbia.

Milosevic was elected by the workers' votes, but he had to attack them. Workers in Serbia had to be made to forget they had nothing to feed their children. They had to have it drummed into them that these were grave times for all the nation, that sacrifices were necessary. Patriotism and treachery became the two dominant words.

Milosevic had to 'retreat forwards' to stay in power but to do so his line of march had to become more headlong, mad and bloody. He had to open the door to the fascists.

He transformed the Yugoslav People's Army, which came out of the partisan revolution, into something controlled by these fascists. At the front lines the Titoist officers were forced to submit to the orders of the fascist gangsters – Arkan, Seselj and others. The red star on the caps was replaced by the white eagle.

In order to destroy the working class, which in fifty years had become a great threat to the bureaucracy, and in order to

"Give me back my brother." Women in Belgrade protesting against the war

stronghold in Belgrade. There was a 65 per cent abstention, invalidating the election, but the 'socialist' leader Milosevic recognised the result. Every night television would show Seselj, strutting around in his khaki uniform, waving the Chetniks' black, death's-head flag.

The Partisan revolution, started in 1941, and this counter-revolution are crossing swords. This filthy war was intended to grind down the working class physically, to deliver all the people of ex-Yugoslavia, exhausted, starving and demoralised, to the mercy of western imperialism which will be begged to buy what is left of the national wealth for a pittance.

That is the real content of this war; the restoration of capitalism. Neither Milosevic or Tudjman dared openly attack collective ownership of the factories and mines before the war. They were not strong enough. Privatisation and the restoration of capitalism could not be achieved in a peaceful manner. The workers' movement had to be crushed. The inter-Yugoslav wars have opened the door to this restoration through the bloody destruction of Yugoslavia – the unity established by the Partisan workers.

But things are not yet finished. In Serbia, after the war-like frenzy and triumphant nationalist songs, will come the bitter disappointment, the discovery of the blood-stained reality and, finally, immense anger. People will come to the conclusion that we have been tricked. This is not our war. We have died for the privileged ones in the rear.

RADOSLAV PAVLOVIC, Belgrade

trap the mass of unemployed youth, this reactionary force was directed against centres where the workers were the most ethnically mixed, where there were the largest numbers of mixed marriages, where the Yugoslav spirit dominated over nationalist feelings. Tuzla had the highest percentage of people declaring themselves 'Yugoslavs'.

Vukovar, the Croatian workers' town, was the experiment for this war unleashed from above. Everything that was later to devastate Bosnia was there. Long range artillery, blind destruction of the town, driving out the population through fear. The armies must not meet. Young conscripts, all speaking the same language and until recently holding the same passports, must be kept apart. News is blockaded, distorted. Terror is brought down on anyone who hesitates in carrying out the orders to destroy. Gangs from the dregs of society are unleashed, fed and armed by the Army General Staff but guided by the fascist parties. Just prior to the attack on Vukovar, the fascist leader, Seselj (Doctor of Business Studies) stood for parliament in a working class

The turncoat heroes who fight for Bosnia

From Emma Daly
in Sarajevo

"NEVER has a Serbian boot stepped on this ground," a Bosnian government commander said proudly to his general, who was visiting the *armija* trenches on Mount Zuc, part of the defensive line around Sarajevo. "Good," replied General Jovan Divjak, No 2 in the Bosnian army, "but what about me?" The commander laughed: "You? You don't count."

General Divjak is the most prominent of several thousand Serbs still fighting against their ethnic brothers for a united, multiracial Bosnia. A bluff, eccentric and former officer in the Yugoslav National Army (JNA), he was born in Belgrade but moved to Sarajevo 26 years ago. "I always felt Bosnian, that I was part of Yugoslavia," he said. "I never felt that much a Serb. I didn't have that sense of national pride — it's more important to me to belong to the city, and to Bosnia-Herzegovina."

Men such as General Divjak are loathed with a passion by those they are fighting; one Bosnian Serb official struggled to find a word in English bad enough to describe him and his ilk, a word beyond "traitor". "They are just . . . *not Serbs*," he said finally, the ultimate insult in a statelet where Serbian blood is everything.

For General Divjak, his enemies are not only the product of "psychopathic thinking", but also savages who must be stopped. His views are shared by his soldiers, even those desperate to escape the army. Aleksa, 25, crossed the line from Grbavica in May 1992 to avoid the Bosnian Serb draft, then volunteered for the *armija*. "When I came to this side, the war had already started, so I knew what was going on. I was ashamed," he said. "We all volunteered for the army. We had to defend this town or the Muslim population would have been exterminated."

But now? "I would give two fingers of my left hand to get out of the army", he said. "After two years, is it still possible to talk about the salvation of Sarajevo and Bosnia? I don't think like this because I am a Serb. I have a lot of non-Serb friends who share my opinion."

General Divjak is aware of such thinking, but insists that his *armija* will triumph if it receives the weapons and technical support so conspicuously lacking. Once the JNA had waged war in Slovenia and Croatia, he felt he had no choice but to fight his old comrades. "It was so clear the JNA stood only for the interests of Serbs. I didn't accept that the Serbian people were at risk in Bosnia."

But even "loyal" Serbs had problems, although the treatment of Serbs in Sarajevo and elsewhere in Bosnia could not be compared to the brutality meted out to Muslims in the self-declared "Republika Srpska" across the front line. "Given the behaviour of [Radovan] Karadzic's extremist Serbs and Chetnik forces, it was very hard for us to win the confidence of the Bosnian side," General Divjak said. The percentage of Serbs in the *armija* had fallen from about 15 to 3 per cent; some had left the country, some had moved to the police force, others had defected. "Serbs are still expelling Muslims from Bijeljina and Banja Luka, so why should Muslims treat Serbs here better?" he asked. But they do.

Dragan, a policeman, insists that, as a Serb, he has never been bothered. A photograph of a smiling teenager is displayed in the sitting room of his flat: Milana, his 13-year-old daughter, lives in Grbavica with her grandmother.

Dragan comes from Foca, one of the nastiest places in the sinister Drina valley. The prewar Muslim majority in Foca has been reduced to just one Muslim man. The rest were "cleansed" or murdered, the town renamed "Srbinje" (Serb place). Dragan, who moved to Sarajevo as a young man, shudders at the thought of Foca.

"When I visited my wife's family in Serbia, they called me 'the Bosnian' — they never used my name," said Dragan, who joined the Sarajevo police force nine months ago. "It didn't matter whether we were Serbs or Muslims or Croats, we were all Bosnian in our hearts and in the minds of other people. In the hearts and minds of normal people, this is how it will remain after the war."

■ Britain would face a serious rift with the US over former Yugoslavia if Washington lifted the arms embargo on Bosnia, British sources said in Usedom, Germany, yesterday, writes Andrew Marshall. EU foreign ministers meeting on the Baltic Sea island approved in principle an easing of sanctions against Belgrade if Serbia allowed outsiders to monitor its blockade of the Bosnian Serbs.

The Independent on Sunday,
September 11th, 1994

The campaign for the northern route

The convoy had been a chaotic helter-skelter. Once the original proposal was made, the convoy took on a life of its own – out of anyone's complete control. This could have been avoided if we had some vast organisation, which we didn't, or if we had turned away all the people who responded to our idea – defeating the whole purpose of the initiative. We had to learn to live with chaos.

After the Manchester meeting there was a clearer idea of how the campaign should develop. A committee meeting was called, open to anyone who wanted to help organise the work. The meeting planned a campaign to get the biggest possible convoy by March. We aimed to capitalise on all the contacts made by the first convoy. However things did not work out like that. Once again, real life intruded on our plans.

Our friends from the Tuzla Logistic Centre begged us to send a few lorries in December. Starvation in Tuzla was getting worse. Desperate for a break-through, they hoped the 'Christmas spirit' might just create a chance of getting through. What could we do but agree to try?

Work began to get four lorries to Zagreb for December. This was a big problem. The first convoy left a £26,000 debt. Some lorries had not made it back. Others were incapable of another trip. New lorries had to be bought. A convoy team had to be got together, though this was the smallest problem. Many of the first team volunteered to go again.

Work to get this convoy ready took all our time. We had no office and few experienced campaigners. Preparations for a big March convoy were inevitably delayed.

Stuttgart   December, 1993

Dear Citizens of Tuzla,

We are refugees in Germany and temporary workers who feel homesick for our beautiful Tuzla. We have been trying to organise ourselves so that all the people from the Tuzla region are involved in collecting aid.

We send best regards to Mayor Selim Beslagic. He is a man we trust. Tuzla has shown its character during the second world war and especially now when all the national parties come in force during this dirty war. Tuzla has always been a positive example. It has morally strong people who always go forward and have not been led by nationalist parties, the national vampires who destroy everything in front of them.

People and property are being destroyed everywhere in Bosnia-Herzogovina. The question is, should we have voted for nationalism or not? Who is the winner? We all have lost everything. Now we live in darkness and it will be very hard to rebuild. Remember the summer and winters spent together and all the actions we took together. Remember our dinners, our weddings, our parties together. At that time we never asked who was who, we sat together – that was civilisation.

National leaders said they were going to save the people, but these 'saviours'destroyed everything: bridges over rivers, bridges connecting people. We did not need national parties like the SDS (Serbian nationalist party), SDA (Muslim nationalist party), HDZ (Croatian Nationalist party). We only needed to work and not go back 300 years.

Try to remember the personal feelings we had; we could go anywhere, we could walk from Slovenia to Macedonia and rest where we wanted, eat and sing. Now we cannot. Love overcame all the borders. People got married without asking the 'national saviours' consent. Now people are 'ethnically cleansed' and pushed into national pens.

The families of the 'national saviours' are not hungry, thirsty or cold. They have enough money. The saviours do not like peace because they make good profit from the war.

Europe and the USA are sorry for ex-Yugoslavia. All the newspapers write about Sarajevo, about how it was a multi-cultural centre. But all of them contributed to the destruction of the city and our peace.

Now we do not know how our neighbours will celebrate Christmas. National leaders made a plan of destruction but they are in a minority. We, ordinary people, have to stop this agony. We are in a majority and that is our power, our arms.

A letter given to Workers Aid in Germany, en-route for Tuzla

The December convoy also took us down a path we had not expected. Our campaign to open the northern route was reported in Bosnian papers distributed among the one million Bosnian refugees scattered across Western Europe. As the second winter of war closed in they were more aware than anyone of the utter misery in the besieged towns, without food, lighting or heat in sub-zero temperatures. In Germany half a million refugees had joined a quarter of a million Bosnians working there before the war. These communities were well organised and had been sending food and clothes to their home towns until the aid routes closed up. Some Bosnians in Stuttgart heard we planned to try to send a few lorries down the northern route in December and they asked if we could take food which they had in store. We sent two empty lorries from Britain. This began joint work with Bosnians across Europe and it was with them and not with the organised labour movement that we really started to prepare the March convoy.

The campaign for the northern route reported in the Croatian press

7.12.94

Nice work if you can get it

Retired Canadian General Lewis MacKenzie, Commander of UN troops in Bosnia from March to August 1992, has taken part in a speaking tour funded by a Serb-American pressure group, SerbNet. He was paid $15,000 plus expenses, SerbNet confirmed.

Gen. MacKenzie never disclosed SerbNet's financial support, despite giving testimony before the House Armed Services Committee in which he re-stated his view that all sides in the Bosnian war were equally to blame:

"Dealing with Bosnia is a little like dealing with three serial killers - one has killed fifteen, one has killed ten, one has killed five. Do we help the one that's only killed five?"

GREAT MYTHS OF THE WAR

● The war was caused by Germany's premature recognition of Croatia

The war in former Yugoslavia has seen an outpouring of anti-German sentiment in Britain. Even though we beat the Germans in two World Wars and one World Cup, they still have not learnt their lesson. In order to expand to the east with their new Fourth Reich, they recognised Croatia. This encouraged Bosnia's secession from Yugoslavia and the resulting war. Such, in essence, was the anti-German view.

Irrespective of this or that Western powers' foreign policy motives, did the Bosnian people have the democratic right to secede from Yugoslavia? Some on the left see in secession a German plot to destroy 'socialist' Yugoslavia, but what kind of socialist supports holding together a federation of nations against the will of its lesser nations? In any case, Germany recognised Croatia over six months after the war had already started.

Whatever plans were hatched between politicians in private, the Bosnian and Croatian people were not persuaded to secede by the slippery tongue of the German Foreign Minister, but by a rabidly nationalistic campaign launched by Slobodan Milosevic in Serbia. This campaign involved:

- A media campaign within Serbia of hate-mongering, directed against Kosovans, Muslims and Croats
- The use of the Yugoslav Army (JNA) to suppress a pro-democracy demonstration in Belgrade
- The passing of laws dramatically reducing the rights of trade unions within Serbia
- The illegal overthrow of the governments of Montenegro, Kosova and Vojvodina
- The use of the JNA to bloodily suppress strikes and demonstrations in Kosova

In the face of these attacks the people of Slovenia, Croatia and Bosnia lost all faith in the Yugoslav Federation, within which they no longer felt physically safe.

British capitalist circles are naturally jealous of the growing power of the Deutschmark in eastern Europe. Their sentiment is echoed by the blinkered left. At a Workers Aid public meeting in London a 'marxist' in the audience denounced our support for Bosnian independence. "Don't you know", he asked, "that the currency in Bosnia is now the Deutschmark?"

A Serb, newly arrived from 'socialist' Serbia, jumped up, pulled out his wallet and, waving some Deutschmarks, retorted, "And what do you think the currency in Serbia is?"

A Kafkaesque journey

" Apparently a simple proposition: take four trucks to Zagreb from Stuttgart. The reality proved to be a strange odyssey. Our first real problem – apart from blizzards, one truck being impounded by the German police, and getting lost in Stuttgart for four hours – was an extreme mismatch of expectations between us and the Bosnians we had met in Germany. Their expectation: we would take 5,000 personal parcels to their loved ones in the Tuzla region. We had two empty lorries – it would have needed another four.

After long, tense meetings with the hundreds of refugees, we loaded what we could and set off from Stuttgart. After further amusing mishaps, made more hilarious by our not sleeping for two days, we finally reached the Czech border to enter the land of Franz Kafka. The Czech border guards made us wait for eight hours.

"Pay us three thousand Deutschmarks," they told us, "and we'll give it back when you leave the country – honest." We had no choice but to pay. We went on, stopping at a truck park for two hours' badly needed sleep. At the point of exit from the Czech Republic we asked for our money back.

"Aha!" exclaimed the Customs man. "You have to pick it up in the nearest town." Two hours later we found the office – a wee room, at the end of a railway station, which was empty apart from a desk and a fridge with some cheese in it.

Eventually a man with a dog turned up to ignore us. An hour later we got our money. Because we were leaving the country immediately they gave it to us in the local currency with the promise that we could change it into Deutschmarks free of charge at the office next door. The woman in the office next door charged 150DM to carry out the exchange.

Slovakia was relatively straightforward – only an hour or so to deal with the bureaucrats. Hungary was brilliant, apart from being ripped off for another £100 at the border. I had my passport stamped and reached the Croatian entry point at 2.30am. An hour later we were told we could move. As we entered Croatia a police officer ran out and stopped us. We were told that we had to go to Split or return immediately. We intended to go to Zagreb and then to Zupanja, the start of the northern route into Bosnia. We refused to go to Split. We returned, and I got my passport stamped on re-entering Hungary. Next day we went again and I got my passport stamped – again. This time the Croatian authorities said we had to go to Belgrade, which is of course the capital of Serbia. We refused, and they said we should contact the British embassy to get permission to go to Zupanja.

The official policy of the Croatian government is to allow freedom of movement within its borders for aid convoys. So why, I asked the border guard, should we ask the British government, and why should we be forced to go to Split? The Customs man was annoyed. We were refused entry. I had my passport stamped.

Next day, after yet another stamping of my passport, we went to the Croatian border. They have a shift system. Each time we went, there were new folk who didn't know us.

"Show us the paperwork", said the official. He looked at it, said it was odd, and walked away. We were sent back. And – you've guessed it – my passport was stamped.

Next day was Christmas Eve. We set out early. After more ritual stamping we approached the Croatian border-post. Our translator stole the Customs man's hat. The Customs man let off fireworks and I ate their Christmas cake.

All this time people in London and Zagreb had been lobbying the Croatian authorities and eventually the word came through that we could go to Zagreb. Just to make sure we reached Zagreb and nowhere else we were honoured with a police escort. In the sky we could see tracer fire as troops celebrated Christmas.

On the way, twenty kilometres from Zagreb, a local police chief decided to stop us and ordered two police officers to search us. We objected strongly. Bad Cop went to check the seals on our trucks. Good Cop stayed with us and sang Christmas carols. One convoy member asked if he could have a shot at driving the police car. Good Cop said, "Yes!"

I will never forget the red tail-lights of the car disappearing in the rain as our convoy member drove away. All around us guns were firing.

At 2am on Christmas morning we finally made Zagreb. The vegetarians among us were fed ham. The barman claimed it was cheese with fish in it! "

GEORGE ANGUS

Our four lorries entered Croatia on Christmas Eve and the team checked into the hostel in Zagreb where they had stayed during the first convoy. It was still full of Bosnian soldiers, injured earlier in the war. They had come to Croatia for medical treatment and their return was then blocked by fighting. They wanted to get back to defend their towns against the 'ethnic cleansers'. Week after week they just sat and waited. Life was on hold. Their bodies were in Croatia but their minds were in Bosnia, a plight mirrored by refugees across the world.

In Zagreb we began another round of meetings with the Croatian Government, the UN and the Logistic Centres of all the towns in the Posavina corridor, towns whose fate hung on the opening of the northern route. The logistic centres now saw us as the leaders of the fight to open the route. This was slightly curious. They had offices, faxes, full time staff and secretaries. We had just about nothing but a few battered old lorries. However, we did have this perspective of a movement of the people of Europe; not governments, but the people. After a year of betrayal by the UN and the great democrats of the world this idea of a peoples' movement, a working class movement, began to make sense to some of the people working for the logistic centres. Unfortunately, people often assumed that since it was us who proposed this mass action we must represent large numbers of people and could somehow mobilise them by a word of command. It led to many misunderstandings.

2nd
Convoy Factfile
DATE: December 1993
LORRIES: 4 lorries
WEIGHT: 15 tons of mixed aid
RECIPIENT: Tuzla Miners' Union.
PEOPLE: 12
ARRIVED IN TUZLA: March 1994

Paris demonstration with French Workers Aid banner

Faruk Ibrahimovic delivers letters on behalf of demonstrators outside the United Nations office in London demanding the opening of the northern route to Tuzla and Tuzla Airport, December, 1993

Our meetings in Zagreb with the various authorities got us nowhere and again faxes were sent from around the world to the UN and Croatian government – Let the convoy pass! Faruk Ibrahimovic, from the Logistic Centre, went to Spain and with help from Ayuda Obrera, (Spanish Workers Aid), had meetings with various mayors and officials where he asked them to lobby the Croatian government. Suddenly, on December 29th, a Croatian Foreign Office official handed us written permission to exit via Zupanja.

Workers Aid, with its four old lorries, had done what no-one else had even tried to do in a year and a half – opened the first door of the northern route. News of this buzzed amongst the logistic centres in Zagreb and the aid organisations. Many of these were huge outfits with big warehouses and budgets that made ours look like tea money. A large percentage of this money, however, came directly from British and other governments who were intent on dividing Bosnia, so it was hardly surprising the aid business had accepted, without challenge, the UN's diversion of all aid to Split.

We wanted to rush off to Zupanja but the Logistic Centre made us wait as they wanted to put more lorries behind ours. A few days later twelve lorries set off for Zupanja and we were soon back on the banks of the River Sava. Instead of the heat and mosquitoes, there was now ice and mud.

The long-awaited permission from the Croatian government to exit Croatia at Zupanja

THE METHODS OF FASCISM
Cultural destruction

Of the hundreds of mosques destroyed since 1992 in Bosnia-Herzegovina, most were not casualties of war, but were deliberately and systematically razed in areas already controlled by Serb or Croat extremists. It is thus hardly surprising that those totally destroyed in 'Republika Srpska' and 'Herceg-Bosna' include the oldest and culturally most valuable: in Banja Luka, fifteen mosques from the 16th or 17th centuries; four 16th-century mosques at Bijeljina; the 18th-century Atik mosque at Brcko; the 16th-century Gradska mosque at Derventa; in Foca, six mosques from the 16th century, and in the surrounding area two 15th-century mosques - the Turhan Emin Beg at Ustikolina and the Stara at Jelec; the 16th-century Krzlar Agha mosque at Mrkonjic Grad; three mosques at Nevesinje from the 15th or 16th centuries; two 16th-century mosques at Rogatica; at Rudo, two mosques from the 16th-century; the 16th-century Hamza Beg mosque at Sanski Most; Semiz Pasha's 15th-century mosque at Praca near Pale; at Stolac, a 16th-century mosque; a 15th-century mosque at Trebinje; a 15th and a 17th-century mosque at Visegrad; the 15th-century Ebul Feth's (Kuslat) mosque and 16th-century Mehmed Celebija's mosque at Zvornik.

From Bosnia Report *(published by The Alliance to Defend Bosnia-Herzegovina)*

A delegation went across on the ferry to hold talks with the HVO commanders in Orasje.

The enclave was still being shelled. Most of the buildings had war damage and the roads were churned to mud. Local HVO commanders listened to our plans for workers' solidarity against the division of Bosnia. The HVO here had little in common with the HVO of Herzegovina and its' bloody war against Bosnia. Here they wanted to fight the Chetniks, who were shelling their town, not the Bosnian army. All day we talked – discussing the war, the future of Bosnia, the future of humanity. They took us for a drink in a bar while mortars exploded in the distance.

Despite their frustrations about the war the HVO were between the hammer and the anvil. They collaborated with the Second Corpus of the Bosnian army under Brigadier Sadic Hazim, who gave written permission for the convoy to travel through areas under his control, but they took orders from Gojko Susak, the Croatian Minister of Defence. Susak, a millionaire with a burger bar chain in the USA, had returned to Croatia and bought his way to power after the break-up of the old regime. The HVO commander contacted Susak. He refused to give consent for our passage through Orasje.

The lorries returned to Zagreb. Most of the team returned to Britain. Four people set off by car round Europe, visiting supporters. In Slovenia they met with Franc Druks, President of the miners' union there, which was helping us prepare the March convoy. Druks returned to Zagreb with us to lend weight to the negotiations. Many Slovenian miners originally came from Tuzla and had families there. They had been taking aid but now couldn't get through.

Day after day negotiations dragged on, sometimes in Zagreb, sometimes elsewhere. Contacts were made in Hungary between the Bosnians and people from Banja Luka, the main Chetnik controlled town supplied via the Chetnik corridor that crossed and blocked our route. Agreements were made to let the convoy pass through the Chetnik lines, but as soon as the agreement was reached it evaporated. Sixty-nine people were killed and two hundred injured in a mortar attack on a Sarajevo market. The UN moved troops into front line positions around Sarajevo and talked about bombing Chetnik positions. It remained talk, but for the moment our deal was off.

Letters to the Editor

Tuzla imprisoned by the UN

Tuzla is a town of 110,000 inhabitants and 60,000 refugees from nearby places occupied by Serbs. The population of north-eastern Bosnia is 1.3 million.

Tuzla is gradually starving, but due to the blockade imposed on roads and telecommunications nobody knows about the sufferings of its people. Electricity is down to 1½ hours a day, and sometimes there is none; the same is true of tap water (there has been no water supply for ten days at the time of writing). Although the electricity and water supply plants are located in Tuzla or within the free territory, these plants need diesel, spare parts and water purification chemicals. There is no heating, there is no food. The people try to produce food by themselves so all green areas in the town have been converted into vegetable gardens. But, they can't produce cooking oil, sugar, flour . . .

In this "safe area" people try to maintain the mutual living among all three nationalities and to resist any partition but if "the poverty comes through the door then love flies out of the window". Is this blockade imposed on purpose? The humanitarian organisations — Merhamet (Muslim), Caritas (Croats) and Dobrotvor (Serbs) deliver some food but is it distributed to all inhabitants of Tuzla and its region equally?

The so-called "northern blue route" (the 75km highway from Orasje to Tuzla) is still not opened, even though it seems likely that the Serbs would pass the convoys through. Supplies to the Tuzla region come via the Split route (650kms and with very bad roads), or via Belgrade by UNHCR or CARE Int. The quantities they bring are insufficient and distributed to the refugees only. What about Tuzla people?

The Tuzla region attempts to organise its own convoys, but the last one reached its goal four weeks ago and three lorries and one tanker were stolen somewhere in Herzegovina. This convoy had waited over four months for permission to leave Split.

The Tuzla airport is still closed. It was the largest military airport in ex-Yugoslavia and is equipped for the landing and taking off of the heaviest aircraft even now.

Medicines brought in by Medicines Sans Frontieres and the World Health Organisation are intended for hospitals. What about the plain ordinary people? No patients may go out of Tuzla for further treatment abroad. Doctors who were away from Tuzla have not been allowed to return.

I went to the Federation Internationale de l'art Photographique Congress in Driebergen, Holland in May and was refused permission to return home. My request was answered with an offer that my family could be brought to me! The Mayor of Tuzla was not allowed to a meeting with Mr Aloise Mock, Austrian Prime Minister recently.

I personally feel as if my country is occupied by the UN since my human rights of free movement are restricted.
Faruk Ibrahimovic.
Radio-Tuzla,
Tuzla,
Republic of Bosnia and Herzegovina.

The Guardian,
March 15th, 1994

In Britain and elsewhere people were busy preparing the March convoy, as well as raising money to keep the December lorries on stand-by in Zagreb. We anxiously awaited news from the negotiations and the war. It was possible for Bosnian refugees to telephone Tuzla – sometimes. It could take hours, even days to get through. The few lines were permanently jammed with thousands of refugees trying to contact relatives inside the siege. From the calls we had a vague idea how things stood. The weak were beginning to die from malnutrition.

There were a number of meetings with Bosnians in Germany during December. It was agreed to hold a conference in Stuttgart in January 1994 to discuss the March convoy.

The meeting was convened jointly by Workers Aid and the Tuzla Logistic Centre. There were Bosnian representatives from Germany and Sweden. Miners came from Slovenia and one of them chaired the meeting. Several members of the December convoy arrived from Zagreb. A few trade unionists and Workers Aid representatives were there from Britain, Hungary, Germany, France and Spain (where Ayuda Obrera – Workers Aid – was growing rapidly). But this was overwhelmingly a Bosnian meeting, with one hundred people present throughout the two days, most of whom had been organising aid supplies. Radoslav Pavlovic, from Serbia, was refused entry to Germany by the border police.

The first day of the conference was chaotic. Amongst the Bosnians, expressions of working-class solidarity had lost their meaning – the 'defenders of socialism' in Belgrade had, after all, become the organisers of genocide. It was hard for us to explain what we were trying to do.

A retired university professor from Tuzla started to speak about the destruction of multi-cultural life and broke down in tears. "Forgive me," he said, "but I have not cried in public before." There was desperation and a hopeless clutching at straws amongst most of the Bosnian contributions. They condemned the UN, but then demanded it should help. They denounced European governments for betraying them, but then voiced the hope that the US government might come to their aid. How could we explain, in the midst of this terrible anguish, that something called the workers' movement, at present silent and dormant, was the only force that could stop the slaughter?

A lot of time was spent arguing, particularly over problems associated with the carrying of refugee's personal parcels on the December convoy. The Slovenian miners, practical and patient, urged everyone to unite to break open the northern route. There were more quarrels over why hadn't some person done this or that. It seemed that the idea of a movement of ordinary people would find no echo until a locksmith from Brcko, Mr Fazlovic, spoke. He supported the working class base of the convoy – that would be its strength. "We need a convoy which starts as tributaries from workers in many countries and joins together as a river". When the meeting resumed the following morning Workers Aid presented a simple resolution calling for a united convoy for the northern route. It was carried unanimously.

Workers Aid: gun-runners for Muslims

"Transport and General Workers (TGWU) bus garage stewards were impressed by the multi-cultural stand taken by Bosnia and Tuzla in particular. Collections were held in our garages and two members gave up driving their buses for a few weeks, took all of their holidays, and went on the first Workers' Aid convoy.

On their return they were able to get the support of the London Divisional Committee of the TGWU, representing 16,000 bus-workers. This committee voted to call on the union's South East Region to ask all TGWU branches to send in money to the union to help a further convoy.

When this matter came before the South East Regional Committee it was referred to a finance sub-committee. When they discussed it, members of the Communist Party of Britain opposed it, claiming that the convoys were gun-running for the 'Muslim' army to kill Serbs.

The two drivers who went on the convoy were never given a chance to answer these lies and money that branches had already sent in to the union was not passed on. "

PETER GIBSON, TGWU member

The Stuttgart conference ended with a new network of people across Europe keen to organise for March, but not the network we had been thinking of in October. We did not focus on our plan to make the existing workers' movement break the blockade. The initial support the first convoy had received from trade unions had not been followed up. Instead we were bringing together people from outside the workers' organisations. Did we go wrong?

The people at the Stuttgart meeting – Bosnians, unemployed people, individual trade unionists – represented those who had actually responded to the original proposal for the convoy, not just verbally but with action. They were the people who had got things this far. Trade union organisations had sent letters, even donated money, but only when prodded. When the prodding stopped, nothing carried on – hardly surprising when most of the union leaders agreed with their governments' lies that it was a civil war with all sides at fault.

We knew we had to find a way to make the unions, which organised the mass of European workers, break from this pronationalist alliance. In an ideal world we would have worked with the Bosnians and also carried on the union campaign

started by the first convoy. Sadly, we lacked organisers to do both things properly. People outside the unions were approaching us and saying, "We want to help – tell us what to do". It was impossible to ignore them.

Nela, Bosnian refugee and convoy organiser in Germany, collecting customs papers.

Velenje, Slovenia　　　　　**January 16th, 1994**

We, Bosnian miners living and working in Slovenia, send this message to our brother and sister trade unionists throughout the world. Our fellow Bosnian miners from Tuzla – Croat, Muslim and Serb – are fighting shoulder to shoulder, defending their multicultural community against the Great Serb nationalists, Karadzic and Milosevic.

Tuzla is a workers' town. We miners have a long tradition of opposing nationalism. Serb, Croat and Muslim have worked in peace together in our salt and coal mines for generations. We do not want the barbarism of ethnic states imposed by Milosevic and the Vance/Owen plan.

We are supporting the trade union convoy organised by Workers Aid for Bosnia. The convoy aims to travel to Tuzla in February along the northern route carrying vital food, medicines and fuel. This route must be opened if our brothers and sisters are not to be starved into ethnic partition.

We appeal to you, fellow trade unionists, to your spirit of workers' solidarity, help us organise this workers' convoy.

Sretno! (Miners' Greetings)

SALKO KAVGIC, Independent Energy Union of Slovenia

Soon after the Stuttgart meeting we were sending out weekly bulletins in English, German and Bosnian, giving details of convoy preparations in nine countries. Things became even more hectic, more impossible to control, than the previous August. Workers Aid representatives were invited to Germany several times to address meetings, including a demonstration of ten thousand in Frankfurt.

After a meeting in a Bosnian Club, we were approached by a few young men who had been brought out from concentration camps. They wanted to go back to fight but their passports had been confiscated as part of the deal with the Chetniks which allowed their release. They supported our condemnation of the UN's troop deployment along the front lines around Sarajevo following the market massacre. These UN troops prevented any Bosnian army moves out of the city. They were acting as reinforcements for the Chetniks, allowing the 'ethnic cleansers' to withdraw troops from the siege of Sarajevo and deploy them elsewhere.

Bosnian paper reports on convoy preparations in Zagreb and the campaign for the northern route

8.2.94

Slovenian miners fighting division

Franc Druks, President of the Slovenian Power Workers Union, announced that the miners would be joining the March convoy and would seek support from other Slovenian unions.

"The appeal of this convoy is that it is to build workers' internationalism and I will be raising it at a meeting of power workers' unions in Rome on February 22nd. We have 500 tonnes of aid ready to move and if the trade unions in western Europe can help by supplying the trucks, together we can take this aid to the miners of Tuzla."

Druks spoke of the Slovenian miners' history of struggle against what he saw as the old bureaucratic regime in the former Yugoslavia.

"Workers in the West should understand that we have been fighting against bureaucracy for a long time and that we have not lost our socialist ideals. I was a young man when I took part in the 1972 strike at the Velenje pit. That strike was part of the fight against the old regime."

"At the moment we have what they call 'social ownership' of the pits and power industry. With the coming of the so-called 'market economy' they are talking of 'state ownership'. We don't know what the difference is but we do know that the unions and the workers are on one side and all the rest are on the other side. We do not want to go into the 'market' as cheap labour. We want the same conditions and wages. Nor are we prepared to give up our health and safety rights."

Druks said that it was shameful that the British miners had been left to fight alone in 1985, resulting in pit closures and the death of local communities. He said he would be working for the re-building of workers' solidarity, east and west. "We must rebuild our connections and make sure that we end the isolation of sections of workers."

These young Bosnians wanted to help our work. Their association had ten lorries, all ready to go. One man hoped that British miners would head the convoy. "They have the strength to break the siege. We watched them on TV in 1984." He would contact friends in the Hungarian mining town of Tatabanja, where miners had supported the first convoy. We talked about how to spread the word to miners further east across Europe.

Mr. Fazlovic, the locksmith, and another organiser, Nela, a Tuzla refugee, invited all German Bosnian clubs to a meeting in Mannheim to discuss the convoy. Bosnian representatives came from across southern Germany as well as a German organisation from what had been East Germany and representatives of the Dutch organisation, Citizens to Citizens.

The meeting was very difficult and tense. Most of the hundred or so representatives had families in the war zone. This was no game. The Bosnians with whom we had been working outlined the plan for the convoy. They were met with great scepticism from a few people. Did we have UN agreement to travel the northern route? Did we have Chetnik consent?

We said that in this war, food was a weapon. Taking a lorry of food down the northern route was no different from going there with a tank. The people strangling Bosnia were not going to give permission simply because we asked for it. We could not hope to start with permission and then organise the convoy. We had to build up a massive campaign for the convoy to force them to give us this permission. This is what the meeting was for – to ask everyone to come to the assistance of Bosnia as reinforcements from the outside – not with guns, but with a political fist.

The sceptics poured scorn on the idea. They doubted the convoy would ever get permission to pass – and the meeting ended without any agreement.

GREAT MYTHS OF THE WAR

- **The Serbs in Bosnia all support Karadzic and want to live in an 'ethnically pure' state**

In 1992 a referendum was organised for Bosnians to choose whether they wanted to stay in Yugoslavia or establish an independent, multi-ethnic Bosnia.

Karadzic's Serbian Democratic Party (SDS) set up armed road blocks and sent armed gangs to prevent not only Serbs but also Croats and Muslims in areas under SDS control from voting in the referendum. These gangs were organised and armed by the state authorities in Serbia. Nevertheless, over 64 per cent of Bosnia's population voted; of these, over 99 per cent opted for an independent country with equal rights for Croats, Muslims and Serbs. Those voting for independence included many Serbs.

The seven-strong Bosnian Presidency established after independence included two Serbs. The Bosnian General in charge of the defence of Sarajevo is a Serb. The editor of Bosnia's leading paper, *Oslobodenje*, is a Serb.

Taking into account the number of Bosnian Serbs who have either stayed loyal to the Bosnian government or who have fled the country, Karadzic now represents a minority of Bosnian Serbs, even assuming he has the support of all the people in the areas he controls.

19.2.94

France's strategy against Bosnian unity exposed

French Foreign Minister Alain Juppé has revealed in an interview with *The New York Times* the strategy of France and allied countries, Britain and Russia, to put pressure on the Bosnian leadership to accept partition along ethnic lines.

He maintained that the Bosnian leaders' refusal to accept both the Vance-Owen and Owen-Stoltenberg plans to divide their country was the main barrier to 'peace'.

Juppe said that plans for concerted international pressure on the 'three warring parties' would shortly be disclosed by the French government. He also attacked the US government for appearing to encourage Bosnians to fight on, which would be a 'catastrophe'.

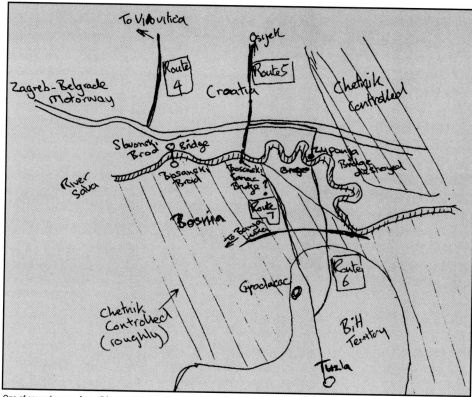

Text on map: To Viroulica, Osijek, Route 5, Route 4, Croatia, Chetnik Controlled, Zagreb-Belgrade Motorway, Slavonski Brod, Bridge, Zupanja Bridge destroyed, Bosanski Brod, Bosanski Samac Bridge?, Bridge, River Sava, Bosnia, Route 7, To Banja Luka?, Route 6, Chetnik Controlled (roughly), Gradacac, BiH Territory, Tuzla

One of several maps of possible approaches to Tuzla faxed to us from Croatia

The Editor,
The Guardian.

February 26th, 1994

Dear Sir,

Whilst Labour MPs Tony Benn, Neil Gerrard and Alice Mahon, are certainly right to warn that 'threats of punitive action [by the UN] may still be issued in the future' (*The Guardian, 25.2.94*), they misunderstand the purpose of the threatened intervention and in doing so completely misrepresent the nature of the conflict as a 'civil war'.

Far from bringing peace, the UN forces have disarmed the Bosnian army in its own capital, Sarajevo, while allowing the besieging Serb nationalist forces to withdraw their guns elsewhere – or to place them in the hands of their Russian allies. Two days after this 'ceasefire', Serb shells started to land on Tuzla.

This much trumpeted intervention has brought the carve-up of Bosnia dangerously closer. Its immediate aim is to complete the implementation of the Vance-Owen plan and legitimise the Serbian and Croatian seizure of territory. In urging the UN to force 'all sides' to negotiate a peace settlement, Mr Benn and his colleagues accept the notion that an ethnically divided Bosnia can be the basis for peace. There can be no better recipe for the escalation of war in the Balkans of which they speak than just this 'solution'. In that sense the only peace-making force in Bosnia is that force fighting to prevent the partition, the Bosnia-Herzegovina Army.

Yours sincerely,

Workers Aid for Bosnia

NOTE: Letter not published

The northern and southern routes to Tuzla, March 1994

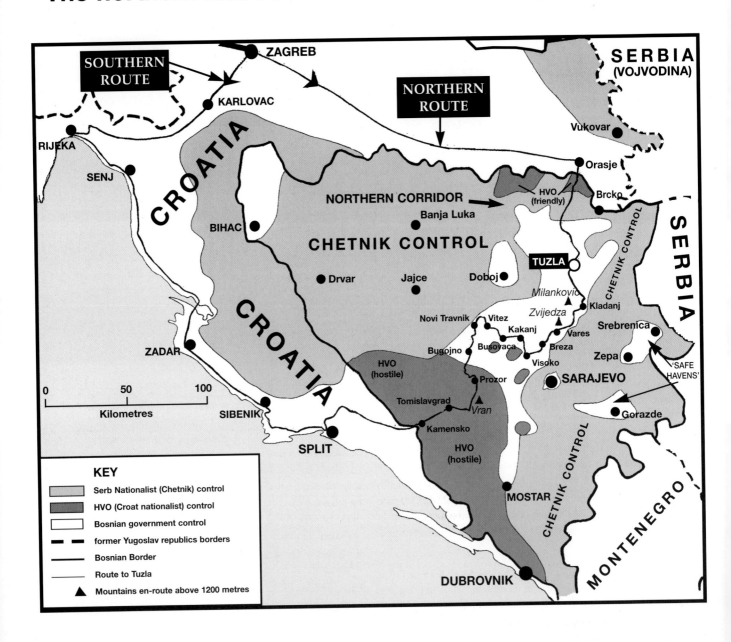

Why the northern route?

The map on the left shows the existing route (south from Zagreb) to Tuzla through which the UN sends aid. Tuzla needs to open the northern route (east from Zagreb) if it is to survive. Why?

1. The existing route (east from Zagreb) is along a 1,200km road, parts of which are dirt track through mountains and are only suitable for small trucks. The route is impassable in winter. The northern route is 400km of motorway suitable for large trucks, passable all year round, and providing quick and easy access to Zagreb and the rest of Europe.

2. The existing route passes through areas controlled by bandits and lorries are often looted. On this route the many front lines between the HVO, the BiH army and the Chetniks change daily. The northern route passes through a fixed army front-line controlled by Croat HVO forces and Serbian forces. Negotiations have taken place between these forces and the authorities in Tuzla. We are confident that convoys will pass through.

3. All existing aid to Tuzla is under the control of the UN. It only distributes aid to refugees *[mostly Muslims]* in Tuzla, not to the people of Tuzla itself *[mixed population]*. In other words, they use aid to deliberately create tensions and divisions amongst people. Even if the UN votes to open Tuzla airport, it will still try to use its control of aid to cause divisions along ethnic lines.

4. The northern route, with its easy access, will make it possible for the Tuzla authorities to bring sufficient supplies for everyone, and for them to control its equal distribution to everyone. Also Bosnia is a recognised country. Its citizens have the right to access to the outside world and the right to trade. The opening of the northern route would make it possible for Tuzla to send out and sell its stock-piles of salt and other commodities, which the workers of the region have continued to produce.

There have been many humanitarian aid lorries sent to Tuzla, but the Tuzla authorities have already got large stock-piles of aid stored in warehouses outside of Bosnia that they have been unable to get in. A recent convoy of eighty-six lorries, which we organised on the existing Split route, saw only eight complete the journey. We lost £150,000 of goods.

The northern route is the key to our survival, and to our continued battle against ethnic cleansing and the division of Bosnia.

The Tuzla Logistics Centre, October 1993
NOTE: bracketed additions by the editors

After the Mannheim meeting broke up, our organisers remained behind, slightly despondent. Someone explained that many of the sceptical people had lived in Germany for a long time. When war started they organised lorries to take parcels from refugees to relatives in Bosnia – but on a paying basis. This money was used to cover transport costs and send extra aid, but some of it went into pockets or into commercial ventures. For their own reasons they had reinforced the feeling of powerlessness amongst the other people.

We swapped reports and made our final plans. Two people from Holland had gone to Zupanja: one of them was a retired army officer who had recently served with the UN in the area. They would report back on the military situation. Bosnians from the Brcko area were sending us information of positions of snipers and road blocks. From Zagreb, the Tuzla Logistics people were continuing their attempts to make a deal with the Serb nationalist forces we had to pass through.

On the political front we had been lobbying hard. Lancashire MP, Colin Pickthall, tabled an Early Day Motion in Parliament, supporting the convoy and many Labour MPs signed it. A Dutch supporter had gone to the European Parliament and after lobbying got Euro MPs to include a statement supporting the convoy in a resolution on Bosnia.

We had faxes coming in from Bosnians in Australia, the US and elsewhere – they wrote with surprise and joy that people from outside the country understood the war and the significance of the northern route. They felt that no-one else had grasped what was going on in Bosnia.

We now had commitments for two lorries from Sweden, two from France, seventeen from Slovenia, fourteen from Germany and three from Spain. All the British Workers Aid lorries were in Zagreb but the search was on for more. We drew up final plans for the convoy route. The west European lorries would meet at the German/Austrian border, then go into Slovenia to meet with the miners and then on to Croatia and Zupanja.

We shook hands and made our farewells until we met again on the Austrian border.

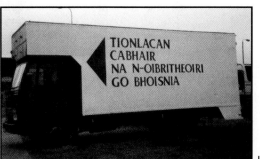

Irish Workers Aid truck

Chapter 4

MARCH 1994   Cease-fire between BiH and Croat nationalists. Federation formed between Bosnia and Herceg-Bosna.

MARCH 1994   Chetnik offensives against Bihac and Gorazde enclaves.

In Tuzla

The December convoy had been stuck in Zagreb for two months. Last minute, frenzied preparations were being made for the March convoy, including urgent appeals to unions to help us get more lorries to transport aid stored in Britain, Slovenia and Zagreb.

Then, days before the convoy was to meet in Germany everything changed. On March 2nd, US President Clinton announced a ceasefire between Zagreb and Sarajevo. The US had brokered a Croat-Muslim federation as part of its' own divide and rule foreign policy. The deal legitimised Croatian control over large parts of Bosnia, but it also gave the outnumbered Bosnian soldiers the chance to turn their few guns on one enemy, instead of fighting on two fronts.

" Clashing cultures

When the convoy was in Zagreb preparing to leave for Tuzla my flat was converted into an office, and in exceptional situations into a dormitory. Dot used to come early in the morning to make plans. As soon as I answer the doorbell, she starts to talk about problems. I interrupt with, "Good morning! Have you slept well? Have you had any breakfast?" She doesn't pay any attention to what I am saying, so I say, "First let us have some coffee or tea and some food then we can speak about problems. We will digest them easier." Dot calls this 'Bosnian style'. When she comes the next day, she passes straight on to problems again. "No, no," I say, "it can't go like that. We have to pass all these stages slowly." She did not understand us and how we could manage any problem. In return, I could not understand that rushed way of living. "

FARUK IBRAHIMOVIC

THE METHODS OF FASCISM
Rape

Journalist Seada Vranic began to collect direct testimonies from women who were raped. At first she believed that rape was simply part of the madness of war – a chaos without rules or system.

"I couldn't accept the idea that rapes were part of the Serbian expansionist war strategy. I thought: rape is a bio-psychological act that cannot be carried out to order. However, after about four months the mosaic took shape for me. I noticed the congruences in events in wholly different localities and I began to enter them on the map. I had victims from everywhere except eastern Herzegovina.

I became aware that rape in such circumstances is not the same as violent sex. It is aggression carried out by sexual means.

In Bosnia during this war there were tens of thousands of rape victims, perhaps as many as a hundred thousand. Behind it lay just one idea: to expel the population of other nationalities from a given territory. Rape is a very effective means for that purpose: if three or four raped women arrived in a village, all the villagers would quickly take flight. For example, Banja Luka was too large a town for them to be able to kill all the Bosniaks and Croats there. Nor could they send all of them to camps, or to the front. So they went into the houses of non-Serbs and raped them. In Banja Luka rapes took place on a particularly massive scale, even though the town was outside the war zone the whole time.

The assault on Foca and its surrounding villages provides another example. This involved lightning terror: bombardment, burning, killing, raping. The aim was achieved very fast: within a few days, even a few hours in the case of the villages, the territory was 'clean'. They took some people off to the camps, they killed some on the spot, and others they raped.

A crime has been committed that in numerical terms is not the greatest in the history of warfare. But for the first time in the history of warfare, rape has become a part of military strategy. For the first time human sexuality has been used for the purpose of what has euphemistically been termed ethnic cleansing, but which is in fact genocide."

Based on an interview in Globus, *Zagreb*

After the ceasefire the bitter fighting between Croatian national-ists and the Bosnian army was halted. UN troops took up positions along the front lines. The fighting had stopped but these 'peace keepers' could not hide the fraud of the 'alliance'. Behind the UN troops, Croatia consolidated its hold on Herzegovina via the facade of the Croatian nationalist mini-state of Herceg-Bosna.

The ceasefire changed the military situation in eastern Herzegovina and central Bosnia. The southern route from Split was passable again. Within hours of the ceasefire, hundreds of lorries, including our December lorries in Zagreb, poured down to Split. Here we were held up again. Lorries could only cross the border into Bosnia with permission from a committee, (whose authority was unclear – UN? Croat?). In a mad confu-sion of bureaucracy, papers and frayed tempers, it became clear that Tuzla bound lorries were being held back. Convoys would arrive and cross the border while the number of waiting Tuzla lorries grew. After two days we organised a meeting of all Tuzla bound drivers, most of them Bosnians. A resolution was passed demanding that the committee allow everyone to move. A Workers Aid driver proposed they block the road with their lor-ries if this didn't happen. One of the Bosnian drivers who had witnessed our protest outside the UN Headquarters told his compatriots, "These guys will do it." Shortly afterwards every-one got their permissions.

There was one final near disaster. Leaving Split, a Workers Aid lorry hit a car. Our driver was taken to the police station. Insurance documents were demanded. We had none. Insurance was a luxury we had not been able to afford. (Some people might accuse us of irresponsibility, but would it have been more responsible to watch genocide and do nothing?) Our convoy representative explained to the police that our papers were in the UK. Could she phone and get them faxed through? Yes. With the police listening she phoned a Workers Aid member in Britain and asked him to fax through the documents. The person at the UK end caught on. After some cre-ative word processing, an impressive looking insurance document was faxed through. The police were satisfied and bailed the driver to appear in court the next day. He was fined 80DM. We paid the car owner 1,000DM for the damage and were finally free to leave. We were jubilant at the prospect of finally reaching Tuzla, but for the first time we saw the effects of the war: massive shell damage, whole villages 'ethnically cleansed', the population reduced to begging. As the lorries slithered down treacherous, ice covered mountain tracks we also saw one of the reasons why it was vital to open the northern route.

UNPROFOR base, Split

12.3.94
Tuzla attacks rise

The price for the Croatian-Bosnian ceasefire may be the abandonment of the working-class-dominated northern region of Tuzla to the Serbian aggres-sor.

Tuzla has come under increased bom-bardment since the UN's Sarajevo deal freed Serbian forces to concentrate their attack in the north.

It is possible that a Serbian push to the south will be made to try and cut off the only remaining roads along which supplies reach Tuzla.

Two views of the southern route

Giving out Sweets

" Got to first town across border. Just about every building burnt out or shelled. Many sad stories to tell. I don't know them, but you could see. Bullet holes everywhere, boarded up houses with tree trunks. Men, women and children lining the streets shouting 'bon bon' or motioning for cigarettes. We keep stopping and giving out ciggies and sweets until we have hardly any left. I think personally this is a bit daft as we have another 250km to go. Everyone will be in a similar boat. We should do our job and get the convoy through. Save the stuff for Tuzla which has very little or somewhere later in the journey. By the time the drivers get there they will be out of sweets and ciggies. Dirk's friend was also saying that we should stop and give people things and not just throw them out of the window. I understand, but we are here to do a job. But I understand that he wanted to show them respect. Different people, different ideas! "

ANDY MILTON

A light in the darkness

"In 1992 about five thousand Bosnians came to the UK, brought here by various organisations. My mother, sister and I were amongst them.

The first few weeks these organisations kept us under their wings, finding us homes, essential equipment and orienting us to our new environment. Their support was reassuring among the confusion that surrounded us. Glad to be safe but torn by separation from friends and family we remained shocked and dazed for months. With minimal knowledge of English, I tried to familiarise myself with a daily routine in an unfamiliar culture. We learned fast the basics i.e. greetings, gratitude and the bus fare to town. However the language barrier rendered simple things, such as shopping and going to the pub, a struggle.

All the time I thought about people back in Bosnia, worrying about their welfare, frustrated by my helplessness and depressed by the apparent hopelessness. The grim radio reports from Bosnia wrought within me a guilt and helplessness and frequently made my stomach turn. I was desperate to do anything to help support the people of my country in their fight against belligerent fascism directed from Serbia and Croatia.

Then I was introduced to an organisation which fully understood the crisis in Bosnia and supported the Bosnian people in defending their country. At last I had the opportunity to get involved practically and politically in the fight against the partition of my country.

When I joined Workers Aid I realised that many Bosnians (especially from the north of England) were already involved and doing a great job in helping the organisation by distributing propaganda, fundraising and preparing convoys. Before long the number of Bosnians involved had grown significantly, Workers Aid being the only organisation which brought Bosnians together as a collective force in the UK, and which united us in our efforts to help the Bosnians back home in their fight to prevent partition.

Through Workers Aid my family made contacts with other families in the UK enabling us to develop a circle of friends, united by separation, sadness, bewilderment, bitterness, and often depression. These social contacts helped to relieve some of the isolation as we shared news from home and our knowledge of the British system.

Apart from its significant contribution as a humanitarian organisation in bringing desperately needed aid, WAB stood alone in acknowledging the overwhelming ignorance regarding Bosnia and the complete injustice of the arms embargo. Unfortunately the British government believed the rhetoric uttered by the Serb and Croat leaders. The arms embargo prevented the victims (Bosnians) from defending themselves. Hence the Serb nationalists ran riot, looting, raping and killing 250,000 innocent, defenceless people in their fascist-minded psychosis.

Workers Aid gave us courage to continue believing in our struggle, and hope that by educating and informing more and more people the sordid impact of the arms embargo would become known. The organisation challenged the ignorant propaganda of the British government and campaigned for the lifting of the embargo. It was under no illusions about the circumstances of the war in the former Yugoslavia e.g. massacred victims were the Bosnians, the Serbs the aggressors, and the Croats the chameleon stalkers. It focused on the real issues and enabled us to increase awareness of the plight of our people in Bosnia. As refugees in the UK we derived enormous encouragement from the thousands of ordinary British people who sought to understand our predicament and support our campaign.

Apart from channelling the efforts of Bosnians in the UK and enabling us to do something to help the fight against fascism, Workers Aid enabled us to maintain contact with our families by carrying letters on the convoys. There were no post or telephone links with Bosnia and without the convoys, months would have passed without us knowing anything of the welfare of our families back home. Through letters carried by the convoys our relatives communicated their greatest needs, especially during the peak of wartime scarcity (the winter of '93/'94). Before the convoys it was very hard to hear our relatives and friends asking for things, which we had in plentiful supply but could not get to them. Thanks to the convoys many of our friends were in receipt of much needed food and clothing and did not suffer as they might, especially throughout the cold Bosnian winter months of war."

AMER IKANOVIC, from Banovici

'Ethnic cleansing'

" Nothing prepares you for it. Pictures and news reports of ethnic cleansing as well as accounts from refugees in Britain – none of this took away the shock of seeing the terrible reality on the drive into Bosnia-Herzegovina.

We had been held up for 24 hours at the border by Croatian nationalists. Now we were through and on our way again. Spirits were high. We were reaching the end of a long journey.

In the distance, down the country road, there is a village. Houses dotted around surrounded by fields and orchards. Things look a bit overgrown but abundant with life. Yet everything is strangely quiet. We pass the first house. Our high spirits evaporate and the silence outside invades our cab. There are no people. Every house has been dynamited from inside. Every broken window has a tell-tale black smudge round the frame. Every roof has a hole in it. Nothing else is disturbed. Not like war scenes on films with bomb craters, blown over trees, devastated scenery – just the systematic driving out of people.

There is no fighting, no bodies, nothing human remains of the nightmare that must have taken place. Only the empty blown up houses as reminders of the families that lived here.

We drive through mile after mile of 'ethnically cleansed' villages. In our cab we are quiet. I know people who come from places like this.

As we drive through these silent, empty villages Faruk tells me their histories – who lived here. Some are Muslim villages, some are Serb.

In Britain there are people who put an equals sign between the different sides in the war. "They are all as bad as each other." If they heard Faruk say, "this was a Serb village, this was a Muslim village," they would say, "I told you so. They all do the same thing." This ignores what happened. The attack on Bosnia came from Serbia, unleashing an orgy of violence against all non-Serbs and non-nationalist Serbs. Bosnian Serb villagers were caught up in the nationalist push whether they liked it or not. Some joined the pogroms with an enthusiasm resulting from the endless propaganda about the Muslim menace. Others joined reluctantly or at gun-point, some managed to slip away – into Serbia to stay there, or on to Germany and elsewhere. Some joined the Bosnian army to oppose the nationalists.

Is it any surprise that in rural areas of Bosnia Muslims, fearing for their lives, would seek to protect themselves by driving out local Serbs who might become the next stepping stone for the nationalist forward drive?

In Britain it is possible for people to take the picture of an empty Serb village and an empty Muslim one and say, "How can we take sides – they are all as bad as one another." This takes only what is immediately visible as evidence. It ignores the long chain of events leading up to the acts of violence. On one side, a well organised campaign of hate and nationalistic rhetoric warning of the Muslim menace. A campaign to create an ethnically pure state, a campaign to organise armed bands of men incorporating openly fascist movements. On the other hand the last minute, panic stricken measures taken by people trying to defend themselves after news of atrocities from elsewhere has reached them.

My heart aches for all the people of these empty villages – Serb, Muslim or Croat. They are all victims of Serb nationalism, including the Serbs.

For the rest of the journey a nagging depression hangs over us in the lorry. As I said, nothing prepares you for it. "

BOB MYERS

To Workers Aid.
From Dot Gibson.

We arrived limping into Tuzla. The road is indescribably bad. Vehicles
witha a low undercarriage WILL NOT MAKE IT. Two of the lorries have
clutch problems. The Logistic Centre will work out how to get them
repaired. The miners have a workshop.
We arrived on a moon lit night. What a way to see a country. The road
goes over the top of the mountains, NOT in the valleys. It is so
beautiful brea thtaking. There is no doubt, ifonly from the point of
view ofc wear and tear on vehicles and nerves, that the campaign for
the northern route is vital. Enough ofall that!
We had a meeting in the town hall with the mayor and various people in
the leadership of the town and the press. Very good. Last night we met
Manjas brother who is the go between BiH 2nd Corpus and UNPROFOR. He
said that what we saying about the UN was exactly right. And also about
need to restore internationalism of the working class. He was so pleased
that he says he wants to tell the people on television. It may be that
we will appear on Saturday.
He read some things in Workers*'s Press and said they were exactly what
they had been saying there. They were excited to find that outside
Bos nia someone had been saying the same as them. "We have felt so alone
so isolated""We have been pleased with Faruk's radio reports showing
that you have been working for us that there were some people who did
care, not to just give aid but to fight for our independence."
When I said that the idea for the convoy came from Rade in Serbia the
Mayor interupted to say "We must meet this man".
The UN is pouring in here. Lynda Chalker was here yesterday. Everything
we said about the west's aim to get control, their effort to isolate
Tuzla leadership etc is right. And known to be right by this leadership.
But they have held on through the whole winter and they desperately need
some respite. The people are hu ngry, tired and stressed. But what a
spirit. What determination and what a tried and tested leadership. They
are proud and humane, without arrogance and it is clear that Mayor
Beslagic has kept a united group throughout these thirteen months of
seige.
They are delighted with the idea of bringing trade union banners on the
next convoy and with getting a leaflet produced. We will fix this up.
Please ensure banners are brought - and also some letters - greetings
from from unions to Selim Beslagic, Mayor of Tuzla, and to the unions.
WE WILL SHOW THEM THAT THERE IS A GREATER FORCE THAN THE UN WITH ALL ITS
HIGH POWERED EQUIPMENT, TRUCKS AND TANKS.

best wishes, Dot.

Fax from Dot Gibson on first arriving in Tuzla

The December trucks arrived in Tuzla, three months after leaving Britain. The miners greeted us with great warmth and friendship. After nine months we could sit down and discuss how to work together to develop the campaign of international solidarity.

It was not an easy discussion. For us our arrival might be a triumph, but for the miners it was only a tiny light in a dark future. A few lorries had reached Tuzla but it was still surrounded on three sides by the Chetniks. The miners, like all citizens, were malnourished and exhausted. The war raged on. Even though the miners agreed with the idea of workers' solidarity, they were sceptical. They had been through a year of siege. No-one had come to help. In the past they had supported other workers in Vietnam, South Africa, Britain. They had waited for similar help. It didn't come. Now they looked to their own efforts to survive. We met many people who had organised the defence of the region: the Mayor, members of the town council, commanders of the the Second Corpus of the Bosnian army, journalists and many others. Everywhere the same response – a great welcome, a great admiration for what we had done and support for our plans but also the same reservation. We had a perspective of workers' solidarity but their problems were immediate: shortage of weapons, food, diesel, medicines, organisers, everything. Everyone we spoke to explained their commitment to the unity of the Bosnian people, their opposition to nationalism and their disbelief that the west could be so indifferent to their plight. We tried to explain some of the problems we faced – the destruction of the British mining industry, the pro-UN policy of the union leaders across Europe and our own tiny forces.

Whatever their scepticism, the miners sat with us and together we planned our future work to bring them the support they needed. It had taken us nine months to make this contact. For a moment we could forget all the problems that frequently threatened to scupper our campaign and that at times had seemed a nightmare. We parted from the great company of the miners whose spirit had survived a year of siege. We had built the first slender bridge between the working people of Tuzla and ourselves.

While the four December lorries had been making their way to Tuzla via Split, outside Bosnia we were having to re-think our plans. With the southern route open, what should we do with our big convoy? The Croat truce did not diminish the importance of the northern route. The southern route was in reality no route as our first drivers were just discovering. Only lorries under twenty tons could even try to get through on the newly made dirt tracks. Every single pre-war road into Tuzla was still in Chetnik hands. No society could function normally under these conditions. The closed northern route symbolised the continuing UN-Chetnik strangulation of Bosnia. It had to be opened.

Our dilemma was this: while the Bosnian refugees had been able to raise money and get lorries and aid, they could do little to make their voices heard. They were Bosnians – invisible. The northern route would not open simply because a large number of lorries turned up. The lorries needed a campaign of protest in the countries where UN policy was being decided.

Originally we envisaged the work in the unions getting us to a point where leading figures in the labour movement would accompany the convoy – giving it clout, creating the kind of international exposure to the UN's policy that was needed to force a change. We had been supported by politicians in Britain and the European parliament. But what action would these people actually take when our lorries were blocked? A motion in the House of Commons was a far cry from support on the ground in Zupanja.

Bosnian clubs in Germany had lorries and warehouses full of aid, but the resources of the workers' movement, above all, their campaigning and organising skills – still remained shut away from us and shut away from Bosnia. Letters went to most union head offices in Britain asking them to put lorries on the convoy. The bakers' union was the only one to even reply.

In all the meetings and demonstrations we spoke at in Germany nobody came from the German trade unions, Social Democratic parties or the huge anti-fascist organisations. The two million strong German metal workers' union told us they had Bosnian and Serbian members in German car factories. There had been fights. The union did not want to inflame the situation by taking sides.

If we sent our thirty-four lorries to Zupanja, what would we do when our passage was blocked? Our plan had been to protest as we had done before. But with Tuzla people starving, how many of our Bosnian drivers would sit day after day on the River Sava waiting for a permission to cross which might never come. They knew they could now get to Tuzla, even if it meant a journey of hundreds of kilometres along almost impassable tracks.

Some of our Bosnian organisers still wanted to try the north. They understood its' continuing importance but after last minute phone discussions, everyone agreed to go via Split.

Commanding officers of the BiH Army 2nd Corps with Mayor Selim Beslagic (2nd left) and Workers Aid members Jackie Vance (3rd left) and Dot Gibson.

One step before the end

" The winter of 1992-3 was neither long nor cold. The coal powered electricity generating plant kept working. It also maintains the steam heating to the modern blocks of flats, but telephones are cut and all roads into Tuzla blocked. The whole region is under a blockade.

Any money that people had saved before the war is gone. Uncertainty has become everyday life for everyone. To survive, to stay alive, under constant shelling, with no money, no job. How do people do it? It is terrible to watch the people, this mass of faces disfigured through starvation, this social misery, this desolate town. Everyone is in a hurry: where, what for? Shells, missiles, explosions in the city centre, chaos, everyone is looking for shelter. Everything else is unimportant. To stay alive, to survive, that's the imperative. Explosions resonate all over the city, children crying in the shelters, a mother's voice, peaceful, coaxing.

Today is the same as yesterday. In the pauses between artillery attacks priority work can be done. Then back to the shelters with new fear, but also some hope that this day at least we will survive. When the situation is difficult, almost critical, it seems time goes very slowly. But this is something which makes the mood of people worse. This helplessness is making itself felt on people's nerves and concentration. They talk without listeners, they beg everywhere. Communication between people is reduced to the lowest level. Friendships are lost, families are scattered all over Europe.

Most people have lost their jobs, the factories are closed. Now there are new activities: selling possessions, searching through rubbish – finding some way to get money. All those pictures about the devastation of war we have seen on TV are now here. The mass exodus of people, the destruction of their homes, factories, communications, robbery and rape, the most violent executions, mass slaughter. Before these were bad dreams, now they are here, around us.

Life becomes worthless, without social purpose, except the fight for survival. It is difficult to explain the hell the civilians go through, even to our soldiers on the front line. Every day there is the fight to find food for the family when nothing comes into the region through the blockade. Almost nothing is in the market. It becomes a daily contest. On one side the black marketeers who raise prices to astronomical amounts and on the other side the miserable, unemployed civil population.

There is humanitarian aid, but it is manipulated. Some fifty humanitarian organisations bring supplies, but only to refugees who have been driven into the region from elsewhere. The Red Cross did give some food to our pensioners, but so little. Tuzla citizens are pushed towards religious foundations for help – to *Caritas*, for Catholics, to *Merhamet* for Muslims, to *Dobrotvor* for Serbs. But even these are little help. Many Croat families, like mine, go to *Caritas* but are told, "Sorry we cannot take any new members." So we starve, we have to search for thrown-out food scraps. Others are more lucky and get one parcel of food each month from the religious foundations.

For the thousands of Serbs though, things are most difficult since *Dobrotvor* has nothing to distribute, as no-one sends them anything despite many appeals to the world. But *Caritas* does give them some help. When large donations arrive they give 50-100 parcels to *Dobrotvor*.

I talk with friends and everyone is angry because of the numerous European governmental and humanitarian organisations that are indifferent to the fate of Tuzla citizens. We are even more angry because we know that their representatives, who are here in Tuzla, are being paid large salaries and drive around all day in brand new, expensive jeeps. We starve, but we can see these humanitarian representatives eating in luxury restaurants every night. We can see that these people come to Tuzla for their own personal gain, using 'humanitarian aid' as their cover.

Starvation grips families tighter and tighter, but old people are in the worst position. They have come to the autumn of their lives and now they are exhausted, weakened by lack of food and the endless hunt for something to eat. And most of all the destruction of their pride and their pre-war place in society that valued their past contribution as teachers, as engineers, as workers.

People who have anything to sell bring it out on the streets and offer it dirt cheap. One day at the street market I see on my left my former teacher of mathematics and on my right my former teacher of geology. We have to run for a nearby cellar during an artillery attack. As the shells whistle the funeral march for someone in the town, we shared some dreams together. One teacher dreams of his family having lunch. "On the kitchen table is roast meat, cakes, drinks. His dream is interrupted by a voice from outside, "Come on out Suljo, the shelling is over." "Nice dream," replied Suljo, "only too short, like everything pleasant."

We go out and Suljo takes his morning's bargainings – two plastic bags of vegetables. His friend whistles. "Heavens, Suljo, you've managed to bargain two bags of food."

"Yes, one bag is for the family and the other is for one of my neighbours, Petra*. She is ill and she gets nothing. I cannot watch it. She will die of hunger. But if Suljo has something, so will she."

Ordinary people help each other, regardless of name, of religion or nationality. Suljo explains that Petra was a nurse and had cared for his son when he was in hospital before the war. He cannot forget these things.

But while the starving people of Tuzla help each other, the world, unfortunately, forgets us. The cultivated, educated, rich people of Europe forget us. Such things cannot happen to them. And no-one here would want it to happen to them. But here nationalism and fascism are devastating society like a plague. And for all their wealth, their culture, their education, when it came to stopping this plague all the organisations of Europe, political and humanitarian, have failed.

Winter 1993-4 started on November 4th. Morning dawned with the sky full of heavy leaden clouds. Soon snow was twenty-five centimetres deep and the temperature dropped to minus five. The spirits of the Tuzla people also sank. Now families only got electricity for two hours after midnight. The communal central heating systems failed. Nobody had enough firewood or coal.

* A Serb name.

Men and women and kids went to collect wood from the nearby forests. Some people stole coal from the trains during the night. In the modern tower blocks there were no flues for fires so people cooked any little food they had on fires on the balconies. Older apartments had stoves and they helped others, sometimes cooking five meals a night. People helped each other over and over. But when illness struck everyone was powerless. Death was everywhere, especially old people who died of hunger if they were alone and forgotten, but younger people died too, sometimes from suicide. Some could not live with their pride trampled in the dirt and live on the level that was now demanded. Some just decided to accelerate an end they saw as inevitable.

Life was difficult for parents, but also for children. Who was attacking them? Where had their neighbours, their Serb schoolfriends gone? Why suddenly is there no food, no money, no medicine? Why are there no more discos? Why must we spend our days in cellars? There is deep snow but no shoes and no money to buy any. How long will this go on? They learn quickly. Soon young boys and girls with dolls are grown-ups, serious people, who know what only older people usually know. But even though they become old they still need everything youth needs. But it isn't there. A few turn to alcohol, drugs.

And then, like the sun on the horizon, the most beautiful news for Tuzla and its suffering people. A CONVOY IS ARRIVING! A CONVOY FOR TUZLA MINERS! Food, clothes, shoes, school materials, medicines. In the town people talk of 200 trucks coming. Some say it is for the town, others say it is only for miners. Some say it is coming from England, Belgium, Holland, Germany. Everyone waits, hoping that it will get through the blockade, either through the Chetniks in the north or the HVO in the south. We just keep hoping. In the evening we miners make plans by candlelight how to distribute the aid. We need everything, we have nothing except for a part of our soul that is still smouldering and resisting. But for how much longer? So we wait to welcome the good people of Europe. You finally remembered us. It is nearly too late for us. But you are coming, just one step before the end. **"**

TIHOMIR BABIC, mining technician, Tuzla

Before they left Tuzla, the December team made preparations with the miners for the arrival of the big convoy. Because of communication problems our people in Tuzla knew another thirty-four lorries were on their way, but little else. They assumed all the lorries were for the miners' union. In fact they were for a number of destinations in the Tuzla region. This misunderstanding almost destroyed the whole campaign.

All the March lorries met in Zagreb. Our empty lorries arrived from Tuzla to refill at the Logistic Centre warehouse. There was considerable confusion, made worse by the lack of any interpreters amongst the eighty people. The English speaking organisers who knew that the lorries had different destinations were in Britain acting as a base for communications. The Bosnian and Slovenian drivers were impatient to see families from whom they had been cut off for a year. They didn't want to hang about and pushed on as fast as they could. The convoy got spread out between Zagreb and Split.

Passing through Bosnia everyone re-grouped and then got spread out again as we passed through endless military checkpoints, passing from HVO territory into BiH areas and back again. The French articulated lorry couldn't pass through a tunnel and had to go and unload in another town. Progress was tortuous and uneven.

Millie goes Smuggling

" Mohammed keeps covering up some badly hidden boxes in the middle of the seat, keeps looking at me and making ssh ssh motions, pointing at the boxes. I start thinking the worst of course. He decides it's a good idea to cover them with my sleeping bag. Maybe he didn't want me in the cab because he's willing to take the risk himself of smuggling guns and grenades, but he was trying to protect me. We are about ten kilometres from the border. My heart is pumping fast. I am trying to ask him what is in the boxes. He just goes ssh ssh and covers them up again. He is sweating now. I look behind. I knew it! We have been separated from the rest of the convoy. But I recognise another Bosnian truck and I know one of the drivers speaks English, so as we slow down to go round a corner I jump out and flag down the truck behind. What's the problem, say the Bosnians. They come over to Mohammed's truck and get him to open one of the boxes. Surprise, surprise. In the box – guns, grenades!! Only joking. TOBACCO!!!! I went phew! "

ANDY MILTON

Workers Aid placed an ad for volunteer Heavy Goods Vehicle (HGV) drivers in *Trucks and Trucking* magazine. Most people who replied had only three weeks' holidays. We couldn't guarantee their return in time. Paul Maddox, a 24-year-old driver from Lancashire, was prepared to take the gamble. It was his first time out of Britain.

21st March. Sunny. Set off crammed into a car with four people / rucksacks etc. Reach Dover 5.15pm. Tedious wait for others bringing a wagon. 7.45pm. Still waiting. Bob, one of the organisers, must have shares in BT. He is on the phone the whole time. Total chaos. I am put to drive a battered Sherpa van and Paul, Bozena and myself take the 9.30pm ferry as we have to get to Heidelberg before 8am tomorrow to get paperwork.

22nd. Dry. Drove all night and reach Heidleberg at 9.45am. Met Nela, refugee from Tuzla, and her father who is providing the lorry which is going to be left in Tuzla. It's weird driving a left-hand drive. First sleep since 6am yesterday.

23rd. Cloudy. We get the truck loaded and weighed then take it to customs to be sealed to avoid border inspections. Set off at 2.45pm for Austrian border to meet other trucks from Germany. Everything going well until Sherpa van blows a head gasket. Limp on to border. The other trucks have already gone on. Get 3hrs sleep.

24th. Sunny. Windy. Up at 6.30am. Get the AA to take van to a garage. What to do with the three extra people and luggage? Take George and Brian to Salzburg to catch train to Slovenia. When I come back to the border to get the other people I get stuck in a lane of traffic that takes me back across the border into Germany. Try to get police to help me get back over. They tell me to wait. Wait 2 hrs. Try to stay calm. I just want to cry. Finally get a customs man to understand. I think 'great, I'll find the others'. When I try to cross back into Austria they say the lorry is overweight and will not let me in. Nightmare. After 4 hrs Paddy and Lisa find

When the December lorries arrived in Tuzla they told the miners that another thirty four trucks were on their way. When the December team left Tuzla to meet the new lorries in Zagreb, the miners' President sent them off with the following message.

With hope in our hearts we have followed all the news about the progress of the Workers Aid all-European convoy to Tuzla's miners. When news of your humanitarian effort came, our hearts filled with pride that we belong to the big family of European workers. Your moral support will make us stand tall even after you leave us. You have been in a position, during your Tuzla visit, to feel that you are part of our fight against the disaster inflicted on us by fascist aggression, and to find out, if only in part, the danger facing us if resistance doesn't come soon. We ask that you do everything in your power so that fascism never appears elsewhere. Thank you for the aid you bring us, which will be distributed to 13,000 miners and 50,000 members of their families.

Sretno!

A city at war

From my window in a high rise block I look down on a patchwork expanse of allotments which people are busy weeding and hoeing. It is Easter Monday and a sunny late afternoon in Tuzla. Along the riverside, whole families are working their vegetable patches, or breaking for a picnic tea. Even on the steep hillside behind the miners' institute, where trees have been felled for fuel, men are cutting furrows for cultivation.

Outside the Bank of Tuzla that morning a man had been leading three small goats to

graze on the lawn. Sound ecology, saving petrol and making protein, I thought. A shaggy pony came trotting briskly down the street with a cartload of firewood. Over the bridge on the main road a peasant is grazing his cow on the central reservation.

The countryside has come into town. But this peaceful-looking pastoral scene to delight any 'Green' isn't out of William Morris's *News from Nowhere*, it's news from somewhere in Europe: Tuzla, where working people and their way of life are tenaciously holding out under siege.

"Did you paint your eggs for Easter?" Tihomir's neighbour asked him. "No," he regretted, "and how about you? Have you baked your baklava for Bajram?" (a Muslim festival). They both laughed. Eggs, like electricity, flour, and festive fare, are in short supply in Tuzla. But not good humour and neighbourliness.

CHARLIE POTTINS

me. Was I glad to see them. They find the head of customs who sorts out everything. Go to sleep in the cab.

25th. Dry. Bright. Breakfast of soup and beans – Paddy's speciality. Slovenians will not let us enter as our Green Card (insurance) has gone on with other lorries. Have to buy new one for 50DM. 5pm. Catch up with convoy on Slovenia/Croatia border. It is like seeing a friend you have not seen for years. My heart is pounding with excitement. Something that people only started in January is taking shape. To get this far has been a lot of hard, stressful work. It will probably get more difficult but for the moment I am on a high.

Next stop Zagreb. Slovenian miners' lorries remain stuck at Croatian border with paperwork problems.

We meet other Workers Aid lorries in Zagreb. Slovenians arrive at 1.30 am. Brilliant. We are all here.

26th. Rainy. Chaos rules. The Slovenians have already left. We try to

organise cash for diesel. A Workers Aid artic arrives from France. Seven trucks head on for Split. The rest wait for more people from France, Switzerland, Hungary and for Dot Gibson and other Workers Aid people who are returning from Tuzla with the first lorries to get through.

27th. Overcast. Dot tells everyone about her first meeting with Tuzla miners. All set off for Split at midday. Stop for a break on a mountain top and have a snowball fight. Roads are terrible. More holes than polo mints. Arrive 3am. Find that one lorry that left Zagreb yesterday went over the side of a mountain road. No-one is hurt. Wagon is knackered and it took 6 hours to off-load all its medical supplies.

28th. Sunny. Woken at 7am by Bronwen, an Aussie woman, wanting to know what my lorry is carrying. Sent off to check with Lisa. Find that Paul and Craig have left and gone home. Not sure why.

Today nothing happening. Go for a beer with Andy and a French guy who can't speak any English and an Argentinean Greek. In the evening we

The Workers Aid lorries from Spain and Britain finally arrived in Tuzla. Some other lorries arrived but not the Slovenians and the bulk of the German lorries. Still expecting them to all arrive, we waited and waited. Diesel shortages in the besieged town meant that there were no local vehicles on the road. The lorries could not be missed.

Eventually we bumped into one of the Slovenian miners in the town square. His truck was empty. All their lorries had gone straight to mining villages around Tuzla and delivered aid directly to families there. They had not trusted the Tuzla union leaders.

Then we discovered the lorries from Germany had passed Tuzla and gone on to Brcko, Banovici and other towns where the refugees who had organised the lorries came from.

As we went to meet the Tuzla miners' union committee it became clear that of the thirty-four lorries that we had been told were on the way, only four were actually going to the union warehouse.

The miners' anger did not go so far as breaking off all co-operation with us, but it came close. They had thousands of starving union members who thought aid was coming. How could the union explain that they did not have it? Fikret Suljic, their president, had received us with traditional Bosnian hospitality, including paying for the convoy team to stay in the Hotel Tuzla. Now they told us they could not give us the meal they had prepared and could not provide accommodation for us. They made it clear that they thought they had been deliberately misled and even used for propaganda purposes.

Their anger was not only driven by the desperate need to alleviate hunger. Tuzla had just survived a bitter winter and was still virtually surrounded. News of our work had reached Tuzla and the miners had seen the convoy as the start of a solidarity movement from the workers' organisations of Europe that could bring about a change in the war. Behind the anger over the missing lorries was bitter disappointment that no such movement yet existed.

We tried to explain, but no words about the future could compensate for the harsh reality of the present. We left the hotel with our bags. Months of trying to build this bridge to the miners, nine months of exhausting, nerve-racking work and here we were, on the streets. Dot Gibson said she felt like throwing herself in the river.

---

light a fire and sit round while Brian plays his guitar. We get through 2 litres of brandy. I am drunk and so is Sue, an HGV driver from New Zealand. I have to carry her to her wagon but can't find her keys so break in. Didn't know the passenger door was open.

30th. Hot. Woken at 7am by Bosnian lady from Manchester. Given a Bosnian ID card.

Nothing moves. I am starving. A warning light has come on on my instrument panel. Water has built up in my air brake reservoirs. Drain loads of water out. Write a letter to Donna. Hope everyone at home is OK. Lot of confusion about when we are leaving. Not today it seems.

31st. Hot. Woken at 3am. Waste of time going to bed. Reach the Croatian/ Bosnian border at 6am. Customs take long time going through all the wagons. Finally we are moving. The dust is amazing. Can't see anything. Finally stop on the top of a mountain. As I fall asleep in the back of the truck I hear machine gun fire.

Today I have finally seen the reality of war. It is not the governments or the armies who suffer – the army will always have food and somewhere to sleep. The people have nothing but what is left of their ruined houses. It has taken us nearly two weeks to get here. So many hold ups and problems. Morale has been high but there have been many arguments.

Bosnian soldiers; some uniforms, but no boots

We had been overwhelmed by the warmth of our reception, including the Mayor and town council. Nothing had prepared us for the acts of kindness shown to us by people who were themselves suffering great deprivation.

But for most of the team there was confusion, and for the people who had reached Tuzla three weeks earlier there was deep disappointment.

As we left the hotel some local teenagers be-friended us and gave us places to sleep in their parents' homes.

We had been unprepared for the level of hardship. We knew the town was starving, but from outside we could not comprehend what it really meant. We hadn't even brought enough food for ourselves for the journey in and out of Tuzla, particularly as the deep, rutted tracks meant long delays for repairs.

Protests in Britain continue opposite the UN in London

People getting stressed out. Impossible now to get in touch with home. No phones.

1st April. Hot. Communal breakfast of baked beans. We stop at a UN checkpoint in a place that has been blown to smithereens. We pass in and out of areas controlled by Bosnian army. Now we are back on Bosnian territory and Addi, who has come with us from Germany, is at the end of his journey. He has come back to fight with the Bosnian army.

What a road! Halfway up a mountain the lorry in front gets stuck. I can't pass and get stuck as well. Stop for the night. Have some soup. It's freezing cold but people have to take turns to guard our diesel supplies which are gold dust here.

2nd Sunny. Woke up in back of my truck. Everything including me is covered with dust. Hard to breathe. What a wild ride down the mountain and into the Tuzla Customs. Wait to be cleared.

4th. Sunny. Go to customs to sort out the problems. Takes all morning. The others are going to a shooting tournament. They enter as a team and come second to last, but beat the police. Charlie, George, Tony and myself went to Nela's uncle and we had some Bosnian biscuits covered in honey called Bosanska hurmasica. I am leaving tomorrow.

5th. Sunny. Left with Dirk from East Germany. We go to the office of the 2nd Corpus of the Bosnian army and get our papers. After leaving Tuzla we take a wrong turn and get stopped by soldiers. The Chetnik front line. I am absolutely shitting myself. We can't understand a word. Eventually they let us go but we are in no man's land. Are we going the right way? Luckily we meet an old man who can speak German and he escorts us back into Bosnian army territory. I have never felt so relieved.

6th. Snowing. Freezing. No breakfast. I just want to go home to some food and beer. Outside it is snowing and we get stuck on a mountain. Put on the snow chains. It is so cold. We leave Bosnia. Pass the mangled remains of our truck which crashed on the way down.

7th. We reach Dresden where Dirk lives and I have a wash. Catch the train for Brussels. A guy in the carriage gave me some biscuits. I was starving.

8th. Woke at Aachen station. Get the ferry to Ramsgate. I am near the end of a journey. Relieved to be near home but will miss my new found friends.

PAUL MADDOX

Truck surfing at Vares

"For those of us who have just arrived in Tuzla, the campaign to open the northern route has taken on a new dimension. Personnel and vehicles seem to age ten years in two weeks during the journey along the southern route via Split. Deprived of food and diesel, frozen after too many nights on mountain tops, it was a dishevelled bunch that pulled into Tuzla.

The southern route is dangerous and frustrating. Chetniks control all roads so the BiH Army and UNPROFOR have carved roads over two mountain peaks. *Route Triangle*, as one road is called in UNPROFOR-speak, seemed to be the worst road I had ever travelled: a two-way dirt track leading away from the coast and climbing well above the snow line and then falling down to Prozor.

It is nothing however to *Route Skoda*. This section begins with not too steep a climb. It is just the surface that's the problem. It's a case of counting the track in the potholes, not vice versa.

A little way beyond Vares there's a tunnel with a stream running through it which has completely eroded away what was an unpaved stretch anyway.

The trucks fall in and out of the huge ruts, throwing people first up to the ceiling and then almost through the bottom of the seat. I have a new-found respect for the men and women who made our lorries. With every corner, you think: surely we can't get over/under, up/down that! However, with the help of some well organised pushing, levering and filling-in, we did.

The southern route saved its tour de force until the end: Mount Milankovic, home of hairpins and one-in-three climbs. Once negotiated, only 40-50km of road lies between you and Tuzla.

Near Kladanj we hit a traffic jam caused by the UN. There's nothing unusual about that. We waited four hours at Prozor because of Britbat, the UN British battalion. One of their lorries refused to stop and got stuck on a corner.

The Kladanj hold-up was different because of a Bosnian truck driver. As a Swedish APC tried to zoom through, it was caught between a fence and a Workers Aid vehicle. The Swedes piled out to have a look. All action-man uniforms and sunglasses (it was raining).

The hero of the hour chose his moment. A Bosnian driver claimed that the UN had smashed his indicator as they had gone past. The UN told him to go away.

In response he lay down under the wheels of their armoured beast. The UN soldiers cocked their rifles, pointing them at the driver.

Workers Aid for Bosnia lived up to its name, however. Certain individuals put themselves between the Swedes and the lorry driver. Stalemate, with a big jam developing. Nonplussed, the UN troops uncocked their weapons.

The Bosnian, scenting victory, demanded 200 DM compensation or he'd be there until they ran him over.

With nationals of several western European countries watching, the Swedes were at a loss. The agreed price was 50DM. This in a region where average wages are 2-5DM per month.

A Workers Aid delegation helped commemorate this victory over imperialism with a bottle of Sljivovica. Delighted with his wealth, the driver toasted the end of the UN. After two more toasts he admitted that his indicator had been broken for several weeks.

The hotel where we stayed in Zagreb is owned by a Bosnian and is full of wounded Bosnian soldiers, recuperating. This sounds fine – a hotelier doing his patriotic duty. However, both we and the troopers paid dearly. Everyone is charged 20DM per night. Workers Aid paid for us; the Bosnian government paid for the soldiers. Last New Year's Eve a drunken soldier harangued our corpulent host. The wounded man told him exactly what he thought of the big, new Audi car and the big, new suits. The owner was incensed. He produced a pistol and waved it at the trooper, who had to leave. He also pointed it at the Workers Aid members who had supported the veteran's outburst.

Bosnia, like anywhere else, is not a single issue. It is a developed, complicated society. Since the start of capitalism's re-conquest of the country, people like this hotelier have grown in number.

This is why a humanitarian effort alone is not enough. If aid is all that we bring, then we simply help to oil the wheels of this restoration of capital; we simply help to turn this country into yet another exploited and unhappy place.

Unless the solidarity of working men and women is established, then it is not the Bosnian people who will be victorious but the profiteers. **"**

TOM BATTERSBY

3rd Convoy Factfile

DATE:
March 1994

LORRIES:
15 lorries from Slovenian miners
13 lorries from Bosnian associations in Germany
5 lorries from Workers' Aid in Spain, France and UK
2 lorries from Swedish 'Unga Liv'

WEIGHT: 220 tons of food, clothes and personal parcels

RECIPIENTS: Mining communities in the Tuzla region, communities around Brcko, Tuzla Hospital and the Tuzla miners' union

PEOPLE: 80

Despite some fruitful discussions in Tuzla, the anger of the miners left us feeling we had let them down. Before we left, though, we began to rebuild trust. A live interview on Radio Tuzla between Dot Gibson from Workers Aid and the miners' president went honestly over the problems and events. The Spanish Ayuda Obrera team made a big contribution by donating their coach and some money to the union.

The Mayor, Selim Beslagic, arranged a meeting with the leader of the Slovenian delegation and explained to him how delivering aid through the union would help to strengthen the workers' own organisations without which the town could not survive. If there were problems with the organisation they had to be confronted, not just bypassed. The Slovenians accepted these criticisms.

These meetings pulled our relations with the miners back from the brink but the warmth, hopes and sense of collaboration that had existed a week earlier was gone.

The people who had been the main driving force behind our last nine months' work were exhausted and disappointment drained what little energy was left. Some had been on the road for almost six months and just wanted to go home to discuss things with campaign supporters.

Some drivers were going back down to Split to help bring up five lorries of medical supplies to Tuzla sent by our collaborators in Sweden. But two young people on the team had other ideas. At a convoy meeting in Tuzla they announced that they planned to go home and organise another convoy as quickly as possible to show the miners we were serious.

Tuzla: a multi-ethnic stronghold in Bosnia

Tuzla, Bosnia-Herzegovina's second largest city, will become either a relic of the past or a model upon which a multi-national Bosnian state is rebuilt. Even now, Tuzla, which had a pre-war population of 120,000 but now has an estimated population of 200,000 (80,000 are refugees), has preserved a great deal of what made Bosnia exceptional. Its' multi-ethnicity and its' rejection of divisions between people are a sore point for all three of the ethnic/national oligarchies.

The fascist aims of Bosnian Serb leader Radovan Karadzic are based on the belief that a shared life is impossible and that territorial division is inevitable. Tuzla stands as a glaring contradiction to this. Karadzic's proposal for an exchange of territory in Tuzla is, in large part, an attempt to destroy evidence that exposes his great lie.

Tuzla highlights the political failure of the Croatian nationalists, too. Even ignoring the preferences of the city's historically cosmopolitan centre, there is very little support, even in wholly Croatian villages, for the ethnic parties. In 1990, the Social Democrats won the elections, the nationalist Croatian Democratic Union (HDZ) attracting only 4 per cent of the vote. In the greater Tuzla region, the Social Democrats, led by Tuzla's mayor, Selim Beslagic, and his Union of Bosnian Social Democrats (UBSD), continue to govern.

Tuzla also represents a threat to the Party of Democratic Action (SDA), the leading Muslim party in Bosnia-Herzegovina. At a meeting of the SDA's executive council this spring, just before the signing of the Washington agreement, Tuzla was targeted as a priority electoral region, where every effort is to be made to undermine Beslagic's political base – from manipulating the Bosnian Muslims' plight for the party's own ends, through using the dispersal of humanitarian aid for the purposes of blackmail, to smearing the authorities of 'Red Tuzla'.

There have been visits to Tuzla by a stream of members of the Bosnian Presidency and leaders of the Islamic religious community (before, the city was avoided like the plague), while SDA leaders have literally been on guard in the town. Hundreds of posters with various political messages are daily being stuck on walls, although the front line is only twenty kilometres away. Many of these posters are financed directly by different organisations in Arabic countries. The nationalist parties as a rule declare all non-nationalists to be either 'disloyal Croats', 'treacherous Serbs', or 'bad Muslims'. However, this vilification of the whole of Tuzla only brings the people together even more in their resistance to aggressive totalitarianism and these attempts to impose feelings of guilt for things they are proud of. The UBSD and Beslagic argue that Bosnia is not divisible, whether between the two or three nations, and insist on the protection of the centuries-old Bosnian identity from being undermined by nationalist ideology.

And so, on the edge of the northern corridor, where thousands of soldiers are poised for what could be Bosnia's next major battle, Tuzla lives its special life. As far as people can see, Europe exists less and less. Indeed, perhaps a united Europe's last hope is this city in northern Bosnia that continues to resist the attacks of national fascism.

by SEJFUDIN TOKIC, MP for the Union of Bosnian Social Democrats (Published in WAR REPORT, London, June 1994)

War cultivation in urban Tuzla

Tuzla - heart of Yugoslavia

Yugoslavia itself was ethnically diverse, but the proportions of the three main national groups were more evenly represented in Bosnia and the different groups were spread geographically throughout Bosnia with many communities living side by side. This ethnic-mixing was particularly common in the urban areas and this factor, combined with a drift away from religion, led to more and more people defining themselves as Yugoslav rather than Serb, Croat, Slovenian etc. In the 1991 census, Tuzla had the highest proportion of people in former Yugoslavia defining themselves simply as Yugoslav as well as the highest proportion of ethnic inter-marriages.

For the first time, Workers Aid members meet the Tuzla miners' leaders, some of them showing obvious malnutrition after two years of siege

	Ethnic Composition (%)			Religious affiliation (%)	
	Yugoslavia	BiH	Tuzla	Tuzla	
Serbs	36.2	31	16	20	Orthodox
Croats	19.6	17.3	17	15	Catholic
Muslims	9.8	43.7	40	16.5	Muslim
Yugoslavs	2.9	6	22	46	None

NOTES: In this table, Muslim is the national designation for all those, irrespective of their own religious beliefs, whose ancestors converted to Islam under the Ottoman Empire. Other ethnic groups – Macedonians, Hungarians, Montenegrins etc, are not shown here. The 1991 census was controversial; the Kosova Albanians, for example, boycotted it.

64

The Independent,
December 29th, 1992

Old and sick suffer as Bosnian winter claims first victims

SARAJEVO — The freezing cold of winter is beginning to claim lives in the besieged Bosnian capital and other parts of Bosnia-Herzegovina. The elderly, the sick and the injured are the most vulnerable.

The number of those killed by the cold in Sarajevo is still low, but people already suffering from injuries or malnutrition are falling prey to pneumonia and other illnesses. Their chances of recovery are slim in hospitals which have no heating.

In Sarajevo's Kosevo hospital Enisa, 16, died not because of the burns she suffered in an accident but because of the cold in her room. A few weeks ago she was badly burnt when she tried to light a lamp with a mixture of petrol and a home-made product. Dr Borisa Starovic succeeded in grafting skin on to her legs and abdomen despite the atrocious conditions and lack of medicine in the hospital. "She was so kind, so courageous. Her life was not in danger because of her burns. It was the cold in her room which killed her," the doctor said.

There is no heating in the maternity ward, where there are between 10 and 15 deliveries a day and as many abortions, and none in the operating theatres. The only place that is heated is a small area reserved for babies' incubators. The number of premature births has risen by 50 per cent

From Christian Millet
of Agence France-Presse

since the Serbian siege of Sarajevo began more than eight months ago. Water is heated in the kitchen, but is cold by the time it reaches the delivery rooms, where there is no emergency oxygen. New-born babies are put into bed with their mothers so they can at least get some body-heat.

Mothers and their new babies are sent home within 15 to 24 hours of the birth. Before the war, they were kept in hospital for four days. Professor Sirecko Simic, head of the gynaecology and obstetrics department, said he had been told that some new-born babies had died of cold after going home.

Most buildings in Sarajevo have electric or gas heaters, but there has been no electricity in the city for more than two weeks and only some areas have a gas supply. Some people have oil heaters, but that fuel also ran out two weeks ago. Few people have a fireplace at home to build an open fire.

Elsewhere, eight old people have died of cold since Christmas at a home in the Sarajevo suburb of Nedzarici. A spokesman for the UN High Commissioner for Refugees said there were 114 people at the home and about 35 had died in recent weeks.

The Guardian, March 17th, 1993

Maggie O'Kane in Tuzla hears, from some of those who have escaped, harrowing accounts of life under siege in the eastern Bosnian town where the UN commander Philippe Morillon has planted his flag

No anaesthetic for the pain of Srebrenica

ON A September night last year a Serb politician who had drunk too much whisky with a British journalist confided: "You journalists were busy with Sarajevo so we could do what we liked in the rest of Bosnia."

Six months later the US air drops and General Philippe Morillon's sit-in in Srebrenica have brought the international press corps up north.

All week American pick-up trucks have been unloaded by young men wearing Raybans, leather jackets and Levis. The American television networks have come to check where Bill Clinton's aid packets are landing and the progress of the "crazy" French general who has defied the Serbian forces and told the people of Srebren-

ica not to be afraid, that he will stay with them.

What has happened in Srebrenica is beginning to emerge from the few survivors who have made it to safety while 80,000 remain trapped inside a town surrounded by heavily armed Serbian forces who refuse to grant the UN High Commissioner for Refugees permission to bring relief.

Last Friday the second Bosnian helicopter to reach the town touched down at 5.30am. The pilot, Mujo Muric, had flown with a national display team of the Yugoslav federal army before the war. Now, dodging anti-aircraft fire, he landed on a football pitch with medicine and food and took 13 of the most seriously wounded on board.

Hundreds of wounded have

been left behind in a town which has four doctors, no electricity, no food, and no medicine. The town has been surrounded since April 18, 1992.

There was no room for the 13th on Mr Muric's helicopter. As they lifted the old man back on to the football pitch he screamed: "God will punish you for this". The helicopter took off after 12 minutes on the ground. "I will remember him screaming· for the rest of my life," Mr Muric said.

In Srebrenica 20,000 refugees from outlying villages and towns are desperate to find space. Many are camped in the snow on the main street where they burn tyres and plastic supermarket baskets for warmth.

When the helicopter flew out, it flew over the hospital where

Jasmina Jakub, aged 20, died last Thursday after 50 hours in labour giving birth to a dead 9lb baby. Her baby turned its back on the birth canal as she walked through 15 miles of snow. There was no petrol for the drive to hospital. When she delivered in the early hours of the third day she had lost too much blood and they had none to give, and no electricity for a transfusion anyway.

The day before, a man who had fled from the village of Vlasnica waited outside an operating room while Dr Nikanovich tried to amputate his daughter's leg with a metal saw. "She's only five. I can't go in," her father told Nezira Bektic who went into the room to collect his shirt. She died on the table from shock while Dr Nikanovich was sawing. There

was no anaesthetic for the pain.

In the streets of Srebrenica the dogs turned wild with hunger. "Once I saw them attack a corpse," said Sebad Catic, who is 25 and escaped from the town with five other men by walking for 10 days over the mountains.

"There were maybe 10 dogs and they started tearing at it on the street. So we shot all the dogs. I don't remember exactly when that was. It happened many times. If there is a big family and one of them gets killed by a shell, then he will be buried. If they have no family they don't get buried. People are too weak from hunger."

Mr Catic's two brothers, Sarid and Nedad, both killed by shells, are buried in the front garden. "Nobody risks going to a cemetery any more. Too many funerals have been shelled."

His neighbour Moushan Curk hanged himself in a cellar on New Year's Eve. His crop up, planted after the spring attack, he went begging in the town for food for his family, but by June Srebrenica was surviving on a diet of maize, pumpkin and acorns. Nobody had anything to spare.

"It is quite logical," Mr Catic said. "When you can do nothing you have to do something."

In Srebrenica the shelling has stopped since Gen Morillon and 14 men moved into the post office in the centre of town and hoisted the white and blue UN flag.

"People are dying from 'hunger, disease and uncured wounds, not from war," Mr Catic said. "Now the world knows what happened to us why is nobody coming to help?"

APRIL 1994	Attacks on Gorazde despite token UN air strike.
APRIL 1994	Chetniks seize Mt. Igman and 150 UN 'hostages'.
JULY 1994	Contact group proposes ethnic partition of Bosnia.

Chapter 5

Regular convoys

Coming back from the war zone was deeply disorientating. In the abnormal atmosphere of besieged Tuzla we had formed strong friendships and on the journey home most people had a feeling of sadness and loss. For some of us, memory of the miners' anger also nagged away. Determination to reach them had kept us going round the clock since the previous June, now mental and physical exhaustion took over. Where would we go from here?

The original decision to send a convoy had started a conveyor belt of action. One thing led to the next, with its own momentum – the first convoy to the meeting with the Logistic Centre, then the campaign for the northern route and the December and March convoys. Now it seemed ten months of campaigning had produced little support for the Bosnian miners, other than in our own, very small ranks.

23.4.94
Human life is cheap in Gorazde

Gorazde's people are being exposed to shelling, sniper and machine gun fire. Water and sanitation systems have collapsed. Food distribution has been halted by sniper fire, as confirmed by a UN High Commissioner for Refugees spokesperson.

Gorazde's hospital has taken a direct hit on its roof, and aid workers report sniper fire being directed at ward windows. Built to hold sixty five patients, the hospital is sheltering at least 200 wounded. The only anaesthetist, wounded in the leg some days previously, is among staff struggling to cope.

"Human life is the cheapest thing in Gorazde right now," an amateur radio operator said. "Life is measured in seconds, not years. There are wounded people trapped on the left bank of the river. NATO planes are flying overhead but doing nothing."

As 60,000 people were trapped in the UN's so-called 'safe haven', it was reported that thirty villages around Gorazde had been 'torched' – Serb General Mladic's own word when giving the order to his troops.

Post-convoy stress

" We had a lot of problems getting back but I was quite happy once we got on the motorway and were bombing along OK, even though we had no tax, no MOT and no insurance. But when I actually got home I felt lost. Within ten minutes of getting back in my house I just felt so depressed; I had got a crate of beer on the ferry and I started drinking. I'd get up, smoke a joint before breakfast, smoke another one, have a couple of cans of beer. My mate would come round, give me some speed and I'd be out of it. This went on for ten days.

I went to see mates, but how can you explain things to them. I mean, they were interested and they do care but they can't understand what I've seen and what can they do anyway? They're all busy looking after themselves, they've got no job, nowhere to live and they've just lost the idea of helping anyone out. If they helped someone else they'd realise they're helping themselves.

Before I went on these convoys my vision of the world was slim. It's still fairly slim now, but not like before. I mean what's money, who gives a shit about money. After seeing what I've seen you just don't care about it.

I got a letter from Zina, this nurse I made friends with in Tuzla Hospital. She told me all about her friends. I felt really guilty because I never wrote back. There I am, in a much better position to write a letter than her, but I just didn't do it. I wanted to forget. I didn't want to sit down and write a letter. Saying what? "I'm feeling quite depressed because I can't get a job," and she writes back, "Six people have just died today." Say I wrote, "the dole have been mucking me about," and then I think, well she don't even get dole. She gets a kilo of flour and a litre of oil a month. My problems are trivia. You don't know what to write. I spent three days trying to write a letter and I just couldn't do it. Do you sound happy, sad or what? In the end I thought, fuck it, I'll just write whatever comes into my head.

It was difficult to get up and do anything. But maybe that's the only way you can sort out some of these problems in your own head. You have to find a way to cope with what you've seen. You do get depressed, it does get on top of you and you can't pretend it doesn't. If I hadn't done that I couldn't have gone on another convoy. I would have just felt too physically drained, because mentally I couldn't cope with it. But once you sort your ideas out, then you can cope with the physical side of the convoy, which is shattering, no two ways about it. Sometimes you might go without food for two days, or drive more or less non stop for two days. But you can do that as long as you know why you are doing it. So when you get back from a convoy you've got to find your own way of dealing with your ideas if you are going to go again. "

TONY MYERS

How was the campaign for to be continued? What could we do about the northern route? When all roads to Tuzla were blocked we gained support from anyone who agreed that aid needed to be got in. However, with most people prevented from understanding even the basic causes of the war, it would be difficult to argue the apparently obscure need to open a blocked route when another was now open.

Most of the Bosnians in Europe who had worked with us to prepare the March convoy returned to organising their lorries through Split. Our bold plan had inspired them. For a short while we held them together with the vision of a workers' assault on the northern route, a united action that people sensed could somehow change the course of the war. It hadn't succeeded and the vision melted away. Bosnians, who had excitedly talked at the Stuttgart conference about a growing river of workers' solidarity, returned to their separate lorry runs. They

Young Bosnians on London demonstration, April 1994

did what they could to stop starvation. Our lorries would sometimes be held up together in a border queue. Drivers would swap greetings without anyone being able to understand more than a few words.

A city at war

" In Tuzla on Easter Sunday, people walked to the Serb Orthodox Church, repaired and repainted after suffering Serb army shelling, perhaps deliberate. Tihomir told us: "They don't need a target. They just fire into the town, knowing they'll hit something, maybe a house."

He remembers running with his wife and small son, trying to reach a shelter, and seeing four children killed, and a piece of still-warm brain on the snow.

On notice-boards outside mosques, churches and the town hall, there are death notices – some with the green crescent of Islam, some with black crosses, some with the socialist red star. The latest is a cameraman from the local television station.

That night, while the power is back on, we turn on the television and watch Gorazde being shelled, big guns pounding workers' flats, flames and clouds of smoke, and a woman sobbing.

On our way back to Britain, we hear that Tuzla has been shelled. I think of the friends we've made, and hope we can make people in Britain understand. "

CHARLIE POTTINS

An economic migrant

" In Split I stay in a house where an old woman lets rooms. I share a room with a man from Sarajevo. He speaks no English and I speak no Bosnian. But with expressions, drawings and drama he tells me his story.

He has been in Sarajevo with his wife and children since the war started. He looks about fifty but is probably much younger. His family are desperate. No work, no money, no food, constant fear. Two brothers and his father have been killed. Then, to his joy, a brother in Germany manages to get him a job, and sends him the coach fare and a letter from the prospective employer confirming his job. From Germany he will be able to send money to his wife.

Now he is in Split – returning back to Sarajevo. They turned him back at the Austrian border. His Croatian visa was valid for one entry into the country instead of multiple entry. This disqualifies him for entry into the European Union.

With a flick of the wrist some border policeman has sent another 'bloody Bosnian' away. To him, nothing more than a couple of seconds of irritation. To the man, the collapse of his whole world and a return to hell.

The man cannot change his Croatian visa in Croatia. He must return to Sarajevo and apply again. He will try again if he can get the money and find the energy, but he will almost certainly fail. He tells me this story and ends with a shrug of despair that no words could convey.

He thinks it is his misfortune that he has been given the wrong visa, an accident or a bureaucratic mistake. He knows other people who have got to Germany. He does not see the overall policy of 'fortress Europe'. The workers of Eastern Europe have to accept the rigours of the free market. They must be conditioned to accept poverty, low wages and unemployment. These restored values come via wars and dictatorships. There would be no point in western capital backing ventures in Eastern Europe if the very labour it wishes to exploit were able to travel west where, for the moment, the working class is able to defend a better standard of living. "

BOB MYERS

4th
Convoy Factfile

DATE:
May 1994

LORRIES:
3 from Workers Aid,
Manchester

WEIGHT: 10 tons of
mixed aid

RECIPIENT:
Tuzla Miners Union

PEOPLE: 10

In the summer of 1994, the
southern route was still dangerous, particularly for Bosnians.
This man was one of two passengers shot by HVO Militia
when the Split coach was
stopped (photograph by a
Workers Aid passenger)

GREAT MYTHS OF THE WAR

• All sides have committed atrocities and are equally to blame

Fact: Killings by Serb nationalist forces are a direct conse-
quence of the Serbian authorities' campaign of stirring hate
against Muslims and Croats amongst Serbs, and of seeking
to expel all non-Serbs from Serbian-occupied land to create
a Greater Serbia. These policies have no equivalent on the
Bosnian side.

Fact: The overwhelming majority of killings – over 90 per
cent – have been carried out by Serb nationalist forces, as
reported by Amnesty International, Médecins Sans
Frontières, and other international monitoring organisations. Of these, the great majority were carried out in 1992,
before the Bosnians had an army.

Fact: While in Banja Luka, the main town of Serb nationalist
occupied Bosnia, every single mosque has been destroyed, in
the main government-held towns of Sarajevo, Tuzla and
Zenica, Serbian Orthodox churches are still standing.

The first convoy was proposed as a way to kick start a movement of solidarity. At that time no-one thought of us becoming
a 'convoy' organisation. Nine months later fatigue and doubts
about the way forward left some people shuddering at the
thought of organising another one. In Manchester, though, two
people carried out the proposal they had made in Tuzla. They
had seen the miner's disappointment and were going to show
them our seriousness. With some friends from the big Hulme
council estate, they raised enough cash and aid in a few weeks
to set off again with three lorries. These were all young, unemployed people with no connection to trade unions or the
labour movement. They just went out to get everything necessary in whatever way they could: money and food from collections in local supermarkets, money from non-stop collections around the pubs.

Unlike previous convoys, there were now people who knew
how to do things. They set off in April and reached Tuzla via
Split in little over a week, gave the aid to the miners and made
new friends amongst students and other young people in
Tuzla. Of course it was not that easy, no convoy ever was.
There were all kinds of hold-ups and near disasters en-route.

This convoy set a pattern for future work. Unemployed people, students and refugees began regular activities to keep the
convoys going, one after another. We became 'proper' convoy
organisers. Warehouses were provided by local councils in different parts of the country. On the first convoy we had accepted anything offered, including old clothes, out of date medicine and food. The comments of a Bosnian doctor brought us
up sharp. "Would you give out of date medicine to your child?
No, well don't expect us to either."

Now we carefully packed only new aid in labelled boxes.
Clothes were sorted by refugees and 90 per cent taken to rag
merchants. We became experts at customs' paperwork and all
the things we had never had time for before. We got spare
wheels, snow chains, communal cooking equipment. The lorries were repaired, inspected, taxed and insured. The days of
turning up at a border and waiting for a shift change of police
to nip through were over, more or less.

A Partisan still marching

Esad Jordanovic, from Zenica, was 17 in 1943 when he joined the Yugoslav partisans fighting Nazi occupation. Now 68, he marched with other Bosnians on the 1994 May Day march in London.

"I have spent my life fighting fascism. In World War II I fought Hitler's fascists. Today we are fighting Chetnik fascism. Today it's Bosnia; tomorrow it could be Macedonia, Kosova, and perhaps Albania."

"In the partisans we were all mixed, Muslim, Croat, Serb. Tito was popular because he took all peoples and joined them together to fight against fascism. In the Bosnian army today we have Serbs and Croats, as well as Muslims. Even when there was fighting between Croats and Muslims at Mostar, we had a Croat brigade in Tuzla region fighting for Bosnia."

When Esad Jordanovic returned from the war in 1946, he became an organiser for the Communist Party's youth movement, but he found his struggles were not over.

"Muslim people still did not have national rights, and Bosnia's status was less than that of Croatia or Serbia. Tito wanted to unite every nation in Yugoslavia, but to keep power himself. He had a very strong police."

Esad spent three years in the forces, working as a flight mechanic at a military airfield. Three times he applied for a pilot's licence. Each time he was turned down, with no reason given.

"I was a Muslim. If I'd been a Serb, I'd have been given a chance. But the Serbs wouldn't tolerate any other nationality in the higher ranks of the forces."

Esad was arrested in 1948 for opposing Stalin's Cominform [the Communist Information Bureau, set up in September 1947], which expelled the Yugoslav Communist Party later the same year.

"Stalin was pressing Yugoslavia to enter a military pact. Because I was a partisan fighter, I did not oppose socialism; but Russia did not care about how people were living, Stalin only cared for power."

Esad was imprisoned as a member of the Young Muslim organisation and for wanting a multi-party system. He spent six months in Sarajevo's central prison and a further eighteen months at a smaller prison. Because he was an ex-partisan, and for his good behaviour, he was released.

"We were not against communism but said we must have more than one party. Tito was a Croat, and personally a good man. But the ministers around him were mostly Serbs. In Yugoslavia, Serbs held important positions in the army, government and management. Towards the end of the war Chetniks and Ustashe, that is fascists, joined the partisans and, after it took power, the party. Tito did not discriminate against any nationality, but his ministers did. Someone like Rankovic, who had killed many Muslims in Bosnia and Albania, joined the partisans after 1944. As a minister he carried out ethnic cleansing of the Sandzak, sending a million people to Turkey."

After release from prison, Esad went home to Zenica, working in the youth organisation and as a driving instructor. But because of police harassment he had to leave for Zagreb where he obtained a job as a printing mechanic at the newspaper *Vjesnik.*

"But my prison record followed me, wherever I went."

Police harassment kept him on the move from job to job, town to town, till he'd had enough.

"In the 1950s I decided to go over the Alps to Austria, but I was caught by dogs on the border. I was held at Kranj in Slovenia, then sent to Sarajevo prison again." This time Esad was subjected to prolonged torture, being held down for long periods with ice-cold water dripping on his forehead, till he feared for his sanity. Tried in secret, he was sentenced to five years.

In 1957, after Esad's prison ordeal, friends helped him find work at the Sarajevo daily *Oslobodenje (Liberation)*, and he stayed there for six years, still under police surveillance. In 1964, he returned to Zenica, and married. He was in Britain on a visit to his son when the war broke out in Bosnia.

"After this war finishes, I will return. I'm too old to fight now but I want to fight fascism politically. I want to talk to young people about the dangers of nationalism and fascism. Because a Serb massacred Muslims we do not want to reply in kind, but if someone is responsible for massacres we must bring them to justice. If Arkan, Milosevic or Karadzic escape justice, they or others like them will do these things again. We must say, "Never again!''

"In our country the unions did not have a chance to say, "We defend the working class." We did not have strong unions. Each bureaucrat defended himself or herself, not the working class. Maybe if we'd had a strong international trade union movement, we could have stopped this war in Bosnia."

While many people got on with the convoy work as the most practical thing they could do, the campaign as a whole never stopped trying to turn this activity into something to set others moving.

Every week new contacts were made in the trade unions, community associations and the like. We tried to assist them to get going inside their own organisations. Members of the Lancashire Fire Brigades Union contacted us, keen to help. They were enthusiastic when we suggested they take aid to fellow firefighters in Tuzla. Talks got under way between us to plan the action, but at these meetings the fire-station management came along. They had worked together before to get aid to Rumania. The managers sniffed at the worker to worker plan and definitely opposed the idea of supporting one side in the war. They were quite happy about aid for starving people, but not for anything that might go against the UN. They persuaded the union members to go by themselves, not with Workers Aid. Their lorry went to Croatia and unloaded at the warehouse of one of the big charities. Maybe the food went into Bosnia, but the firemen didn't and firemen in Tuzla knew nothing about it. That essential link wasn't made. It was charity for the starving, not solidarity with the united workers' communities of Bosnia. For the Lancashire men it became just another trip alongside Rumania, Albania and all the other places where people went hungry. They never found out what was happening in Bosnia, or understood the Tory Government's involvement.

Every time a spark appeared in the unions we tried to help it catch fire. There was no attempt to make support for Bosnia into 'something for us'. We offered whatever technical assistance people might need, passed on what we had learnt, and tried to encourage organisations to do things in their own name and on their own terms. Desperate as we were for money, we always tried to persuade union branches to organise their own lorry, or make their own contact with Tuzla, rather than simply supporting our work. However, many did just give us money. Without the unions acting as an organised whole, it was difficult for a single branch or workplace to do anything else.

Even donating money could have been a starting point of something bigger. However, almost every spark of solidarity we kindled in the unions was snuffed out. This was not because people were unsympathetic to what we were doing, far from it. We spoke at hundreds of factory and union branch meetings. Refugees came with us to explain about the war. Most of the people we spoke to began to understand what had happened in Bosnia. After twelve years of Tory rule it was not so hard to see the British government's divide and rule strategy in foreign policy as well as at home, providing the connection was pointed out. But how many people could we actually speak to? In four years of work it was less than a single union mail-out could reach. Our efforts were neutralised by the barrage of propaganda poured out by the media and government about 'ethnic war', 'civil war', 'all sides committing atrocities' and the 'brave British soldiers trying to bring peace'. The union leadership did nothing to counter this propaganda. To the extent that they said anything about Bosnia, it was simply to reinforce these lies – not surprising coming from people who had refused to support the British miners during their battles.

Campaigning outside TUC headquarters: Dot Gibson seeks help from TGWU leader, Bill Morris

Aida's mother

" We arrived, numb from the freezing mountain nights and choking on the dust from the roads. The strain on Tuzla was immediately obvious. Every public building is bursting with refugees, six-lane roads which haven't seen traffic in two years teem with people who walk everywhere. All grass areas, including verges, railway embankments, and even parks in the centre of town now grow crops. People are visibly under-nourished. Soldiers, who according to nutritionists' law of priorities normally have the highest food entitlement in wartime, look thin and sallow-skinned. During the past winter's total blockade, people died of starvation every day.

The Tuzla spirit survives, with no romantic illusions. Soldiers at the entrance to the free territory brought glasses of Bosnian 'moonshine' (sliva). They overlooked peace-time, drink-driving restrictions and gave us their traditional Tuzla welcome.

Our first task in Tuzla was to find the mother of Aida, a Bosnian refugee in Manchester who has spent months collecting food and money to help buy our trucks. Aida was forced out of her home by Chetnik soldiers and with her husband and two-year-old daughter began the refugees' mountain trail to safety. We found her mother in a basement flat close to the centre of town. We had been so preoccupied with finding the flat that we had not prepared ourselves. She opened the door and looked puzzled. We looked too healthy to come from Tuzla. We couldn't speak, because we didn't share a language. We simply said, "Aida," and held out the envelope. The old woman burst into tears – her daughter, of whom she had received no news for two years, was alive and safe somewhere far from the war. It was such a happy moment – everyone cried.

We had brought a box of food, containing the essentials of flour, oil and sugar, and within a short time it was Bosnian hospitality all over again. The food was clearly cooked from what we brought in the box. It was very difficult to eat, even more so to refuse.

Aida's twelve-year-old brother Amir spoke good English and became our translator. He introduced us to his friends who earn a living with this precious skill outside the Hotel Tuzla where aid workers from international agencies spend their nights. Here they watch cars, carry bags, and act as guides and translators. In the upside down war economy they can earn twenty times their parents' monthly wage, but this isn't really difficult with the average wage only one German mark per month.

On the black market, the only place you can buy food, one kilo of sugar costs 20DM, a kilo of flour 40DM.

These prices cause great divisions in Tuzla. The obvious question is who can afford to pay them? People have spent their life savings on flour alone, but now, with no money and no customers, prices are falling rapidly. The Tuzla Logistics Centre tries to supply each family with a kilo of flour and a litre of oil as part of their monthly wage.

Many of the mental hospitals' patients can be seen on the streets of Tuzla. The story is that the hospital, in the suburbs, was shelled and the patients fled in terror towards the town. They are housed in municipal buildings but during the day wander around with hands outstretched, some making wild gesticulations, some staring off to somewhere distant in their minds.

The war has had a marked effect on the population. Western psychologists are paying close attention to this modern European society under siege and the resulting psychotic behaviour of some of its citizens, civilians and soldiers alike. One night a grenade was thrown near a group of young people. A girl was seriously injured. No-one knows who made the attack or the motivation. The following night on the same spot a man, presumably an ex-patient, attacked a soldier who collapsed in front of us. We rushed to help but there was nothing we could do. The soldier died, when only moments before he had been telling us of his trips to Australia before the war.

After many sad goodbyes we prepared to leave. There were three boxes of food in our truck for the journey home, but it was only three days to Croatia, so we decided to give it away. A humane but foolish move. The young boys, who have all now written letters for school children in England, were there and we began passing them packets of food. Within minutes there were crowds, everyone shouting for a packet, but by that time, only one left – who gets it? How do you choose from fifty hands?

This was supposed to be our last trip. We ought to get paid jobs in the summer to return to college in the autumn but now things have changed. In Tuzla there is only four hours of electricity and water per day. To make bread for her daughter's friends from England, Aida's mum got up at four in the morning. It's so precious, but you have to eat it.

Next month we will take her more flour. College must wait. "

PADDY McCLOY and LISA MEADE

The floppy boot brigade

" We took six trucks to Tuzla with $500,000 worth of medicine for Tuzla hospital from the Swedish *Unga Liv* organisation, who asked Workers Aid for help.

We got there on a shoestring – literally! The fan-belt broke on one of the 1950s Swedish army trucks, so shoestrings came in handy and we became the floppy-boot convoy.

We were stuck at the Croatian/Bosnian border for a day at Kamensko. It was hard to tell why – our papers were in order. Perhaps it was because we were with a Bosnian, or we didn't offer a roasted pig – as someone else did – or beer or Deutschmarks.

Finally, Tony's threat to block the border if we weren't over that day seemed to cause a ripple.

Going up Milankovic in the dark, we had to drive with one truck towing another without lights because the battery was dead. I flashed my hazard lights so the driver could at least see a little.

A UN truck backed into one of our Bedfords, breaking the windscreen. After that the Bedford driver would drive with his legs out the window or mime cleaning the non-existent windscreen for the entertainment of those around.

Tuzla had changed from the previous month. It was spring. Bosnia is very beautiful – wild herbs grow all over the landscape. We drove through a town. One house was completely destroyed by the shelling, but the front garden was in full bloom – red, lilacs and golds.

When shelling broke out in Tuzla I told the people I was staying with that I wanted to hide. They said that that was how everyone used to be, but now people refuse to live in fear.

The hospital was pleased with what we had brought. We were given a shower and food. Having spent the previous night sleeping upright in the cab of my truck at a checkpoint, this was much appreciated. But to be there, surrounded by many men my age in wheelchairs or with missing limbs, was hard. The hospital is a favourite target of the Serb nationalist forces, along with the marketplace.

The woman I stayed with was from India. She had eloped with a Bosnian because her parents were arranging a marriage for her. They thought that my home country of New Zealand must be nirvana. They talked of music. Eventually all conversations led to the situation in the former Yugoslavia. It was very painful. So much is happening to try and create ethnic division.

It is nearly a month since we got back to Britain. I miss the people on the convoy. So much happened between us. Walking into a supermarket here is a shock – so much food, so much choice.

Last weekend I collected for Workers Aid in Bath with a young Bosnian woman of sixteen. Old beyond her years, she could gently and firmly go up to people and ask for their support for Bosnia. She had seen her home destroyed and her brother and father taken to a concentration camp. "

SUE MORRISON (Heavy Goods Vehicle driver)

After the truce between the HVO and Bosnian forces the frontlines between them became fairly static. The Croat-Muslim Federation, which the US had sponsored, remained a diplomatic fiction to cover Croatia's annexation of parts of Bosnia. Heavily armed checkpoints either side of no-man's land testified to the complete absence of any 'federation'. The Croat nationalists built their statelet of Herceg-Bosna – controlled by Zagreb but administered by local bureaucrats, mass murderers who were becoming some of the new rich of ex-Yugoslavia.

To cross Herceg-Bosna we had to fax our convoy papers to the Bosnian Humanitarian Aid office in Zagreb. There they would be stamped and sent to the Herceg-Bosna officials in Siroki Brijeg. The HVO would counter-stamp them and send them to another Bosnian office in Split. We could then collect them and go to join hundreds of other lorries queuing at the Herceg-Bosna border.

Getting the papers stamped in the first place, however, was the problem. It could take days. In August, Spanish and British lorries sat waiting in a lorry park in Split. No toilets, no washing facilities, nothing. Every day we went to the Bosnian office but nothing came from Siroki Brijeg. We started our usual fax campaign – let the convoy pass! After five days we unloaded one lorry. Empty, it could cross the border. Six people from Britain and Spain drove into Herceg-Bosna to try and get the papers.

Sue, with Bosnian children and floppy boots

In Herceg-Bosna an HVO official met our team.

"Maybe I can help you and you can help me." In other words, how much aid will you give me to let you pass. Most humanitarian organisations automatically gave a third of their cargo to these nationalist gangsters. Our team pretended not to understand, and he shrugged. "Come back tomorrow." The following day they went again. Still no papers. On the way back they were stopped at a checkpoint, ordered out of their lorry at gun-point and bundled into the back of a van.

The rest of the team in Split waited anxiously as night came. No news. Messages were sent to Britain. "Six of the team have gone missing near Mostar" – a notorious killing ground. In Britain, MPs were contacted and eventually their calls to the UN located the missing people. They had been held in a police cell for nineteen hours. On their release they re-joined the convoy in Croatia.

After more faxes and protests our papers eventually arrived. The convoy passed through Herceg-Bosna without giving away so much as a tin of beans. We would not give a thing to these 'ethnic cleansers'.

18.6.94

Ceasefire Broken

The one month ceasefire in Bosnia, agreed at Geneva on June 8th, was broken last week when Serb Chetnik guns fired on Brcko.

Chetnik leaders had called for a six month ceasefire in order to consolidate their control over 70 per cent of Bosnia. The so-called 'contact group', of US , Russian and European Union foreign ministers, met in Istanbul to draw up a map carving up Bosnia – 51 per cent for the Bosnia/Croatian federation and 49 per cent for the Chetniks. Moscow pressed for the lifting of sanctions on Serbia at the meeting.

Mostar

" As we drove along to the east of Mostar and looked down we could see that almost every house had been shelled. When we went down into east Mostar the impact became greater. The place was in ruins. The people – old men, women and children – carried on as if things were normal. The young men have all been called to serve in the Bosnian army.

East Mostar is a Muslim area – the predominant flags were green with the star and crescent of Islam. There were very few flags with the Bosnian shield. Multi-ethnic Bosnia-Herzegovina seems to have been destroyed in this region.

With the destruction of their homes and mass murder it's not hard to see why the local people have turned to Islam. First they were shelled by Serb nationalists from hills to the east and then by the Croat nationalists from the west side of the town. When you cross the river into west Mostar where the Catholic Croats live the buildings are hardly touched. Occasionally you see a wall that has been hit, but that's about it. Unlike the nationalists, the Muslims of east Mostar had no heavy weapons. Their best 'military vehicles' are old Yugo cars covered with camouflage paint.

In west Mostar, post offices are open, phones are available and cafes serve beer. Life goes on. The journey between the once unified sides of east and west Mostar is not easy. The three bridges across the river, including the famous mediaeval one, have been blown up. 'Normal' traffic has to cross a pontoon bridge built by the Spanish UN battalion (Spanbat). Vehicles then have to make a long detour around the demilitarised zone on a dry, dusty dirt track.

A Spanbat escort took us through the demilitarised zone, which reminds you of the pictures of Hiroshima and Nagasaki. Lamp-posts at crazy angles. Buildings burnt out, with no roofs or windows. Suddenly the destruction stops and you are in west Mostar, near all the government offices.

I tried taking photographs from inside the truck. But, when we were arrested for nineteen hours by Bosnian-Croat (HVO) forces outside Capljina, the film was confiscated. It's not surprising that the HVO does not want the world to see pictures showing the contrast between west and east Mostar. "

MICK COOKE

Mostar's East Bank

Metkovic

"The lorries join the back of a queue that stretches for a kilometre up to the border at Metkovic. In the newly torn-apart Yugoslavia there are borders where a little while ago there was only a line on administration maps. A country road, a village street, a river; before they signified nothing. Now the clutter of portacabins, uniforms, guns, hangers-on, customs, passport controls, queues, gates, barriers, warning notices, angry people – all indicate this is now a border.

Police with dark glasses and guns hang around. Rat-faced officials walk importantly up and down flapping pieces of paper. This border is no better, no worse than the most long established frontiers but it is new and this one is controlled by nationalist forces trying to rapidly install a sense of nation into the little patch of land ruled over by their guns. In the turmoil of social upheaval the scum of the earth have come to power. They are lords of the border portacabin. The huge queue of lorries are waiting on their decisions. These queues are repeated at borders across former Yugoslavia.

Like dating geological strata you can judge the age of the border: wooden huts, six months; portacabins, nine months; portable prefabricated offices, one year. As soon as these barriers to travel emerge so does the possibility of making money. The crudest wooden hut border post has its even cruder wooden bar alongside. All the time at Metkovic there is a hammering of construction: pizzarias, import-export offices, currency exchanges and one day, maybe, even duty free shops. Progress.

A turmoil of human activity, shouting, quarrelling. But nothing crosses the border. For twenty hours our lorries wait. All that happens is that more lorries join the back of the queue. The only vehicles to pass belong to the UN. Huge convoys pass without ceremony. Amongst the UN vehicles are the aid organisations that go under their wing, this charity, that charity, charities for Catholics, charities for Muslims, specialists, experts, helpers, all with their UN Blue Cards which only accredited people carry.

The day passes. Drivers sit in their lorries or by the road-side. Most are Bosnians bound for Tuzla. Another UN convoy passes, this time a group of young British men and women volunteers driving humanitarian aid. They are dressed in white t-shirts and have their UN cards dangling round their necks. As they drive past they probably do not understand why a Bosnian driver is using an imaginary machine gun to blast them sky high.

How could they understand? Haven't they come to help Bosnians? But this is the border of Bosnia and Bosnians cannot enter their own country while the new power – the UN – can come and go at will. What are all these experts, helpers and advisors in their brand new jeeps going to do? Was there a shortage of teachers in Bosnia? Or doctors? Do Bosnians need advice on forestry, agriculture, baby care? The problem for Bosnia is not the lack of skills or expertise. It is the Chetniks' artillery, which the UN protect. The white UN vehicles are divided into two main categories. One group have a nice sticker – a circle with a red line through a gun – indicating 'no weapons aboard'. The others have no sticker. They have guns.

Everyone agrees that the 'no weapons aboard' people do a good job. They provided experts to get the sewage running and trams moving in Sarajevo. They have provided mushroom compost for a mushroom growing project. When communities have been surrounded, bombarded, threatened and terrorised the United Nations High Commission for Refugees (UNHCR) helps evacuate the people, leaving the area 'ethnically' pure in line with the overall UN policy to divide Bosnia. They help graduates re-train, provide doctors when local doctors are too tired or hungry. They help teach mothers to look after their children. And of course all these acts help dispel anger against the other UN vehicles – the ones with guns. The 'no weapons aboard' people are an essential part of a public relations campaign.

Everywhere in Bosnia-Herzegovina ordinary people mutter that UNPROFOR – the armed wing – protect the Chetniks, help carry out 'ethnic cleansing', run the black-market, encourage prostitution etc. Against this unfocussed muttering is the evidence of UN good intentions when they bring in food supplies and help.

Aid helps hide that the UN are here to divide Bosnia, to halt its popular self defence, to clear the ground for the 'New World Order'. To ensure that there is no resistance to cheap labour and the construction of a MacDonalds in the Market Square."

BOB MYERS

Workers Aid and Ayuda Obrera members waiting in the lorry queue at Metkovic

Why Bosnia should concern anti-fascists

If anybody wonders what exactly it is that today's fascists aspire to, then you need look no further than Bosnia.

I recently returned from a Workers Aid convoy to Bosnia. Before I went I had serious doubts about the situation there. If you believe what you see on the telly, they're all just a bunch of dodgy nationalists and religious nutters blowing the shit out of each other whilst the poor old United Nations valiantly tries to 'keep the peace.'

Well, not quite. Bosnia is a multi-ethnic country. Its' people are fighting to remain a multi-ethnic country. They are fighting fascism. Fascism in Bosnia usually takes the form of the Chetniks – the army of the Serb nationalists. They are fighting for a country free of all 'ethnically undesirable' elements, e.g. anybody who isn't a full-blooded Serb.

What 'ethnic cleansing' means in practice is that if, for example, you are from a family of Muslims living in a predominantly Serb area, then your house will be blown up. The male members of your family will probably be brutally tortured and then executed. The females will be gang-raped. It is very likely that all the 'racial undesirables' from your village or town will be herded together and forced into specially made concentration camps where all the torture, rapes and killings can take place in a more orderly fashion. Sound familiar?

Rape is an officially sanctioned tactic of the Chetniks. There are two obvious motives behind this. The first is that if a Serb Chetnik rapes a non-Serb then, presumably, this will cause an anti-Serb response from the victim and her family, friends, neighbours etc, who will not want to live alongside Serbs any longer. The second 'motive' is that if a young Muslim girl is raped then, in strict Islamic eyes, she will no longer be a virgin and is therefore 'unclean' and unfit for marriage – henceforth, no Muslim babies. Unfortunately in some areas of Bosnia where Islamic groups such as Mojahedin

International fascist solidarity: the Russian Zhirinovsky with former Milosevic coalition partner, Seselj

have gained influence, this tactic is having the hoped-for effect.

In Tuzla the people still believe fervently in keeping Bosnia multi-ethnic, in having Serb, Croat and Muslim living side by side as they have done for generations. I believe it is our duty as anti-fascists to assist the people of multi-ethnic Bosnia in any way necessary. After all, the fascists of Europe and America have already picked their sides. Whilst I was in Tuzla, I saw a news report that showed dead Russians who had been fighting for the Chetniks. Many Russian and Eastern European Nazi groups send supporters over to fight for the Chetniks.

The other side to this is the Bosnian people and their army. When you speak to Bosnian soldiers they tell you how much they hate fascism and that is what they are fighting. They are overwhelmingly working class, of all ages and ethnic backgrounds (although predominantly Muslim). Most are male but I was surprised at how many women are in the army – a far greater percentage than in the 'civilised' UN forces.

Most had given up their jobs in the mines, factories and fields in order to go to the front. They are pitifully under-equipped. They have to share guns. Many don't have boots, just trainers and sandals! They don't have much transport so they walk and hitch-hike to the front line.

The resilience of the people is tremendous. The Chetniks' front line is a few miles out of town and every day they shell the city. A number of people were killed and injured by the shelling whilst I was there. Most men are in the army fighting at the front. Two days fighting, then two days home leave in Tuzla. Those who still have jobs have not been paid in years.

Many people spend their days chopping wood with their neighbours, preparing for the harsh winter – or working on allotments. Despite all this hardship, the people are full of generosity and good humour. They are committed to keeping Tuzla at the heart of multi-ethnic Bosnia – to smashing fascism. Most people have lost family and friends. Everywhere are fresh graves with pictures of young men and women on them – hundreds of small white crosses. Each cross marks the spot of somebody who died in this war against racism and fascism.

JAMES TAIT (Originally published in Anti-Fascist Action)

In Tuzla, members of the August convoy team met the Tuzla District Trade Union Committee. This included the Presidents of various unions – salt miners, road builders, chemical workers, local government, teachers, health workers. The committee contained four Muslims, three Serbs and two Croats – all Bosnians. They spoke of the destruction of the unions, of poor communication between their committee and the committee in Sarajevo and the need for international solidarity against ethnic cleansing and fascism. They reported that none of their members received any food from the UN or aid organisations. They asked us to work with all the unions in Tuzla and not just the miners.

Students on the convoy revisited Tuzla University and meetings there with Tuzla students began to have an effect back in Britain. Student Aid for Bosnia societies were formed at Leeds, Leicester, Brighton, Cambridge and Lancaster universities. Bosnian campaigners such as Professor Adrian Hastings, Lee Bryant and Melanie MacDonough came to speak, but it was

Through Bosnia-Herzegovina

" The route is breathtaking as only a road can be that goes through territory where no road should sensibly exist. Sometimes we are on country roads then on to newly made dirt tracks through forests or over a mountain. We edge round a gorge with a dark, cold river rushing below. The track heads towards the valley end, with towering rocky hills out of which there appears to be no exit. At the last minute a tunnel appears in front of us – part man-made, and partly a natural underground river system with the roof recently cut higher. The big French lorry got blocked here in March.

The villages, often no more than a cluster of old wooden buildings, look as they have probably looked for centuries. The towns are different. Many show signs of heavy fighting. The streets are full of people, many in uniform, men and women. Everyone appears to be on the move. There is no public transport because of fuel shortages so many people are trying to hitch lifts: soldiers going to and from the front, people going to see relatives. Children walk in groups to school, all neatly dressed with their school bags on their backs. Everyone waves.

Horse drawn carts bring timber out from the forests. In town people cart things around in wheel-barrows. Everywhere is the smell and sound of wood cutting with axes or chain saws. Not just in the rural areas, even outside the tower blocks in town.

Last winter people were unprepared. They couldn't believe that the world would let them starve and freeze to death. When the heating systems to their flats failed people froze. Food in freezers rotted when the electricity went off. This winter they are better prepared, wood is cut, food is bottled. They know no-one from outside is going to help.

Each town has road blocks around it. But for the first time on our journey the 'officials' are not bloody minded bureaucrats. These are mainly young people defending their communities. A quick check of our

papers and we are through.

The biggest driving hazard is UN convoys. They drive at speed and slow down for no-one. At one bend several huge UN tankers pass us at speed going in the opposite direction and the rear of the final tanker spins out and smashes the side of our door. Glass showers in over our heads.

We stop at the next UN base to demand payment for the damage. Waiting for the military police, we chat to some young tank drivers. They tell us they are instructed to drive like crazy to avoid becoming targets. They cannot believe we are driving these roads without military protection. This seems strange to us. After ten days travelling along motorways in our clapped out lorries, always expecting police to pull us in or to be blocked by customs or border police, we have only felt safe since entering Bosnian controlled territories. The UN obviously don't feel the same way.

A military policeman comes out and asks us to fill in forms. He turns to Faruk and in childspeak says, "You can fill this form in Croatian." Faruk looks at him and replies in perfect English, "This is Bosnia and the language is Bosnian." "

BOB MYERS

22.10.94

Serb forces threaten Tuzla route

Serb nationalist forces went on the offensive in three areas of Bosnia last week, threatening the aid route to the northern town of Tuzla, and leading the United Nations to halt relief supplies to the capital, Sarajevo.

Six people were reported killed at Bihac, in the north-west, by shells fired from Serb-held territory in Croatia. A relief convoy came under fire near the beleaguered town of Gorazde, killing a driver.

never possible to get the supposedly anti-fascist or socialist student societies to take an interest. The worst of them, the Revolutionary Communist Party (*Living Marxism*), put out material denying the genocide. The Socialist Workers Party called us 'non-political humanitarians', contrasting our 'well-meaning' convoys with their proposed 'working class solution', which consisted of doing nothing. However, a number of students, including groups of Spanish, Jewish and British Asian students were attracted by the idea of solidarity convoys and started to collect money around the pubs and colleges to send educational supplies to Tuzla.

5th
Convoy Factfile

DATE:
August 1994

LORRIES:
4 from UK
2 from Spain

WEIGHT: 24 tons

RECIPIENT:
Tuzla Miners' Union

PEOPLE: 18

Kava? Dobra! Convoy veteran Andy McFarlane enjoys Bosnian hospitality in the offices of the Tuzla Trade Union Committee

From *Leeds Student*

Bosnia for most people evokes the image of a distant, ongoing war – another of the world's disasters about which the ordinary person can do little. Workers Aid has proved this is not the case. It is an independent aid agency, comprising small committees throughout the country. Those working for the group are volunteers, many without the relevant qualifications or previous experience required by larger groups such as the Red Cross or the UN.

Students Paddy McCloy and Lisa Mead, who will be visiting Leeds next week, went on the convoy and had the opportunity to meet students from Tuzla, and to find out how the war had affected them.

"There used to be three Halls of Residence, but refugees have taken over two, so all the students are crammed into one. They live three to a single room, and can hardly move. Student poverty is rife. There is no detergent and the buildings are infested with cockroaches. Students lack knowledge of recent developments in their subjects because they have no recent books."

"Anyone can help. It doesn't matter if you feel you don't have anything to offer. Everyone does, and just being there makes a difference. Ordinary people can have an impact on the Bosnian war in many ways."

TAMSIN LEWIS

In October 1994, a British/Spanish convoy took aid to the miners and to the Tuzla District Trade Union Committee. Meetings were held with union representatives in different factories – all silent and empty. Unlike much of Bosnia, the industrial areas of Tuzla remained relatively undamaged. In other places they were targeted by Chetnik bombing early in the war.

Before the war the Yugoslav People's Army (JNA) had barracks in all the republics and during the invasion of Croatia large reserves of troops were stationed in Bosnia. They remained there, supposedly to protect Bosnia but by this time the JNA consisted largely of Serbs and Montenegrins. Other nationalities left as it fell under the control of rabid Serb nationalists and outright fascists.

Milankovic

" The southern route is best explained by saying that to go from London to Manchester you go by back roads to Lands End, along the Welsh coast and finally over Snowdonia by forestry tracks. Milankovic is Snowdon. A zig-zag road has been cut through the forest to get over this mountain. Some lorries cannot make it. They don't have the power or clutches burn out.

We arrive at the bottom of the climb. Faruk in the little Leyland Roadrunner goes first followed by the old Bedford. Two hundred metres up the dusty earth track it grinds to a halt. Not surprising as it is two tonnes over-loaded.

We discuss what to do. The track on this part of the mountain is a one way system – one track going up, one coming down. They meet further up. We reckon from previous trips that the 'down' track is not so steep as the 'up'. It starts about half a mile away. We drive the lorries round. Before we try again we stop by the side of a small group of old wooden farmhouses to off-load some of the Bedford's cargo into another lorry.

We begin to move the loads over. Straightaway a woman, in rural peasant clothing, comes over and watches the sugar and flour being transferred. Within minutes there are

more women watching. We carry on working. The crowd grows. They start to make begging signs.

We finish moving the load as quickly as possible and lock the backs of the lorries. I tell the others I will walk up the track to let Faruk know what is happening. I find him and tell him what has happened. We leave his lorry and walk back down the track to see if the Bedford can now make it.

Faruk is telling me that on the previous convoy the lorries had problems here. When they finally got to the top they found the canvas sides on a lorry had been cut and computers stolen.

We round a bend and see the lorries surrounded by a huge crowd. Women are walking away carrying armfuls of sugar and flour. Faruk starts running and yelling, "Thieves, Bandits, Bastards!"

At the back of the lorry some of the guys look flustered. They say they couldn't resist the appeals of the women and gave them a few bags each.

Faruk is still shouting "Give it back you robbers."

Then some local men arrive and turn on him. "Call us robbers, we'll smash your head in."

Two of them move to attack Faruk. I shout at Faruk to get in the lorry. After a few seconds he angrily climbs up into a cab. One man picks up a rock and is about to hurl it through the windscreen at Faruk. I grab both his arms as maybe only an outsider could have done at that moment. Some women come up and also hold his arms.

The other man turns, "I'm getting my gun." I grab his arm and say something in English about fighting the Chetniks and not each other, which they could not have understood. But the anger of the moment has passed. We all jump in the lorries and, to get out of the village as quickly as possible, drive back to the 'up' track.

Once more the Bedford sticks. We talk of unloading more cargo. Here there are no houses, no people. Then along the track comes a tractor, driven by one of the men who wanted to kill Faruk. He offers to try towing us up. But he gets us no further. The tractor wheels just turn up dust, stones and the smell of burning rubber.

Finally salvation. Another man from the village arrives with an empty haulage truck. He tows the Bedford to the top for 50DM – more than most people have earned in a year in Tuzla. His mate asks for some bags of sugar and we give them to him.

Faruk berates people for giving aid away in the first place. He tells them the peasants made money during the siege of Tuzla, selling food at high prices.

So many cultures clash. The urban Bosnian, bringing a convoy for the defence of multi-cultural Bosnia. The peasant farmers, trying to survive a war in whatever way they can. The British drivers for whom war and its effects on people are still strange. "

BOB MYERS

In 1992, with Serb nationalist paramilitaries erecting barricades across roads in Sarajevo and elsewhere, 50,000 Bosnians, including bus-loads of Tuzla miners, gathered in the capital to demonstrate their opposition to all the nationalist parties and their squabbling politicians. The demonstrators were shot at from the Holiday Inn by Chetnik snipers. Tuzla miners managed to seize the snipers and handed them over to the police, who soon set them free. The Chetniks' war had started.

Ignoring everything the JNA had done in Croatia, Bosnian President Izetbegovic called on the JNA Generals to keep order and stop the growing violence of the Serb extremists in Bosnia.

Many people in Tuzla, including the municipal authorities under their anti-nationalist Mayor, Selim Beslagic, were not so blind to what was coming. When a column of JNA troops tried to leave Tuzla with their artillery and weapons they were ambushed by Tuzla workers.

The ambush not only gave the Tuzla people weapons, but also the time to organise their defence lines before the Chetniks could counter-attack. Miners' battalions were formed to protect their multi-ethnic communities.

In other towns people were not as organised. In Mostar a JNA column also tried to leave with their weapons. Women sat in the road and blocked its exit. Bosnian politicians came and pleaded with them to let the soldiers depart for Serbia. Eventually the women let them pass. The artillery and heavy guns went no further than local mountains, from where they began to shell the Muslim side of the town. Throughout most of Bosnia, Serbian nationalists held the hill-tops and with their total control of artillery were able to terrorise towns and villages. This would have been the case in Tuzla if people there had been less organised.

Early in the war, the Chetniks tried to push their way into the Tuzla region. They constructed an armoured train and moved down the railway line towards Gradacac, a strategic town 30km from Tuzla, but people from the area derailed the train and siezed its' colossal arsenal of weapons. They joked that the first people to break the UN's arms embargo against Bosnia were the Chetniks. The long history of workers' organisation in the region had made itself felt. Many other places were not so fortunate, particularly the small villages, where it was everyone for themselves.

Durham Miners' Gala, 1994

6th Convoy Factfile

DATE:
October 1994

LORRIES:
4 from Workers Aid
1 from Ayuda Obrera

WEIGHT: 20 tons

RECIPIENTS:
Tuzla District Trade
Union Committee
Tuzla Miners' Union

PEOPLE: 18

19.10.94

British General helps strangle Sarajevo

Nationalist forces have tightened their stranglehold on Sarajevo and British United Nations commander Lt. General Sir Michael Rose is helping them to do it.

Sarajevo is facing its third winter under siege. Nationalist forces have cut off water, electricity and gas supplies. They have closed all roads into the city. Last week Bosnian forces tried to weaken this stranglehold with a mortar attack on a nationalist held road. General Rose threatened to call in NATO bombers – against the Bosnians!

Elsewhere in Bosnia racist 'ethnic cleansing' has been stepped up, forcing more than 3,000 Muslims from their homes in the Bijeljina district, beating and robbing them before herding them over the front lines. The UN protests, but does nothing.

Instead, the brave British General, knowing the Bosnians have neither planes nor air defence, has threatened to bomb them for defending their own people and capital city!

As in World War II, Tuzla region once again became a 'free territory', a sanctuary for anyone. Its mines, power station, chemical industries and infrastructure survived. However imported raw materials and machinery spares soon ran out. Huge factories, such as Sodaso producing soap powder, cosmetics and chemicals, formerly suppling markets across Yugoslavia and abroad, now ground to a halt. Nothing could leave the region. Factories closed. Workers went to the front lines.

Tuzla (Turkish for 'salt') had been a salt mining centre for centuries. In the salt works the research director explained that production had stopped. Vital machinery was worn out. They had asked the UN and various humanitarian aid organisations to bring replacements. They told the aid organisations that people wanted to live by their own work. A lorry load of food was soon eaten and everyone was back to square one, but if production equipment was brought people could work. Food aid came, including salt, but no machinery. The salt workers concluded that it never would, not until Tuzla capitulated to the ethnic cleansers.

It was after hearing reports like this that we suggested to the Tuzla Union Committee that we should help them send a delegation to Britain to talk directly to trade unions, to see, for example, if they could help get the machinery for the salt works. Maybe an explanation of the war and its consequences would have a greater impact coming directly from a Tuzla union delegation rather than from us.

The committee suggested it would be best to send a joint Bosnian delegation - Serb, Muslim and Croat. We all drank a toast of slivovitz to this new cooperation and returned to Britain to prepare their visit.

A city at war

" Tihomir, with whom I stayed, studied in England, and proudly showed us a souvenir – a National Union of Mineworkers' badge. His dad and elder brother were miners. Now he teaches mining engineering in between serving as an army officer. "It's not a Muslim army," he stresses, "there are lots of Croats and Serbs serving."

Tihomir doesn't like the way the Bosnian government is promoting 'Muslim identity' in schools, and Muslims to important positions. He suspects the government in Sarajevo doesn't care about Tuzla, "because we never voted for [President] Izetbegovic's party." But he is proud of the young men in his unit. "They all take care of each other, from whatever background they come." "

CHARLIE POTTINS

Preparing for winter

Collecting: picking up aid, Leicester

Workers' Aid for Bosnia.
27th September

The following vehicles are carrying humanitarian aid to Tuzla, BiH.

1 Ford Cargo E548 WGP   total wt 1700kg.   cargo 8000kg
Vosac - E Cansdale   016049796

2 Leyland Daf J412 KJR   total wt 1700kg.   cargo 8000kg
Vosac- J Ward   L907815 F

3 Ford Iveco L196 XDD   total wt 12000kg   cargo 5500kg

Repackaing: sorting aid en-route

All passports are UK.

```
1     Ford Transit    N132 GAR
Driver     Keziah-Jehnne Featherstone     005403511
Educational Aid
24 packets A3 white cartridge paper
11 boxes A4 paper,
15 boxes A3 colobr
14 boxes A4 colobr
52 packets of 50 F
35 black lever arc
1 box A5 file hold
8 boxes small plas
3 weather charts
3 packets of 10 co
7 boxes maths felt
6 boxes registers
50 packets of 10 b
70 packets of 10 b
22 packets of 12 b
1 packet of 12 pen
12 pentel cartridg
2 packets of 6 pen
12 hybrid roller p
3 packets of 8 pen
3 packets of 8 pen
94 pentel ball pen
12 pentel correcti
24 hybrid pens, go
12 flip chart mark
4 packets of 12 su
35 pots and mouses
50 staplers
5000 packets of 10
7 boxes rental bri
5 boxes landscape
5 boxes watercolou
6 boxes oil pastel
1 box first aid ki
1 box medical band
4 boxes sanitary t

To be donated to:
OS. Breanska Malta
75000 Tuzla
for: Jala School
     Brcansha Malta School

Total value of aid in this donation: 800DM
```

Lifting: the big load-up in Manchester

Mending: Millie on his back as usual

Pushing: Come on McBride, put your back into it!

Sweating: London bus driver Paddy helps re-load in Slovenian customs

Eating: a hungry driver

Steering: keeping an eye on the edge

Shivering: Stuck in Slovenia with frozen air-brakes, -15°C

Cooking: just for a change...... spaghetti and beans

Being escorted: in Bosnia with a Bosnian soldier

Unloading: finally in Tuzla, delivering miners' lamps

Chapter 6

MARCH 1995   Fikret Abdic and Chetniks tighten noose around Bihac.
MARCH 1995   35 killed in Tuzla shelling.
MAY 25th 1995   Shelling atrocity Tuzla. 76 dead.

A trade union delegation from Bosnia

The Tuzla Trade Union Committee wrote a letter to trade unions in Britain asking them to help a multi-ethnic delegation visit Britain. We forwarded this letter to the TUC International Department and a number of individual unions.

While we waited to see what response Tuzla would get to their letter a delegation from the Workers Aid committees in Britain, France and Spain attended an international conference in Tuzla organised by the Tuzla Civic Forum. All the international visitors were deeply committed to Tuzla's defence of multi-culturalism but their only perspective for defeating the 'ethnic cleansers' was by appealing to the UN and the high and mighty in general to come to Bosnia's assistance. Throughout the war these people would condemn the 'inaction' of the UN and catalogue its complicity with the ethnic cleansers, then end up with no other way forward than appeals for a change in UN policy. Workers Aid submitted a resolution making clear that the UN were not passive bystanders, that they were behind the division of Bosnia and that the only force that could stop this division was the workers' movement. The problem was that few people at the conference could see a 'workers' movement'. What had it done to show that it could be a force capable of stopping the killing? The UN, on the other hand, clearly did have the physical means to intervene. So these well intentioned people continued their appeals. In Tuzla, however, the value of these appeals to the UN was met with growing scepticism.

A Bosnian mechanic comes to the rescue

Is Europe possible without multi-culture?

Many people travelled to participate in the Tuzla Civic Forum conference, but journalist Mirza Mukic was disappointed that instead of explaining how they were going to defend multi-cultural society, they came to preach.

For decades the people of this town have taken their multi-cultural society for granted. In Tuzla it is called 'the neighbourhood'. There are plenty of examples of multi-culture in Tuzla that nobody mentioned at the seminar. These would have been of great benefit to the people attending from Britain, Germany, Italy and France. If an elderly Tuzlan from Konjicka Street (also known by the ancient name of Atik Mahala) had spoken, then some things would have become clearer to the intellectuals, philosophers and journalists.

What could an elderly Tuzlan tell the European elite about multi-cultural society? Konjicka Street runs from the Skver towards Tusanj. With your first steps you will see the yellow, single-storey house of the Dusek family. Before World War II Karlo Dusek, a pastry-cook from Bohemia, came to Tuzla looking for a better life. He managed to live very well selling cukreninas in his shop at Korzo. Today his son, Cestimir Mirko Dusek, is a highly accomplished musician and conductor. The second house on the same side of the street – now the *Kucica* restaurant –

Tuzla Serb Orthodox church, repaired after shelling by Serb nationalists, looks down on young people of all backgrounds enjoying music at the Umjetnost Slobode festival, August 1996

belonged to Mrs Vrabecka who was born in Vienna. She lived very quietly. Opposite the *Kucica* restaurant once lived the Tuco family, who were Croats. Over the years, the family left for other parts of the world, never to return. The Tucos shared their yard with two Muslim families. In a neighbouring house lived Nua Ceta, the well-known Tuzla goldsmith, an Albanian Catholic. The life of this family was influenced by their traditions and language. They kept themselves to themselves and did not disturb anybody. The house at the beginning

of the lane on one side is today occupied by the scouts and mountaineers organisation. This was the house of the Poletika family, who were of Russian origin; in another part of the building lived Haim Pinto, a painter and a Jew who fled to the US to escape fascism. In another lane there lived the Hudinski family, who were Poles. In time they married into other families. At the entrance to the same lane there is the house of the Sacir Salihovic family, Albanians who have retained their family name. This family includes very good pastry-cooks such as Husnija and Rasid. The house in which Rasid made sweetmeats is still there near the hill of Kicelj; but Husnija's house was demolished 'by order of the people' because of 'subsidence'.

This order was used by the Yugoslav federal authorities to destroy things that remind the Tuzlans of their traditions or family homes. In another lane nearby lived the Hajsler family, who were probably of German origin, and in the house opposite there lived the Perkovics and Krekovics, who were Croats.

Also here were families of Muslims, Serbs and Gypsies. In another house, now gone, lived people who spoke a strange tongue; they were dark-skinned, cheerful and friendly. It was said they were Tzintzars, but this was just a rumour, since in this street it was considered impolite to check. A little bit further towards Tusanj there is the villa *Maria* where the Italian, Vidjis family lived. They have left and today the house is in disrepair and uninhabitable. And so the examples go on; in 300 or 400 metres there was Europe in all its richness, with different languages and cultures, flourishing, supplementing and enriching each other. Atik Mahala gave to the world people of international repute as painters, musicians, sportspeople, and writers. But there also lived there idlers, ruffians, drunkards, and thieves. All this should have been said to the elite who came from around Europe to the seminar.

Reprinted from the Tuzla newspaper, **FRONT SLOBODE**

Money or aid?

" We brought many trucks to Tuzla. Language was not a barrier to understanding or friendship, but the objective and message of convoys was sometimes misunderstood in Tuzla itself. Often I heard officials in Tuzla saying that it would be better and cheaper to bring money. By the cold logic of numbers, they were right. But they did not have any idea of the nature of our campaign and how the aid was collected. They neglected the importance of bringing people who could return to Britain as convinced campaigners for a multi-ethnic Bosnia. They had little idea of building a movement. Some bureaucratic union officials in Tuzla were against sending representatives to other countries and they undermined the idea of sending a representative to work in London. Nevertheless, many convoys followed, big and small, and some people in Tuzla started to understand what we were trying to do.

To me a curiosity with convoys was people and trucks. Many people on the convoys had never been employed although they were over thirty. Some of them did not have a licence to drive a truck either. But they had a brave heart to travel into a war zone to convey solidarity from ordinary British people. The trucks we used were all old, except one. Tyres, engine problems and clearance from the ground were the most common problems. On one convoy we got two Volvo trucks from Sweden full of hospital aid. They hadn't done a lot of miles, but they had been built in the 1950s. All the rubber parts in the engines disintegrated – hoses, gaskets. We travelled at a snail's speed. One truck was towing another. The mechanic took parts from one and fixed them on the other. "

FARUK IBRAHIMOVIC

During the conference there was a noisy clash between supporters of the Muslim political party, the SDA, which controlled the government in Sarajevo, and the people from the Tuzla Civic Forum. The SDA supporters, mostly students from Tuzla university, argued that the genocide against Muslims made it necessary for them to have their own state to defend themselves. This was rejected by the majority of the Bosnians present, including local army commanders. They refused to accept this ghetto-like future, which was for them a mirror image of the Chetniks' 'ethnically cleansed' state.

By the beginning of December the Tuzla TU Committee had received no replies to their appeal to British trade unions. We informed the committee that Workers Aid would organise their visit in February 1995.

Kreka miners' van adapted for military use

7th
Convoy Factfile

DATE:
November 1994

LORRIES:
3 with aid from Lille Sarajevo Committee

WEIGHT: 10 tons

RECIPIENTS:
Tuzla University,
Tuzla Hospital

PEOPLE: 10

North East Workers Aid lorry sponsored by the Fire Brigades Union

This was not easy. The travel costs would be about £1,500. Our members were fund raising round the clock, but always for the next convoy. Without the convoys there would be no fund raising – they were what motivated all our supporters – but each convoy tended to take us further into debt. We were constantly jug-. gling payments to irate lorry salesmen, accident claimants, mechanics etc. For us to fund an activity outside of the convoys would be difficult.

Two further convoys were sent over before the delegation came. The first took supplies collected in Cumbria and by our friends in the Sarajevo Committee in Lille, France. The second, in December 1994, was a joint convoy with Student Aid for Bosnia, Ayuda Obrera and the rave sound system, *Desert Storm* .

When other aid organisations later heard of the *Desert Storm* rave, they criticised us for wasting money taking a lorry full of sound gear over the snow covered mountains. Didn't we know people were starving? But as one person in Tuzla said, "We have got used to doing without bananas but we can never get used to the lack of culture." Even when Tuzla market was almost bare the stall selling bootleg music tapes was doing business, and much of the music was from Serbia, a testimony to Tuzla's opposition to all forms of nationalist narrow-mindedness.

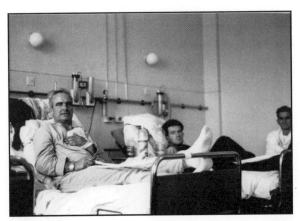

Tuzla hospital

Humanity is not enough

" Guns and bombs are not the only weapons being used in the attempt to destroy the multi-cultural community in Bosnia. In a starving, desperate country the distribution or non-distribution of aid is an equally powerful tool. In the Tuzla region, three large agencies pursue policies which serve to increase the divisions which are fuelling the war.

The United Nations is the grandest of the group. Only refugees, via the UN High Commission for Refugees and all the big aid agencies, receive food from the supposed protectors. Those not fortunate enough to have already suffered military defeat and 'ethnic cleansing' get nothing. So the logic of starvation dictates that people are better off 'cleansing' themselves and heading for the nearest refugee camp. People are penalized for actually defending their homes.

Two religious organizations, *Caritas* and *Merhamet*, pursue similar ends though more covertly. In theory both work closely with the local government in Tuzla. Again, in theory this means equitable distribution to all citizens regardless of creed using all available collection points and vehicles. This amicable pooling of resources sounded excellent.

After asking around a rather less rosy picture of the activities of both *Merhamet* and their Catholic equivalent *Caritas* emerged. These agencies give preferentially to Muslims and Catholics respectively. For example, a Croatian family living on the outskirts of Tuzla told me that their house had never been blessed by a priest. They were not on the *Caritas* register and they were rejected when they went to 'their' church for aid.

Having witnessed the desperate situation it is not difficult to imagine a long queue for the priest's services. *Merhamet* are not to be outdone and Tuzla's first Islamic school has been opened.

But their use of aid as a weapon is dwarfed by the Western powers. Michael Portillo, British Minister of Defence, was asked if he thought the Bosnian Government would abide by a certain agreement that he had forced on them. He was sure they would, as they knew that the whole of Sarajevo depended on Western governments for food to stay alive. "

TOM BATTERSBY

Tuzla schoolchildren, with convoy artist Ed Cansdale

Members of north-east Workers Aid are paid a visit by a Bosnian trade union delegation, whilst collecting outside a supermarket

Jackie Vance of the first convoy team marching with Timex workers before setting off from Dundee, July, 1993

Driving through the silent, empty 'ethnically cleansed' and looted villages

Dust and mountains: the southern route to Tuzla during summer

In Tuzla,
winter,
1994

Serbian road
member see
page 93

Workers Aid
members with a
Britbat soldier in
Herzegovina,
July 1995

Workers Aid delegation marching at the Durham Miners' Gala, summer, 1995

Workers Aid member Sead Masic plays the accordion in front of the Bosnian miners' banner at the 1995 Durham Miners' Gala

RUDNIK SOLI I SONI BUNARI TUZLA   1984

TUZLA by Ed Cansdale

Desert Storm

Sound systems do not have to seek trouble these days. Under attack from a parliament which considers them criminals, they work with the constant risk of arrest and seizure of equipment. Most party crews face all this for no more reward than seeing people dance.

In the beginning the parties had an entrance fee, "but," says founder member Keith, "we were starting to get some really dodgy people hanging around.... so we went back and built

our first RDV (Rapid Deployment Vehicle) which was a camouflage Transit with a 1.5K rig on it. We could just drive in anywhere and start playing."

By 1994 the campaign against the Criminal Justice Bill was politicising ravers everywhere. *Desert Storm* were the only sound system to apply for permission in time to play on the July march, and consequently entertained an audience of some 70,000 in Trafalgar Square on a glorious summer's day. Three months later this celebration was overshadowed in Hyde Park by possibly the only riot in history to have been started by police determination to stop people dancing.

Keith recalls: "Amid all the mayhem we'd broken down, but we were still playing. There were riot cops everywhere and this crazy Glaswegian stuck his head through the van window and said, "I've got to have your phone number." A week later we were home in Glasgow and I got a phone call from the guy asking if we wanted to go to Bosnia in three weeks. I mean, what could we say? It was definitely fated, we just had to go."

The resulting trip took them to Tuzla with a Workers Aid convoy. James describes the events of the evening: "We started playing on the move and we had thousands of people following us through the streets in two foot of snow and minus ten degrees. We played techno records with a chorus that went, "get going to the beat of a drum, BANG!" and all the soldiers fired their AK-47s in the air, "kakakakaka," and it was such a fucking buzz it was incredible. We played the same record about ten times."

Three trips later and the desire to take techno to the front line is as strong as ever. The ethics of taking a party to the most miserable man-made hell in Europe is an on-going source of debate, and not only among themselves.

Danny admits: "It's something that comes up repeatedly when we're collecting money, how can we justify taking a large van all the way to Bosnia with only ourselves, but then I think back to that first New Year in Tuzla and I know we're doing the right thing. Most of our money is raised among young people here in the UK and most of the people who go to the parties there are young. What we do is a cultural gift from the youth of Britain to the youth of Bosnia."

From SQUALL magazine, January 1995

The *Desert Storm* rave was planned for New Year's Eve, but the convoy only arrived in Split on Christmas Eve and the Herceg-Bosna offices had shut for the holidays. The convoy waited anxiously. Three days later they got permission papers and crossed into Bosnia. The route to Tuzla was bad in midsummer but in winter it was a nightmare. Luckily the BiH army had recently won territory around the foot of Mount Milankovic so when the convoy arrived, soldiers told them they could go over the mountain or round it, via a recently captured road. There was, however, sniper fire in one place. The convoy team met. All the people who had driven up Milankovic before voted to chance the sniper fire.

Our convoy crept into Tuzla on December 31st, just in time to unload aid and organise the first ever war-time, New Years' rave.

8th
Convoy Factfile

DATE:
December 1994

LORRIES:
5 from UK, Leicester, London, Brighton, Manchester, Tyneside
3 from Spain
Desert Storm Sound System

WEIGHT: 35 tons

RECIPIENTS:
Tuzla District TU Committee and Tuzla Miners Union

PEOPLE: 28

Keith of *Desert Storm* with Bosnian soldier

Storming to Tuzla

"We arrived in Tuzla about 5am on December 31st, completely worn out. We couldn't get a venue for the rave. The club managers were scared to open for fear that celebrating soldiers might do damage. Then one of our drivers said: "Why don't we take the 17tonner, pull the curtain sides back, stick all the gear on and drive around Tuzla with the music?"

We had to unload the 17tonner, and take the equipment out of *Desert Storm's* truck. The drivers who had the keys to the 17tonner had gone off – so we couldn't start it! He only arrived in the nick of time at 11.45pm, fifteen minutes before the New Year!

We set off around Tuzla. The first place we stopped was the town hall. The police started dancing and turned on the flashing lights on their cars to increase the effect, but their commander asked if we had permission. We shrugged. He went off to check with the Mayor. A few minutes later he returned. "The Mayor orders you to TURN THE VOLUME UP!"

The mayor invited us in for coffee but we were too busy. We drove around for a while and parked in a housing estate of high-rise blocks. Within minutes there were hundreds of people dancing near the truck and many more waving and dancing on their balconies. The people brought us coffee and sljivovica. I've never been in such a friendly atmosphere, although most of the soldiers had AK-47s. I had the most unusual but wicked night."

TONY MYERS

The *Desert Storm* truck, between Sarajevo and Zeneca

Where is my parcel?

"Personal packets were a real nightmare. Bosnian refugees living in Britain wanted to send things to their relatives. Although we gave a weight and size limit for the packets, understandably this was seldom respected. Some packets were lost on the way or unloaded with other goods by mistake. We exercised the utmost care with these packets but mistakes happened. Sometimes it was not possible to deliver them because either the address was incomplete or damaged, or the convoy had to return quickly to Britain. Then my wife

came under attack on the phone. I was reported to the local police for stealing packets several times. Once, a packet went back to Britain on a lorry and I was blamed for that. The sender reported that there were some medicines in it urgently required by his mother-in-law. Later, in Manchester, when the packet had to be re-packed, we discovered a TV set inside. After every convoy we said 'no more personal packets', but how could we refuse to help a refugee who wanted to send something to their husband or children who had nothing?"

FARUK IBRAHIMOVIC

The seventh and eighth convoys had used up all the money we had raised, so the tickets for the Tuzla delegation were bought on credit cards with the hope that the money would be recouped during the visit. A bigger problem than finding the money was setting up meetings for the delegation.

This was a crazy situation. Here was a union delegation coming to Britain. The British trade union movement, with eight million members, had a network of communications that could ensure information about their visit was circulated to all sections of the movement. But we had to work from the outside, as if that whole movement did not exist, which in a sense, as far as the Bosnian defenders of multi-culturalism was concerned, it didn't.

We had to write to as many factories, workplaces, union branches, trades councils etc as possible – a laborious and costly process and one which, with our resources, could get to only a fraction of the movement.

During February we started to get calls from various places that did want to meet the delegation. Bill Speirs, from the Scottish TUC, who had visited Tuzla the previous autumn as a result of a meeting with Faruk Ibrahimovic, offered to organise several meetings in Scotland. The post and telecom union, CWU, circulated the Tuzla letter to all their regions and people from the Midland and North West regions contacted us and started to organise meetings for the delegation. The National Union of Teachers' international department invited the delegation to visit them. The North West TUC proposed a meeting. Calls also came in from across the country from shop stewards' committees and local branches interested in holding discussions with the Bosnians. The Secours Ouvrier committee also asked for two members of the delegation to visit France for one week.

Tuzla had proposed sending a three person delegation but during February they informed us that the Serbian delegate felt it was too dangerous for him to travel out of multi-cultural Tuzla. As we had just realised that the Miners' Union were not actually part of the Tuzla T.U. committee we invited them to nominate the third person.

So the President of the Tuzla committee, Fikreta Sijercic, another committee member, Segat Ivica, and Resad Husagic,

secretary of the Tuzla miners' union, set off from Tuzla on February 20th. This was a tense time for us. First the delegation had to reach Zagreb by coach – a twenty-seven hour journey along the southern route – never a safe journey, especially for Bosnians. Then they had to go to the British Embassy in Zagreb and obtain visas, which might be refused. Finally they had to get to the airport on time. We had bought the cheapest, fixed date tickets.

We went to meet the delegation at Heathrow airport. They were not on the plane. Many times the campaign arrived at a point where the whole forward drive seemed to hang on a thread. We had a growing movement around the convoys, but

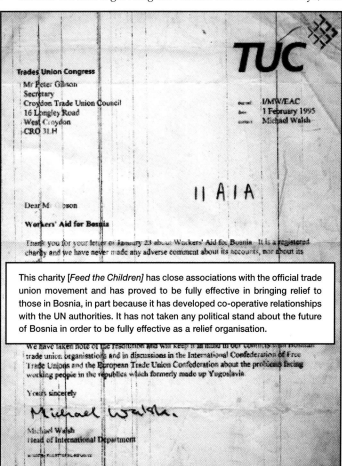

This charity [*Feed the Children*] has close associations with the official trade union movement and has proved to be fully effective in bringing relief to those in Bosnia, in part because it has developed co-operative relationships with the UN authorities. It has not taken any political stand about the future of Bosnia in order to be fully effective as a relief organisation.

TUC International department advises Croydon TUC that aid for Bosnia is better channelled through *Feed the Children* rather than Workers Aid

how much longer could these be sustained with debts growing? The meetings that were lined up for the delegation held out the prospect of a break into the workers' movement. It was hard to think how the fight for solidarity would proceed if these didn't happen. Frantic calls to the Croatian trade unions revealed that the Bosnians had missed the flight by one hour. They would catch a plane the next day – but at an extra cost of £540. At that moment the relief that they would be coming was only slightly greater than the panic about the debts the visit was piling up.

When the delegation finally arrived we talked together about what they were going to propose to people they met. It was agreed that the best way to try and get support was to work for direct union to union contact, rather than asking people to support Workers Aid. The Tuzla Committee would propose a trade union convoy for the summer and ask European unions to support it. Workers Aid would provide logistical help to organise the convoy but it would not be 'our' convoy.

In France they met with various unions, and the post and telecom union, Sud PTT, indicated a strong desire to help. In Britain their visit was also a great success, except that the delegation was soon exhausted. During the day they would meet local trade unionists, go on local radio or meet civic leaders. In the evening there would be public meetings, a few hours' sleep and then on to the next town.

Everywhere the Bosnians stressed their fight for a united Bosnia, for the right of all workers to live and work together free of division. Resad Husagic, from the miners' union, met with miners in different parts of the country, but not with the union president, Arthur Scargill, who had not replied to letters from the Bosnian miners' union. Resad attended a rally in Ollerton, organised by Nottingham NUM to celebrate the tenth anniversary of the British miners' strike. He was invited to speak and his short appeal for solidarity with Tuzla received a standing ovation from miners and their families.

Resad Husagic (in white coat) marching in Ollerton

Council of Tuzla District Trade Unions
February 16th, 1995

Dear Friends,

For three years the people of Bosnia-Herzegovina have faced a barbarous attack aimed at dividing our people and partitioning the country into ethnic ghettos. In Tuzla the workers have stood firm in defence of our multi-cultural way of life. Our Unions make no distinction between Serb, Croat, Muslim or anyone else. We only try to defend our right to work and live together.

But we cannot continue to resist this attack without international solidarity from the working people of Europe. Our mines and factories are virtually at a standstill through lack of spare parts and raw materials. Our people are hungry. We lack everything that is needed for a normal life. If multi-cultural Tuzla is defeated can there be anywhere in Europe that is safe from racists?

The Tuzla District Trade Union Committee and the Tuzla Coal Miners' Union are therefore calling for the workers' organizations of Europe to come to our side. We are organizing a convoy to bring food, clothes, medicines and other essentials to Tuzla from all over Europe in July.

We appeal to your organizations to do everything they can to make this convoy as big as possible. We ask factories to collect food and money from every worker and organize your own truck. If you cannot organize a truck yourself collect food and money and we will organize transport.

We know there are many charities that have brought food to Bosnia for which we are grateful. But in Bosnia the working people face a future of division. We need more than food. We need you all to take sides – the side of an undivided people against those who wish to herd people into 'ethnic concentration camps'.

Come with your supplies to Tuzla. Talk to the people in Tuzla. See for yourselves what is happening. Let the people there see that they are not alone in defending the right of workers to live together in peace.

Sincerely yours,
FIKRETA SIJERCIC, President

The delegation met with Michael Walsh, the head of the International Department of the TUC, who could just as well have been an official of the Foreign Office. He talked of keeping lines of communications open to all sides in the war, without making any distinction between the sides – in other words the same policy of neutrality, the same lie of civil war.

The delegation handed him a letter asking the TUC to support the trade union convoy, particularly by providing resources for one of their members to come to Britain to take charge of the convoy organisation. Michael Walsh took the letter and promised to forward it to the TUC general council. Later the TUC denied any knowledge of the letter and when it was sent again Walsh replied that the Tuzla proposal had already been widely circulated (by Workers Aid, not by the TUC!) and he made no proposal for the TUC to give any assistance.

At the TUC Headquarters, before meeting the International Department

A death in Tuzla

❝ Emina was sixteen in 1945. She joined the Communist Party and was a communist for the rest of her life. With great enthusiasm she joined the people trying to make a new society. Her father was an Imam – a Muslim cleric. Much of his property was expropriated and in place of this private wealth his daughter joined with other Tuzla citizens in creating a new town with health clinics, hospitals, kindergartens, public transport, cultural associations and better housing.

She became a communist, an atheist and a Yugoslav and never went back on this. Now we are sitting by her bed in the modern Tuzla hospital as she lies dying. Tonight she is still just conscious, able to eat from the spoon offered by her son-in-law and to give a smile as I am introduced. She begs me not to tell her daughter – a refugee in Britain – how old she looks. Her tired smile still shows a flicker of life. Her photograph portrays a beautiful woman but now her face is gaunt. She has had a stroke, but it is the war that is killing her.

For a year people starved. Now six months after the end of the total blockade things are still tough. There is cheap food in the market – cheap to us outsiders that is. For most people it is unobtainable since they have no money, unless relatives outside the country send some. Pensioners get no pensions. Savings have been wiped out. But somehow or other people now get enough food not to starve as they did before. A lot of people have recovered their strength, put weight back on. But here and there you see painfully thin, mostly old people. They cannot recover. It's not just the deprivations they cannot get over or the fear of the shells. They cannot get over the destruction of Yugoslavia, the collapse of the society they helped build. Emina's husband sits by her bed and shakes his head sadly. He was in the Yugoslav People's Army. In his house a picture of Tito hangs on the wall. His army pension is no longer paid. Instead he sells cigarettes from a pavement stall. With him at the bedside are his two sons-in-law and one of his daughters – the other one took her children and they became refugees. She was a founder member of Workers Aid in Britain. Now she is unable to be with her dying mother. She has no travel documents.

This night her mother can still make a little joke but the next night she is unconscious and the following day she died.

She was an atheist and a Yugoslav but they still gave her a Muslim burial. Her daughter in England was brought out of the war by a Christian organisation and has made friends with the people who helped her. She goes with them to Church sometimes. She doesn't exactly believe in God but wishes she could, to make everything easier to cope with.

With people's lives under a daily chance threat from the grenades or the bureaucratic rejection of a piece of paper, with fate once more apparently beyond the control of human beings, God is regaining his old territory. ❞

BOB MYERS

At the end of a three week tour, the delegation were given a farewell party in the London offices of the National Union of Journalists, attended by representatives of the Communication Workers Union, the National Union of Teachers, the Inland Revenue Staff union and many rank and file union members in London as well as Bosnian refugees. Bill Speirs, from the Scottish TUC, handed over a donation of £4,000 for the miners.

The previous day Tuzla had been badly shelled in response to an advance by the Bosnian forces around Tuzla. They had surrounded a Chetnik artillery position on Majevica and demanded its surrender. The Chetniks' response to any Bosnian army push was to shell the civilians. Bosnian soldiers knew that a successful action on the front could cause the death of families in the town. For several days mortars hit Tuzla every hour and thirty-five people were killed. This was the reality that the delegation had tried to convey to their audiences in Britain and it appeared that they had started to get their message across. A number of faxes were read out at the farewell meeting from unions deploring the attacks on Tuzla. Among the messages was one from the North West region of the Transport and General Workers Union: "We support the unions and working people of Tuzla in their resistance against 'ethnic cleansing' and condemn the recent attack on Tuzla." The No. 9 region of the Fire Brigades Union wrote, "We will do all in our power to assist the workers of Tuzla in your attempts to secure freedom and peace. Please take this message back to the workers and comrades in struggle – International workers' solidarity on the move."

The next morning we took the delegation to the airport feeling that we had succeeded in bringing the voice of resistance out from its isolation so that it could it be heard by working people elsewhere.

Dot Gibson (right) being made an honorary member of the Tuzla District Trade Union Committee, by Fikreta Sijercic, President

A sack of flour

" On our way to Tuzla, we had passed through Vares, a small mining and industrial town set in a deep river gorge. Rusting machinery and rolling stock reminded me of some depressed town in Britain. On the steep hill out of town, we were stopped briefly at a Bosnian army checkpoint. The soldiers checked our papers, and read our leaflets. A young military policeman in battle fatigues came over to our minibus, clutching a Workers Aid leaflet. "You are from England, Germany, Spain .. .?" We nodded. "International workers' solidarity?!" His eyes lit up. "That's great!" Then he noticed we had a spare seat. Could we help this old lady? She appeared from the roadside, not exactly old, but plainly exhausted, a little woman carrying a big sack of flour up a steep mountainside, trying to reach her family near Tuzla.

That night, we stopped on another mountain, because one of our vehicles couldn't make it. Over towards the hills to the east we could hear big guns, then nearer in the woods, what sounded like rifles. The woman, anxious to see her children, wept silently, accepted a consoling hand from a comrade, and a cigarette. Then she mumbled a few

Convoy driver's Bosnian ID card

prayers, from which liturgy I'd no idea, but I gathered she included us all.

The following morning, we reached a customs checkpoint just outside Tuzla. While we were checked for contraband a crowd of small children swarmed over in the rain to beg sweets. Many had no proper shoes and, we learnt, no parents alive either. Here Edna came into her own. She doesn't speak Bosnian, and the refugee kids don't know Geordie, but by some magic she soon had the entire crowd of kids forming a conga behind her to run round the rainswept customs yard. For a few moments the war was forgotten. "

CHARLIE POTTINS

The step forward represented by the first delegation was achieved at a price. During the visit the delegation raised a large sum of money from union donations but due to communication and translation problems it all went back to Tuzla with them. None was left to cover the final £3,000 cost of the visit as we had all agreed it should be. Workers Aid had to pick up the bill, chicken feed for the unions that had met the Bosnians, but crippling for us.

The following week several local Trade Union Councils contacted us to investigate the possibility of getting trade unionists from Bosnia over to speak at May Day ceremonies. We organised for two other members of the Tuzla Committee, including the President of the Chemical Workers Union, Ramo Ramic, to come over. At the same time the Bosnian Trade Union Federation President, Sulejman Hrle, invited a Workers Aid member to attend the Tuzla May Day ceremonies.

The road mender

" "They want to divide Bosnia. So what am I supposed to do," demanded Adzic, "divorce my wife, split up my family? Where will my children go? My wife is a Serb. I am a Muslim...ha! me a Muslim! I've not been in a mosque since I was a kid."

"But now they put a label on you. And for people trapped in Bosnia it is different. You must go to the church, or go to the mosque, if you want to eat. I could never believe that this would happen in my country."

We'd been collecting for Bosnia, on a cold winter afternoon, and were in a cafe in Leeds. Adzic had heard from his sister, after months of worrying whether she and her children were still alive. But her letter told of burnt homes, friends taken away, 'ethnic cleansing'.

What was I thinking of? Could I continue with routine meetings, gossiping with my old friends on demonstrations, going for a meal, contented I'd done my bit? Maybe somewhere at the back of my mind a picture of that Bosnian woman fleeing with her children resonated with something I'd heard as a kid, about a young girl fleeing a pogrom in Russia, carrying her baby brother, my grandfather.

Earlier this year, fed up with hearing why we could not, or should not, do anything, I told friends I was going to Bosnia. Workers Aid for Bosnia were sending a convoy to Tuzla. Though I'm not a driver, they agreed I could go.

We assembled in Zagreb. Seventeen lorries with food from the miners' union of Slovenia. Thirteen from Germany, driven by Bosnians who'd been working there. Jacques from Normandy, with a huge, long truck loaded with milling grain. Sue from New Zealand who had fetched a lorry load of medical supplies from Sweden; Paddy, from Glasgow, ex-soldier reading politics at Cambridge, putting his lorry-driving experience to use. Lisa doing the same with her studies in nutrition. Young Andy from the Lake District, long-haired and scruffy, who proved ace at repairing lorries, and handling them on iced-up mountain roads.....

At Prozor, as dusk fell, drunken Croat militiamen stagger out of bars. One of them rammed a rifle butt through Jacques' windscreen. At Gorni Vakuf, a British officer told us we must wait till morning, but not step off the road as there were mines. We saw a lot of young people with legs missing. The British government exports such mines, but refused export licenses for mine detectors under the arms embargo to Bosnia.

.....We've a crooked rock-hewn tunnel to pass through, and more climbing. We spend a night on a windswept Mount Milankovic, hearing Serb artillery. Next morning a man with a wheelbarrow and shovel is out mending holes in the road. We share tea and cigarettes with him. He is a Serb, keeping the aid route to Tuzla open, unpaid. "When this war is over we must not forget people like him," says Faruk. Someone gets a mandolin out of a lorry and the old man plays us some great songs. Whenever I hear the BBC refer to Dr. Karadzic and his gangsters as "Bosnian Serbs," I remember this decent man mending the road to Tuzla. "

CHARLIE POTTINS

Reprinted from the bulletin of the Jewish Socialist Group

The people from Bosnia came and spoke at May Day rallies in Lancaster, Leeds, Coventry, Leicester and Norwich and had other meetings with trade unionists during the following week. This time all the money for their visit was raised by the local unions. The Workers Aid representative set off for Tuzla but a bus that was supposed to pick him up in Split never materialised. A message from Workers Aid was sent into Tuzla where they held a large May Day gathering, but fear of shellings kept many people away from what is traditionally a huge day of festivities.

With the Mayor of Kendal, whilst campaigning in Cumbria

On the southern route

9th
Convoy Factfile

DATE:
April 1995

LORRIES:
4 lorries from Ayuda Obrera, including 2 organised by the Spanish firefighters' union

WEIGHT: 13 tons

RECIPIENTS:
Tuzla miners' union

PEOPLE: 13

NUJ member Tim Gopsill with Faruk Ibrahimovic at farewell party for Bosnian trade union delegation

Julius Zupan and Ramo Ramic in Lancaster as guests of Lancaster TUC

Who is UNPROFOR protecting?

" We stopped on the outskirts of Vares to make a cup of tea. Some Bosnian soldiers came to check our papers and stayed to talk. The men were all in their twenties. Spirits were high.

"The Chetniks are finished. We are starting to push them back. The only problem is the U.N. Protection Force. They protect the Chetniks. Yesterday we mounted an attack on a Chetnik stronghold. We would have taken it, but French UNPROFOR intervened and seized fifty of our men. Soon we will have to fight UNPROFOR."

We explain to them about our campaign for workers' solidarity and say that we have to work for the day when such action by the French UNPROFOR is answered with demonstrations in Paris against French government collaboration with the Chetniks. The soldiers agree with this. One young man asks the question, "We are fighting against fas-

Bosnia, but the problem is UNPROFOR."

cism. Why is no one coming to our assistance?"

In Tuzla we hear the same story we heard from the soldiers – "If this was a war between the Chetniks and us we would free the whole of

One soldier tells us: "Now when we prepare to take some ground we block the roads around us first so UNPROFOR cannot intervene." The day we left Tuzla we heard on the news that Bosnian soldiers had attacked French UNPROFOR. "

BOB MYERS

Workers Aid publicity from Ukraine, Spain, France and Hungary

UNPROFOR pontoon next to destroyed bridge at Jablanica (southern route)

On Mount Milankovic

A short while later, Tuzla was to suffer its worst catastrophe of the war. On May 25th, Tito's birthday and Youth Day in the former Yugoslavia, hundreds of young people gathered in a square in the centre of Tuzla. Spirits were high. Tuzla had survived three years of war and siege and on this day, the first warm day of spring, the local basketball team had won a regional tournament. It was years since the young people had money or entertainment but the one thing they could still do was come together, talk and joke. A single shell fired from a Chetnik gun hit the square and killed seventy two young people – from all ethnic backgrounds.

They were buried under the cover of darkness to prevent a further massacre, but instead of burying them in Muslim, Orthodox, Catholic or atheist cemeteries, as was customary, their families and loved ones decided to bury them together in a public park to show the world, that knew only 'ethnic war', that they had all lived together and died together.

MAY 25th

A spring May day, shattered by death,
Gay young voices gasp a last breath,
Evil struck from the hills that day,
In Tuzla town, on the 25th of May.

72 bodies lie bloody and shattered,
Serb, Muslim, Croat – it hardly mattered
To the faceless men, dealers in pain,
Clinical death through explosive rain.

The innocent die in a sunny town square,
Cordite and coffee smells blend in the air,
People stand silent, stare in disbelief,
The rest of the town united in grief.

Numbed by shock, they can only shed tears,
For a lost generation of such tender years.
Hate is the reaper, he gathers the crop,
When hate is abandoned the killing can stop.

Tony Parker
(Wallsend People's Centre)

Two messages from the Mayor of Tuzla, Selim Beslagic, to the United Nations

MAY 25TH

On May 25th, a terrifying crime happened in Tuzla at 8.55pm. Karadzic's fascists hit the centre of town where the youth of Tuzla were gathered and killed over sixty five girls, boys and children. More than a hundred were wounded. The final number of victims is rising from hour to hour.

Do not expect me to address you in diplomatic language in this most painful moment of the history of this town. Tonight parents of Tuzla were collecting the parts of their children's bodies from the streets of Tuzla. Their children had left their homes a few hours earlier with the belief in a better future. You must know that at this moment when the pain is all over Tuzla there are no longer any dilemmas – the UN, who should be the protectors of world peace and basic human values, participated in this crime through its inaction. To tolerate the crimes in Bosnia over the last three years amounts to nothing else but being a spectator of our destruction.

If after this terrible crime you again stay silent, if after this you do not act with force, the only legal force left to protect innocent people from Karadzic and Serbian crimes – then without any doubt you were and you remain on the side of evil, darkness and fascism.

You declared Tuzla and other besieged cities in Bosnia-Herzegovina to be Safe Areas. You have worn out all diplomatic means. Innocent children and people are being killed continuously.

For the sake of God and humanity, use force at long last.

MAY 26TH

I am addressing you again after less than twelve hours of the criminal attack on Tuzla. Today in the early morning at 8.30am new missiles again hit the town centre. The citizens of Tuzla have nothing to say to you. The civilisation of the 20th century has nothing to say either. You stand by in silence as innocent people are killed and you do nothing to stop it. Your behaviour is nothing else but collaboration in this crime against humanity.

On the Yugoslav revolution

During World War I, Austro-Hungarian control of the Balkans collapsed and the Treaty of Versailles established the Kingdom of the Serbs, Croats and Slovenes under the Serb royal family. Its non-Serb people came under Serbian domination, and in 1929 control was further centralised in Belgrade and the country re-named the Kingdom of Yugoslavia.

In World War II the Nazis occupied the region, establishing a puppet regime in Croatia run by the Ustashe. They set about murdering Serbs, Muslims, Jews, Roma and communists with a ferocity that sickened even the Gestapo. Serbia came under German military rule. The Serbian nationalists, the Chetniks, fought the German occupiers but directed most of their fire against Muslims and Croats.

The Partisan forces grew, drawing together opponents of fascism from across the region. Bosnia, with its multi-cultural society and its powerful workers' movement, was the heart of the Partisan resistance movement.

In 1943, the Anti-Fascist Council for the Liberation of Bosnia-Herzegovina met in Mrkonjic Grad, in the free territory liberated by the Partisans. The Council passed the following resolution:

For centuries the people of Bosnia-Herzegovina have lived together, intermingling and interlinked by their common interests. For centuries the foreigner has introduced conflict and hatred. This policy of spreading hatred and intolerance was continued in pre-war Yugoslavia. Today the people of Bosnia-Herzegovina desire their country, which does not belong to Serb, Croat or Muslim but to all, to be a free and brotherly Bosnia-Herzegovina in which full equality of Serb, Croat and Muslim will be ensured. The people of Bosnia-Herzegovina will play an equal part with others in building a people's democratic federal Yugoslavia.

But as the Partisans were driving out the German fascists and their local allies, the future of Yugoslavia was once again being decided far beyond its borders. In 1945, Churchill, Stalin and Roosevelt met at Yalta to discuss the post-war map. They shared a fear of revolutions, such as those which were sweeping Europe in the aftermath of World War I. They met to ensure the war ended without such a challenge to their powers. There was a mutual recognition that they needed each other to do this. Neither the rulers of the capitalist west nor the regime that suppressed the workers in post-capitalist Russia were strong enough by themselves to keep the lid on things when the war ended.

At Yalta they drew lines across the map of the world marking out the regions in which each of them would suppress revolt. One line passed through Yugoslavia. Part of the territory would fall under Soviet control, the rest under western control.

Most of the leaders of the Partisans were members of the Communist Party, but when Stalin passed down the orders concerning this division of Yugoslavia there was uproar. The Partisan army could not accept that the region and its people would once more be divided, nor that in the 'western' territories control would be returned to the local capitalists and landlords who had participated in fascist murder.

The Yalta agreement was enforced in Italy, in Greece and in other countries where the Communist resistance movements had control following the collapse of the Nazis. They obeyed Stalin's orders and handed back power to the capitalist politicians. But in Yugoslavia the memory of ethnic cleansing, of colonial rule and oppression was too strong for the Partisans to swallow the Yalta deal.

In defiance of Stalin's orders the Federal Republic of Yugoslavia was established with the Partisans in control, and from 1945 until Stalin's death in 1956 Yugoslavia kept its independence from east and west. In 1948, the Yugoslav Communist Party was expelled from Stalin's Cominform.

Menaced from east and west, the Partisans and many Yugoslav people worked to reconstruct their country with enthusiasm. For the first time in their lives they felt in control of their own destinies.

Their revolution rolled into one social action two great historical movements:

1. The struggle of people to establish a democratic nation, free from external oppression.

2. The struggle of working people to free themselves from exploitation.

The first process had been completed in countries like Britain, long ago. But the very emergence of Britain and other powerful imperialist nations thwarted national emancipation in the Balkans and elsewhere. As the 20th century progressed, the Balkans remained firmly under foreign domination, but the continent-wide development of capitalism proceeded, creating, even in the oppressed Kingdom of Yugoslavia, a powerful workers' movement.

In the midst of World War II the local oppressed bourgeoisie, while dreaming of national freedom, felt more threatened by the organised workers and peasants than by the imperial masters. The struggle for national self-determination and the creation of a united people was led, not by the Yugoslav bourgeoisie, but by the workers' movement. It was they who finally succeeded in throwing off foreign rule and creating a nation.

But in completing this old process, they also began the second, completely modern task – the freeing of all people from exploitation by capital. The revolution saw the transformation of private property into socially owned property in 1950. Production would be organised collectively by and for the producers.

But while the Yugoslav people achieved national emancipation by themselves, a permanent advance of the social revolution required international co-operation. Socialism could not be created in one country. Capitalism had taken the nation state to its peak of development and the carnage of two world wars indicated that its' limits had been reached. Further development of society called for the pulling down of all national borders, of all the divisions between people. A society based on the collective, social activity of the producers could not be created within the confines of the nation state. It could only be done on a global basis. In 1945, the fate of the Partisan revolution depended on it becoming part of a continental and global movement for change.

Yugoslav independence did start to become a beacon to working people across Europe. From Britain and other countries people went to help in reconstruction (our first convoy had with it a Hungarian communist who as a young man had helped build the Banovici-Brcko railway).

The Yugoslav revolution was a growing threat to the politicians, east and west. In the west, millions of people were demanding 'no return to the 30s', and pushing for social reform. In the east, the Red Army was establishing Soviet rule in the occupied territories, but having great difficulty suppressing the workers' movement. On the Yugoslav-Hungarian border there were frequent clashes between the Red Army and the Partisans.

For the Yugoslavs, the future depended on the growth of internationalism and solidarity. For the rulers, east and west, their continued power depended on regaining control over the Yugoslav people.

Scared that their plan to divide Yugoslavia was in danger of igniting wider protests, the Western politicians agreed to move the line slightly to the west and accept a united Yugoslavia. This move, and Stalin's death in 1956, led to the restoration of relations between the Soviet regime and Tito.

The revolution could not easily be undone and Yugoslav people kept a freedom unthinkable in Hungary, Poland or East Germany. But politically their revolution was absorbed into the Soviet system of control. The national independence was maintained but the momentum for international solidarity to expand the process of socialised property was halted. The Yugoslav people were sold the lie that the consolidation of their socialist future lay in an alliance with 'real, existing socialism' in the east. Over the next few years the suppression of workers' revolts in East Germany (1953) Poland (1956), and Hungary (1956)

showed exactly what 'real, existing socialism' was, and also why Stalin had so feared the untamed Yugoslav revolution.

With the Yugoslav Communist Party safely back in the Soviet fold, Tito, like Stalin, tried to build socialism in one country.

Without a political perspective of extending the Yugoslav revolution beyond its borders, there came in its place, slowly, silently, lurking in dark corners of Yugoslav government offices, the restoration of all the old ideas of nationalism, of ethnic supremacy and eventually, fifty years later, the idea of capitalist production. The Partisan revolution, like all revolutions, had been chaotic and partial. When it became clear they were going to emerge victorious from World War II all kinds of people climbed aboard. Many Serb nationalists joined the Communist Party and the politicians that emerged as leaders of the new Yugoslavia included people who had organised 'ethnic cleansing'. In the Belgrade political elite the dreams of a Greater Serbia were never extinguished. Even in the new Yugoslavia many Muslims continued to suffer discrimination and the Albanians in Kosova never rose above the status of a colonised people.

The revolution opened a road to the future, but a thousands ropes still bound Yugoslavia to the past. As long as the working people were able to make their imprint on events this past declined in influence, but as Russian bureaucrats promoted the growth of a Yugoslav bureaucracy and the weakening of popular influence, the nationalists and reactionaries felt more able to flex their muscles.

In the 1980s, following the collapse of the Soviet regime, western capital sought to regain its lost territory of Yugoslavia. To do this it had to undo the unity that survived from the Partisans.

Capital pumped in the oxygen which the nationalists needed to breathe. Meetings took place in boardrooms and government offices in which the west made plans with the politicians of Yugoslavia, encouraging their various enterprises, encouraging their nationalist aspirations.

Throughout the war the UN and the superpowers backed the 'ethnic cleansers', not for their cause of Greater Serbia, or Greater Croatia, but as a battering ram against the legacy of the partisans – above all, the united workers' communities of Tuzla and other Bosnian towns.

In the midst of the carnage of World War II the partisan revolution took a first step towards a new stage of human development – of co-operation, freedom from exploitation and unity of people. For fifty years this first step remained frozen, waiting for the next step. As the 'ethnic cleansers', backed by western capital, seek to undo even this first step, the fate of this new society still depends, exactly as it did in 1945, on building a movement of internationalism and solidarity.

CAMPAIGN LIFE

Dot Gibson at the TUC Conference, 1993

The first Workers Aid demonstration, June 1993, where fifteen people marched

At the Féte de l'Humanité, Paris, August, 1993

After a supermarket collection, Newcastle, 1994

North-East group supermarket collection

On the march, spring, 1994

Outside a well known London club

Fundraising concert at the Royal College of Music, 1994

Young Bosnians marching in London, spring, 1995

On the streets, July 1993

Bosnian Solidarity Campaign demonstration, summer 1996

At the Timex picket line, August 7th, 1993

The first convoy, in Sheffield, July 1993

Waiting to march off, The Durham Miners' Gala

Chapter 7

The trade union convoy

The site of the Tuzla massacre was well known to Workers Aid members. We often sat in the bars round the small square, drinking coffee or beer with Bosnian friends.

The killings received a mention on British radio, a paragraph in the papers, and that was it. The world's media focused on the 'hostage crisis'. The UN had bombed some Chetnik 'arms stores' around Sarajevo. Even though the strikes missed any significant targets (by design?) the Chetniks retaliated by taking UN soldiers hostage to prevent further air raids. Later, British squaddies told us that when the 'hostages' complained about the food their captors took them to a supermarket to choose whatever they wanted. Their weapons were just left in the room where they were being 'detained'. The UN promised to stop air strikes and the hostages were released. While this charade was played out Tuzla buried its dead youngsters.

Durham
Miners'
Gala

May Day greetings sent to Tuzla by a Workers Aid representative, stuck on the Bosnian border, 1995.

Dear Comrades,

I am sure that you have had enough of those May Day speeches when everyone makes fine noises while the actual problems get worse. In Britain we have no war but our conditions are getting bad. Since the miners' strike of 1984, nearly all miners have lost their jobs and the mines have closed as the free market makes use of cheaper labour in Poland and elsewhere, and in Tuzla if it can. The tragedy is that many of those attacking the rights of working people are the same people who a few years ago were making May Day speeches about socialism and internationalism. Milosevic's guns bombard Tuzla in the name of defending 'socialist' Yugoslavia. Reality is being turned inside out. The ideas of generations of working people are trampled in the mud. The army founded by the partisans to fight fascism has been turned into an instrument of terror against the workers. This destruction of ideas of the workers' movement is not confined to Yugoslavia. On this May Day why will none of the workers' organisations of Europe speak out against the aggression aimed at dividing the people of BiH?

The European trade unions and workers' political parties have refused to take sides in this war. They hide behind the so called 'peace' plans of the UN, ignoring the fact that these plans call for the division of BiH – the division of working people.

On this May Day we cannot just make fine speeches. We have to discuss what has happened to the so-called socialism of eastern Europe, otherwise we are left with the conclusion that the only way forward for society is capitalism, which itself is inflicting untold suffering.

At this moment two trade unionists from Tuzla are in Britain speaking at May Day meetings. In February, three Tuzla trade unionists toured France and Britain. Their visit has begun to change the situation. Last week the Scottish TUC voted unanimously to support your union's convoy and urged all their unions to try and organise lorries.

It is too early yet to know how far this action will spread by July – the paralysis will not be overcome that easily – but in July, lorries will be brought to Tuzla by trade union and student representatives from several countries. We must ensure that when they return they spread this spirit of internationalism.

In Britain they will return just before the annual conference of the British TUC. We want to make sure that this conference votes to extend this solidarity work. We have to make the European trade unions speak out against the actions of the western governments who collaborate with the Chetniks.

So when the people come to Tuzla we need to organise meetings and cultural activities. Let people talk to each other about their everyday problems. Help them to know the truth.

On this May Day our hearts are heavy for the tragedy of this barbaric war but our hopes are high for the rebuilding of real international solidarity between working people. As long as the spirit of multi-cultural Bosnia survives we will be working with all our energies to support you.

Support for the trade union convoy began to grow – the two Tuzla delegations had made an impact. It was one thing for Workers Aid members to speak to a union meeting and quite another for people to hear their fellow trade unionists from Bosnia give a first hand account of their problems. The Midlands and North-West regions of the CWU made preparations to put a lorry on the convoy. The Scottish TUC annual conference voted to support the convoy. A conference of the Association of University Teachers voted to send aid to Tuzla university. The National Union of Teachers put out an appeal to their members to collect educational aid. The General, Municipal and Boilermakers Trade Union conference voted to back the convoy after a delegate, a supermarket worker, called for action. The Greater London Association of Trades Councils voted to back it, as did the annual conference of local Trades Union

Councils. The National Union of Journalists published an appeal on behalf of media workers in Tuzla and found a journalist to go with the convoy to produce a report about the visit. Members of student unions at various colleges also started to make preparations.

Local union branches and trades councils also began to collect aid and money. UNISON branches in the North West circulated publicity to workplaces and UNISON branches in Camden and Hertfordshire organised a delegation to go with the convoy. Financial donations came in from workplaces where workers were unable to go, but wanted to show support. The Fire Brigades Union in the north west offered to cover the travel costs of a Workers Aid lorry. In the north east the firefighters helped the local Workers Aid group buy a new lorry after theirs was burnt out by vandals.

The internationalism of UNISON's International Committee

" My branch asked the Standing Orders Committee to read to our national conference the letter circulated by the Tuzla union delegation during its' visit, seeking support for the trade union convoy.

The Standing Orders Committee agreed to read a shortened form of the message. But then the International Committee intervened! First of all they said that the message was still too long and should simply be a message of greetings to UNISON from Tuzla. They said that the part of the message that calls on workers, "to take sides against those who wish to herd people into concentration camps," could not be read out, because UNISON had to remain neutral in order to have dialogue with all sides.

The chair of UNISON's International Committee, John McFadden, came along to say that Fikreta Sijercic's letter was not signed and could have come from anybody. Louise Richards said they would only read out a message faxed directly from Tuzla. I had to explain that it was not easy to send faxes from a war zone where the electricity is only on for a few

hours each day!

McFadden was overheard telling Richards that he wasn't happy with a message being read out and he didn't know whether Bosnia should be considered to be a state at all!

Both McFadden and Richards made it clear that if the convoy was organised by Workers Aid for Bosnia, UNISON would not support it. The following day they had not been able to reach Tuzla by fax. They agreed that a shorter version of the message could be read out. The message had still not been read to the conference by Thursday morning, and more pressure and lobbying was required before it was. I then discovered that a fax from Tuzla had arrived on Wednesday. I obtained a copy and took it to Louise Richards. She did not want to discuss it, saying: "It's not on headed notepaper, it could have come from anywhere." This was not just a case of fighting through layers of bureaucracy to get something done. Several members of the standing orders committee and UNISON staff were very helpful. The problem is that influential people, like McFadden and Richards, are opposed to the defence of Bosnia against Chetnik attempts to impose ethnic division. "

STUART CARTER, Secretary, Salford Mental Health Branch, UNISON

Just as the convoy plans were beginning to take shape, the fighting in Bosnia suddenly escalated. For a long time there had been little movement of the front lines. The Bosnians had lacked the weapons to do anything other than defend their small patches of territory. But this lack of movement was leading to a collapse of morale amongst the Chetniks. Earlier offensives had gained them fanfares and even more importantly, loot. Villages and towns were ransacked. These advances, though, had been against unprepared civilians. Resistance in Sarajevo, Tuzla, Bihac and elsewhere became better organised and better armed as every month passed. The Chetnik advance stopped. In the spring of 1995 the Bosnian people began to turn the tide. Fighting broke out on several fronts as Bosnians tried to break the sieges around their towns. Large numbers of Bosnian troops moved up towards Sarajevo to try to free the city from its' three years of hell. In response, the UN threatened to attack the Bosnian soldiers.

The BiH army push, as always, resulted in heavy retaliatory artillery fire of civilian areas. In Britain the fighting was reported only as a meaningless escalation of 'ethnic war'. We had to work hard with the various unions that were considering sending delegations to keep them to their plans as the fighting escalated. One union official telephoned the Foreign Office to ask for advice about going and, not surprisingly, was told it was too dangerous. However, rank and file members who had met the Tuzla delegation were determined to go. When CWU officials asked for four volunteer drivers, forty members put their names forward.

Chetnik tanks captured by the BiH army

GREAT MYTHS OF THE WAR

● **UN forces were in Bosnia to protect convoys and innocent civilians. Their humanitarian efforts saved many lives**

The following extracts are from a letter sent to the French government by a French UNPROFOR soldier after his tour of duty in Bosnia in 1994.

For five months I helped with the delivery of humanitarian aid....I do not want to deny what the UN soldiers are doing on the ground.....but you can't ignore that....in November the Serbian forces entered the Bihac area not from the south...but from the Bosanska Bojna area on the north of Bihac. This region was officially demilitarised and under UN control. But after the August 25th, we allowed the Serbs to re-install 155mm cannons and T55 tanks in the area. After about September 15th we ceased to patrol the area. All this was despite the UN promises to the Bosnian government to demilitarise the Bosanska Bojna area. So the Serbs first entered the Bihac region through a French controlled zone. After that my humanitarian aid deliveries do not count for much.

When I see the pictures of men, women and children now trapped in Bihac...I am sure I see the same people I met previously....When they saw us they had their hopes raised....We looked impressive....Our military clothes are ironed and our boots well polished, our weapons shine. The people gain confidence from this.... they found some hope in our presence.

Then when the fighting increased we abandoned all the people we had made promises to. Every time danger threatened, the UN soldiers disappeared into their shelters. Shouldn't we admit that the only security we were concerned about was our own....?

What actually is the policy of the UN when its leaders say, "Of course we have not been able to stop the Serb invasion, but look at all the food we have distributed and all the people we have helped medically?"

Notes for people considering going to Tuzla on the Trade Union convoy

from *FARUK IBRAHIMOVIC*

The events of the last few days in Bosnia raises the question, "Can the convoy go ahead?" We will not take stupid risks but we cannot organise for a convoy in two months on the basis of what is happening now. We have to prepare on the basis that it will be safe to travel.

The recent attack shows that Tuzla is in range of Chetnik guns but after three years of war Tuzla remains largely undamaged by shelling. This is not to pretend the recent events do not matter, but to help you get a better picture.

It can be hard to remember the convoy's purpose when you are on the road and tired, facing some hold up. A Spanish Workers Aid convoy was recently held up for eight days by the HVO. The convoy included a group of Spanish firefighters. When the hold up went on day after day they proposed to deliver the food to refugee camps in Croatia. But these convoys are not simply to feed hungry people. If your aim is simply that, then stay in Britain. There are hungry people there. This is a convoy to strengthen resistance to the division of working people and Tuzla is at the heart of that resistance.

So it is important that everyone keeps in mind the purpose of this convoy.

What you will need. Full passport, no visas needed for UK passports. E111 Health Insurance form for free treatment in EU. Sleeping bag. Clothes – not many. Sun block lotion – it will be very, very hot.

The journey. From Dover to Dunkirque, then a continuous journey through Belgium, Luxembourg, Germany, Austria, Slovenia and Croatia. This is the end of the motorways. In Croatia you will begin to see why we have campaigned for the opening of the northern route which was a five hour drive. Now you have to go round the world. A ten hour drive down the Dalmatian coast road to Split. Here we have to wait for permission papers to cross the border. From Split it is four hours to the Bosnia border. Then you drive along country roads past Mostar, through Central Bosnia and north to Tuzla. From the border to Tuzla is about twelve hours' drive, but it will take longer as curfews necessitate an overnight stop en-route. The final part of the journey is along dirt roads.

The journey time will depend on hold-ups for papers, break-downs etc. With only normal stoppages it should take seven days but it can take much longer. The wait in Split can be the hardest as the lorry park there has no toilets etc. People will sleep in the cabs or in the back of the lorries all the way.

Inside the EU, borders have disappeared but at Slovenian, Croatian and Bosnian borders there will be customs' delays, usually several hours. At the Croat/BiH border we need permission to travel through Herceg-Bosna. The HVO have a truce with the BiH army but remain very hostile to Bosnia and to traffic passing through to Bosnia – especially our convoys. Many humanitarian groups avoid problems by handing over 30 per cent of their cargoes. We will not hand anything over to nationalists.

The convoy will be run as democratically as possible but the aid, the money etc. involved in the convoy has been raised by a large number of people, not just the people on the convoy. It is the convoy team's job to get the lorries to Tuzla.

There is often a lot of frustration when people feel they are not being informed of what is happening, particularly during long hold-ups. The greatest asset is patience. Often the convoy leaders are dealing with bureaucrats and using all their energy to overcome some obstacle and cannot let everyone know what is going on.

It is important that during the journey progress is made quickly. There will be hold-ups due to circumstances beyond our control so it important that no time is lost unnecessarily. If the convoy stops, everyone should stay in their vehicles until the lead personnel let you know what is happening. If everyone gets out of their vehicles at every stop, for what may only be a small problem on one lorry, then every five minute stop turns into an hour. Never leave your vehicle unless you have been told that there is a definite stop. If you go off to buy post-cards you may hold up twenty people for half an hour - a sure way to lose friends. It is vital that people get ready to move at the pre-arranged time. It is no use going to bed agreeing to leave at 7am and then getting up at seven, looking for breakfast etc..

Remember this is a team. Think as a team, work as a team. It is not just you who is tired – everyone is tired. If the convoy stops for the night and there are things to do, cooking, repairs whatever, don't just go off to sleep and leave it to others. Non-drivers have a special responsibility to help during stoppages.

Booze. Don't get drunk on the journey. It doesn't help with driving or human relations. The more people keep away from drink the better.

Entering a war zone. In Croatia you are entering a war zone even though you may see no signs of it. At all times take the advice of the convoy leaders who know the score. Never intervene in arguments with police, army, etc. Wait for a report of what is happening.

Photography. Obey 'No Photography' signs 100 per cent or you will have trouble. Once you enter Bosnia all cameras must be put away. Do not try and sneak a picture of devastated Mostar. Drivers have ended up in jail for taking photos. People will want to take photos. Don't. It will not just be you who will be stopped. It will be the whole convoy. Cameras are fine when you reach Tuzla.

Aid. Everywhere children will ask for sweets. You can take a bag of sweets in the cab and give them out (don't throw them out of the lorries – you may get someone run over) or biros but NEVER give aid away. This is hard. You will meet people who beg for help. If you give away one bag of sugar to an old woman you will be surrounded very quickly by many other people and can find yourself in an ugly situation. Your job is to get these supplies to Tuzla. So you must hold in your feelings of sympathy and just say no.

Driving in Bosnia. You are on small roads. Your main problem is UN convoys. They consider they own the road. They never slow down for fear of attack. Do not stay in the middle of the road and see if a UN lorry will move over – it won't. Never drive close behind any UN vehicles. They can stop very suddenly.

In Tuzla. When you reach Tuzla you have achieved what you set out to do. Once the aid is delivered, enjoy yourself. Remember you are representing the idea of solidarity from the ordinary people of Europe. Enjoy yourself in a way that does not give ammunition to those who oppose this struggle for unity.

Use your time in Tuzla to make friends and find out what is happening. It is not easy in a short stay with language problems. Things you see can be confusing. You have driven food all the way from UK yet Tuzla market is full of food. But many workers have no money and can only look at the market. Other people have made a good living out of the war. There will be meetings and events organised and it is important that people attend these.

Finally, there will be breakdowns, hold-ups, personality clashes and arguments. Your job is to ensure the convoy is completed in a way that inspires thousands of other people. In Bosnia-Herzegovina our future depends upon it.

UNPROFOR exposed

Most political parties and public opinion are currently demanding a reassessment of UNPROFOR's role. Relations worsened when General Janvier, commander in chief of UN forces in ex-Yugoslavia, secretly met General Mladic at Zvornik and promised him he could re-supply his troops from Serbia, through the occupied territories. Nothing was done to secure supplies to the encircled Bosnian towns.

The news that UN representative Akashi had written to Karadzic to re-assure him that the Rapid Reaction Force would have the same mission as UNPROFOR – none at all – was also very badly received. The Japanese diplomat was declared *persona non grata* by the Sarajevo municipal assembly.

At that point UNPROFOR ceased all activity in Bosnia-Herzegovina. The exclusion zones ceased to exist, as did the so-called 'security zones'. The Serb terrorists' planes flew over Bosnia, which is explicitly forbidden by a UN resolution.

The army of Milosevic and Karadzic rakes Sarajevo with the fire of 600 artillery pieces and 30 tanks. Civilian targets are shelled using shells filled with phosphorus. They are banned by international convention as so-called asphyxiating chemical weapons.

In June, several home-made bombs containing enormous quantities of explosives were launched at Sarajevo. Often made from washing-machine drums, these bombs have a huge destructive power and were also used by the HVO forces during their war against Bosnia. The worst damage is done by quarter-tonne and half-tonne flying bombs. The Serb aggressors launch them from a special ramp at their base in Lukavica near Sarajevo.

MILENKO VOCKIC (re-printed from **Sarajevo Fax***)*

BILLY PYE, sacked Lancashire miner and former National Executive member of the National Union of Mineworkers, circulated the following open letter to the NUM, its members and former miners.

Comrades and friends,

The British media's reporting of the Yugoslav war has been at best selective and at worst full of lies. None of us who have been involved in the fight to prevent the destruction of our industry need any convincing of what the media is capable of. We hear 'stories' of a war centred on an inter-ethnic dispute, a war which has the broad support of the Serbian, Croatian, and Muslim people. This has been the justification for a whole string of 'peace plans', some authored by former friend of the Union of Democratic Miners, Dr David Owen, based on carving up Yugoslavia along ethnic lines with the objective (at least the stated one) of keeping the warring factions apart.

The actual facts of the war are too complex to go into here, but it is not true that the war has the support of the mass of the Serbian, Croatian, and Muslim people. In Bosnia-Herzegovina, the Tuzla region is a prime example of a multi-ethnic community doing its utmost to resist the war.

We can perhaps empathise with a community fighting to defend itself, we have our own experiences in this respect, but we can little imagine the tremendous hard-ship and suffering that these people experience every day.

Over the last two years Workers Aid for Bosnia has organised several convoys of aid for the Tuzla region. These convoys have provided the material aid which the Tuzla trade unions have requested, although the aid thus far provided has only scratched the surface.

The convoys have also served another important purpose, namely, the need for people from other countries to see for themselves what life is like in Bosnia-Herzegovina, so that the truth about the situation there can be brought back.

The next convoy to Tuzla will leave Britain in July. The Tuzla region has many industries, but the main one, and the one which is of crucial importance to the people of the region at the present time, is the mining industry. The Tuzla miners are continuing to operate their industry, albeit at much reduced capacity, working without wages. The question remains, however, as to how long the miners of Tuzla and their families, as well as the Tuzla people as a whole, can continue to resist without assistance from outside.

The United Nations stands by while the community is bombarded and starved into submission; the Western 'peace makers' have nothing to offer the people of Tuzla other than ethnic division.

Whilst it would be foolish to suggest that the labour and trade union movement in Britain could somehow intervene in the war itself, it should not be beyond it to respond in a united way to the pleas for help brought to Britain on behalf of the people of Tuzla by the trade unionists who have been here in the recent past.

I will be going to Tuzla in July and I hope that with the circulation of this letter other miners and former miners will join in raising support for the convoy in their own communities.

If enough people within the mining communities respond to this call, and would consider actually accompanying the convoy to Tuzla, a lorry or two specifically from mining communities could form a part of the convoy. With this objective in mind, I would like to hear from anyone or any NUM branch or area willing to help in raising support.

A day in the life

Dateline August 1st, 1995. Secretary of Workers Aid for Bosnia is Bob Myers. It's only days before WAB's eleventh convoy leaves and he's still getting offers of aid, lorries and drivers, although most offers of transport are retracted when the owners are told that no insurance policy will cover them in Bosnia. Transport continues to be the organisation's biggest headache, and it usually has to buy its own.

However, union involvement is making this easier. The Communications Workers' Union has bought a van and has members on the convoy; so does Leicester Trades Union Council, and in the course of the afternoon the Gas Board offers another. It costs about £1,500 to get a vehicle to Tuzla so the funds are almost impossibly stretched. Bob hopes a demonstration in London the next day will help raise money.

Creative chaos and nervous energy spill into every corner of Bob's Manchester house. It has been taken over by sacks and boxes, volunteers and the ceaseless ringing of the telephone and fax. His family have de-camped until the frenzy is over.

It's almost impossible for Bob to sit still. Our interview is punctuated by phone-calls, deliveries, faxes of CVs from volunteers, instructions to eager helpers. His patience seems limitless despite the whirl of activity which seems to get faster all day. There's a lot to be done – picking up a van from auction, collecting £6,000 worth of mining equipment which has been donated by its manufacturers and the Scottish TUC, organising custom's lists, ringing around for more lorries, and, if there's any time left, picking up more aid from around the region.

Bob and his nephew Tony have already been on local television today – filmed loading up parcels donated by shoppers from a supermarket. He says they wanted a fluffy 'mercy

Over £2,000 collected in one day; Cambridge Student Aid members Tom Edwards and Rachael Robertson

mission' angle and were peeved that he kept emphasising the political side of Workers Aid.

British trade unions have been slow to lend their weight to the movement, hardly surprising given the nature of reporting from the former-Yugoslavia and the prevarication of the UN.

In March a delegation of Tuzla trade unionists visited Britain mobilising union support and issuing an unequivocal invitation for support. The result is this convoy, co-ordinated, but not on this occasion initiated, by Workers Aid for Bosnia.

International workers solidarity has a strong tradition in, for example, the Spanish Civil War, and supporting Workers Aid is a way of con-quering the sense of helplessness aroused by chilling news reports. It's not just about money and fund-raising – it's about getting your com-pany or union to donate equipment and other types of support. Alternatively how about giv-ing your time to paint lorries, to picket embassies and the Foreign Office, to box up aid in the organisation's warehouse, to arrange food collections, or simply write letters of sup-port. Just before I left, four boxes of musical instruments and reams of sheet music arrived. The music had been sent from a group called *Raging Grannies*, based on an island off Vancouver. Now that's an international effort.

HARRIET HANMER (from **Red Pepper**)

Trades Union Congress
North West Regional Council

24 July 1995

A MESSAGE TO THE WORKING PEOPLE OF TUZLA

Dear Friends

We send this message with the Workers Aid convey at a time when you are facing great dangers and suffering. Our hearts and thoughts are with you and we most earnestly commend your efforts for peace in your country.

The recent trades union delegation that visited us here in Britain was invaluable in helping us to understand your situation and was critical in ensuring that the convoy came together. I know that there is the possibility of further delegations and we believe that such continued dialogue is of upmost importance if we are to build solidarity between us.

With the convey will be a number of leading trades unionists from this region, including Jerry Brookes from the Communications Workers Union and a member of the Executive Committee of the TUC's North West Regional Council. The NW TUC brings together some 50 individual trades unions who represent close to a million workers in this part of Britain. They will be able to underline this message of solidarity and they will report back to us so that we can learn from you and organise for the future.

Yours in solidarity

ALAN MANNING
Secretary

Truck sponsored by the Communications Workers Union

Transport House, 37 Islington, Liverpool L3 8EQ
telephone: 0151 298 1225 fax: 0151 298 1240

Regional Secretary: *Alan Manning* General Secretary: *John Monks*

24. 7. 95

Beaten, handcuffed and sent to war

Serbian President Milosevic, presented by the British government and media as a peacemaker for Bosnia, has sent tanks, missiles and unwilling conscripts to reinforce the Serb nationalist forces in Bosnia and Croatia.

Interviewed in *TIME* magazine (July 17th), Milosevic says modestly: "I'm just an ordinary man who, by the circumstances of his position, can help by having a policy of peace, one that is honest and objective to all sides."

But a report from Belgrade says, Serbian police have rounded up thousands of Serb refugees from Croatia and Bosnia, and sent them back to be cannon fodder for the nationalists.

"In most cases police used force if met with resistance," says Milos Vasic of the Belgrade magazine *Vreme*. "People were handcuffed, occasionally beaten, and in at least one case a man was shot in both legs whilst trying to escape."

Men have been arrested in night raids on refugee centres and hostels, or just taken off the streets. Serbian police were accompanied by military police from Karadzic's so-called 'Republika Srpska' in Bosnia, or from the 'Republic of Serbian Krajina' in Croatia.

Sources in Pale and the Krajina say new arrivals have been beaten as 'draft dodgers' and 'deserters.'

"There is a concern that conscripts might be used as spear-heading forces in future battles and deliberately wasted," Vasic says.

No-one in the unions openly opposed the convoy or its support for undivided Bosnia, (with the exception of Arthur Scargill, who claimed Bosnians had destroyed 'socialist Yugoslavia'). Noone proposed alternative action. Clearly the aim of the convoy went against the prevailing outlook of the TUC leadership but they were unable to justify opposition to this simple act of solidarity. In practice, they stifled it by preventing all mention of the initiative. For example, at the UNISON conference the International Committee tried to prevent a message from the Tuzla TU committee being read out. The TUC International Department, who had received the Tuzla delegation, did not so much as issue a circular.

This bureaucratic opposition was aided by the prevailing confusions amongst union members. Three years of fascistic aggression in Bosnia had gone by without it even being discussed inside the unions. Union members in Britain were so far behind events, so cut-off from the experiences of their Bosnian comrades, lacking even the understanding that the young convoy teams had acquired, that the response to the Tuzla delegation, however heartfelt, was far from being coupled with the defence of multi-cultural Bosnia. The Tuzla delegations could easily convey the misery of their people, their hunger and hardships. To get across who was fighting who, and why, was more difficult, especially in an imperialist country like Britain that for centuries had never experienced national oppression. Union leaders, unable to oppose the union to union convoy because of the basic sympathies of their members, did all they could to keep it at the level of 'humanitarian aid', rather than solidarity with the cause of unity that the Bosnian trade unionists were fighting for. The Scottish TUC's resolution backed both the convoy and the UN 'peace initiative'. At the CWU conference, where practical rank and file support for the convoy was strongest, a collection raised thousands of pounds for their lorry but a resolution on Bosnia was pushed off the agenda.

Elsewhere, resolutions supporting the convoy, or promises made to the Tuzla delegation, were not translated into action. This was partly because this activity was so different from what the unions were used to organising, but mostly because of the way in which the UN and government policy was transmitted down through the whole movement, blunting all sense of purpose.

Where there wasn't any close local contact between trade unionists and people who had been on previous convoys, the initial reaction provoked by the Tuzla delegation faded away and vanished in the confusion of 'ethnic war', 'neutrality' and 'leave it to the UN'. Where there was such local collaboration with Workers Aid members the impact of the delegation was sustained and practical preparations went ahead – getting lorries, collecting aid, raising money and finding volunteers. Workers Aid members were also busy campaigning throughout the local communities. In Leicester, for example, young Muslims who shared our support for multi-culturalism asked to send their lorry with us.

On the eve of a pre-departure meeting of convoy participants we heard the news of the fall of the 'safe haven' of Srebrenica.

For three years, Srebrenica had been a large concentration camp, in the heart of Chetnik held territory. In 1992 and 1993 thousands of people had been driven into the town from other towns in eastern Bosnia. In April 1993, the defenders of Srebrenica ran out of ammunition and the Chetniks prepared to move in for the kill. The UNPROFOR Commander, General Morillon, went to Srebrenica to see how things stood. As he tried to leave the town women blocked his exit, taking him hostage. He was released after promising the people, "I will never abandon you." The UN, desperate to prevent the total discrediting of its role, pleaded with Milosevic to stop the attack, and eventually a deal was done. The UN disarmed the Bosnians in Srebrenica and promised them UN protection. From 1993 to 1995 people lived with hardly any food, electricity or medicine and in perpetual terror of the ethnic cleansers still surrounding them.

Two years later the, "I will never abandon you," was forgotten. On July 11th, 1995 Chetnik tanks once again advanced on the town. The UN refused to call in air cover for the Dutch battalion 'protecting' the town. Dutch troops surrendered and drove out of the town in their tanks – running over and killing an unknown number of people in their hasty retreat. For the Muslims in Srebrenica there was no such escape. The Chetnik Commander, General Mladic, arrived in the town and told people not to worry. They would be bussed to Muslim areas of Bosnia. Chetniks separated all males between 16 and 65 and marched the women and children out of the town. The men were taken to nearby fields and shot – some 8,000 of them.

THE METHODS OF FASCISM
Mass Execution

There were twelve of us in the small truck. We were driven for about two to three minutes, and when the truck stopped we were ordered to get out by twos. My cousin Haris called for me.... I saw grass underneath the blindfold. Haris took my hand. He said, "They're going to execute us." As soon as he said that, I heard gunfire from the right side. Haris was hit and fell towards me, and I fell with him....

I heard the Chetniks talking. They sounded young....Someone was ordering them to finish us off individually. This process continued all day. I was frightened during the next 'tour' of prisoners, which was to be shot after us....I heard all the bullets whizzing by and thought I would be hit. During the day I also heard trucks continuously driving....I also heard a bulldozer working in the background and became horrified. My worst nightmare was that I would be buried alive....

I kept hearing people gasping, asking for water so they wouldn't die thirsty. Others kept on repeating, "Kill me. Just finish me off." I lay on the ground with no shirt on all day; it was extremely hot, and ants were eating me alive. There were moments when I just wanted to get up and have them shoot me. I woke up, I wasn't sure whether I blacked out or fell asleep, and it was drizzling. It was night and I saw light beams from a bulldozer's headlights. I still heard the same noises as before – trucks driving up, people getting out and gunshots.....Later, I heard a truck pull up and someone saying, "...We won't finish tonight. Leave some guards and we'll take the bodies away tomorrow." The Chetniks started arguing, because no-one wanted to stay and guard the field of corpses. They said, "They're all dead anyway," and they left.

....When I finally decided to get up, I couldn't; my whole body was numb....I saw corpses littering a meadow about 150 metres by 100 metres. Suddenly I heard someone ask, "Are you wounded?"... It was I.T. from Ornica....I tried to make my way over to him without stepping on the dead. It was impossible, so I tried at least not to step on the chests and torsos,...We saw two other wounded men.....We checked and realised there was no way we could help them. They realised this too, and told us to run away as quickly as possible....The last thing I heard them say was, "Run brothers, save yourselves."

N.P. (edited from *Human Rights Watch/Helsinki Vol 7, No 13*)

Lurid Stories

Of course there have been atrocities committed in Bosnia, as in all wars. To date, however, and despite three years of searching, nobody has produced any hard evidence to substantiate the claims of genocide. Instead, lurid stories, based only on hearsay, about ethnic cleansing, death camps and mass rape, suffice to damn the Serbs....before they even reach the dock.

LIVING MARXISM *July/August 1995*

Many women and children fled and began a desperate journey on foot through the mine-strewn forests, trying to reach the safety of Tuzla. On the way they were shot at and gassed.

Scenes of these pitiful human beings pouring into Tuzla hit TV screens around the world. The following morning newspapers carried a picture of a young woman who could take no more and had hung herself from a tree in the midst of thousands of other traumatised women.

A shock went through Europe. Not just the horror of the massacre but the dawning suspicion of an awful truth – the UN had handed Srebrenica over to the 'ethnic cleansers'. For three years the UN and the western governments had managed to persuade people that they were 'doing something' about Bosnia – they were taking food to civilians, they were trying to separate the 'warring factions'. They had argued that the arms embargo was saving life. Now a flash of lightning went through the mood of many people worldwide. The reality of the war had always contradicted the UN's claims but, lacking information, people could not make sense of things. With Srebrenica, the haze began to clear – the UN were not neutral 'peace keepers', they were supporting 'ethnic cleansing'! People began to see that they, themselves, had to do something. Things could not be left to governments.

Our pre-convoy departure meeting went ahead, but it was clear that we could not just proceed with our plans as if Srebrenica hadn't happened. The shock over the genocide was widespread. The Muslim community, refugee groups and others joined in voicing their protests. A group of Jewish academics and intellectuals organised a candle-lit vigil opposite the British parliament and, with the mood of anger growing, it was decided to call a meeting to co-ordinate the protests. Here, four organisations, the Jewish Socialist Group, the Muslim Solidarity Campaign, the Alliance to Defend Bosnia-Herzegovina and Workers Aid, agreed to combine forces as the Bosnia Solidarity Campaign. A national demonstration was called for the following Saturday, July 22nd. The various groups set to work immediately. There was a terrible sense of urgency. General Mladic's troops were moving towards the next 'safe haven,' Zepa. Eastern Bosnia was finally going to be totally 'cleansed'.

Workers Aid decided that £3,000 we had raised to finance our lorries on the convoy, due to leave in one week, should be diverted to pay for advertisements in the national press for the demonstration. We could only hope to recoup the money on the demonstration. It was a risk we had to take. Not to try and mobilise the outrage would leave the convoy looking like a futile gesture.

In France a conference of writers, artists, actors and film directors passed a resolution condemning the UN and many of them started a hunger strike. We received faxes from the USA and Europe with information about demonstrations and protests. In Tuzla, young people protested outside the UN military base and stoned its vehicles.

Extract from a statement by the International Union of Food, Agricultural, Hotel, Restaurant, Catering, Tobacco and Allied Workers Associations (IUF), composed of 312 trade unions in 110 countries.

The outcome of the July 21st London Conference constitutes another chapter in the 'international community's' refusal to respond effectively to the threat against the entire population of Bosnia-Herzegovina.

Governments which proclaim their willingness to organise a 'tactical' defence of Gorazde stand by while inadequately armed Bosnian troops fight on at Zepa after refusing to deliver the male population into the hands of their executioners. Daily attacks continue on Sarajevo and Bihac, Tuzla airport remains closed, and up to 15,000 residents of Srebrenica remain unaccounted for.

The sinister farce being enacted under the auspices of the United Nations must come to a stop.

The war against Bosnia-Herzegovina is not an 'ethnic' war. It is a political war waged by a regime combining the fascist ideology and practice of 'ethnic cleansing' with Stalinist authoritarianism, a war against a state and a society committed to the fundamental values of democracy, pluri-culturalism and tolerance. The failure of western governments to rise to the defence of the people of Bosnia-Herzegovina constitutes a threat to the survival of democracy in all of Europe.

The international labour movement must approach this conflict not in a spirit of deference to governments that have proven unable to act in the defence of the most elementary human rights, but by recalling its own best traditions of resistance to Fascism and to Stalinism in defence of the right of every people to life, free from oppression.

Dear Sir,

Your front-page report today on the expelled population of Srebrenica contains two striking details which, taken together, do much to explain why the response to four years of aggression and genocide in former-Yugoslavia has been so inadequate in this country.

First, what 50-year-old refugee Mujo said: "This is Major's doing. This is a result of his pro-Serb policies, and Major has convinced Clinton." You could hardly get a crisper formulation of the essential truth about why the Srebrenica tragedy happened. The mass deportation is part of a planned, racialist project organised in Belgrade, with which the British government has, from the outset, been complicit. Mujo shows a perfect grasp of 'our' reality, contrasting sharply both with widespread readiness here to accept the official line however implausible, and with the protestations of bafflement that constitute the standard conversational reaction in Britain to events in the Balkans. But why this contrast?

Part at least of the answer is supplied by the second detail from Julian Borger's report, when Sabira Huseinovic begins her account with the words: "The Chetniks came at 7 o'clock in the morning," – and a sub-editor carefully inserts the word 'Serbs' in square brackets, thus totally distorting her account. To the victims, their attackers are not 'Serbs' – a category, after all, to which they may well themselves belong – but Chetniks, or fascists or whatever. Their attackers are not people, but the bearers of a specific political project – an ethnically pure Greater Serbia.

The distinction made by Sabira Huseinovic – standard in Bosnian political and media parlance – indicated both political understanding and democratic aspiration. To call the destroyers of Vukovar, and the genocidal 'ethnic-cleansers' of eastern and northern Bosnia, Chetniks – or to call those who devastated East Mostar, Ustashe – is the very opposite of what TV pundit Michael Ignatieff argues in Time Magazine this week: not a brutalisation of language, but a mature use of it; not a demonisation of Serbs and Croats, but a refusal to demonise them; not a blanket identification of them with their war criminals, but a determination to give the latter a specific and appropriate name.

QUINTIN HOARE (Alliance for the Defence of Bosnia-Herzegovina)

Published in The Guardian, August, 1995

STOP
THE RAPE
OF BOSNIA!
DEMONSTRATE!
SATURDAY, 22nd JULY 1995
1pm The Embankment
(Temple Tube)
0113-2622705

WORKERS AID FOR BOSNIA AND ALLIANCE FOR THE DEFENCE OF BOSNIA-HERZEGOVINA

The Srebrenica demonstration

" We decided to organise a demonstration protesting at the Srebrenica massacre. We wanted to place adverts in *The Guardian* and *The Independent*. This was the only way we could let many people know in a couple of days. But we had the usual problem: money. The first ad cost £4,000. A Professor who was paralysed from a traffic accident phoned us and offered £2,000.

Nobody knew how big the demonstration would be, it was organised so quickly. Everybody was busy. I was doing translations and designing leaflets. In just one night all the underground trains and public places were covered with 'Stop the Rape of Bosnia' stickers. The response was tremendous. People were ringing in from all parts of the country to find out details of the demonstration. It was the first time that I saw my friends Dot and Geoff crying. The Islamic community promised to pay for a large hall opposite Parliament for a meeting after the demonstration. I was invited onto a BBC News programme. The presenter introduced me as a Bosnian Muslim to which I objected, saying I was a Bosnian and that my religion was my own affair. We started receiving messages from abroad of similar demonstrations and protests – the phone was going non-stop. Geoff used to have a short sleep on the office floor, folding a cushion from an old armchair as a pillow.

The demonstration came on a nice, sunny day. The Observer reported that 6,000 people came. The police were taken by surprise and had to call for extra men. At the head of the march was a Scottish piper in front of a huge banner with a photo of the young Srebrenica woman who hung herself. Demonstrators called out many slogans but I remember one in particular: 'Self-defence is no offense – lift the arms embargo!' The demonstrators marched through the Strand, Trafalgar Square, then down Whitehall to the Houses of Parliament. Outside Downing Street we stopped spontaneously and shouted and whistled. The police forced us to move.

Westminster Hall was packed with about 3,000 people. After the meeting we started picketing in front of the Ministry of Defence. "

FARUK IBRAHIMOVIC

With the honourable exception of one or two individual journalists, the media played their usual role. They could not hide the horror of Srebrenica in the way they hid the Tuzla massacre, but by continuing their parroting of 'ethnic war' the coverage of Srebrenica worked to camouflage the complicity of the UN and the British government in the single biggest mass execution since World War ll.

The Bosnia Solidarity Campaign was asked to participate in a TV programme about Bosnia, hosted by Jonathan Dimbleby. He told the participants that the programme would be broadcast uncut that evening. He then repeated all the usual lies about 'atrocities on all sides'. Most of the programme was taken up with 'experts' and was 'even handed' – two of Karadzic's media-friendly liars followed by a hesitant Bosnian refugee. Towards the end a Bosnia Solidarity member managed to speak, arguing for the lifting of the arms embargo and criticising the programme for repeating the lie about ethnic civil-war. The programme was indeed transmitted uncut – with the sole exception of this speaker.

All week we had newspapers and TV stations ringing up for interviews. Bosnia was news. They heard we had a large convoy about to leave and wanted pictures. A BBC journalist interviewed people loading a lorry but when they began to speak about the fight against fascism she cut them off. She didn't want a 'political' interview. She sighed and said that the war was so 'complicated'. "No," they told her, "it's very simple."

The following Saturday six thousand people gathered in London behind a banner saying, 'Stop the Rape of Bosnia'. At a meeting after the demonstration messages were read out condemning the massacre. One was from the Croatian Trade Unions, another was from anti-war protesters in Serbia. When the chairperson announced this message some Muslims in the audience began to boo and jeer. A Tuzla woman took the microphone. Speaking in Bosnian she said that if Serbs were willing to risk their lives by speaking out against their government's aggression they should be cheered not jeered. The two thousand strong audience fell silent and listened to the message from Belgrade.

Before the demonstration the organisers discussed how to strengthen the growing mood of people to take action. At the demonstration it was announced that the union convoy would be leaving for Bosnia in two days with its message of solidarity and that a round-the-clock protest would be starting outside the Foreign Office immediately.

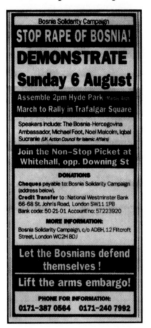

Bosnia Solidarity Campaign
STOP RAPE OF BOSNIA!
DEMONSTRATE
Sunday 6 August
Assemble 2pm Hyde Park March 4th
March to Rally in Trafalgar Square

Speakers include: The Bosnia-Hercegovina Ambassador, Michael Foot, Noel Malcolm, Iqbal Sucranie (UK Action Council for Islamic Affairs)

Join the Non-Stop Picket at Whitehall, opp. Downing St

DONATIONS
Cheques payable to: Bosnia Solidarity Campaign (address below).
Credit Transfer to: National Westminster Bank 66-68 St. John's Road, London SW11 1PB Bank code: 50-21-01 Account no: 57223920
MORE INFORMATION:
Bosnia Solidarity Campaign, c/o ADBH, 12 Fitcroft Street, London WC2H 8DJ

Let the Bosnians defend themselves !

Lift the arms embargo!

PHONE FOR INFORMATION:
0171-387 0564   0171-240 7992

All my life I have been a Pacifist

Speech made by a Sarajevo refugee, on behalf of the non-stop picket, to a demonstration in Trafalgar Square, London, August 6th, 1995.

All my life I have been a pacifist – against militarism, against weapons and against the use of force. Most Bosnian people are the same. That is why we have no weapons.

Devastated and confused by sudden fascist aggression, we waited a long time for someone to rescue us. We trusted the promises of the United Nations and the European Union.

And under UN protection, fascists are killing us systematically day by day.

Under UN protection, concentration camps are held where people are kept and exterminated.

Under UN protection, a new holocaust is gathering strength in Europe.

The UN has fallen into negotiating with war criminals as Chamberlain tried to negotiate with Hitler. Words then were not enough. Military force was needed to stop Hitler, and all the others who share his ideology of purity of race, of Greater Germany or of Greater Serbia. An ideology that understands only force, that trains its followers to rape, to kill and to displace; that can be stopped only by force – unfortunately.

We have gathered thousands of signatures in our support. I am proud to say that they come from people from all over the world, all political backgrounds, all religions and races. I am proud to see you here, Jews together with Muslims and Christians. I am proud because that is what we used to have in Bosnia – and still have, in the parts of the country we still hold. We are not only Muslims, as the UN defines us.

We are Bosnians all together.

There are a vast number of Serbs living in Bosnian-held territories, sharing the same life and the same fate under aggression. There are Serbs shot by Serb snipers, Serbs committed to democracy shot by Serbs following a fascist ideology. Serbs are present in the Bosnian government; one of the commanders of the Bosnian army is a Serb.

So don't believe in the UN's excuse for not acting.

This is not a religious war.

This is a war between fascism and democracy.

Why do we stand day and night in front of John Major's official residence? Symbolically, to show John Major that our killers do not rest over the weekend.

We can't see Mr. Major. He looks down on us in the same way that a sniper looks down on the people of Sarajevo.

We can't see you, Mr. Major, but you can see us; if you were interested in us, in any of us Bosnians, you would hear our individual, tragic stories. Stories in which you have an important role. If I had the opportunity to speak to you, I would tell you of my hopes.

After the experience with Serb fascism in Slovenia and Croatia, I had hoped that you would prevent the occupation of my own neighbourhood by the fascist army.

But you did nothing.

After I woke one morning surrounded by armed fascists, who forbade us to leave our own home, I still had hope that you would free us from our imprisonment.

But you did nothing.

After my husband was dragged out of our

home and massacred, together with his mother and his brother, I still had hope that you would prevent this happening to other families.

But you did nothing.

After I passed through torture, I still had hope that you would prevent this happening to other women.

But you did nothing.

After I was rescued by a Serbian friend, who risked his own life to help me, I still had hope that you would remove the need for democratic Serbs to risk their lives by helping others.

But you did nothing.

Although you knew everything, you did nothing.

For three and a half years I believed in the all-powerful world organisations, and in you.

It took a long time for my hope in you to die.

Now, after the fall of Srebrenica and Zepa, tens of thousands of men have been slaughtered, thousands of women have been brutally raped, entire populations have been expelled from their homelands.

After all of this has happened under your and the UN's protection, I have no hope in you any more.

I don't believe in your empty words of support.

I don't believe in your endless conferences, while we are dying, and in your futile and stage-managed air strikes.

Even though not in you, I still have hope.

I have hope in our supporters throughout the world.

I would like you to see all the people in front of me and to know that we, together, recognise your empty promises. We know you are not willing to help the Bosnian people. Probably because we don't have any oil. But never mind, Mr. Major. I haven't lost hope in our heroic men and women, who are willing to fight fascism in the name of humanity.

We demand the basic human right to defend ourselves. Provide us with weapons, so that we have more than our bodies to use against tanks and heavy artillery. If we are to be killed, we would prefer to die with dignity defending our-

selves than to die slowly, in miserable conditions, under your so-called 'Protection.'

But enough of Death; we are alive.

We have brave hearts. We don't need support from the UN any more.

We need support from the people at this meeting, and everywhere.

I know that you people here will pray for us. I know that the Catholics amongst you will put a candle in church for my mother-in-law, and for all Catholics killed by the fascists.

I know that the Muslims amongst you will pray Al Fatiha for my uncle, and all other Muslims killed by fascists.

I know that the Jews amongst you will pray Kaddish for my friend, and for all Jews killed by fascists.

I know that the Orthodox amongst you will pray for my Serb neighbour, killed on Serbian-held territory because he refused to be a fascist, and for all democratic Serbs killed by fascist snipers and mortars.

I know that you will pray in your own way for my husband and his brother, who respected all religions but were not religious.

But praying is not enough. We need to be free. Charity, too, is not enough. It only serves to prolong our suffering. Once we can defend ourselves, we can feed ourselves. So help us to be free. Come and join us on our picket. We can all do a lot. Act, and act quickly, before it's too late.

THE FIRST SREBRENICA DEMONSTRATION, JULY 31ST 1995

Scottish piper about to lead the demonstration from Hyde Park Corner

Above: Kosovans join the demonstration

Approaching Downing Street

Michael Foot, former Labour Party leader, speaking at Central Hall, Westminster

Above: Trade Union banners on the march

British Muslims express their anger

The trade union convoy set off for Tuzla, the largest convoy we had helped organise since March, 1994. Lorries from France, Spain, Ireland and Britain converged in Split. During a two day hold up on the Herceg-Bosna border the escalation of the war led to nervousness amongst the many 'first timers'. People listened for news bulletins. Rumours came and went. After we crossed into Bosnia the fears vanished.

The following night, in a queue of lorries waiting to be escorted down 'snipers alley', with young, unshaven Bosnian soldiers outside preparing us for the blackout dash, it was possible to dream that maybe this convoy, with its trade union delegations and the growing protests over Srebrenica, might mark a real change. Maybe at last real allies were appearing on the horizon to support those tired, care worn faces, moving around outside in the dark and rain, defending their multi-cultural bastion.

10th Convoy Factfile

DATE:
August 1995

LORRIES:
1 from Ireland.
2 from France, one from PTT SUD (Telecom workers' union), one from Secours Ouvrier / SOS Balkans
2 from Ayuda Obrera, Spain
10 from UK, including lorries and aid from Communications Workers Union, Greater London Association of Trade Union Councils, Leicester TUC, Coventry TUC, NUT, AUT, UNISON, STUC, NUJ, Parkside Women Against Pit Closures, Muslim Aid Leicester, Student Aid for Bosnia, Desert Storm sound system and Workers Aid from Leicester, Tyneside, Manchester, Brighton, Nottingham, East London and Exeter, plus cars and a minibus

WEIGHT: 90 tons

RECIPIENTS:
Tuzla District TU Committee, Tuzla military Hospital, Tuzla Schools and University, Tuzla Post and Telecom Workers, Tuzla Miners Union, Association of Women Miners, Tuzla orphanage

PEOPLE: 85

At Mostar

" We halted at a UN check-point just after the road had circled above the devastation of Muslim east Mostar. We had become accustomed to seeing in the villages we passed through, seemingly selected houses, their walls riddled with bullet holes. Here, as we waited on the side of a road bordered by meadows, a UN soldier told us how a large number of Muslim men had been brought down from the villages in the hills and shot in this meadow. I remember how the three young British Muslim men driving the lorry from Leicester stood at the gate looking across this now tranquil meadow in the gentle evening light. I could only guess at their thoughts. "

JILL OXLEY

University teachers in Tuzla

" When I appealed to the Association of University Teachers National Council in May I pointed out that this was a convoy of solidarity, not charity. We support the right of Bosnia to exist as a multi-cultural society. The response was immediate, and the Council members raised £500 in a collection, which was made up to £1,000 by the Executive.

I went to Tuzla as a delegate from the Association, carrying with me a letter of support, books, computer software and stationery for the University of Tuzla.

In Tuzla, I was able to go to a meeting of people involved in education, and also discussed with the Rector of the University of Tuzla, Professor Sadik Latifagic.

They pointed out the problems that arose from the war. Buildings had been destroyed and staff killed, especially in outlying areas. 120 teaching staff had left the University at the beginning of the war. Male students and staff had military duties, completely disrupting patterns of study at the university. The University was also contending with a 'knowledge blockade'. Faculty buildings in outlying areas had been taken over by Chetniks and the teaching staff 'cleansed'.

In spite of these problems, 500 students had graduated in the first year of the war, as had twenty PhD and thirty Masters students.

Serbs and Croats occupied leading positions in the University and the ethnic 'mix' of students approximated to the proportions outside the University. All pointed out that Bosnia was defending itself against division into ghettos of Muslim, Serb and Croat.

The Rector emphasised this point. "We consciously and deliberately preserve and even repair all religious and cultural property, Serb, Muslim and Croat," he said. "When the Serb nationalists take over an area, they destroy everything that is not Serbian. That is the meaning of 'ethnic cleansing'."

In Bosnia as a whole the university in Sarajevo had been destroyed as had the one in Mostar. In Banja Luka, in the occupied territories, all non Serb staff and students had been expelled. "

PAUL HENDERSON, Secretary, Leicester University AUT

National Union of Teachers' members in Bosnia

" Teachers' associations in Bradford, Leicester, Croydon and East London supported this convoy. Four National Union of Teachers' (NUT) members went to Tuzla. Many schools and individual teachers, parents and children donated aid and money, and campaigned to make it possible. The NUT contributed £500 worth of educational material.

On behalf of the Greater London Association of Trade Union Councils we bought a six and a half ton van which proved surprisingly reliable over the treacherous mountain roads. In all we took three tons of food, clothing and educational materials. The British section of the convoy was made up of ten vehicles from Brighton, Leicester, Newcastle-upon-Tyne, Manchester, London and Leeds. Unions represented included a delegate from the Association of University Teachers, Leicester Association of Teachers in Further and Higher Education and the Journalists' Union, four delegates from the Communication Workers Union, two delegates from Transport and General Workers Union and Engineering Union, and six delegates from UNISON. Along with the Workers Aid trucks there were two Student Aid trucks from Leeds and Cambridge University. They were joined in Split by the *Desert Storm* truck with the sound system.

We made Split in record time. With two French trucks, a Spanish truck and the Irish converted ambulance from Limerick we totalled eighty-five people and fifteen vehicles. Bill Speirs from the Scottish TUC went in to Tuzla ahead of the convoy to meet the miners.

At every meeting in Tuzla people introduced themselves as Bosnian Serb, Bosnian Croat and Bosnian Moslem, not to highlight the differences but to emphasise their unity as a community. There are 15,000 mixed marriages in Tuzla alone. The head of science at the university is a Serb from Serbia. In Tuzla the Serbian Orthodox church has recently been repaired and repainted after Chetnik shells damaged it.

We visited two elementary schools for children aged 8 to 15. Pazar School was the best equipped, with money from a Norwegian aid organisation. Though newly decorated, it had only one cupboard containing the books for all 700 pupils. The teachers receive no salaries and survive on food parcels from the convoys or what they can grow in their gardens. The teachers spoke of the increasing number of

Engineering and Transport Union members from Brighton on the convoy

traumatised refugee children who desperately need specialist help.

We delivered a letter to Tuzla teachers from the NUT General Secretary, Doug McAvoy, who hoped the aid would be of some assistance. The Secretary of the Tuzla teachers trade union had previously written to the NUT but without a response. On this occasion, following the massacre at Srebrenica and after a meeting in March between a trade union delegation from Tuzla and the Union's International Dept, an appeal was circulated by the NUT. It was only followed up, however, largely by those who were in direct contact with members of the Workers Aid campaign. "

JILL OXLEY and PHIL EDWARDS

Why I got involved

" My reasons for getting involved came from a feeling of helplessness when watching the news from Sarajevo and thinking, this could be me. I found there was a group of people in UNISON organising a truck and I started to help. In UNISON there was a very good response to fund raising.

The journey itself was an adventure – travelling on good and bad roads, through some of the most beautiful countryside and waiting at borders, check points and hours and hours on end in incredibly muddy lorry parks. As soon as we crossed into Bosnia the atmosphere changed. People were very friendly and glad to see us. In Tuzla we took the aid to schools, hospitals, an orphanage, a therapy centre for refugee women, the university and Town Hall. We met many people involved in the trades unions and expressed our solidarity with these workers and asked what we could do. We all came away fired up with ideas. People spelled out exactly what they needed to rebuild their communities. On a personal note the convoy is one of the best experiences I have ever had. Some of the people on the convoy will be friends for life. I feel a great sense of loss since coming home. The abiding memory is of people in Tuzla, of all creeds, talking to us about their community and how they want to keep it together without division. I will never forget the families who opened their homes to us as complete strangers and who we left as friends. "

ELEANOR SMITH (Camden UNISON)

Mind games

" We've been stopped at the Croatian/Bosnian border for more than fourteen hours and there is no sign of moving. It's three in the afternoon and still no news. Last night, standing next to our lorries on this switchback mountain road, we could see both the milky way and flashes in the distance.

From our isolated position bits of news and rumour from outside took seed in people's minds. "They're bombing Mostar, you can see the gun flares." All of us felt vulnerable, but a glance at a compass showed that the flashes were coming from over the Adriatic. Today we laugh about the heat lightning that we saw last night.

I find myself worrying about our children and what they must be thinking. We were expecting to be in Tuzla tonight and of course we won't be as, even if everything goes to plan, it will take at least fifteen hours. The heat is tremendously oppressive, and all that most of us can do is lie around and sleep. Earlier, some of the younger members of the convoy went exploring on the shit-encrusted hillside and discovered a decomposed body. "It did my fucking head in," said one of them. We did not need too much reminding, but there is of course a war going on. "

POLLY HENDERSON

Tony Benn's night of shame

Rightwing Tory Sir Alfred Sherman has, "nothing against Muslims," he assured a House of Commons gathering on June 26th, but Muslim countries were neither "civilised" nor "democratic".

Maybe rape camps, 'ethnic cleansing', killing children and systematic destruction of libraries and mosques are Sherman's idea of democracy and civilisation, because he boasts of his pride in backing Serb nationalist war criminal Radovan Karadzic.

Speaking at a meeting to launch a *Committee for Peace in the Balkans*, organised by Labour CND supporters and Labour leftwingers like Tony Benn, he said, "I am Karadzic's adviser and I am proud of being Karadzic's adviser."

As Quintin Hoare, of the *Alliance to Defend Bosnia-Herzegovina*, told them, looking straight at Tony Benn, whom he had supported in the past, "This is a shameful, and shaming, meeting."

Purporting not to 'take sides' in the war, this 'peace' committee says it's against 'outside intervention'; but it knows the Serb nationalist forces have all the weapons whilst insisting that the arms embargo must be maintained.

Labour MP Alice Mahon, chairing the 'peace' meeting, regretted it had taken so long to do anything. A young Bosnian commented, "Now, when we are starting to drive back the Chetniks, these people shout for peace!"

Sir Alfred Sherman was among the signatories to the 'peace' committee's leaflet. When people shouted, "Where's your friend Le Pen?" the French fascist whom Sherman had invited to Britain in 1987, chairperson Alice Mahon insisted on Sherman's right to speak without interruption.

The platform speakers – Labour MPs Tony Benn and Tam Dalyell – made no attempt to disassociate themselves from his reactionary diatribe. Rather than condemn the crimes committed against the Bosnian people, Benn evoked atrocities committed by Ottoman Turkey in the last century.

Bosnian refugees ably answered the platform's hypocrisy and lies.

A young man expelled from Chetnik-held Banja Luka said, "You want to treat all sides equally, but they are not equal. Bosnia must be for all. Nobody has the right to create 'ethnically pure' states. If you support that, you support fascism." Another young Bosnian, Ismet, said those who wanted Bosnia disarmed should apply the same recipe to their own states.

Answering talk about what NATO or the UN should do, he declared to applause, "We do not want foreign soldiers in Bosnia. We only want to have the right to defend our own country."

A letter, sent to the meeting by the Tuzla TU Committee, was read out. It condemned the organisers for refusing to support Bosnia's fight against ethnic division.

The strong support for Serbian nationalism in the leadership of the labour and trade union movement often takes a disguised form. This common platform of fascist sympathisers and 'socialist Yugoslavia' supporters gives the game away.

CHARLIE POTTINS

This was the first and last meeting of Committee for Peace in the Balkans and gave a good insight into the thinking among upper echelons of the labour movement. However, the work done by the Bosnian community, Workers Aid and the Alliance to Defend BiH ensured the Committee was still-born.

UNISON delegation

The GLATC van
and delegation

Ayuda
Obrera
truck

THE
TRADE
UNION
CONVOY

Tea-break

In Tuzla, the trade unionists delivered their aid and held meetings with their Bosnian counterparts. Some of these meetings made deep impressions. A press conference for local TV and newspapers was held and different people from the convoy spoke. The communications workers from Britain and France read out a joint statement. The British CWU members had previously disagreed with the call to lift the arms embargo. They thought it would just lead to more killing. Now, having met Tuzla communication workers, they promised, in their statement to the press conference, to return to Britain to campaign for the British government to lift the arms embargo.

We also informed the Bosnian media of the London demonstrations and the non-stop protest outside Downing Street.

Teachers met with teachers and delivered aid to schools. UNISON members visited hospitals, clinics, old people's homes and orphanages. Billy Pye, former-executive member of the National Union of Mineworkers, and two members of Women against Pit Closures went to stay in the mining town of Banovici.

To, the Labour Group Leadership
   All Labour Controlled Councils
   All Labour Party Members
   In Britain

Tuzla, 08. 08. 1995.

Dear Comrades,
   We firstly write to thank you for the aid from Labour Councils in Britain brought by the Trade Union convoy which arrived this week in Tuzla, so desperately needed here. As you know our workers get no pay and rely solely on food parcels which they receive once or maybe twice each month. Most of our workers alternate work and military service including duties on the front line to defend Bosnia and Herzegovina and its multi-ethnic and multi-cultural communities from fascist attack. Our soldiers are poorly armed due to the arms embargo, but morale is high because we believe the right is on our rights.
   With the help of people from all nationalities and backgrounds we will continue to fight for a free and multi-ethnic and multi-cultural Europe. We also call for your support for coordinated demonstrations against fascism across Europe.
   We hear from Bosnian refugeees in Britain and others who visit us that there is a great feeling of support for Bosnia and we hope that you will soon adopt a policy of support.
   We are in the fore front of the fight against the rise of fascism in Europe and make a sincere call for your support.

Yours Comradely,

Selim Beslagic
Mayor of Tuzla

Sulejman Hurle
President Trade Union Council Of Bosnia

Interview with CWU branch secretary, Ian Young, a postman from Bolton.

How long did it take you to organise your part of the convoy?

Planning started in April and continued up to the day we left Manchester.

Why did you decide to go?

After listening to a plea for help from a Tuzla union delegation who spoke at our regional office.

Were you nervous about making the trip?

Not really, but if bad news came on the TV, it started me wondering just what I was going to encounter.

What did you like most about the journey?

Going over some of the very high passes which were no more than dirt tracks.

What did you hate most about it?

Being stuck on the Croatian-Bosnian border for two nights and days where we found the remains of a child which we buried.

Did going to Tuzla change your views about the situation?

Yes, I now firmly believe that the arms embargo should be lifted. I wasn't sure before, but these people must be allowed to defend themselves.

Was Tuzla how you expected?

It is smaller than I thought and the people more friendly. It is truly multi-ethnic.

What was your most memorable moment in Tuzla?

An afternoon at a nearby lake with one of the families.

Which person made the biggest impression on you?

A young man from Tuzla Post Office who in one day early in the war found over 200 bodies on his delivery round. He had been blasted by shells ten times while at work.

What did you learn that you think others should know?

That not all the people in former Yugoslavia are warmongers. Most are ordinary people like you and me who want an end to the fighting.

How will you use this experience in the trade union movement?

I have already made a couple of reports and, hopefully, I will influence others to take up the challenge.

From Solidarity not Charity, a report of the TU convoy by NUJ representative, Tony Samphier.

Some people went to Tuzla airport where the thousands of women who escaped from Srebrenica were camped in tents.

The Tuzla authorities had coped with 50,000 refugees coming into Tuzla during the war. This was a huge material problem and it also led to serious social tensions. The refugees were mainly Muslims driven from rural areas and there were deep cultural differences between themselves and the urban workers. However, the town tried to shelter and feed everyone seeking safety. Now another 20,000 traumatised people were living in tents on Tuzla airfield. The irony could not have been greater. People desperate for food, clothes, for everything, all camped on Bosnia's biggest airstrip – a federal airforce base. The UN had declared the airstrip open for aid flights a year before and landed one plane. The Chetniks complained to the UN about using the airport and no more flights came. So everything for Tuzla had to keep travelling the mud tracks from Split.

For a week, everywhere you went in Tuzla you would see groups of trade unionists, unemployed people and students from the convoy sitting talking with Bosnians, sharing experiences. The President of the Bosnian Federation of Trade Unions, Sulejman Hrle had come from Sarajevo to meet the trade union convoy. Meetings were held with him and the Tuzla committee to discuss how to develop the work amongst the trade unions.

It was agreed that the Bosnian unions would call for an international day of demonstrations in October to commemorate the thousands of Yugoslav workers and trade unionists who had died fighting fascism in World War II and now, fifty years on, the thousands of Bosnian workers killed in a new fight against fascism. It was felt that bringing the past and the present together was the best way to try and turn the outrage over Srebrenica into a clearer understanding of the war. We promised to do everything we could to mobilise support from the trade unions of Europe to make this day of action a success. and agreed to organise for Mr. Hrle to visit Britain so he could campaign for it.

Media Workers in Bosnia

Mark Bareham and Greg Dropkin are Broadcasting, Entertainment and Cinematograph Union (BECTU) members in Liverpool.

" In the morning, we meet TV Tuzla. Editor-in-chief Jasna Zunic says three of their journalists had been at the cafe, near the site of the May 25th massacre, with a colleague celebrating his wedding anniversary. His child was killed in the slaughter. "We are probably naive, but we just can't understand that someone could do such a thing."

TV Tuzla offered six minutes of their footage exclusively to World Television News for distribution. But no broadcast channel outside Bosnia was interested. A Reuters camera was also on the scene, but no-one wanted that footage either. So why was the cafe kept out of sight? Jasna observes that UN troops had just been taken hostage by the Chetniks and were receiving international media coverage.

TV Tuzla was formed in 1992 when the war started in Bosnia. Local events are the focus because their transmitter can't reach beyond the city. That also means people living in the Chetnik controlled areas can't tune in, though some apparently listen to Radio Tuzla in secret and video cassettes of TV Tuzla circulate on the black market.

"We are funded with very modest donations of cooking oil and flour," Jasna says. When they do get the odd commission from a foreign TV unit, they have to accept whatever wages are offered. "We worked for three days in the field, preparing and videoing raw material for a film. Our journalist and cameraman worked from 8am until ten in the evening. We are educated and trained and we know the price in the international market. We asked 7,000DM. They said they were ready to pay 2,000. We feel angry because they belittle our work, our value, but we have to accept such commissions."

We also spoke with Sinan Alic, Editor of the newspaper *Front Slobode (Freedom Front)*. It began as an anti-fascist title on November 7th, 1943, and still appears under the same name. "I could not imagine I would be fighting fascism here in Europe fifty years later," Alic says.

The front page blurb reads, 'The title will appear again when the money is collected.' They are running 2,000 copies twice a month, with a cover price of 1DM, enough to buy 1.5kg of bread. Each copy is read by eight people, Alic reckons. They print on everything except toilet paper. There are no wages.

Alic and other journalists tell us that the influx of refugees from Srebrenica may threaten Tuzla's multi-ethnic society. Partly, this reflects a clash of cultures between urban Tuzla and its rural surroundings. There have been incidents of Serbian houses near Tuzla being raided by Muslim refugees, presumably in retaliation for their treatment by other, very different, Serbs who also shell Tuzla. The media has reported these issues and the police have responded to ensure that the Serb owners retained possession.

There is some fear that the Union of Bosnian Social Democrats could lose power in Tuzla to the Muslim nationalist party (the SDA) which heads the Bosnian government, as the refugees from rural areas are recruited into party politics. But at this time the town remains visibly multi-ethnic and proud of it.

Our brief visit to Tuzla came before the Nato bombing – which Workers Aid opposed – and the current US-led diplomacy, which amounts to the division of Bosnia on ethnic lines. In Tuzla, the demand was clear: a united, multi-ethnic Bosnia with full civil rights for all its citizens. "

GREG DROPKIN (from the BECTU journal)

Salima

Xavier Perez-Moreno, a Catalan, became involved in Student Aid for Bosnia while studying at Leeds University. He wrote the following story after visiting an orphanage in Tuzla which houses children from Srebrenica and other Bosnian towns.

She does not know for sure what day it is today. She is barely seven and memories sometimes get mixed up. She remembers the house where she used to live before being moved here. They had an old cow, but she still gave enough milk. She also remembers the river, and the trunk in which she used to play with Husein. She is still aware of afternoons sitting in the kitchen, hearing the rain, and Semiya singing quietly; Daddy and Mummy, sitting by the fireplace, drinking milk and eating bread.

All of these are well remembered by Salima, so that her pictures are full of cows, houses and rivers. Trouble begins when she tries to remember beyond that dark night. Mummy woke her and took her hand. Since that moment every memory has become blurred. Anxiety, fear, darkness, unknown people's faces. Men from other villages, some of them smiling, some of them sad, giving hope or full of anger, but all of them strange; a series of bodies overlapped in a fragile image of disaster. And deep down, the scream of the cow, a strident whine that shakes Salima. Salima wants to go back for the cow, but Mummy does not allow her to go, and it is hot, very hot, and her hand sweats.

Sometimes, Salima's pictures get full of grey colours and night and sinister figures. She wants to draw a river and a cow, but suddenly she hears the scream and then she knows they are back again. She closes her eyes and tries to cry, but she cannot, and when she opens her eyes again, she finds a frightening picture on the paper. And if she shuts her eyes to the picture and listens, it seems that the weeping cow is calling, "Salima, Salima."

Then Mrs Karovic arrives. She looks at Salima with a disapproving face. Mrs Karovic tears up the paper with majestic movements. Salima knows that making pictures when nobody has asked for them is forbidden. Salima does not speak. Her silence makes Mrs Karovic more nervous, and she finally slaps Salima.

Salima only wants to go to bed now, to sleep where nobody can see her. But she has to go back with the other children and play with them as if nothing has happened. Mrs Karovic is watching them, and if they are bad she will send them back to the place they were before, far away from the city.

Today everybody seems to be very excited. In the morning the children were woken up and dressed with clean clothes, as if it had been one of those days when the people from the city come. Everything has been thoroughly cleaned and the children are sitting in the classrooms. Mrs Karovic is wearing a new dress, a pink one.

Somebody has come to the orphanage. Salima watches them arrive with a small bus and some cars. They are odd people. They have strange hair and wear coloured clothes. They take up positions in the playground. There are no children.

Mrs Karovic gives permission to go out, one by one, in a row. The younger children are holding hands and stand in a corner.

The foreigners have brought musical instruments that Salima has not seen before and they give the children the chance to play them. The most easy-going take some maracas, but no-one gets too close. The foreigners are a little frightening, Salima thinks. They smile and sing. None of them can speak Salima's language.

Salima discovers something. The foreigners have brought a very big, heavy box. One of the older children who can speak their language explains to her that the box is full of crayons and markers. Salima watches the box.

If she could bring colours to the cow and the sun would shine yellow and red in the sky, a blue sky and not a black one, and the river would have water and coloured fishes........Maybe if the colours would stop being grey, maybe then Salima would stop seeing the men who are watching her through that piece of paper, and she would be back singing with Daddy and Mummy.

The foreigners start collecting their instruments. Salima stays near the box and watches. One of the foreigners seems to be arguing with Mrs Karovich who in the distance gestures to the box and shakes her head.

Salima feels something close to fear. No-one moves the box. The foreigners finish packing and all of them get into the cars. Mrs Karovic is still arguing. At the end the foreigner leaves her and makes a sign to people in the car.

The car stops in front of the box and three men get out and load it into the boot. One of them looks at Salima for a moment with a helpless face. Salima turns round and joins the other children. They go together into the orphanage through the front door, while, in the distance, they hear the noise of the cars leaving.

XAVIER PEREZ MORENO

Delivering aid

We delivered mostly food supplies – pasta, cooking oil, flour, rice, sugar etc, but also toiletries, baby food and clothes, school and university equipment and medical supplies. Workers Aid often discussed how aid should be distributed. Most convoy members spent many hours collecting the food and money for the trip. They did not want aid wasted or for it to get into the wrong hands. But how do you do that? Which are the right hands? Here's how complicated things can be.

Some people proposed giving the food to refugees in Tuzla since they had suffered the most. But refugees received aid from the UNHCR, occasionally enough for them to sell some at high prices to the Tuzla citizens who got nothing from the UN.

We always gave boxes of aid to the families we stayed with. This seemed such a good 'one to one' relationship that some other people thought this could somehow be extended. But the Bosnians who accommodated us became the subject of envy from neighbours. We were a small organisation and could not deliver to everyone. Every time you gave to one person it caused friction and division. 'Pomoc', Bosnian for 'aid', symbolised the Bosnian peoples' dependency on the whim of outsiders. Many Tuzla citizens had a proud disdain for everything to do with the 'pomoc' industry.

There were aid distribution networks like *Caritas* and *Merhemet* but they were religious based, using their control of desperately needed food to 'catch' their flock, causing more division. Some people proposed just delivering directly to the ordinary Tuzla folk. But how? Hand it out from the back of the lorry? Not only would you soon have a riot,you would have no idea who it was going to. These many complications will give some idea why the problem of how to best deliver aid is not confned to the big aid organisations.

Our value judgments often differed from those of people under siege. Food delivered to the unions was given to the working members. Some of our people found this odd. Shouldn't it be given to the unemployed? But workers didn't get paid – except for inadequate parcels of food delivered by people like us. The unemployed were worse off, but from the point of view of the whole community it made sense. Without the coal, the electricity and the medical treatment which working people provided, everything would collapse and without food people cannot work.

For Workers Aid, delivery had to relate to the purpose of the convoys – the defence of a united Bosnia. That needed two things: the self organisation of Bosnians, and the growth of international solidarity. It was for this reason that we nearly always delivered to trade unions or student unions. As outsiders we could not play god and decide the merits of this person's need against another's. We delivered to the unions and left it to them to decide the criteria for distribution.

Could we trust the union representatives? Some of our aid ended up in shops and on the blackmarket. At the university we could find few students who had received any of the aid delivered to their student union. But even this kind of thing was not straightforward. When you deliver four lorries of aid to the miners' union, for example, with ten thousand members how many are going to get anything? At a convoy meeting in Tuzla some people proposed that we ask the unions for a list of people who received aid. A British miner replied that if anyone had brought aid to his union during the miners' strike and asked for such a list he would have told them to shove the aid up their arse. "If you don't trust me, don't bring it." When we first arrived, in the chaos of war and with language problems, it was not easy to know who to trust. As we got to know more people we tried to deliver aid directly to a specific destination, via the union. Lorries would go and unload at a hospital, or orphanage or school, making the unloading closer to the recipients. Even then things were not always easy. In these institutions there were hierarchies of power. When several lorries of medicine were delivered to Tuzla hospital the nurses, who received a litre of cooking oil and a kilo of flour a month for 'wages', told us that some of the 'higher ups' dipped into the medical aid and sold it.

Nothing could narrow the huge gap between what we delivered and what was required. In the midst of hunger rumour, jealousy and corruption thrive. One Tuzla friend told us that the working people have no voice in Bosnia. This was the real problem. If there is a shortage then those with power always get their hands on an unequal share. The one thing that would greatly help the Bosnian people assert their control over events was to see the European workers organising themselves to assist their sisters and brothers in Bosnia. It was here that delivery to the trade unions made real sense. They were organisations that many people in Britain could relate to. A letter from the Tuzla teachers, union might inspire British teachers to act. Delivering to the union was not some ideal solution, but it was based on a perspective of international workers' solidarity. Each convoy taken by itself was far from perfect, but overall we had a strategy which we stuck to.

Sulejman Hrle and members of Workers Aid spent a week visiting union committees in other towns in the area – Lukavac, Gradacac and Kalesija.

In each town local committees asked us to extend our solidarity actions to include their unions. We had to explain that we were a small organisation and that everything depended on developing the kind of support the union convoy had built for Tuzla. We said we would pass on their appeals to the unions in Britain.

In Kalesija the union president, a woman who had maintained production on Bosnia's largest co-operative dairy farm throughout the war, took us to see the town centre. At the outbreak of war the Mayor, a Serb, had armed local Serbs and driven out all Muslims. Later the BiH army had fought a bitter, house to house battle. Now the town was back in Bosnian territory, but the centre was deserted – every house and shop burnt out and still in easy range of the Chetnik artillery we could see on the nearby hills.

Everywhere we went expectations in us were so high. We were the first people to come and talk about the defence of multi-cultural Bosnia and about working class solidarity. These people met us with civic receptions and laid on police and army escorts. Did they understand that we were nobodies, a bankrupt organisation with a fleet of battered old lorries? We told them the truth, but could their desperation allow them to understand that we were not the leaders of powerful British trade unions which they had all learnt about at school – the people who should have been there to meet them?

We returned to Britain with their appeal letters, as we had previously returned with appeals from Tuzla, but at least we now had some British addresses where we could deliver them, confident they would be read.

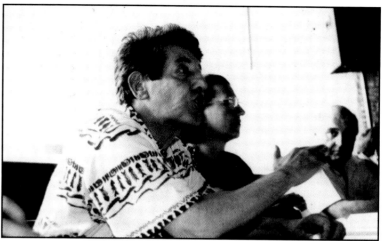

Sulejman Hrle at the Tuzla press conference

A Workers Aid representative lays flowers at the site of the May 25th massacre

Pub crawls, supermarkets and the opera – a guide to WAB finance

In 1993, Tuzla was under siege. If the proposal from our friend in Serbia for a convoy was to be taken seriously, a campaign had to be undertaken immediately. Our act of solidarity, which we hoped would act as a catalyst, could not await costings, targets, and thorough logistical preparations. The critical situation in Bosnia made such things a luxury.

We had never organised a convoy and knew little about the military or political situations in BiH. Speaking for myself, I knew still less about the country's geography. We were also faced with confusion or outright opposition within the labour and trade union movement.

So the first convoy was not simply a matter of drawing up a budget to get some lorries from A to B. It was a campaign with lorries, in which we learned a lot very quickly and managed to win support which helped sustain future convoys. However, we spent over two months on the road, with a large group of people needing food and acommodation. On further convoys we slept in the lorries and did communal cooking by the road side, but on this first convoy we were not so prepared. We also spent two frustrating weeks up a mountain at an off-season Slovenian ski hostel as we tried to discover the safest route to Tuzla. All this cost a lot of money and some of it had to be borrowed. We had hoped to sell two of our trucks, particularly a large lorry and trailer which cost £11,000, to pay off half of our debt on our return, but both these vehicles were lost when a small section of the convoy decided to go to Tuzla via the long Split route.

Although this first campaign was necessary for the future development of Workers Aid, it left us with a £28,000 debt. We have carried this debt through all the convoys since then, sometimes reducing it, sometimes when new problems arose, seeing it expand.

In the two years from June, 1993 we raised about a quarter of a million pounds. This is a very rough figure as not all the money went through the central accounts. As local groups became more organised, buying their own vehicles etc, most of the funds were spent locally. A lot of money was also raised just before convoys departed and was taken as cash for diesel etc, so it didn't go through any bank account.

How did people, who had never been involved in large scale fundraising, find this amount of money? We first got an inkling of the kind of response that awaited us from conventional labour movement methods. Comrades set up a table with leaflets and a collecting tin in Crawley town centre in July, 1993 and raised over £70 in a very short time. A Labour Party member in Leeds, Edna Stubbs, organised a collection at Tescos where we collected two van loads of food

and over £1,000 in two days. This pointed us in a new direction and we put a lot of time into getting collecting permissions from supermarkets all around the country. We got better at it, producing laminated display material, stickers, campaign t-shirts, proper ID and large boards listing the aid required.

Not everyone gave when you asked. I had many refusals to my request, "Will you make a donation to the miners of Bosnia?" some unprintable. My favourite was, "No. I'm from Bolton." Fortunately we had many more who did give money and respond to our notice saying, BUY AN EXTRA ITEM FOR BOSNIA. Some shoppers donated full shopping bags and we usually had a struggle not to block the entrance.

Supermarkets also gave an opportunity for Bosnians to help. Although a few of the younger refugees, whose English was very good, did help do pub collections, supermarkets were where we depended on our Bosnian members most.

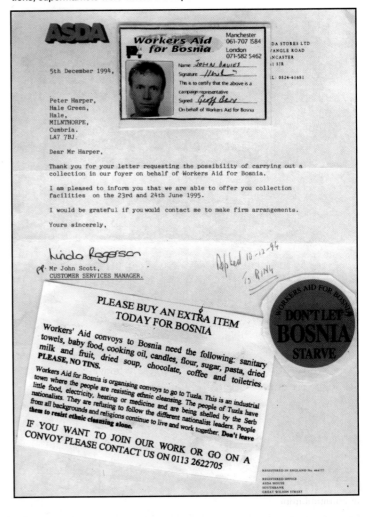

In Newcastle and Gateshead for example, large amounts of food and money were collected, much of it by former inmates of the notorious Omarska concentration camp.

We also discovered that we got a big response from collecting with tins on the streets. To begin with we had permit problems with the police, but it didn't usually stop us. As the city centre collections became more organised they raised large amounts – usually over £1,000. We collected in Cambridge, Norwich, Leeds, Edinburgh, Exeter, Derby, Kendal and other towns.

We also raised a lot of money during the first convoy through the support of the rock group U2, who were in the middle of their ZOOROPA '93 tour. After exchanging faxes with their management we were invited, at three hours notice, to collect at their concert in Roundhay Park, Leeds. A startled Texas Homecare cashier sold us thirty-five buckets which we rushed up to the park and used to collect over £4,000 that night. Some of us, including thirteen-year-old Jasmina, went back-stage. At one moment she was overwhelmed at being given a U2 sweatshirt and signed photos, the next she was describing, with a seriousness way beyond her years, her experiences escaping from Sarajevo in 1992. She wrote a letter appealing to Bono for help. He did help by mentioning the convoy and we collected at three other U2 concerts that summer.

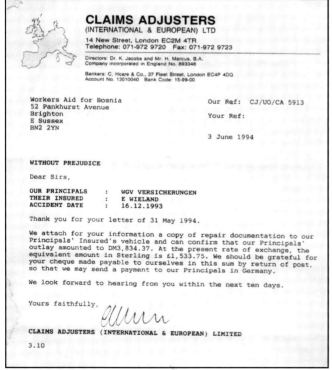

An unwanted surprise

John Davies,
36 Burnside Road,
KENDAL,
Cumbria.

228 Mansel Road,
Winch Wen,
SWANSEA,
West Glamorgan.   Sal 7JT

Dear John,

On behalf of the Swansea Branch of the National Union of Journalists I have pleasure in enclosing a cheque for £150 towards the excellent work you and your colleagues are doing in providing aid for Bosnia.

The award is one of many made recently from our Press Ball Account and was nominated by one of our members, Mike Burrows.

It's not a lot in terms of your mammoth task, but we hope it will be of some assistance.

Yours sincerely,

Brian Walters

May 7th 1994

We raised large sums from pub collections and the message of international workers solidarity got a ready hearing. For example, we raised over £360 in one evening amongst holiday-makers in Lake District pubs.

Other regular collection methods included car boot sales, leafleting theatres and the opera, and one-off events. The latter ranged from union conferences, benefit gigs by *Jethro Tull* and *Showaddywaddy*, Ulverston Carnival, Buxton Opera Festival, the Bradford Mela (the biggest Asian festival in Europe) and the Durham Miners' Gala.

The percentage of our income which came from trades unions donations was relatively small, but we did receive a trickle of cheques from branches and trades councils and occasional big donations; the North-West Firebrigades Union paid about £1,500 for one lorry to go to Tuzla.

Our limited resources meant that we could only buy old lorries which in the long run required huge sums on repairs. If you add up the costs of buying lorries, servicing them plus the insurance, ferries and diesel for each trip, then the total far exceeded the value of our cargoes. We weren't, though, only transporting aid. The people who travelled with us helped to build the movement of solidarity that was growing up at both ends of the journey.

What are the costs of a convoy? There are the obvious ones like diesel, ferry tickets, tolls, road tax and insurance. Then, if you are faced with delays, you have to feed a large number of people on the road. You need plenty of spare tyres and snow chains in winter. You have to make on the spot repairs to wing mirrors and windscreens when they get broken by reckless UNPROFOR drivers. You also have travel costs within Britain, before you leave. Collecting aid from different parts of the country is an expensive business. But at a very rough estimate, the cost per lorry per trip was £1,500.

Everyone involved in Workers Aid was an unpaid volunteer, but there were big campaigning costs. Telephone bills frequently went over £1,000 as we were having to use satellite links to Croatia and BiH. There were the mundane campaign items like leaflets and printing, and collecting materials such as tins, stickers and information videos, but also more exotic ones like repairs to the doors of the warehouse we had been lent or paying for a trailer stolen outside a pub in Liverpool whilst collecting aid. On occasions the sudden urgent need for an extra lorry could only be met by a Workers Aid member taking out a personal bank loan and this had to be repaid in monthly instalments over the next year.

Sometimes everything came at once and the situation was black farce: a convoy is leaving next day requiring £3,000 cash, two of the bank loans have re-payments due totalling £700, a letter has just arrived demanding the immediate settlement of a 3,500DM insurance claim or legal action will follow, telephones will be cut off next week unless you pay the £1,500 owing and.....you have no money. After writing a few stalling letters, you get on the phone. Maybe Paddy, Lisa, Andy Mac or Ed can do a pub collection? We've got the Asda collection next weekend (at least £700) and the Opera North concerts the week after. That's good. And we can count on £1,000 from the Norwich street collection next month (we must order some more tins and stickers). We just need someone to lend us the 31,000 now. Failing that, rob a bank?

Despite the problems, we showed what could be done. Our accounts are not a financial document so much as a balance sheet, showing both the lack of solidarity from the bureaucratically controlled workers' movement and the efforts of many, many people to build a movement that can react when workers are in need.

JOHN DAVIES

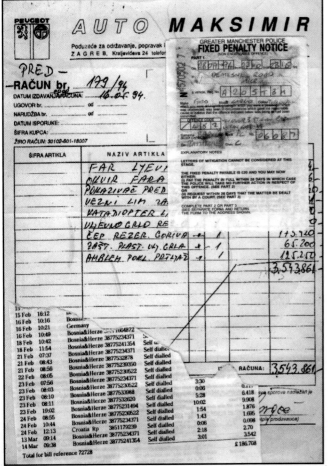

More bills: truck repairs, parking tickets, telephone bills

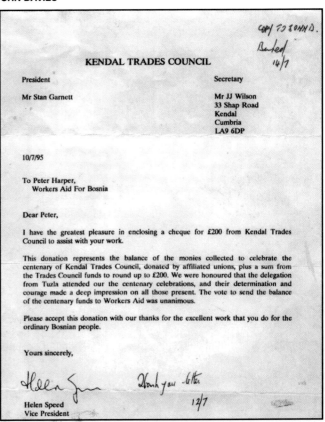

Chapter 8

AUGUST 1995   Croatian Army recaptures the Krajina; Seige of Bihac raised; rebel Abdic army smashed.
SEPTEMBER 1995   20,000 rally against Milosevic in Kragujevac, Serbia.
OCTOBER 1995   Mass graves begin to be uncovered in liberated areas of north-west Bosnia.
DECEMBER 1995   Dayton agreement signed in Paris.

The aftermath of Srebrenica

The Srebrenica massacre was rapidly followed by military developments on other fronts. Even as the trade union convoy was on its way to Tuzla, the Croatian army was re-taking large parts of Croatia, seized by the JNA in 1992.

In Bosnia we had found horror and anger over Srebrenica counter-balanced by an optimism that the tide of war was changing. The Croatian offensive weakened the Chetniks' hold over parts of western Bosnia, and in September the Bosnian army, in co-operation with HVO units, attacked Chetnik positions. The siege of Bihac was swiftly broken and Bosnian troops liberated large areas of the region pushing east towards the nationalist stronghold of Banja Luka. The Chetniks were in major retreat for the first time.

Outside Bosnia there was growing criticism of UN policy. The arms embargo was supposed to save lives and yet eight thousand unarmed people had been slaughtered in Srebrenica.

Banner and shrine at 24-hour picket opposite Downing Street. The Ministry of Defence is behind the railings.

Bosnia in Mauritius

Rama Valayden, a young lawyer from Mauritius visiting Britain on a case before the Privy Council, joined the picket

It is an accident that I came into contact with you. I asked my friend to stop the car in front of the picket so we could meet the courageous soldiers on the line. But the police would not allow the car to stop and it was only the next day that I got there. I was very impressed by the dedication of the picket, who not only seem to understand the nature of the problem in Bosnia, but also seem to be dedicated to a fight against the system on a world-wide level. This internationalist aspect of our fight is very important.

Mauritius is a very mixed country, with people coming from many parts of the world. You have Hindus, Muslims, a small Buddhist community, as well as Christians; there are people of Indian, African, and Chinese origin.

When the Bosnian crisis occurred we believed it was a struggle against fascism. This crisis has been spurred on by the IMF policies imposed on Yugoslavia to 'liberalise' its economy.

When we received information about the 'ethnic cleansing' it was clear, especially to people living in the sort of society we have in Mauritius, that we must support all those being oppressed in the former Yugoslavia.

We felt we had to alter pubic opinion about the issues and to explain to Mauritians that it is not a Muslim problem, but one that is fascist in nature and fascist in substance.

Mauritius is a small island with 1.1 million people but within ten days we had held twenty meetings up and down the island. We held a big meeting in Port Louis, the capital, which was attended by nearly 800 people. This was very good, given the short notice. Everybody wanted to have their say.

Two days later we held a demonstration which, according to the police, attracted more than 3,000 people. Our slogans were 'Stop fascism!'; 'No ethnic cleansing!'; 'Arm the Bosnians!'

The offensive by the poorly equipped Bosnians made a mockery of the UN's 'inability' to maintain the 'safe havens'. People compared the UN's 'defence' of Srebrenica with the military campaign to defend 'democracy' in oil rich Kuwait. Even before the fall of Srebrenica Robin Cook, Labour Party Shadow Foreign Secretary, told Parliament that he had come to the conclusion that the UN had pursued the wrong policy. They had tried to divide Bosnia. Now he recognised that this was against the wishes of most Bosnians and could only be achieved through force. Cook called for the UN to change its approach and give support to people trying to maintain multi-cultural society.

Cook and the Labour leaders had been fully informed by the Union of Bosnian Social Democrats of the real nature of the war two years before this 'discovery'. Their silence over the fate of their fellow Social Democrats mirrored the TUC's response to Bosnian trade unionists. But Cook's speech showed that the determined resistance in Bosnia was forcing its' voice to be heard. Bosnians could not just be silently eliminated as those who planned their division hoped. The first cracks were appearing in the international conspiracy against them.

Recollections of the picket – 1

" Over the course of two months, bright summer evenings among a crowd of volunteers gave way to torrential rain and freezing nights when one waited for replacements who were delayed or who never came, while struggling for conversation with one's single bored, companion.

I recall the picket with pleasure because it let me feel, after four years of hand-wringing, that there were people who saw Bosnia the same way as I did, and that we could at least do something about it.

I first came to the picket a week after it had started and was surprised to find a small community, surrounding an elaborate display, made up of posters, placards and poems. The presentation sometimes included the human candle, Erica from Sicily, whose act was certainly eye-catching, even if its symbolic reference to Bosnia was never entirely clear to me. It was a pitch that nobody passing by, other than MOD civil servants and occasional ministers, could easily ignore – although we made sure they had no chance to ignore us anyway.

My only famous 'victim' was Clare Short MP, who said she wholeheartedly agreed with our position, but wouldn't sign the petition because she thought she might already have signed it.

Some of the most interesting conversations I had were with sympathetic people who didn't feel able to sign a petition calling for further war. But most people knew exactly what they were signing. I remember long discussions and debates about the motives for western non-intervention, rising excitement as the Bosniak-Croat forces finally started to drive the Serbs back and the anti-climax when the 'peace' of Dayton was imposed, at just about the same time that we closed the picket down. "

NEIL THOMSON

The 24hour, Whitehall picket

PICKET RULES

1. There must always be one person designated as the chief steward who wears an arm-band to indicate this.

2. Only the chief steward speaks to the police.

3. The chief steward is responsible for money collected on the picket -— he/she must make sure full tins are collected and emptied, and that no tins are lost. The number of tins must be counted when he/she takes over, and checked with the previous chief steward.

4. No drink or drugs on the picket.

5. There must always be at least two persons on the picket.

6. Everyone coming on the picket must sign into the picket book.

7. Everyone coming on the picket must read these rules and agree to them.

Bosnia Solidarity Campaign - how we came about

July 1995. The unthinkable happened to the people of Srebrenica. In Britain four organisations joined together to enable the voice of ordinary people to be heard. We organised two mass marches through London on July 19th and August 7th, behind the main slogan, 'STOP THE RAPE OF BOSNIA!' The marches demanded the lifting of the one-sided arms embargo, and an end to genocide.

Rallies were held after each march at which politicians, trade unionists, religious leaders, actors, journalists and others condemned the atrocity. After the first march, outraged demonstrators started a non-stop picket outside the British Foreign Office and 10, Downing Street with the same demands as the marches. The picket went on 24-hours every day from July 19th until September 29th.

People of all nationalities and all ethnic backgrounds, of all religions and none, from a variety of political parties and no party, spent their days and nights on the picket. Picketers collected 35,000 signatures on a petition, demanding the lifting of the arms embargo.

A high point of the picket was a visit on a rainy September morning from the Serb Civic Forum, supporters of the multi-ethnic Bosnian government. Among the delegation was General Jovan Divjak, deputy Commander in Chief of the Bosnian army. The Civic Forum made it abundantly clear that war criminals like Karadzic and Mladic do not represent all Bosnian Serbs.

Many people joined the picket in Whitehall, who were not members of the original four organisa-

tions, so we decided to carry on as a new organisation in support of multi-cultural, multi-ethnic life in Bosnia.

We have continued to meet (every week at first, now once a fortnight) since the fall of Srebrenica because we recognised that Dayton was not a solution to the conflict but a reward to Serbian nationalists for ethnic cleansing and a means of legitimising it.

We decided we would campaign for three basic principles to assist the struggle for multi-cultural life: justice over the war crimes, for the right of all Bosnian refugees to return to their homes, and for the reconstruction of Bosnia.

We have continued to meet, demonstrate, hold public meetings, raise money and distribute a newsletter to further these aims.

BRONWEN HANDYSIDE

PICKET NEWS

No 1; 20p. Bosnia Solidarity Campaign, ADBH, 12 Flitcroft St., London, WC2H 8DJ. tel: 0171 240-7992

FLYING START FOR 24HR. NON-STOP PICKET

GENOCIDE in Srebrenica has shocked and saddened millions of people throughout the world. The heroic stand by the inhabitants and displaced people holding out in Zepa, refusing to hand over their menfolk to the Chetniks has both inspired and shamed millions. The aggressors are armed to the teeth and these people have been denied arms by the so-called 'international community'.

Over the past three years we have watched representatives of the Big Powers preside over 'negotiations' which were really a method of pressurising Bosnia-Herzegovina into accepting the break-up of their multi-ethnic sovereign state.

On 21 July, while thousands of men, women and children faced and experienced genocide the London Conference was a 'green light' for further Bosnian Serb aggression.

But this so-called 'international community' does not represent the millions of ordinary citizens who really do say and really do mean that they will not stand by and let fascism triumph in Bosnia.

Four organisations came together to hold the 22 July march and rally in central London: the Alliance to Defend Bosnia Herzegovina, Workers Aid for Bosnia, Mulsim Solidarity Committee, Jewish Socialist Group. Thousands of people responded and hundreds more are blocking our telephone lines to tell us that they want to act to defend multi-ethnic Bosnia-Herzegovina against genocide and demand that the arms embargo be lifted so that the people can defend themselves.

In response to this demand these four organisations campaign as BOSNIA SOLIDARITY CAMPAIGN - please join us - and to take part with us on the picket in Whitehall, on the 6 August march and rally (see advert below and on back page). Please take this bulletin, leaflets and petitons far and wide to meet up with all those like-minded people who want to do something to stop the genocide and ensure that the legitimate government of multi-ethnic Bosnia is not defeated.

SUNDAY 6th AUGUST: BOSNIA SOLIDARITY CAMPAIGN INVITES YOU TO MARCH FROM HYDE PARK (MARBLE ARCH) ASSEMBLE 2.00 p.m. TO RALLY IN TRAFALGAR SQUARE BREAK THE ARMS EMBARGO - LET THE BOSNIANS DEFEND THEMSELVES

Rush hour at the picket

2.9.95

Sarajevo Slaughter

The United Nations was clutching at its tattered reputation todayafter Serb nationalists mortar bombed a marketplace in Sarajevo, killing thirty-seven people and wounding eighty-eight. Several children were among the victims.

The shell was no stray shot, but part of a barrage aimed at the Trznica market area from Serb held positions. Serb forces are the only ones with the type of ordinance used. Nevertheless, the UN forces' response was to send soldiers out studying the shell craters to ascertain where the shells came from.

They were still deliberating as shells hit the Koseva hospital where the wounded had been taken and continued shelling took the lives of more children.

Recollections of the picket – 2

" I had been involved in past anti-racist campaigns in Britain, and what was happening in Bosnia seemed a nightmare come true. Then I heard about Workers Aid – a campaign that combined practical distribution of aid with a clear and principled political analysis. This seemed a different sort of campaign from the posturing that often poses as politics in Britain.

The picket soon became the focus of our work in the Bosnia Solidarity Campaign. I remember the warm feelings of solidarity that came from collecting signatures and donations from people from all over the world, tinged with sadness as I realised how many homeless and disturbed people wander the streets of London at night.

Did the picket make a difference? I believe that it helped in many ways. The frustration and anger of Bosnians in Britain at the complicity of the British government could be expressed directly – right opposite Downing Street. British politicians soon became aware of our existence. British and Bosnian people, along with many others from around the world, were campaigning continuously at the heart of government in Whitehall to ensure that the politicians could not ignore or forget our anger. Robin Cook acknowledged our picket in passing, but will he and a Labour government make a difference? We will see. "

DAVE LAWRENCE

When the union convoy returned to Britain, the Bosnia Solidarity Campaign non-stop picket was continuing opposite Downing Street, bringing new people into activity. Other protests were being made across the world. Workers Aid was invited to speak at Srebrenica protest rallies in Bradford and Teeside, where local solidarity campaigns had sprung up. The main organiser in Teeside was a UNISON member from the Asian community. She told a meeting that after Srebrenica she felt she had to do something to show her solidarity with multi-cultural society. The leaders of UNISON and other unions remained as silent about the massacre as they had about the whole war, but how many union members felt as the Teeside woman did? Probably thousands.

Naseem Akhtar, Teeside Bosnia Solidarity Campaign organiser, prepares for a fund raising parachute jump

Kalesija Trade Union Committee	October 25th, 1995

Dear Workers Aid,

First of all I would like to express my gratitude for the aid sent to Kalesija, we appreciate it, not only because of the aid but because the truth about Kalesija and its people was heard in Britain.

I would like to express my admiration to all those who brought the convoy headed by Mr Geoff Robinson in spite of different tortures. I express them my gratitude and apologise for everything they suffered just to bring the aid to us.

Now I would like to write some words to Mrs. Marica Croft as well as her two daughters Sarah and Claire. I have no words to express my gratitude for the aid they brought to Kalesija. They were impressed by the farm and with nice landscapes and with people who they saw and met. I would like to pass them love from me and all people who received the aid.

In this occasion I would like to say that all aid aimed for Kalesija was not received since the truck which left for Gracanica had some aid for Kalesija as well. The whole lot was presumably unloaded in Gracanica. I think it should not be done that way. I had big problems therefore. The reason that I write you with such a long delay is that I was seriously ill, now I am all right.

Concerning the general situation it is peaceful only sometimes Chetniks in the mountains fire the rifles, but it is not so dangerous. We all are looking at the talks in the USA with great anxiety. We hope that Bosnia will not be divided since the people who stayed here fighting for its unity and democracy will not allow it.

SENADA SEHANOVIC, President

Bradford demonstration

We hoped that the 'Day of Demonstrations', proposed by the Bosnian unions for October 22nd, would give people like the UNISON steward the opportunity to make their own organisations take a stand for the first time.

When we left Tuzla, Sulejman Hrle, the Bosnian TU Federation President promised that he would return to Sarajevo and fax the appeal for the Day of Demonstrations to the various European TU Federations. We made arrangements for him to visit Britain in September, at the time of the TUC conference.

While we waited for his fax another convoy was being organised. We had never had two convoys in such close succession but a number of trade unionists who met the Tuzla delegation and wanted to help had been unable to go with the August convoy. Lorries from the CWU, the Municipal and General Workers' Union in Consett (Derwentside), Bradford Bosnia Solidarity Campaign, whose group included a Labour Party Councillor and grandmother, as well as several from Workers Aid and Muslim organisations set off in September.

It had always been a problem that our convoys went only to Tuzla. It appeared we were concerned with the fate of one town rather than the whole of Bosnia. We had previously planned to send lorries to Hrasnica, near Sarajevo, but our limited strength made it impossible to open up a new 'front'

Now we were able to send lorries and union representatives to several towns, some of which we had visited in August: Kalesija, Lukavac, Srebrenik, Gradacac, Zivinice, Lipnica. We also sent three lorries to Bihac.

The September convoy faced enormous problems. Three of the lorries had just come back from their eighth trip trip and needed major repairs

Chemistry laboratory in a Bihac school, trashed by retreating Serb nationalists

Workers Aid was very active in the North East where a group, including a large number of Bosnians, bought a lorry and collected large amounts of aid. Some of the Bosnians were former inmates of the notorious Chetnik concentration camp at Omarska. A number of their fellow countrymen, likewise 'ethnically cleansed' from their homes, joined the 17th Brigade of the Bosnian Army. Their fearless attacks on Chetnik positions earned them the name of the 'Muslim Jihaders' in the western press. Maggie O'Kane, a *Guardian* journalist, managed to reach the 17th Brigade's camp and found that the 'Muslim Jihaders' were in fact Serb, Croat and Muslim Bosnians, fighting to regain their homes from the Chetniks.

The following poem was written by an ex-shipyard worker who was a leading member of the north-east group.

MAN OF THE 17th

Darkness shrouds you once again,
Creeping shadows across the plain,
Falling shells make bright the night,
Illuminating faces touched by fright.

Tracers reflected in your eyes,
death dealing fireflies,
searching out a deadly path,
searing pain as aftermath.

Barrage of death, will it cease?
Will the daylight bring release?
Thoughts of home flood your brain,
they carry you above the pain.

Omarska camp is your inspiration,
and now you thirst for liberation,
Some day you will sit in the shade,
and never have to be afraid.

Tony Parker
Wallsend People's Centre

repairs, which fortunately were accomplished in record time by Bradford Council workers. Unlike the previous union convoy, this convoy was stopped at every possible border point. At Mostar, all the Asian drivers were arrested and the lorries attacked by stone throwing youths. The convoy had to spend the weekend hiding in a derelict factory. Finally, in Tuzla, it was stuck for two days in the Customs' compound. For thr trade unionists, all of them making their first trip, it was a frustrating experience. The aid was delivered, but the long delays on the way meant that the convoy had to return almost immediately to Britain and most of the members did not have the chance to meet and talk to local Bosnians. Tiredness led to quarrels on most convoys, but the delays and resulting problems caused frictions on this convoy which were out of the ordinary.

Apart from th tension caused by external factors, two new members of Workers Aid constantly criticised and argued with our attitude to aid and the United Nations. They stated that we were using aid to further unstated political objectives, as though these were somehow secret and devious.

Back in Britain the two people wrote a report criticising the convoy's organisation. By itself this wasn't anything new. Many people had come back with criticisms and suggestions. Some were positive, some less so. Too often people thought they had discovered the wheel. For example people would experience the problems of lorries getting separated en-route and criticise us for not having two-way radios, like the UN convoys. We explained that everyone had recognised this from the very first convoy. The problem, as with most things, was lack of money. This present report, however, contained something quite new and startling – allegations that we were involved in smuggling children out of Bosnia, with the innuendo of sexual abuse. They sent this report to the trade unions.

We immediately asked Professor Adrian Hastings, from the Theology Department of Leeds University, to investigate the allegations. Although his report completely exonerated Workers Aid, there must have been smiles on the faces of the union bureaucrats who had opposed our work but who, until now, had been unable to justify this opposition to their members.

Within the Communications Workers' Union, and other unions, there were people who had come to the defence of multi-cultural Bosnia, others who supported the 'humanitarian' side of convoys whilst understanding little about the war, and finally people who flatly opposed the growth of workers' solidarity. Our work with the Tuzla unionists had begun to strengthen one end of this spectrum. The allegations against Workers Aid helped tip the scales the other way.

11th Convoy Factfile

DATE:
September 1995

LORRIES:
8 from UK, including lorries from GMB Derwentside, CWU, Muslim Aid in Leicester and Blackburn, Bradford Bosnia Solidarity, and Workers Aid from Newcastle, Manchester, Brighton, Exeter and Devon

WEIGHT: 40 tons

RECIPIENTS:
Community of Trzacka, near Bihac, Trade Union committees in Gradacac, Kalesija, Lukavac, Banovici, Zivinice and Srebrenik

PEOPLE: 22

---

10 Nothing in the Brighton report appears to provide any reliable ground for major criticisms of WAB. It is strange that it should have been written and circulated without any prior consultation with anyone in WAB. There were meetings and opportunities on the convoy to raise these issues but I am assured by different participants that at no point did the writers of the report do so, at least in public. One can hardly refrain from asking what motivation there was behind subsequently producing the report.

In conclusion it appears to me to be the case that WAB has nothing to hide and no serious charges to answer. Hitherto it has done a very difficult job rather successfully and it fully deserves continued support.

Professor Adrian Hastings
Leeds
14 December 1995

The CWU broke off collaboration with us. The momentum of their contact with Tuzla carried on for a while. They independently organised several more convoys of aid to their fellow communication workers in Tuzla but the whole operation became separated from a political campaign of support for a united Bosnia. The question of the arms embargo and British government policy, raised in Tuzla by their members, never saw the light of day in the union.

Afternoon mayhem

" When we return to the compound I am totally taken aback by the mood of the convoy. After the long delays and frustrations at other borders the final straw is obviously being stuck in the Tuzla Customs. All the problems of whom to trust and the black markets have come to a head. There is a general suspicion of the customs, the Tuzla Trades Unions, Workers Aid and me. Some people think that they are being kept in the compound to be squeezed for money or aid. Then the customs come round to inspect us at about 3.30pm. There are four inspectors, a couple of our translators, several wagons being inspected at the same time and large numbers of other people from the surrounding Trades Unions and affiliated organisations who are arriving to try and make contact with the wagons that are delivering aid to their area. Complete chaos is brought to a head when the food inspector looks in the back of the convoy kitchen wagon and finds out-of-date food which is for our journey home. He is not willing to clear the convoy until every van has been unloaded. It is too late in the day to do this so now we face another day in the compound. I return to Jeki's pretty fed up. Jeki is unloading the winter wood supply and is obviously relieved to have got a dangerous task out of the way. Talking to the family about conditions in Bosnia begins to put things in perspective. I also get a phone call from Bob Myers. He explains that on the last convoy a French vehicle had out-of-date baby food which is maybe the reason the food inspector is being so obstinate. This seems reasonable and at least I know what the problem was today. "

GEOFF ROBINSON

The Bihac no-fly zone

" Friday. Within seconds of getting out of the wagon in Bihac an air-raid siren went off, there was the sound of a plane and three loud explosions. All this happened within thirty seconds. The ground shook. I asked myself: what happened to the ceasefire and the so-called no-fly zone?

We found that the doctor whose signature was required to clear the aid and remove the seals on the wagons to allow distribution had left at 4.30 pm. He was not going to return until Monday. In future we should arrive by Thursday at the latest.

Having checked with the Bihac Logistic Centre, the convoy decided, on hearing of the plight of the people of Trzacka in Cazin, to take the aid there. We were the first convoy that the village had received.

Up to two months ago the Cazin area was totally surrounded and no food reached the people for a period of fifty weeks. The population nearly starved. We heard reports of three year old children who weighed only fourteen pounds at death.

Trzacka has been so devastated from being on the front line that the houses have no roofs, and plastic and wood board up the windows.

When Chetnik forces occupied the area they trashed people's homes before being pushed back by the Bosnia-Herzegovina/Croatia military alliance.

I was taken to the house of Irfat Rekic (a refugee in Britain), which is in a prominent position on a hill. It must have been used as an HQ by the Chetniks because the roof was intact.

Trenches and fox-holes had been dug across his back garden and neighbouring properties. From these positions snipers could aim at farmers working in the fields.

We found the village community to be very honest and sharing with each other. When we offered food from drivers' packs to individuals they refused saying they would wait until it was shared out properly by the Logistic Centre. "

DAVE MCKENZIE (Wallsend People's Centre)

A book in one hand, a gun in the other

" An appeal for books and all relevant literature was made to us at Tuzla University.

The lecturers and students have kept the University functioning under the most extreme conditions. Not only do they not have enough to eat, both students and lecturers alternate their studies with postings to the front line where they fight the Serbian fascists. An armed soldier in full battle dress was introduced to us as the Dean of Philosophy!

The whole town is extremely proud of the University. It is based on the industries which have been the mainstay of the town for generations, in particular the mines. Out of the seven faculties, four are technical but all need text books.

Sabid Zekan, international secretary of the students union said:

"All of the male students are soldiers. We spend one month at our studies and one month at the front line.The Chetniks destroyed my house, and my family had to flee to Zenica. I study my books in the mountains, and in my other hand I hold a gun.

In my faculty we have Serbian, Croatian and Muslim students. My home was destroyed by the Serbs – but the Serbs in Bosnia are occupied too. They hate the war as well, I know it. My friends in western Bosnia are Serbian, they were at school with me, they write to me, and they hate the war."

Zekan ended by saying, "I am sure the students of Europe will help us."

Part of the Workers Aid delegation which visited the University were Spanish and Catalan. The University principal told them that the students' social club was named after a citizen of Tuzla, Zvonko Ceric, who was killed fighting the fascists in Spain in the 1930s. "

PAUL HENDERSON, Leicester University

In the weeks following the convoy and its aftermath it was possible to feel the support from the unions slipping away. It seemed to start with the child smuggling allegations. Soon it became clear that this was not the real cause. In other circumstances the lies could have been pushed aside. They flourished because other events, on a much bigger scale, were making themselves felt.

The proposal for the 'Day of Demonstrations' never emerged from Sarajevo. We made many calls to Sulejman Hrle's office but got no clear answer. Two days before he was due to fly to Britain his secretary called to say he could not come.

We had closely watched the Bosnian offensive and the change in popular opinion outside the country. Other people in high places, however, also noted these things and took them as warning signs. Our human resources were small and our energy was so focussed on the task of helping the defenders of multi-culturalism break out of their isolation, that we had been unable to pay sufficient attention to the activities of world diplomacy, the greatest enemy. We only belatedly began to see what connected separate military events.

The little grey mouse

" It took me fourteen months of hard thinking before I finally decided to go to Bosnia. It was only when I'd decided that I might be of some use that I made up my mind. Like anyone else in Britain I had watched the news, and thought it best to leave wars to those in high places; but then I decided to intervene personally, as it became clear that those with the power were not prepared to use it.

I joined a team of people helping restore some houses. My first night in Bosnia was spent in the tiny home of a family in the village of Ostrozac, near Jablanica. Four women and five children in a 'house' the size of a well made shed. Being

Bosnian they offered everything they'd got. I didn't understand much of the conversation, but I did catch the word 'misha' – 'little grey mouse'. Our PM, John Misha. It turned out that all the men in this family were dead. All the women were underweight. Their TV was showing a dubbed film of Captain America engaged in battle with Nazis. It seemed a touching naivete. The little grey mouse had failed them, but maybe our super-hero, super-power would step in to help. When we left it was raining. We walked in silence, mainly because I was speechless with rage. I never felt so angry, frustrated in my whole life. I stood outside the house we were re-building for over an hour, stamping around in the rain.

Later I saw a Workers Aid convoy driving past.

Back in Britain I got in contact with them and went on their next convoy.

I drove us all into the wrong crossing point (Bob reckons) at Mostar and subsequently got all our Asian members arrested; apparently they were all Mujihadeen and we were all criminals and gun runners. There was a Swedish policeman nearby, who arranged for EU officers to find our friends, whilst I and a Swiss lady went to the police station. At the station we found all of our crew in a spare room sat behind desks. Now and again excitable HVO policemen would crowd around the door to see the Muslim fanatics. I doubt if they could work out why there were two pushy redheads sat there too. "

PHIL O'CONNELL

The UN abandonment of Srebrenica was the first indication of a secret deal. Croatian President Tudjman and Serbia's President Milosevic had always hoped to carve up Bosnia-Herzegovina between them – of course both wanting the lion's share and each backed by different super-powers. After three years they were stuck in a war they could not finish. Moreover, resistance to their plans might not only turn the tables in Bosnia – it could politically destabilise their regimes in Serbia and Croatia. Military defeats would weaken their use of nationalist flag waving to suppress mass discontent at home over poverty and unemployment.

Western politicians had seen the dangers for the restoration of the 'free market' if workers in Bosnia managed to cling on to their unity and turn the tide against nationalism. On top of this there was now the danger that people across the world were starting to question western policy and the myth of UN neutrality. The war had to be stopped before everything the nationalists had achieved in Bosnia started to unravel.

It is now known that early in 1995 the US, taking the diplomatic initiative away from the European powers, sent envoys to talk with the Croatian and Serbian leaders. If they would settle for less than they had hoped and tolerate the survival of a small rump 'Muslim' state, the US would use its power and influence to sell a three way partition to Bosnian Muslim leaders.

US envoys told the Bosnian leaders they could never win the war. The slaughter of Muslims would continue. If they accepted a deal Muslims would have a state which the US would arm and help protect. There were signs that some people amongst the Bosnian Government could be pressurised to accept. Bosnian Prime Minister, Haris Silajdzic, resigned when he saw others moving away from their defence of a united, multi-cultural Bosnia.

All that was left to be done to make a deal possible was to move all the people still living in the wrong places. This could never be achieved by negotiations. No politician could sign away sections of 'their' people and survive. Removals had to be presented as a fait accompli. Srebrenica was inside 'Greater Serbia' and so its' Muslims had to go. The UN handed them over to the 'ethnic cleansers'. The massacre was not the result of UN weakness, incompetence or indifference, it was their coldly calculated plan.

The Croatian army's 'heroic' recapture of Serbian occupied Slavonija and Krajina was secretly agreed in advance between Belgrade and Zagreb. The Croat troops met little resistance. Belgrade had withdrawn its army commanders. Thousands of Croatian Serbs were driven from their homes. The Greater Serb politicians and commanders had invaded Croatia in 1992 claiming they were defending these people. Now they abandoned them – Serb victims of both Serb and Croat nationalism.

Militant *is a left-wing group that remained neutral over the Bosnian 'civil war'. This letter published in their newspaper was from one of their members who went on a Workers Aid convoy.*

Dear Comrades,

I must take issue with *Militant's* position on Bosnia as expressed in Judy Beishon's article. It makes some very useful observations, but doesn't put forward a clear position, in particular dodging the question of whether to support Bosnia against Serb and Croat nationalists. The article does say *Militant* is opposed to UN intervention and supports 'workers self-defence'. Well, in central Bosnia, particularly in Sarajevo and Tuzla, there is a mass movement for workers' defence of multi-ethnic communities.

Yet *Militant* has consistently failed to openly declare its support because (God forbid!) it would mean taking sides in the war.

Undoubtedly, the Muslim leaders of the ruling SDA party have quite different aims from this mass movement, namely a Muslim dominated if not fundamentalist state, but this is no more a reason for neutrality than it would have been in the Spanish Civil War.

For as long as this mass movement – in defence of a multi-ethnic Bosnia – exists, then the SDA's nationalist ambitions won't get very far.

Just because the workers' brigades in Tuzla don't call themselves 'Marxist' and 'the forces of Marxism are weak', doesn't mean that we shouldn't support their fight.

In their own terms, they are fighting for workers' unity against nationalism – isn't that what we want?

This sort of easy opting for neutrality, as in Northern Ireland, only ends up repeating a left-wing version of imperialism's arguments – that the war is simply one between three groups of psychopaths determined to kill each other.

MARCUS SEAL

This negotiated 'end game' forced on its planners by the Bosnian resistance, was not yet clear to us or to the world at large. What Bosnian soldiers saw was the collapse of Chetnik occupied areas in Croatia. It gave them great encouragement and their soaring morale was in sharp contrast to the dispirited Karadzic forces, many of whom had no faith in the plan for an 'ethnically pure' Greater Serbia. The Bosnian offensive against Chetnik forces in western Bosnia may have been part of the plan but it quickly threatened to go beyond any deal agreed in secret. Milosevic had certainly not volunteered to relinquish control over Banja Luka, from where he controlled large parts of Bosnia. Now BiH troops prepared to take the town. Could the secret deals stop the Bosnian fight back?

The first signs of the US's successful negotiations with leaders of the Muslim SDA, the Bosnian ruling party, came on September 8th. The Foreign Ministers of Croatia, Serbia and Bosnia signed an accord in which, for the first time, the Bosnian leaders accepted the occupying forces would remain in Bosnia.

Bosnian soldiers were then ordered by the government to stop their advance towards Banja Luka to allow international negotiations. Bosnian army commanders reacted in fury. What had 'international negotiations' ever done to help Bosnia? The Chetniks were on the run. The Bosnian forces could take Banja Luka and free all of western Bosnia. They knew that the superpowers only pressed for a cease-fire because the Bosnian army was winning the war. Despite these angry exchanges the advance was halted.

The 'Peace Plans' for ethnic partition

October, 1991 – The Carrington Plan Whilst recommending a loose association or alliance of 'sovereign or independent republics', the Carrington Plan takes the first steps towards Bosnian partition by accepting that Bosnian Serbs should have their own government, administrative structure, police and judiciary. Rejected by Milosevic.

December, 1991 – The Vance Plan Calls for the setting up of three United Nations Protection Areas (UNPAs) and the deployment of UN troops to in effect freeze the existing front lines in Croatia and so leave the ethnically cleansed areas of Croatia (the Krajina and Eastern Slavonija) in the hands of Serb nationalists. Implemented in February 1992.

February, 1992 – The Lisbon Agreement Whilst formally preserving Bosnia-Herzegovina as a unitary state, introduces for the first time a plan for the country's ethnic 'cantonisation'. After Izetbegovic initially accepts the plan, it is rejected by the Bosnian government.

January, 1993 – The Vance-Owen Plan Whilst again formally recognising Bosnia's existing borders, Vance-Owen proposes the partition of the country into ten, ethnically defined provinces. Rejected by the Bosnian Serb nationalists.

May, 1993 – The Joint Action Plan Put forward by the US, Russia, France, the UK and Spain, the plan reinforces the 'ethnically cleansed' areas by proposing the deployment of further UN troops along their borders as well as the creation of six Bosnian 'Safe Areas'. It also formulates, in embryo, the next stage of the 'peace' talks: the three-way partition of Bosnia.

August, 1993 – The Owen-Stoltenberg Plan Proposes the three-way ethnic partition of Bosnia-Herzegovina: Serb (53%), Muslim (30%) and Croat (17%). Rejected by Itezbegovic government.

February, 1994 – The Washington Accords Establish a federation between Bosnia and the Bosnian Croat nationalists. Although this agreement takes the Bosnian Croat nationalists out of the war and thus allows the Bosnian Army to concentrate on its' battle with the Serb nationalists, it too is based on the idea of ethnically based cantons.

July, 1994 – The Contact Group Plan The 'Contact Group' (Russia, the US, Britain, France and Germany) propose the ethnic partition of Bosnia between Muslim-Croat federation (52%) and Serbs (48%). Despite, like the previous plans, consolidating Chetnik military gains and rewarding their 'ethnic cleansing', the Bosnian Serb nationalists reject the plan.

September, 1995 - The Dayton Agreement The tide turns. Serb nationalist forces in the Croatian Krajina and Central Bosnia are defeated. Bosnian forces threaten to re-take Banja Luka, the Serb nationalists' only Bosnian city. The US government intervenes quickly. Bosnia-Herzegovina is partitioned in all but name at the Dayton Airforce base, Ohio.

FOOTNOTE:

At no time did any of the great powers ever express support for the right of the Bosnian government – the government of an independent country recognised by the UN – to expel the invading Serbian and Croat forces and to exercise its' control over its' own territory, in accordance with the multi-ethnic constitution voted for by the majority of Bosnian people in a referendum in 1992.

The Socialist Workers Party (SWP) was the main force involved in establishing the Anti-Nazi League, which organised many protests against fascist attacks in Britain. However, they organised no such protests against ethnic cleansing in Bosnia. An ex-miner from Durham wrote to them.

Dear Comrades,

Your article in *Socialist Worker* argues that it is impossible for workers here to take sides in the Bosnian war or advance any anti-fascist position. According to you Serbs, Croats and Muslims are all in the grip of nationalism, all equally prepared to commit atrocities, all equally misguided.

The workers of ex-Yugoslavia are not stupid. On the eve of the war in Bosnia tens of thousands of workers, with the Tuzla miners at their head, marched on the Sarajevo parliament to denounce the nationalist politicians. This protest was broken up by Serb nationalist snipers. Did that working class opposition to nationalism just vanish? Your article doesn't give any hint that it ever existed or of the huge protests of workers against Milosevic in Serbia. If the communities are all in the grip of nationalism how do you explain that in Sarajevo – after three years of siege and murder – there are as many mixed marriages taking place as before the war? Like David Owen, you describe an ethnic war. But this is a complete distortion.

Take the mining town of Tuzla, for example. There are Bosnian Serbs in both the attacking and the defending forces. In Tuzla there are still thousands of Serbs who refuse to leave. Why don't you mention them? Their existence makes a nonsense of the popular myth that this is an 'ethnic' war. Tuzla is not being attacked by Serbs. It is under attack from Serbian nationalists. The miners in Tuzla are Croats, Serbs, Muslims, Hungarians and many who before the war would have simply described themselves às Yugoslavs.

They have maintained the front lines around Tuzla. What are they defending? What are the Serbian miners in Tuzla defending? Surely it is the right of all workers to live together.

Your article implies that the Bosnian Serbs in the nationalist forces have their rights and grievances. I heard this argument during our 1984-85 strike. The Tory government were able to organise a section of the miners to scab. The media, the Tories, Labour politicians and union leaders all discovered the rights of the working miners – their right to work. As good democrats they conceded our right to strike but when we went to picket we were violating the scabs right to work. Whose side were you on in that situation? The strikers or the scabs?

Now, in Tuzla or Sarajevo, whose side are you on? The Serbian nationalists, who are fighting to divide communities along cultural lines (ie divide the working class), or on the side of those, including Serbs, remaining inside the besieged towns to defend the right of all people to live side by side? You must answer this question. It is no use throwing up a smokescreen about Muslim nationalists in the Bosnian Government. Nor is it acceptable to start counting how many people in the communities still support multi-ethnic Bosnia. As long as there are people in Sarajevo, Tuzla and elsewhere, including Belgrade, standing up for an undivided Bosnia they should be supported by our workers' movement and by you. If the National Front here attacks a Muslim do you refuse to protest because some Muslim leaders are Tories?

Despite your opposition to UN intervention your analysis echoes the UN's. You describe communities totally caught up in nationalism. The only difference is that the UN uses this false description to justify their imperialist intervention to divide 'the warring factions', while you use it to justify working class silence. But working class 'neutrality' – that is the refusal to oppose the for-

eign policy of the Tory Government and their spokesman, David Owen – allows the UN to divide the working class in the Balkans.

Your article ends up saying the way forward is for workers to unite. But these are just empty words. The workers in Tuzla are united – against nationalists and fascists, and you refuse to support them. What could the unity that you call for look like, other than what exists now in Tuzla? If the working class of Europe cannot act now to defend this existing unity what chance is there of moving to some wider unity across the region?

In the miners' strike we wanted unity of all miners. But what unity? Unity of scabs or unity of strikers? There was no other possible unity. Working class unity could only be won by the scabs joining the strike. Was our picketing of scab pits fighting for unity or disunity? In Bosnia the working class is under attack. There cannot be an abstract unity on some airy-fairy principle which ignores the present war. Unity can only be on the basis of the defence of the right of all the people of BiH to live and work together – a way of life that was won by the Partisans in their fight against fascism. The only other basis for unity is unity with the nationalist aggressors.

Victory for the nationalists' policy of division, supported by the UN and Major, will strengthen the forces of racism across the continent. We are all under attack in Bosnia and to refuse to take sides is to open the door to disaster for our class.

Miners and other workers in Britain are now preparing to take mining equipment and food to Tuzla miners. We are taking sides. This is what fighting fascism means. I ask you to support this work and propose that you send representatives with this convoy to talk to the workers in Tuzla and actually find out what is happening.

DAVE TEMPLE

FOOTNOTE: There was no reply to this letter.

Alongside the secret negotiations, US diplomats went on a publicity offensive to prepare the ground for a deal. After the Srebrenica massacre they called, with breathtaking hypocrisy, for stiffer UN action against the Serbian nationalists. Stern warnings were given that no other 'safe havens' would be surrendered. With a huge fanfare of publicity and media attention, US planes bombed Chetnik positions in Bosnia.

Once again the raids caused little damage on the ground. Despite having 'smart' bombs, every one that was dropped on a Chetnik airfield missed the runway. However, to people who had lost patience with the UN after Srebrenica, it did seem that at last something was being done to stop the slaughter. Bombing raids, top level negotiations, condemnations of the nationalists, US criticism of European leaders' weakness – it seemed that the US had forced the west to act.

Sulejman Hrle's failure to call the Day of Demonstrations was almost certainly because in government circles in Sarajevo it was being said that at last the superpowers were intervening. The proposed demonstrations in Britain and elsewhere might hinder this change.

So the shift in attitudes inside the CWU came in the midst of a wider shift in public mood. Peace was now within reach. There must be no more talk of war or victories. Everything must be settled by negotiations. Leave it to the politicians.

In November, the US took the leaders of Bosnia, Serbia and Croatia to an air force base in Dayton, Ohio and demanded they accept the US peace plan. They all had to be forced to give up something – but only the Bosnians had to give up their country. After days of secret talks and arm twisting, a deal was done. In order to sell it in Bosnia and to hide western support for ethnic division, the opening sentences of the agreement made an abstract recognition of Bosnia-Herzegovina as a single country and promised its re-unification. The rest of the deal went straight on to legitimise the territorial conquests of the 'ethnic cleansers', preparing the way for their annexation into Serbia and Croatia.

Serb Civic Council, Sarajevo.

Sir,

The Serb Civic Council represent the Serbs of the territories controlled by the legal authority of the Republic of Bosnia-Herzegovina. We are convinced that we express the interests of the majority of the Serb population, both within Bosnia-Herzegovina and refugees abroad. We are members of different political parties, but many of us hold positions in the Bosnian government. We come from different parts of Bosnia, including Sarajevo, Tuzla and Zenica. We are convinced that at this critical moment it is essential to point out that Radovan Karadzic and Ratko Mladic cannot be given the right to represent the Bosnian Serb point of view.

It is as much in the interests of Serbs as anyone else to maintain a unified Republic of Bosnia-Herzegovina. We are fully committed to pluralist democracy and the equality of all peoples. We are particularly opposed to any division of Bosnia and above all one based on ethnic principles. We request that the Serb Civic Council be included as representative of the Bosnian Serb community in the peace negotiations.

Yours,

Mirko Pejanovic (member of the State Presidency of Bosnia-Herzegovina), Tatjana Ljujic-Mijatovic (BiH ambassador to the UN in Geneva), Zarko Bulic (President of the BiH Bar Association), Gen. Jovan Divjak (Deputy Chief of Staff, Army of Bosnia-Herzegovina), Mico Rakic (former Ambassador of Yugoslavia to the United States), Vojka Djikic, Milojka Hadziabdic, Mirjana Hadzikaric, Nenad Jovanovic, Dragoljub Stojanov and Marko Vesovic.

Edited version of letter published in **The Guardian,** *September 12th, 1995*

Croat People's Council of Bosnia-Herzegovina

Sir,

The September 8th 'Accord on Principles for Bosnia-Herzegovina' which was agreed between the foreign ministers of Bosnia-Herzegovina, Croatia and the so-called Yugoslavia, in a politically scandalous and morally unacceptable manner rewards the aggression by Belgrade and Pale against our country, and accepts the results of the expulsions, 'ethnic cleansing', crimes and genocide inflicted upon our country, confirming the 'entity' created by such means – the 'Republic Srbska'.

We once more warn of the invalidity of all such ethnic-territorial divisions of Bosnia-Herzegovina. Based upon the recognition of force and crimes, such 'solutions' inevitably lead in the direction of new cycles of chaos, blood, violence and war, and the definitive disappearance of the state of Bosnia-Herzegovina.

Yours,

Stjepan Kljuic (Member of the State Presidency of Bosnia-Herzegovina, Vice-President of the Croat People's Council of Bosnia-Herzegovina), Ivo Komsic (Member of the State Presidency of Bosnia-Herzegovina), Ivan Lovrenovic.

Edited version of a letter published in **The Guardian,** *September 19th, 1995*

Workers' Aid resolution on the Dayton peace deal (extract)

After three years of refusing to defend the victims of aggression, the US and UN politicians are now imposing a 'peace' which endorses 'ethnic cleansing'.

The present peace deal is aimed at advancing US influence in the region by supporting different nationalist politicians and using them to divide and control the population. Sixty thousand NATO troops will pour into Bosnia to protect the hold of nationalist politicians and war lords over their various territories.

Any Bosnian who now tries to continue the struggle to reunify the country and restore its multi-cultural way of life will be attacked by NATO forces. Their guns are not aimed at the Chetniks. The Serbian regime has got what it wanted. Once Milosevic has whipped the Bosnian Serb nationalist leaders into line, Belgrade controls half of Bosnia.

Resistance to the division of Bosnia by the majority of its people prevented the outright victory of the nationalists. Indeed, that resistance was turning the tide of the war. The timing of the present US intervention had more to do with the collapse of morale in the Chetnik army and the possibility of its defeat, than with a search for peace.

The determination not to accept the destruction of Bosnian society destroyed all the previous UN 'peace' plans that openly recognised the nationalist's conquests as permanent.

This resistance to division is acknowledged in the present deal. It recognises the prewar boundaries and calls for the election of a single government for the whole of Bosnia-Herzegovina. It forbids the annexation of parts of the country. But united multi-cultural Bosnia cannot be rebuilt while most of its regions are under the control of nationalist forces who have carried out genocide. The recognition of a united Bosnia is meaningless unless it is made clear how the nationalist forces are going to be destroyed.

The peace plan does the opposite. Fifty percent of the country will remain under the control of Belgrade. Other areas are under Croatian rule.

The peace plan protects and perpetuates nationalist influence. They can continue their tyranny over people, whipping up racist fervour against Muslims.

Rape committed in Dayton, birth expected in Bosnia (from *Front Slobode*)

The plan endorses the right of return for the millions of refugees, but who will return home while the influence of the nationalist murderers continues? Even as Clinton was announcing the 'peace', people were still being driven from their homes or killed. European governments are preparing to force over a million refugees to return to Bosnia despite the fact that many of them will be in danger if they return to their homes.

The peace plan calls for prosecution of war criminals, but will the real criminals be prosecuted? Milosevic, chief architect of the war, is now the 'great diplomat'. Tudjman, who presided over the murder of east Mostar, is another 'great statesman'. What about the UN military and political leaders who handed over Srebrenica? Will any of these people who have played a part in genocide ever be indicted in court as war criminals?

The only basis for peace is a united, multi-cultural Bosnia brought about by the defeat and destruction of nationalist forces and their ideology of 'ethnically pure' states.

Such a victory is possible.

The Chetniks only managed to inflict defeats because the Bosnian people were left to defend a united society alone.

The US and the Great Powers are only able to impose this deal because the Bosnian people are without powerful allies. They have been denied weapons, blockaded and starved. They have gone without a friend to the treacherous tables of international diplomacy.

Where are the mass demonstrations in the capitals of Europe that opposed apartheid rule in South Africa?

Multi-cultural Bosnia is being strangled because the people of Europe – above all its' labour movement, its' trade unions, socialist parties, anti-fascist groups – have not yet come to its' defence.

People now ask the question: 'Will the peace hold?' This is the wrong question. What should be asked is: 'Are we prepared to accept this consolidation of ethnic division? Are we prepared to allow our governments to send their armed forces to protect the division lines created by barbarism?'

Take the side of an undivided Bosnia-Herzegovina!

Speak out against an unjust peace!

Speak out against your governments and let all those Bosnians who refuse to accept this shameful 'peace' know that they have allies.

November 24th, 1995

12th
Convoy Factfile

DATE:
December 1995

LORRIES:
2 from Spain
7 from UK including
Workers Aid from
Edinburgh, Manchester,
Newcastle, Liverpool
Leicester and Muslim Aid
from Rochdale and
Blackburn

WEIGHT: 45 tons

RECIPIENTS:
Schools and hospital in
Cazin, near Bihac, TU
District Committees in
Gradacac, Kalesija, the
Tuzla Miners Union and
Public Sector workers in
Tuzla Town Hall

PEOPLE: 20

War criminal Mladic enjoys a drink with Dutch-Bat commander, Karremans.

I suspect a fraud

The big imperial policeman, NATO, headed by the biggest imperial power, the USA, descended, with a military force not seen before, on the small and unlucky country of Bosnia.

According to the Dayton 'peace', in the next year these multinational forces should implement peace in the former multi-cultural, multi-ethnic and multi-national Bosnia-Herzegovina. The international community will teach us how to live together again. It seems that 200,000 Muslims have been slaughtered to give the international community the chance to say, "A big tragedy has happened!"

If it had not been for the Bosnia-Herzegovina army and our stubbornness things could well have gone the other way. Even with the arms embargo our soldiers could have reached the River Drina. But the world's map creators said, "Stop! It would be too much for you!"

Staring at the dead plum tree in my yard at the bottom of Gradovrh hill, I meditate, "Everything is the same, but you aren't there, Bosnia, a country damned to sleep...."

I suspect a big fraud.

CAZIM SARAJILIC (from FRONT SLOBODE)

While the Dayton negotiations were proceeding and Workers Aid was dealing with the problems of 'child smuggling', the Bosnian Solidarity Campaign in London was broadening its work. The round-the-clock picket received a visit from a Bosnian Serb delegation which included General Jovan Divjak, second in command of the Bosnian army ('Muslim' army according to the press!). This delegation, and a similar Bosnian Croat one, carried the message that Karadzic and other nationalist leaders did not represent Serbs or Croats, as they falsely claimed. The Bosnia Solidarity Campaign also started the first steps towards an enquiry into western governments' complicity in war crimes. The first mass graves were being uncovered and the Dutch Government in particular was having an uncomfortable time trying to silence its soldiers who had witnessed the handing over of Srebrenica and the subsequent massacre.

In January 1996, 60,000 NATO troops poured into Bosnia and replaced the nationalists on the front lines dividing the country. Weeks before this, in December 1995, Workers Aid and Student Aid convoys went to Tuzla and Bihac. For the first time there was no fighting, but Bosnia was still starving. Production was at a standstill. The country was devastated. Ask anyone if they needed aid and they would say, yes. However, the regular team members sensed the convoys lacked the previous sense of purpose. Workers Aid was not set up to simply run convoys. It was formed to help stop the division of Bosnia. People were happy that the fighting had ceased, but this also put an end to a military perspective for overcoming division. Even the bitterest opponents of the unjust peace lacked the stamina to think of resuming the war, except in maybe six months or a year.

B.S.C. protest against Tudjman's attempts at press censorship

In the midst of nationalist aggression, the convoys had been a way to create a spirit of internationalism, of solidarity with multi-cultural Bosnia.. With peace, maybe this was no longer the way to proceed.

A national meeting of Workers Aid was held in January, 1996. We had reports from the December convoy teams and from a November delegation that had gone to a Tuzla conference on the future of multi-cultural society. It was clear from these reports that the question of how to continue the struggle for a united Bosnia after Dayton were not only concerning us. We decided to send a delegation to Tuzla to talk with our collaborators there, to find out how they saw things.

A Bosnian christmas

" Our journey had been meticulously planned to provide every chance of mishap, and it did not disappoint. Take some death-trap lorries, young drivers, pick the coldest time of year and just to be on the safe side, make sure it's a holiday period. It's a wonder we made it to Calais.

Clutches broke, brakes froze, tempers rose and storms blew, but after twelve days and nights we crawled into Tuzla; exhausted, filthy and greatly relieved. Time to unload our cargo into the grateful hands of Tuzla's students. Time to find the student union leader who was eagerly expecting us. Time to find out that no one was expecting us at all.

Eventually the university rector sorted out some room-sharing arrangements, and I got to stay with a student called Nermin and his family. We struggled in English and Bosnian, made do with sign language, and his mother stuffed me with good food. Nermin's mother was a Serb and his father was Muslim, which made him (as he saw it) neither one nor the other. Apart from that, we spoke little of politics.

Over the next four days we had to find a home for the books, foodstuffs and geriatric computers we had brought with us. We split up and made friends. After all, that was half the point. Some of us paid a visit to the cemetery, where all the young people from the May, 1995 mortar blast were buried. I had walked past the explosion site with Nermin, who just said, "It tore the heart out of this town."

We had driven through hundreds of miles of destruction and ruin, both in Croatia and Bosnia, which none of us will forget. In Tuzla, the infrastructure was intact; but everyone had lost friends. Some had lost much more. A couple of young kids on the street turned out to be from Srebrenica; and I met a soldier, nicknamed Rambo, who had escaped the massacre but without his family. He had nothing left, and he knew it.

Before leaving, I exchanged addresses with Nermin. He dictated his to me, finishing proudly with "Republic of Bosnia-Herzegovina." I didn't have the heart to tell him that no such thing existed: it had been signed out of existence at Dayton. His town was now in the Muslim-Croat Federation, and the only place deemed to be a republic was the Serb Republic, which had tried and failed to smash his town and its people. Such are the triumphs of diplomacy. "

DAVID MOSELY

Sussex University Student Aid

" Sussex University Student Aid was set up in the autumn term of 1995 by Alyoscia D'Onofrio who had been a member of Workers Aid. There were about eight active members of the group of differing ages and backgrounds. Some of the members had previous experience of Bosnia (either from working there or from knowing people from the area), while some actually came from Bosnia and had left the country in 1992. In the first meeting we decided to raise money for the lorry and to raise the awareness of students at Sussex about the situation in Bosnia. We organised meetings which covered the beginnings of the war and the role of the international community. We were also paid a visit by one of the professors from Tuzla University where we were hoping to deliver the aid at Christmas. Our attempts at raising money went fairly well, but it was hard work as there was competition from other societies and Bosnia was failing to make the front pages. However, through street collections and a club night we managed to raise enough to fund the journey. Everything was going well until the offer of a free truck fell through. However, a few days before Christmas I received a phone call saying that an extra person was needed on the national Student Aid convoy. So far they had trucks and aid from Leeds, London and Cambridge and a huge donation of packages from Lancaster. We had no truck, but we could donate the money we'd raised....and me. "

KIM WARD

Workers Aid members with Bill Speirs from the Scottish TUC and Tuzla miners' representatives outside their union offices

Rhian and Christine, an Edinburgh HGV driver, campaign for the Christmas convoy

The Workers Aid delegation went to Bosnia in February. For the first time it was possible to travel along the northern route. It was strange to reach Tuzla in five hours from Zagreb rather than the usual three to six days and even three months at the beginning of the war. The forty minute drive inside Bosnia started in Orasje, under Croatian control, past US tanks at a check point, into the 15km under Chetnik control, past more US tanks, and finally into BiH territory. The road was open. There was no more fighting, but this short journey was through a divided Bosnia. Were the NATO forces, positioned along the dividing lines, going to oversee the re-unification of the country, or

behind their guns was division being consolidated and made permanent?

In Tuzla the main meetings were with the miners' union. In the course of the convoys we had found that the Tuzla District union committee, despite the principled outlook of the various union presidents who sat on it, was only a shell. Most of the unions it represented had ceased to function after the war started. Factories closed down and workers had joined the army. The miners union, on the other hand, did speak for the 10,000 miners who had carried on working. The union had also tried to look after the well-being of another 10,000 non-working miners – those who had joined the army or been laid off due to lack of equipment in the mines.

So we went to the miners to discuss the future. We also talked with the Tuzla Civic Forum, a citizens' organisation that worked throughout the war to hold Tuzla's multi-cultural society together.

24.2.96

Hands off Nazi death Camp Memorial

Croatia's President Franjo Tudjman has been warned he'll face legal action if he goes ahead with a plan to turn the memorial centre to Nazi victims at Jasenovac into a memorial for Croatian war dead.

Slavko Goldstajn, editor of the independent magazine *Erasmus*, has written an open letter to Tudjman, warning that he'll file a lawsuit against him. Goldstajn says Croatia's Jewish community strongly opposes the plan.

Some 80,000 people, including 17,000 Jews from Croatia and Bosnia, thousands of Serbs and Gypsies, and many Croat and Muslim resisters, were killed at Jasenovac during World War II.

M92s

" In Zenica we met with journalists working for an independent television station – NTV Zetel. It is committed to an undivided, multi-cultural society and has come into conflict with the local authorities controlled by the government party. The government tried to cancel their licence. The journalists broadcast an appeal for all their viewers in one area of Zenica who wanted them to keep broadcasting to turn their lights off. They kept doing this and a TV camera on a hill-top showed area after area flashing their lights. The local generating station rang them up and asked them to stop as it was causing problems at the distribution end.

The journalists tell us there are many 'M92s' – people who have become Muslim since '92. There is conflict between them and people who were practising Muslims before the war. A local Muslim priest had arguments with an Iranian mullah who now works in the town. The Iranian says people must stand in a certain way to pray. The Bosnian replies that Bosnian Muslims never stood that way and that there is no reason why they should. "

BOB MYERS

Ramiz

" A journalist from Edinburgh was looking for an interesting story from Tuzla. She was interested in children born to Bosnian women who were raped. We started to inquire but everything was wrapped in silence.

Nobody wanted to talk about it or to point us in the right direction. The first person who told us anything was a director of the orphanage. We managed to see about thirty children. They were nearly three years of age and were playing carelessly like any other children. They crowded around us, touching my cameras, taking different poses. When we asked if their mothers visited them the reply was in the negative. Except one. She came that day to visit her beautiful son, Ramiz. She permitted me to take his photo.

When we asked her for an interview, she refused saying: "I have been interviewed so many times. Everybody could learn from those interviews what I and my fellow women had experienced but nothing has been done so far to bring the criminals to the tribunal. Mladic and Karadzic, the creators of all crimes committed in Bosnia, are still free."

While she was talking with us she kept her son on her lap and caressed his hair. Tears started to glisten in her eyes. We decided to leave. I wondered what would happen when this boy and other kids realised the truth. "

Oxford   October 4th

Dear Friend,

Who are Workers Aid, and how did they come about? I have only just found out about the organisation after three frustrating years trying to get messages and aid into Tuzla. A chance meeting between my dear friend in Tuzla and a Workers Aid driver, who contacted me on his return, has opened up a very valuable supply line to our friends there and we are very grateful.

Having contacted the driver, he was almost reticent about the part he and his mates (at Birmingham Post Office) play in getting supplies into Tuzla. He is a wonderfully modest, ordinary humanitarian 'worker'. Thank god for people like him!

As he would not be 'interrogated', I vaguely gathered that his part as a trade unionist committed him to the cause. As a life long trade unionist myself I would be proud to think that the 'boys' have organised themselves in this, but know nothing about it. Please enlighten me.

I am sixty four years old and of course, unemployed. My daughters have spent a fortune on buying supplies, sent via what can only be described as 'hero seekers'. Up till now all this has been lost until the lads at Birmingham Post office delivered much needed aid. I hope you can manage to carry on.

Kindest regards,

David

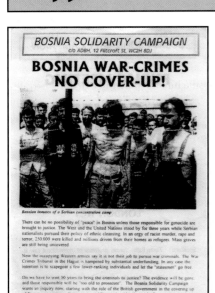

The silent, empty, frontline town of Kalesija, near Tuzla

When we arrived in Tuzla we found the response of the miners and the Tuzla Civic Forum was quite different. The Civic Forum, organised mainly by professional people, knew the peace deal meant support for division and understood that had it been forced on Bosnia to stop it winning the war. For them the struggle against division had to continue, but by other means. The 'peace', unjust and unstable, gave them a chance to restore contacts between opponents of nationalism across ex-Yugoslavia.

The miners' horizon was closer to home. They were exhausted, hungry and happy the fighting had stopped. Now they were concerned about the future of their industry. Where would new machinery come from, what would happen to all the miners who were not working? Like all Bosnians, they had received no pay for four years. From January 1st the working miners had been promised £20 a month, but it hadn't been paid. They had organised a strike and the money appeared, but what would happen in the future? During war they had been prepared to make sacrifices and work for nothing. Now they expected better things.

Miners in Banovici spoke of their worries about privatisation. If their mines were bought up by private companies what would happen to their miners' holiday homes, or other facilities which the miners and their families could use?

The miners' representatives felt that if we could help them find information and answers to these kinds of problems it would be more use to them than aid.

For the first time Workers Aid members travelled to Zenica and the mining town of Kakanj, along roads that had been under Chetnik control until the BiH army push the previous autumn. Some of the recaptured villages were being used to house the survivors from Srebrenica. Only women, children and old men could be seen moving between the houses.

In Kakanj the miners also spoke of their determination to get their promised wages and to improve them.

For the professionals of Tuzla Civic Forum, and for intellectuals world-wide, the fight for multi-ethnic society was a defence of cultural and human values. For the miners it meant the defence of their unity, which they had fought for over many decades and were still determined to defend.

The Dayton Agreement was based on the outlook of the ethnic cleansers. It spoke of a Bosnia inhabited by three distinct peoples. This was the starting point for all its proposals. It denied the existence of Bosnians, a people who had existed for centuries and whose twentieth century culture had been developed in a struggle against nationalism and fascism. In Banovici the Workers Aid delegation were taken to a miners' bar. We were introduced to the men and women sitting round the table, singing and drinking. Serb, Muslim, Croat, Muslim, Hungarian, Muslim. The door opened. A new drinker entered and everyone laughed. "Slovene! We are complete." This was the Bosnia that the nationalists and the great powers had wanted to destroy. They had failed.

As a result of various meetings it was agreed that we would make arrangements for a delegation of miners from the Tuzla region and middle Bosnia to visit Britain.

**13th
Convoy Factfile**

DATE:
December 1995

LORRIES:
3 from Student Aid for Bosnia with aid from London, Leeds, King's College Cambridge, Brighton and Lancaster Universities

WEIGHT: 8 tons

RECIPIENTS:
Tuzla University Students Union, the orphanage and schools

PEOPLE: 14

The Kakanj miners

The union has been maintained throughout the war. We had a committee of eight men and we have been determined to keep the union going, helping the workers as much as possible. Sadly in the mines in Zenica the union has collapsed as no-one there was willing to keep it going. In the future we will have to make sure the union is properly recognised. We want equal power with the government. We need the kind of unions that exist in Britain. But this is going to be very difficult. Because of the war we have no money and no resources of any kind. I am paid by the mine director. During the war we co-operated with him very closely, but being paid by him and not by the union means we are not properly independent. We have applied to be recognised by the European Federation of Trade Unions and we hope that we will get that soon. But the basic problem is to increase production at the mine. Only if we restore production can the union really become strong again. For this we need help, we need machinery. Throughout the war we received no wages. Only some food parcels. With the end of the war the government promised that we would start to be paid from January. We should have received 70DM a month. But we did not get paid. In February we went on strike for five days. Everyone in the town supported us as they knew we only wanted paying for the work we had done. Eventually we were promised we would receive our pay and we went back to work. Now there is a lot of talk about privatisation but no-one here knows what is going to happen.

LUKA BRADARIC, President, Kakanj Miners' Union

Hate

> My two young companions are in love with each other. They met two years ago. The first convoy was stuck in Croatia trying to find a way through to Tuzla. The drivers all went drinking in a bar where Jasna was working.
>
> We are driving back to Tuzla, the February sun hot through the car windows, the snow stretching away from the fields up through the trees. Suddenly on top of one of the rocky hilltops we can see the tower of an old Turkish castle. We park the car and start to wander up a track. Below is a river. Apart from its' murmur, there is a wide, eternal silence. We stop to take each others' photos. The castle is small, built on an impossible outcrop of rock, and outside its' walls, balanced on even more crazy pinnacles, are a few houses and a tiny, plain mosque. Some teenagers are hanging around chatting. They eye us coming up the path, the first visitors since the war started, before they were even teenagers.
>
> We say, "hello," and ask the way in to the castle. They point to some steps and at the top of them is a good joke. The entire area inside the old walls has been turned into a football and basketball pitch. It's the only level ground in the entire district.
>
> From the tower you look on the river far below, on both sides. We are on an island and the river forks round us.
>
> We pass the teenagers again and turn the car back onto the road. It is one of those days. The totally carefree days from years before, before the world pushed its' way in.
>
> A few kilometres down the road a woman is walking along. We stop and offer her a lift. We stop for everyone. There is no public transport. She gets in and thanks us, asks where we are going. Jasna translates between us. The woman is short, about 35, short boyish hair. Bright red lipstick and a shopping bag.
>
> Then without warning she starts crying. Her eyeshadow is running down her face. There is confusion. She and Jasna are talking, she between tears. Jasna gives her a packet of tissues and she begins to wipe her eyes and starts apologising. We can't understand and don't have a clue what is wrong. We ask Jasna but she is silent. We ask again.
>
> "She was out walking with her small boy in her arms yesterday. A man, a 'Croat man' she says, came up and asked her name and when she told him, he shot the boy. She got the boy to Turkish IFOR troops and they flew him to hospital in a helicopter. She doesn't know where or how he is. It was her only child. She was married for ten years and wanted children but didn't get any. Then she got pregnant. A few months after the boy was born her husband was killed. He was in the Bosnian army"
>
> The woman has cleaned up her face and offers us a packet of biscuits from her bag. She explains she had a Spanish friend who used to visit her for holidays. They used to drink brandy. She asks us to come and have a drink someday.
>
> We come to the turn off for Tuzla and she asks to be put down. We say goodbye and I see her out of the rear window walking down the road.
>
> On Sarajevo television that night there is an interview with Admiral Leighton-Smith, US commander of the IFOR troops. He is asked why the British troops under his command have twice that week allowed Karadzic to pass through their checkpoints even though he is on the war criminal list – wanted for organising the violence that has left a quarter of a million people dead. Leighton Smith defends his troops. Karadzic travels with an armed bodyguard and if the British had tried to apprehend him then there may have been shooting and civilians may have been killed. Leighton Smith has 60,000 troops at his disposal.
>
> It was 'a Croat man' our woman passenger had said. But who stirs the filth? Who incites, who plans and who organises? And who watches and does nothing, 'in case civilians get killed'? "

BOB MYERS

TRUCKS AND TRUCKING

Andy Milton was an unemployed HGV driver when he became involved in the convoys. He spent much of the next eighteen months lying on mountain tracks in blizzards or dust storms, trying to improvise repairs to our ageing trucks. His skill and unflappable good humour saved us on many occasions.

Trucks were mostly bought at auction for £1,300 to £3,000. With this you pay your money and take a chance. We tried to borrow trucks. Big companies were sympathetic until they realised there was no insurance cover for a war zone. But British Gas did lend us a few and the Water Board sold us one for a tenner.

Fitting snow chains

In the beginning, the vehicles lacked various legal necessities. This was partly down to cash, but also to pressure of too many things to do and not enough people with the right skills. After a while we got everything in legal order – well, more or less.

My first experience of convoys was March, 1994. The route was mainly rough roads that meandered through beautiful valleys, over three main ranges of mountains, and through settlements 'cleansed' by nationalist forces. There were many vehicles scavenged for parts or smashed and burnt out, on or over the edges of the roads. Not all of these vehicles had come off the road accidentally. The UN used these roads and if a broken down vehicle was in the way, it would be pushed down a bank or into a river. But it was also incredibly easy to slide and end up with your wheels over the edge, especially in winter.

Much of the road was single track and when you meet another convoy, of fifty plus trucks, coming in the opposite direction, things get a little complicated! Trucks jam together, usually with lots of lively discussions. If in doubt, in true Bosnian style, stand on your horn (if it works) and shout a lot. On one occasion we were jammed up for six hours like this. But that is nothing to the queues at borders – one hour to two weeks.

We were not like other aid convoys. Their aim (at least their stated aim) was to simply get aid through. For this you need the biggest trucks with two drivers. For us it was how does each convoy help build up further support, so we always tried to take as many people as possible. All available space is utilised, with generally three in a cab, even if it was made for two. Once we had six people travelling

in the 'Big Blue' – a 17ton Ford Cargo. All the trucks got nicknames – Big Blue, Little Blue, Bread Van, Geordie Wagon etc.

Mostly we used 7.5ton Ford Cargos. Anyone can drive these on a car licence. Early on in the war it was impossible to get big lorries to Tuzla. (Our artic from France couldn't get through a tunnel and another one got stuck. We had to let air out of the tyres to get it through.) But once it became possible to get the forty tonners to Tuzla, from a purely aid point of view, we should have stopped using the small lorries. We kept on using them, partly so there were more vehicles and thus more people, but also because in Britain the local Workers Aid groups could easily raise the money for a 7.5ton truck and find drivers. So they were local campaign boosters. People could see 'their' truck and go and get the aid and the money for the next convoy. If we had only used HGVs it would have separated most campaigners from the convoys themselves.

Many drivers developed a deep relationship with their truck, and sometimes had to be shoe-horned out of the seat when it was clear they were asleep. This was a common hazard as the driving demanded full concentration. Most other vehicles on the road were built to cope with extreme temperatures and demanding road surfaces. With our old trucks, designed for the British climate and road surfaces, our drivers had to become experts in avoiding hazards.

We travelled on tracks which got churned up in wet weather and there was the danger of 'bottoming out' on monster potholes created by UN trucks. We had to drive around each one, going for miles at a snail's pace. How deep is that puddle? On one occasion it was about four feet and my truck almost toppled! Even smug HGV drivers make mistakes!!

Inevitably there are problems when trucks, communications and people are being pushed to their limits and beyond. Trucks took wrong turnings if the convoy got too stretched out. The art of convoy driving is to 'follow' the truck behind you, ie always adjust your speed to the one behind, then providing the lorry in front of you does the same everyone is alright. Great in theory. But it only takes a little daydream and when you look in your rear mirror – no convoy behind you!

A few other convoy problems: inadequate diesel tanks meant fuel had to be carried in jerry cans, dust would often find its way into the fuel causing many blockages; running out of fuel, generally in inappropriate places; watered down fuel; waxing fuel (in sub zero temps); getting ripped off at fuel stops; losing air pressure, which makes all the brakes lock on; brakes freezing on; driving with no clutch; much 'bump' starting due to flat batteries/stolen batteries; towing out of holes; constant towing on sections of the route; trucks with faulty electrics; no windscreen wipers/lights (though this did help where there were night time snipers); temperamental brakes; dodgy steering; constant engine overheating; extreme heat (summer), intense cold (winter); the wandering hands of desperate peo-

ple while we stopped – diesel, lights, batteries all going missing; broken fan belts with no spares; 80Km round trip to get a spare part worth £3; being stuck on a mountain pass in heavy snow with no snow chains; no interior cab heating in winter – Brrrr; Croatian border guards not allowing us out of Bosnia as some of the trucks were "not suitable for Croatian roads" after being bashed in Bosnia; tail-lifts falling down after puncturing hydraulics on potholes, nearly causing severe personal injury on one occasion; in strong winds on a cliff-hanging road, one truck carrying mainly rave/music equipment blew over onto two wheels – a couple of tons of ballast (tins of pineapple chunks) were required in order to continue the journey. And so on.

There are four trucks in Bosnia that never made it home. Another three in Zagreb. Two in Germany and several in Britain which were not fit to go again. Two trucks burnt out by vandals. But all the lorries served us well as our ambassadors. When we stop Bosnians can see for themselves that we are normal(ish) folk, like themselves. Not like the thousands of 'official people' in brand new 4x4 jeeps that have taken control of Bosnia. Also the trucks have Workers Aid for Bosnia in Bosnian and English written on them. This is well received in Bosnia, as many people there felt the world had forgotten them.

Setting aside the political situation, and the massive preparation effort, the actual journey has been an artform in itself, with a 'mixed bag' of people pulling together (well, most of the time!) and making the best of many good/bad/stressful situations. I personally have met many new friends, on convoys and within Bosnia. We all stayed in people's houses and we've had a real window into Bosnian people's lives, witnessed changes in their fortunes and listened to their personal stories. I can't say I have lived it, but I've had a highly privileged look.

ANDY MILTON

Levering a wheel out of gulley

Smashed windscreen thanks to...

...middle of the road drivers

Wanted – cash to help Bosnia

AN AID convoy from Leicester still needs cash before it can set out on its journey to Bosnia.

The lorry will be carrying books donated by local universities to Tuzla and is set to leave on December 16.

The books will go to universities in Tuzla and Sarajevo and the assistance came after a plea from the rectors of the two universities during a recent visit to Leicester.

While enough books have been gathered, organiser Mr Paul Henderson has admitted the project still needs £400 for various expenses.

He said: "We have raised pretty much all the money we needed to get out there but we still need about £400 to send the lorry.

"The university has been very good and we've had lots of geology and medical books.

"We've also had to do some work on the lorry but I think it should be alright."

The driving will be done by Mr Mark Oseland and Mr Paul Collins — two postgraduates at Leicester University — and a local youth club has been busy decorating the lorry.

The trip is expected to take two-and-a-half weeks in total.

Mr Henderson can be contacted on Leicester 2707730.

Workers Aid features in local news reports in Teeside, Leicester, Newcastle and Cumbria

Burning an aid lorry is sickening

Moronic act of vandalism puts in jeopardy vital mission to Bosnia.

IT SEEMS incredible that a lorry which has carried aid undamaged through war-torn areas should meet its end on Tyneside.

The vehicle stood in a car park waiting to be loaded with much-needed food and clothing for the people of Bosnia when some idiots set fire to it.

Generous people in and around Wallsend who donated to the mercy mission will be sickened to learn that their efforts have been put in jeopardy by the act of mindless morons.

The lorry was clearly marked as being an aid vehicle, which makes the actions of the arsonists even more difficult to comprehend.

It is to be hoped that some company who reads of the aid workers' plight will respond with offers of help.

If the aid is allowed to rot in a warehouse it will be victory for those of sick mind.

Tusla terror for Ed

A KENDAL man was part of a convoy of volunteers from Workers Aid for Bosnia who were arrested and intimidated overnight in the war-torn country.

Former soldier Ed Cansdale, 26, who is a student at Kendal College, was one of the drivers with the volunteer aid convoy heading for the multi-ethnic city of Tusla.

Rebel Croatian nationalists - who object to aid going to Tusla and other multi-ethnic towns - stopped six of the convoy's volunteers and threatened them with guns. Their belongings were thrown into the road and they were put in prison overnight without food and water. One volunteer, a Macedonian, was interrogated, but was not beaten.

Ed and the other volunteers who escaped arrest were left in a state of panic over their colleagues. They contacted Workers Aid for Bosnia in England to get help, and a number of MPs who support the organisation were able to use their influence to get the aid workers released without harm, according to national treasurer of Workers Aid for Bosnia, John Davies, from Kendal.

Mr Davies said the convoy, which arrived in Bosnia about ten days ago, had got through despite the setback and had been "very successful", delivering 35 tons of food - flour, oil and sugar - to its destination.

● Workers Aid for Bosnia plans to send out another convoy late in September.

Her leap to help Bosnia

NAZEEM Akhtar reached for the sky to bring hope to strife-torn Bosnia.

Nazeem, a bi-lingual assistant in Ayresome Infants School, Middlesbrough, took advantage of a gap in the weather to make her sponsored parachute jump.

She raised more than £600 - cash which will help set up a children's clinic.

Nazeem, of Teesside Bosnia Solidarity group, is on her way to join a group of six other people who are travelling by truck and car with aid to Bosnia.

Nazeem, of Tavistock Street, Stockton, said: 'I was very lucky because you can only do parachute jumps at Topcliffe at the weekends. I had been waiting for a month.'

And the timing of her latest trip - she has been there twice already - is also crucial.

'July 11 is the second anniversary of the massacre of Srebrnica when thousands were slaughtered,' she said.

Chapter 9

FEBRUARY 1996   First post-war strike by Bosnian miners over underpaid wages.
MAY 1996   Financial links revealed between Tory Party and Radovan Karadzic.
SEPTEMBER 1996   First post-war BiH election.

After Dayton

The raft ferry at Zupanja

During our visit to Bosnia everyone we had spoken to was desperate to resume a normal life. But how was this to be done in a country, not only devastated by war, but now partitioned into three parts? The fighting had stopped but the main issue of the war – unity or division – was not settled. Nationalism had almost succeeded, but not quite. The battle would continue in a different form.

The Dayton Implementation Force, IFOR, replaced the UN Protection Force, UNPROFOR. For British, French, Spanish, Russian, Pakistani and other troops already in Bosnia it simply meant a change of badge, but a large contingent of US soldiers now joined them. At Orasje the Americans constructed two large pontoon bridges across the River Sava, for the use of IFOR vehicles only. Other traffic for Bosnia, commercial and private, still had to queue for the ferry. In winter, when the river often rose to flood levels, the wait could be ten to twenty hours. Money was supposedly set aside to rebuild the blown up motorway bridge, but no construction took place.

The new power in the land made their authority known. US troops turned up at the gates of one of Tuzla's idle factories. A US officer told the factory security men to open the gates as the factory was being requestioned for a depot. They refused, saying they needed authorisation from the factory manager. The officer replied that if the gates were not open in five minutes his troops would break them open. Under the Dayton Agreement IFOR troops had the right to take such buildings as they needed.

Though US military convoys passed through Tuzla with their gunners on alert, by and large the IFOR troops were kept at a distance from Tuzla citizens. Bars, restaurants, cinemas and so on were set up inside army bases away from the town. IFOR went about their business and the people of Tuzla went about theirs, for the moment occupying separate worlds.

Banovici District TU Committee   **May 1st, 1996**

To Leicester Trade Union Council

Dear Friends,

We were moved and greatly cheered by your letter and your efforts to make known the truth about the struggle by Bosnian people against Serbian fascism through your publicity material. Your contribution to our struggle for a multi-national and multi-cultural Bosnia is great.

Banovici is a town 30km from Tuzla with a population of 30,000. The building of the town began in 1946, after the completion of the Brcko-Banovici Youth railway, in whose construction, International Brigades from England, Denmark, Holland, India, France, Belgium, Austria, Switzerland and other European countries took part.

With its' completion, the foundations of the mine were laid. It developed, and in 1991, before the outbreak of the war, Rudnik achieved an output of 2,300,000 tons of black coal and employed about 4,000 workers.

The aggression against our country, both by the Serb aggressor, and from local Chetniks, led to a blockade of all road links to Tuzla and the economy practically ground to a halt.

The best sons of this state went shoulder to shoulder on the defence lines to protect their families, the factories and all that has gone to make this city a multicultural centre.

This city did not fall, the population did not suffer genocide, but opened its doors to the casualties, the dispossessed, the refugees from Brcko, Bijelina, Zvornik, Bratunac, Srebrenica, Zepa and other places in which the fascists carried out atrocities.

We fought to survive, and we succeeded. Our wish is that all Rudnik's industries continue production and through this provide schooling, health and culture – all that a city must have.

We know that some trade unions in Western Europe assisted the Chetniks. The truth about Bosnia will surely reach them. A large number of corpses were found in the mine at Ljubija near Banja Luka. This is how the Chetniks used the mines.

Sincere greetings from the Banovici District Trade Union Council, to all my friends in Britain and in particular to the workers of Leicester.

DZAFER RAHMANOVIC, President

Powys to Bosnia – Schools' Aid for Banovici

In April, four Bosnian miners, the union's President from Tuzla, the Vice President from Kakanj, the Tuzla union secretary and a mining technician acting as interpreter, came to Britain. On arrival they went straight to a meeting discussing the campaign of 500 Liverpool Dockers. The dockers had been sacked over a year before for refusing to accept the use of casual labour in the docks which had already destroyed trade unions and workers' rights in every other British port. The rapport between the dockers and miners was immediate. Two groups of working people, both fighting to defend rights won in the past, both in very beleaguered circumstances, both trying to gain international solidarity.

The dockers heard a report from the miners and a bucket collection in their mass meeting raised £400 to help with travel expenses, even though the dockers themselves had not been paid for a year. The dockers also invited the Bosnians to address the Liverpool May Day rally a few days later.

Women to women

" *Teeside Bosnia Solidarity Campaign was formed after the Srebenica massacre. In March 1996, with help from* **UNISON** *branches in the north-east, they took a lorry of aid to the* Hands of Friendship *women's organisation in Banovici, travelling via the northern route.*

"We wanted to go as a women-only group because Bosnian women and children have suffered so much, because we had made contact with a women's group in Banovici, because we thought as women we'd have less hassle getting through and because we as women knew we could do it.

We are just ordinary people. It is always ordinary people like us who suffer in wars. The people of Bosnia seemed so far away, out of reach, but they are not. We decided it was time to reach out and touch them.

Our journey to Bosnia was frustrating and worrying. Would we cross the border – the River Sava? All the bridges had been blown up in the war. There were miles of waiting trucks and vans. Could we cross by ferry?

We felt helpless. We'd come so far. Now the police were turning us away. We waited and waited and spoke to the military forces and police in Slavonski Brod until we were finally given permission to move on. We were in Bosnia! I felt so relieved, so happy.

Banovici was a bigger town than I had imagined with some tall buildings and lots of people hanging around the town centre – youngsters with nothing to do, nowhere to go.

The welcome we had from the women of the Hands of Friendship Association was so warm.

One of the head-teachers told our group, "we've got the strength to fight. We don't want people to feel sorry for us. But in the name of our dear children, help us to re-build our school. Help us to get some desks, some furniture, some books, equipment."

Banovici is a multi-ethnic town with many intermarried families. Many people have left and some families will never be re-united. I cannot comprehend the enormity of this tragedy. Curfews, people still short of water, gas, electricity, most shops still empty, tensions high. People are exhausted but they still have great resilience to survive and fight for their multi-ethnic identity.

We did reach out to touch a few of the people of Bosnia, like members of a new-found family. And now we are back to say thank you so much to the people of Teeside, to UNISON and Workers Aid for Bosnia, and other aid groups that have supported us." "

NASEEM AKHTAR

Bosnian miners' President Fikret Suljic, addressing the May Day rally from the balcony of Liverpool Town Hall:

Dear Friends,

I bring you Mayday greetings on behalf of the Autonomous Trade Union of Coal Miners of Bosnia Herzegovina.

On this international workers day I want to appeal to trade unions and working people here in Britain and throughout the world, to act in solidarity with miners in Bosnia.

During the war our union has fought to keep alive basic trade union principles – to defend the rights of all miners. No-one has left our pits because of nationality. Muslims, Croats, Serbs and others all still work together and we are rebuilding contacts with miner's organisations in other countries of former Yugoslavia. We are all miners.

Our miners and our union are without any money to enable us to carry out our union functions. We do not want to be dependent on government or the mine management, or political parties, or on religious groups. The only people we can turn to is you. Without your solidarity our miners' trade union will not survive. We have been the victims of racist and fascistic aggression aimed at dividing people. If we are defeated then where will it happen next?

During our visit here we have been made aware that you also have big problems. We must act together to defend the rights of working people. I hope that together we can begin to rebuild the spirit of international solidarity that used to exist and which Mayday celebrates.

Greetings from the miners of Bosnia-Herzegovina.

On May 1st, the miners marched with dockers and other workers to celebrate internationalism and solidarity. In Fikret Suljic's short speech to the rally there could be heard the spirit of workers' unity that war and starvation had failed to crush.

Amongst the listening crowd few people could have known anything about our convoys, about the triumphs, the tragedies, the exhaustion or about the times we had all felt like giving up. It didn't matter. Our work had made possible this coming together of resistance, east and west, in Liverpool.

A Bosnian student in Britain

" People tend to ask, "Are you a Bosnian Muslim, Bosnian Serb or Bosnian Croat?" My answer to this is that I am none of these. I am a Bosnian. My best friend is from a 'mixed marriage,' so how could she answer this question? I know that most young people in Bosnia would agree with me. The only way in which I can relate to these sub-divisions is to look at Tuzla. Here is a city where no single national party won the elections in 1992, and the stated view of the Tuzla people is for unity.

In former Yugoslavia we have seen the country disintegrate, with broken homes and broken families, not to mention the barbarity of rape, torture and genocide. A whole generation is growing up brutalised and if we don't support the people who are fighting against this, we will not be able to fight it in any country.

I have had to watch my fourteen-year-old sister grow up with hatred in her heart. She has not been allowed to be a youth and future generations worldwide will pay for the tens of thousands of youths who are like this.

I heard about Workers Aid through its, first convoy, when a massive effort was made to get food to Tuzla. As I got involved I realised that it was more than a charity issue. Although aid is required, it is also important to build an understanding in all countries of why we should fight for unity and solidarity.

I hope that at Leicester University we can follow the example of other universities which have set up branches of Workers Aid. "

Edited from an interview with Emina Atic in RIPPLE, the Leicester student union paper

The delegation went on to meet with various union leaders. With Bosnian miners on pitiful wages following four years without pay, the union desperately needed money to function properly. They needed a fax machine, a copier and other basic office equipment, small things by British union standards. On a bigger scale they needed safety equipment, boots, hats, lamps etc, that would allow some of the non-working miners to return to work. About half of the twenty thousand miners could not work due to equipment shortages and a drastic fall in demand for energy with industry at a standstill. These people were paid an even smaller pittance than the working miners. The union was scared that the Bosnian government and its appointed mine managers would try to dismiss the non-working miners. The union's attitude was quite firm. Until other jobs were available no miner was going to be dismissed.

No offers of financial help for the union were forthcoming from the union leaders they met in London. The head of the TUC's International Department, Michael Walsh, claimed that the TUC had already helped the Bosnian unions. Fikret Suljic, the miners' President, angrily retorted that throughout the war the miners' had received nothing from the TUC.

The Liverpool Dockers contacted the National Union of Miners (NUM) head offices and arranged for Fikret Suljic to meet Frank Cave, the Vice President. He offered no explanation as to why their letters to Arthur Scargill had gone unanswered. Instead he gave a lecture on the problems of miners in Cuba. When Mr. Cave was asked what the NUM could do to help the Bosnians, he replied that this would depend upon which of the international mining union federations they intended to affiliate to.

A programme of meetings that was supposed to have been organised for the Bosnians by the Greater London TUC was

The poor have sown, and the poor reap

If from the Srebrenica cul-de-sac you go twenty kilometres along a half-flooded dirt road, you will come to the 'Slapovic' reception centre. Some twelve hundred Serbs live there. Following the territorial losses in western and central Bosnia in the summer of 1995, Srebrenica became the destination for the inhabitants of Donji Vakuf. A few also came from Bihac and Krupa.

"It's a miserable life," says seventy-three-year-old Drago Naerac, who is one of the camp's oldest residents. "I read in the 'Hundred Year Almanack' that a time would come when fools would rule. That's what we've got now." He also offers a solution. "The people have been ruined by all the bigwigs – Muslim, Serb and Croat alike. The best thing to do is change the leaderships, so that we can go back to our homes, each to his own." "Eh, Grandpa, it's all right for you, you didn't fight in the war. I'd return tomorrow too, if Serbs were in control," says Andjelko, a youngish man who spent the war

on the Donji Vakuf front. "When the command to withdraw came, you took with you what you could. The women could only collect the children. The men went directly into exile from the front, in the uniforms they're still wearing. When I go to Bratunac, they ask me why I'm still in uniform; as if I had anything else to put on."

Each person receives 10 kilos of flour per month, a cup of oil, half a kilo of rice, half a kilo of beans (which nobody wants, because they can't be cooked) and, most important, a 340-gram tin of some meat product or fish. "Five or six of us get together, and we walk up to 20 kilometres in search of a few onions or potatoes that the Muslims planted for themselves." "The poor have sown, and the poor reap," was Grandpa Drago's comment.

We ask a sixteen-year-old youth how they spend their time. "We play football, what else?" he retorts aggressively. There is no electricity, so they cannot have music. They sit and talk. There are no guitars or accordions - who would have taken such things, when they had less than an hour to flee?

The people in the camp worry about their future. The brook is polluted, there is no sanitation, the warm weather is coming and they fear epidemics.

They were told on arrival that nobody would spend more than four days here. A year later, they are negotiating with the Swedish government to relocate the camp, though they have little hope. The new Srebrenica authorities have promised to let them settle, 20 bungalows at a time, in the neighbouring villages, where they will be able to work the land and slowly repair the houses. Significantly, one of the villages he mentions is Osmaci, made famous by General Mladic's remark: "no Serb foot ever trod here until we liberated it." Now any Serb who wishes may tread there – but many, used to urban life, have no wish to become peasants. In the meantime, there is no electricity and no transport and the most they can hope for is that someone may send them shoes.

From a report by Srboljub Bogdanovic in NIN, Belgrade, April 12th, 1996

called off at two days' notice and members of the International Department of UNISON failed to turn up for an appointment at the UNISON offices. This hostility of union leaders contrasted with the warm welcome they received in Liverpool, from the Scottish TUC and from union members up and down the country.

They visited mining areas in Scotland, Northumberland and Durham and saw for themselves the destruction of the industry and its effects on mining communities. They began to understand some of the problems we had faced during the war in trying to bring them aid on the scale they needed. Not just the problem of the union bureaucrats who had no sympathy for their struggle, but also the problems of British miners and other working people.

In Durham, local NUM representatives invited them to send representatives back to Britain in July for the famous Durham Miners' Gala. Workers Aid delegations, with many Bosnian refugees, had participated in the previous two gala parades, but 1996 was an especially proud moment when two Bosnian miners marched with their own union banner amidst the Durham miners.

Both the April and July delegations were funded by trade union branches and Trades Councils through a solidarity fund established by Durham NUM.

The visits did not produce financial support on anything like the scale the Bosnians needed but they were happy they had begun to make direct contact with many workers' organisations in Britain.

Chetniks in Leicester

" We held a public meeting in Leicester for the three visiting Bosnian trades unionists. I was chairing the meeting. I should explain that living in Leicester are about 4,000 individuals of Serb descent, most of whose families came to Britain as opponents of the partisan revolution. Leicester even boasts a Chetnik club. Of the sixty or so people present at our meeting, around thirty five were from this community. Many of them were young, most of them were extremely vociferous, and all of them were determined that our speakers were not going to be heard!

Our interpreter was alarmed when he saw one of the Serbs bolt the entrance door from the inside. I half anticipated a riot, but this did not happen, possibly because the older Serbs wanted to impress on the British trades unionists that the Serb nationalists were those with right on their side. In the general hullabaloo, the only violence that was done was carried out on the table, which I had to bang up and down in a fruitless attempt to keep order.

Unfortunately, Bosnian refugees in the meeting were intimidated, and most left early in the expectation of trouble. On a more positive note, members of Workers Aid spoke to some of the younger Serbs at the back of the hall, and found them more receptive to discussion than their older relatives. Later, we toyed with the idea of campaigning amongst this group, but decided against, in view of the feelings of our Bosnian comrades.

The meeting ended quietly. The Serbs went home, having done their bit to ensure that, on that night at least, the truth about the struggle for a multi-ethnic society would not be heard. **"**

PAUL HENDERSON, Secretary, Leicester Trades Union Council

The United States Suppresses the Evidence

20. 4. 96

Former US Secretary of State Lawrence Eagleburger has been accused of trying to bury the truth about atrocities by Serb forces. An official says he was told the Bush administration "could not afford" to confirm reports of concentration camps.

Having backed Serbia's President Milosevic, the Bush administration feared public outrage in the US would force it to alter policy.

Speaking on an ABC News special programme, former state department east European expert John Fox said the US government, "had in its possession credible and verified reports of the existence of Serbian run camps in Bosnia and elsewhere as of June, certainly July, 1992."

But after TV reports of the camps in August, 1992, Assistant Secretary of State Thomas Niles testified to Congress that the administration had no "substantial information on the matter."

AN EXCHANGE OF CORRESPONDENCE

Samostalni sindikat radnika Rudnika uglja R/F BiH
Republički odbor

Adresa : Mije Keroševića broj 1., 75000 Tuzla
Telefon : 212-111, loc. 594, telefax : 9938775821422

29. 4. 1996

The situation is very bad for miners throughout the countries of
former Yugoslavia, but worst of all in Bosnia. There are 20,000
employed miners in middle and northern Bosnia. Out of these only
10,000 are able to work due to the shortage of personal safety
equipment and mining machinery.Many of the unemployed are
soldiers who have now been demobilised.
For four years miners received no wages but only a rare food
parcel. From 1 January 1996 working miners have been paid 70Dm
per month. Non-working miners receive 30Dm. Food prices are
roughly the same as in western Europe. So called
'reconstruction' funds from international governments will not
include any provisions for the welfare of miners or their
families.
In the past, our union has always come to the assistance of
working people in need. We have given generously to people in
Vietnam, South Africa and South America, and during the British
miners' strike we gave one days' pay per month. Throughout the
war our union has fought for the basic principles of trade
unionism. Now without international solidarity our union cannot
continue.
We need solidarity and help in three ways. Firstly we need
financial and moral support to maintain a functioning union,
independent union. Most of the union's property and equipment
has either been destroyed or requisitioned during the war so we
are left without any copiers, faxes, telephones, office
equipment.The poverty of our members makes it impossible for us
to restore these things so that we can carry out our trade union
activities. We do not want to be dependent on any political or
religious group. We need to be accepted into the appropriate
European and international trade union organisations.
Secondly, the war and poverty has not just hurt miners but also
their families. We need the assistance of working people and
their trade unions to re-equip our schools, hospitals, clinics,
libraries and to restore a normal human existence.
Thirdly we need 1000Dm for each miner to be able to return to
work. This will pay for personal safety equipment, boots,
helmets, overalls, lamps as well as mining machinery.
Throughout the war our union has always tried to defend all
working people and many of our members have made great
sacrifices in order to maintain the right of all people to live
and work together. We are confident that our principled defence
of basic trade unionism will help us re-establish cooperation
between miners in Croatia, Serbia, Slovenia, Macedonia and BiH.
To do this we need the assistance of the working class movement
internationally. If you can assist us in any way please fax us
on 00 387 75 821 422 or contact Durham NUM, 01191 384 2515.

Miners' greetings,

Fikret Suljic
President.

Donations to miners denied

My attention has been drawn to an article titled: *A Call to Alms* which appears in the *The Big Issue 114*. This article, dealing primarily with the situation of the Miners' Union in Bosnia-Herzogovina, contains a number of allegations which are, quite simply, inaccurate.

This article is the latest in a long line of claims that mineworkers in Britain received financial assistance during the 1984/85 Miners' Strike from mineworkers in former Yugoslavia, in particular, Bosnia: claims that are simply untrue.

I feel it is essential to respond.

1. I want to make clear that neither the National Union of Mineworkers nor the Miners' Solidarity Fund (set up to look after striking miners' family and communities) have any record of monies, goods or any material aid received from miners anywhere in what was Yugoslavia during the 1984/85 strike.

If mineworkers in the former Yugoslavia were giving up a day's pay a month to help the British miners, I for one, would like to know to whom that money was sent.

2. The article also states that Fikret Suljic and his three comrades from the Miners' Union in Bosnia-Herzogovina were in Britain in May "as a guest of the National Union of Miners". No such invitation was organised by the National Union of Mineworkers.

I would like to know who – both in the former Yugoslavia and here in Britain – is behind these inaccurate claims.

ARTHUR SCARGILL
PRESIDENT
NATIONAL UNION OF
MINEWORKERS

Samostalni sindikat radnika Rudnika uglja R/F BiH
Republički odbor

Adresa : Mije Keroševića broj 1., 75000 Tuzla
Telefon : 212-111, loc. 594, telefax : 9938775821422

10. 7. 1996.

We are writing to you concerning information that Bosnian miners did not give aid to the British miners during the strike of 1984-85. We are sorry to have to speak out in this way against people who want to deny the truth.

As you know the big miners strike started in Britain in 1984 and it was reported by all the news agencies. As soon as NUM president, Arthur Scargill, sent an appeal for help, miners at 'Kreka' colliery organised meetings in all departments and unanimously voted to send financial and moral support to British miners.It was decided that the 10,000 miners would give one days' salary every month as long as the strike lasted. Following this other mines in BiH joined this solidarity action. The coal industry in BiH is one of the largest parts of our industry and its miners are known for their solidarity throughout the world.

Naturally all the money we collected was passed on to the Trade Union Council of Yugoslavia as, at that time, we were part of this Federation. Its leaders were well known to all the union leaders in Britain.

Now, for whatever reason, people want to deny the help Bosnian miners sent to their fellow miners in Durham, Yorkshire and other mining regions of Britain. Today, we would do exactly what we did in 1984 because miners across the world must help each other because today we might need help and tomorrow it will be someone else. Solidarity must be defended.

We are sorry to have to address the general public in Britain but at the same time we would very much welcome those people who deny our past solidarity to come to Bosnia and see that the mines and miners still survive and are fighting to live by their own work.

Miners' Greetings,

Fikret Suljic,
President.

Meanwhile Workers Aid was facing its' own problems. Even before the Dayton agreement was signed the mood of outrage over Srebrenica was subsiding. Inside and outside of Bosnia people felt the UN and the super-powers were finally going to do something. With the peace deal this seemed to be confirmed. They had stopped the fighting. The most barbaric war in Europe since 1945 was halted. Public attention shifted away from Bosnia, which had been at the centre of the news for almost four years. For most people the cause of the war and the nature of the 'peace' was unimportant. Dayton and the western politicians had finally brought an end to the killing. That was what mattered.

This was also felt inside Workers Aid. People who had joined because of a general hatred of war drifted away. More important though was the winding down of the convoys. There were differences of opinion about this. Some people wanted them to continue, pointing out the dire poverty continuing in Bosnia. Others felt the convoys were no longer the way to continue our

Let's go

" Our convoy is four trucks from Britain and one from Spain. This convoy is pretty much like others in terms of its' personnel. There are Tony and Dave from Wallsend People's Centre, trade union activists. Dave worked on the dust carts and Tony worked in the shipyards till he was made redundant. They have been helping the convoys ever since the first lorries stopped overnight at their Centre. On the convoy their Geordie humour is a great source of stability. They are also our cooks. Everytime the lorries stop they are in the back of their truck, where they have a gas stove, whipping up some new combination of pasta, rice, tinned tomatoes, tinned peaches and condensed milk. In three weeks, they never repeat the same combination.

From Scotland there is Andy from Dundee and James from Edinburgh. Andy is a lifelong socialist and was active in the Timex Support Group. James is a young member of Anti-Fascist Action. Its good to have him on the convoy as the anti-fascist organisations in Britain have mostly been silent on the war in Bosnia. Then from the North West of England there are Ed, Andy and Marcus. Ed is at art school with a marriage and a stint in the Royal Marines behind him. Whenever the convoy stops Ed gets out with his sketch pad and makes drawings. We find out later that he was suffering from a bad stomach hernia that had to be operated on

back in Britain. He never said anything on the trip but only ate tinned peas. It must be the marine training.

Andy and Ed come from Kendal in the Lake district. Andy is a heavy goods vehicle driver. Like many other young people he long ago decided that there were better things in life than just working to pay the mortgage. He lives in a caravan and travels round to various music festivals. He is an ace mechanic. After a long day's drive and faced with some mechanical problem in the middle of a cold night he will get out of his lorry and get on with the job – all night if need be.

Marcus, from Manchester, has just finished his A' levels at a fairly posh school and is taking a year out before going to Oxford. He recently resigned from the left wing Militant group who have an 'all sides are equal' attitude towards the war.

From the south of England is Alyoscia, a Brighton student who has taken a year out between his degree and a postgraduate course to help Workers Aid build links between students in UK and Tuzla University.

Finally there is Faruk from Tuzla who has been a leading member of Workers Aid since the beginning.

This particular convoy is peculiar in only one respect – there are no women, the only convoy where this has happened.

Through Britain, France, Belgium, Luxembourg, Germany and up to the Austrian border has all

been fairly straightforward. One of the lorry clutches burnt out fifty miles after leaving Manchester. The lorry was full not just of aid but also about one hundred parcels from refugees in Britain to their families in Tuzla.

Two lorries headed on to Lille in France to meet a deadline for meetings with local trade unionists and the press. The other two lorries stayed behind to try and sort out the breakdown but this was an old 12ton Bedford – an obsolete make – and we really only expected the one lorry to follow on behind.

Like every convoy, we have set off without enough money to get to Tuzla. Street collections continue while the convoy is on the road and money is forwarded to Croatia. But on this occasion we have hardly enough money to even get to Croatia.

We got to Lille and spent the day there campaigning and collecting money in the town square. A woman gives us 1000Frs (£120) In the evening we were enjoying a meal with young members of the local Sarajevo Committee when news came that a Workers Aid truck was coming up the street. We went out to meet it and a great cheer went up when we saw not just one truck but the Bedford, as well. They had managed to get a new clutch. It cost £600.

"Where did you get the money?" I asked.

"Andy's credit card."

Credit cards do not have to be repaid for a month. That's so far away it's as if the clutch was free. "

BOB MYERS

support for multi-cultural society. As well as these differences there was the hard reality that money was no longer coming in. Whether this was due to a changed response to our collections from the public or to our own members no longer feeling the same sense of urgency to go out day after day collecting food and money was a 'chicken and egg' question. The two things had a common source – the fighting had stopped.

Workers Aid was always run on the basis of supporting anything people wanted to do, providing it was in line with our general principles. So over the next two years a few lorries were sent from Britain and Spain but the non-stop programme of convoys ended with Dayton.

Even while we were discussing our perspectives, post Dayton, we had to begin getting rid of our lorries. With the sudden drop in income there was no money for tax, insurance or repairs. There was no longer money to pay other urgent debts like phone bills and the lorries were our only asset. Big Blue, Little Blue and others were taken to the auctions. It was a sad parting. For us they were no longer lumps of metal but the embodiment of a thousand dramas, their cabs inhabited by a spirit of comradeship. The warehouses were cleared out and vacated.

Convoys had been an activity which anyone could participate in and help organise. Workers Aid and convoys had become synonymous. Even for the people who argued against continuing with convoys it was hard to imagine life without them.

What could people who wanted to oppose Dayton's imposed division do now? There was not much our refugee and unemployed members could do in relation to the Bosnian miners' visit except come and listen to their reports. It was also hard for many people to see the connection between the fight to stop ethnic division and a visit by miners who wanted to talk about their wages and jobs.

Car boot sale in Middlesborough

GREAT MYTHS OF THE WAR

- **During World War II the Partisans were Serbs and the Fascists were Croats**

This myth is encouraged by those who defend Milosevic and 'the Serbs', because they think they are in some way 'defending socialism'. In fact the Partisan movement was progressive precisely because it was a multi-national movement – Serbs joined in large numbers, but so did Croats, Muslims, Slovenes, and all Yugoslavia's other nationalities.

By the end of 1943 there were 26 Partisan divisions in existence, of which 18 were Bosnian or Croatian. These Bosnian and Croatian divisions included large numbers of Serbs, but even larger numbers of Croats and Muslims. It was precisely their ability to appeal to all of Yugoslavia's nationalities that enabled the Partisans to defeat the Nazis, their puppets and all the remnants of the old regimes.

15.6.96
Chetniks hide the evidence

UN officers investigating mass graves near Srebrenica in Bosnia dug a 'test trench' at Nova Kasaba on June 5th, and found at least six corpses, with more thought to be nearby.

Survivors and US satellite photographs suggest up to 2,700 missing men and boys may have been massacred.

Serb authorities claim any Bosnians buried there were soldiers killed in battle. But the latest bodies found were in civilian clothes.

Near Brcko, in Serb-held northern Bosnia, IFOR troops were guarding a mass grave after a Serb contractor arrived with bulldozers to level the site for a factory.

Primrose Hill is a typical inner city school in Leeds, with children from many ethnic backgrounds. The following article is reprinted from their school magazine.

The war in Bosnia has stopped, but only now are all the victims being discovered – in the mass graves near the 'safe-havens' that the United Nations could not, or would not, protect.

We read of the death, fifty years ago, of Anne Frank, the fifteen-year-old Jewish girl who died in another 'ethnic cleansing', and we wonder how the world could have let such things happen. And yet last year we could do nothing.

Last December an aid convoy went from Leeds to Tuzla, a Bosnian city which tried to stay multi-ethnic throughout the war, with Serbs and Muslims living peacefully in the same community.

We sent over £100 in cash and several boxes of goods, along with some letters and Christmas cards to the school children of Tuzla.

When the convoy returned, it brought a pile of letters and messages for Primrose pupils. Azra, aged 15, wrote, "I'm very happy to know that someone in a foreign country thinks about us, here in Bosnia....We didn't want that war, but we were attacked and had to defend ourselves. There were many massacres, like the one on May 25th, 1995 in front of the Kapija. There, 72 young people were murdered and about 150 injured. There were many of my well-known friends....but we are continuing to live. Many schools are open again. We just try to live like we did before this awful war."

Another convoy is leaving on July 27th, taking more letters from Primrose.

In London the Bosnia Solidarity Campaign centred their activity on investigating the British government's complicity in the war. Some Workers Aid members co-operated with a number of other people and organisations to stage an arts festival in Tuzla in August under the name of *Artists for a United Bosnia*. A hundred or more people, from a number of countries, travelled out to put on a whole range of cultural events ranging from art exhibitions, Mozart recitals, to a pop concert with Bosnian and British bands.

Even with these various activities the reality was that there was nothing to replace the convoys. They had been made possible by the huge tremors that had shaken European society during the war. For the moment the tremors had subsided.

Some of the veteran convoy members moved on to other things. Two people got jobs inside Bosnia, partly in order to learn the language properly. Some people became involved in other struggles and others, like people in Bosnia, resumed 'normal' lives.

It was hard to see this great team of people, who had become so close during the convoys, drifting apart but if the convoys were no longer appropriate, then it had to be accepted. The knowledge people had gained was not going to be lost. People were not dropping their determination to change the world. They were moving on to doing it in different ways.

Young Bosnians at the National Theatre of Tuzla, during the Tuzla Arts Festival

Bosnia Solidarity Campaign statement on the Tory Funding scandal:

Allegations that the Tory party have been receiving financial handouts from supporters of Serbia, and have apparently maintained friendly relations with them to the point where a leading spokesman for the ethnic cleansers plans to stand as a Tory candidate should come as no surprise.

While repeatedly refusing on the grounds of 'neutrality' to protect the people of Bosnia, an internationally recognised sovereign state under brutal attack, Western governments, and particularly the British, have worked to an agenda of covert support for the Serbs that constitutes complicity in war crimes.

The extent of this support, and its practical results, should be subject to the widest possible public scrutiny so that we can judge for ourselves the morality of the politicians who purport to lead us.

15th
Convoy Factfile

DATE:
July 1996

LORRIES:
2 from Workers Aid and 2 from Artists for a United Bosnia

WEIGHT: 8 tons

RECIPIENTS:
Tuzla music school, Amica Theatre Company and the community of Celic

PEOPLE: 15

First anniversary of Srebrenica massacre, Whitehall.

Durham Miners' Gala, 1996

As Workers Aid was going through this metamorphosis other avenues of work were opening up. In Bosnia people were trying to resume their lives and began to confront the huge social problems, not just those resulting from the destruction of war but also those arising from the forward march of the 'free market' into the former socially owned economy. Western banks were overseeing the 'reconstruction' of Bosnia. The miners were the first to strike over pay, followed by Tuzla health workers and teachers. 10,000 refugees from Srebrenica and other towns staged a demonstration in Tuzla on the first anniversary of the massacre. They turned their anger on buildings associated with the UN, who they correctly saw blocking their efforts to know the true fate of all their men.

Bosnia is raising its head again

During my previous, brief visits to France from Serbia the Bosnian friends I have met have all more or less been beaten down by the catastrophe which engulfed their country.

They struggled to defend it, trusting more or less in Western governments, but the more these governments showed their complicity in the bloody partition of their country, the more beaten they felt.

But Mevlida is something else. She is a mature woman with two children and a confident bearing, direct gaze and energetic voice. She knows what she wants. People of this calibre make good leaders.

Mevlida Altumbabic is a teacher at the building trade technical college. She is President of the Secondary School Teachers' Union. She comes from a family which has lived in the city for several generations.

"Before the war I was a Communist Party member for twenty years. It wasn't me that left the party, it was the party that left me."

The League of Yugoslav Communists broke up wretchedly in 1989. Swearing loyalty to the working class and to socialism, it had long since become the party of the ruling bureaucracy. It abandoned Mevlida and thousands of honest communists to the demagogy of militant nationalism.

Since then, Mevlida has been distrustful of parties. That is why she chose the trade-union slot, where she is near to her rank-and-file colleagues and where her energy and capacity for work can find expression without her becoming a transmission belt for her superiors.

"At the height of the Chetnik aggression in 1992 teaching stopped. From October we planned to continue schooling in cellars, but that was impossible for the secondary and technical schools. We went back to work in the buildings we shared with refugees, living with the constant fear of a shell landing on the classroom."

"Karadzic's army fired at random on the town, but there was a sort of a pattern. Whenever the Bosnian army advanced anywhere, the Serbs would shell civilians. The worst thing was the shelling of schools during lessons. The pupils were our responsibility and we had them on our conscience."

The shell which murdered seventy-four civilians in the main street put the whole town in mourning.

"They were clearing away the blood when I was there. I lit a candle, but thinking about all the blood in front of me, I went numb for I don't know how long."

"We worked without wages throughout the war. What the soldiers did at the front, we did at the rear. The schools did not close, we fed the young people with knowledge. What would have become of them without the schools where they could forget the war for a few hours?"

"We were all Yugoslavs, but Yugoslavia was destroyed, starting from Serbia. Now I am a Bosnian. Fascism tried to destroy Bosnia, but it did not succeed. Bosnia is raising its head again. Bosnia is the first line of defence for the whole of Europe. Because if fascism crushed Bosnia, it could only spread all across Europe."

"At the most difficult time in the war, my husband and I thought about leaving this hell. Now, there is no question of that. Our struggle for the future was a struggle for our children. Defending our country was to educate the children, to give them knowledge."

If Yugoslavia was murdered on the body of Bosnia, the renewal of the trade union and political movement of the workers of the former Yugoslavia will come from Bosnia.

The surest guarantee of this is the new people who have arisen in Bosnia. Mevlida is one of them.

Interview with MEVLIDA ALTUMBABIC by Radoslav Pavlovic, August, 1996

The UNISON branch which had helped Teeside Bosnia Solidarity Campaign send supplies to Banovici asked us if we could help them bring over a Bosnian health worker for the UNISON annual conference. We arranged the travel for Raisa Gulamovic, Vice-President of Tuzla Health Workers' Union and for Faruk Ibrahimovic as translator. UNISON leaders did not invite her to address the conference but some local branches organised a fringe meeting and she was able to talk with many nurses and other health workers.

In 1994 Workers Aid had leafleted delegates going into the UNISON conference. The following year some UNISON branches who supported our work tried to get Bosnia discussed at the conference and did manage to have a message from Tuzla read out. Now, in 1996, a Tuzla representative was inside the conference. Even if our own members were drifting apart, the momentum of their work was setting new things in motion.

At the same time the President of the Tuzla Secondary Teachers Union, Mevlida Altumbabic, visited Paris and met with Radoslav Pavlovic from Serbia, who first proposed the convoys to Tuzla. They discussed the need to overcome the barriers that nationalism had created between people, not just in Bosnia, but througout the region. Together, Workers' Aid and the Tuzla teachers began to make plans for a meeting of education workers from across ex-Yugoslavia.

While the mass of people were now effectively penned in their ethnic ghettos, the nationalist leaders, western politicians and representatives from western banks and industries could all travel freely throughout the region, taking advantage of the divided and weakened people to pursue their own plans. The defenders of multi-cultural Bosnia needed to break out of their ghetto to pursue their aims and we hoped the education workers' meeting would be a way to do this.

This idea of working against the wider division of people came up not just with the teachers. The miners also spoke of their desire to regain contact with miners across ex-Yugoslavia. The President, Fikret Suljic, always made the point at meetings that there had never been problems between miners, they were all just workers. It was the nationalist politicians who had driven a wedge between them.

Interim report by Bosnian Solidarity Campaign into western governments' complicity in war crimes

PRIJEDLOZI ZA ISTRAŽIVANJE RATNIH ZLOČINA

Dana 17. marta 1996. Bosnia Solidarity Campaign odlučila je pokrenuti kampanju za istraživanje sljedećih činjenica:

1. U JULU 1995.g. nakon pada Srebrenice, britanski general Rupert Smith potpisao je tajni dogovor s Ratkom Mladićem za evakuaciju žena, djece i starih osoba iz UN "zaštićene zone". Odrasli muškarci i mlađići nisu obuhvaćeni dogovorm (Roy Gutmann "Nema mira da se čuva", strana 99). Postoje dokazi da su UN trupe već ranije vidjele ali i zanemarile srpske zločine. Smith je morao znati da muškarce i dječake iz Srebrenice prepušta na mučenje i ubijanje. Uprkos obznane UN-a o masakru britanska vlada je prikrivala činjenice. U brifingu MI6 datom novinarima nakon čega su vijesti saopštavale da su Muslimani muškarci napustili Srebrenicu još prije njenog pada i da su se probili do teritorije pod kontrolom bosanske vlade. I holandska i američka vlada učestvovale su u prikrivanju činjenica (John Sweeney, "Observer", 10.9.95.)

2. U NOVEMBRU 1994.g. britanski general Sir Michael Rose naredio je pripadnicima SAS-a da ne otkrivaju položaje srpske artiljerije oko UN "zaštićene zone" Bihać kako bi spriječio zračne udare NATO-a a koji su se trebali biti upereni protiv njih (Ed Vuilliamy, "Guardian", 26.1.96.) Rose je tvrdio da se bojao da bi zračni udari mogli ugroziti pripadnike UNPROFOR-a. Ranije je s velikim oklijevanjem zatražio zračne udare iz zraka i sa zemlje oko Goražda (aprila 1994.) a poslije čega je govorio o ozbiljnim gubicima nakon srpskog napada na Goražde, vjerovatno da ne bi ugrozio najnoviji "mirovni plan" (Silber i Little, "Smrt Jugoslavije", strana 362-363).

Djelovanje Rosea (i Smitha u Srebrenici) navodi nas da se zapitamo ko je komandovao britanskim trupama u sastavu UNPROFOR-a – čini se da nije bila razrađena posebna politika UN-a, ili se njima komandovalo iz Whitehall-a? Ako se komandovalo iz Whitehall-a da li je njihova taktika bila da se slijede već poznatu politiku britanske vlade, ili je postojao još tajanstveniji plan o brzom porazu Bosne kako bi se ojačala Srbija? Bilo bi dobro pogledati u diskusije u Parlamentu i u zvanične zaključke o britanskoj politici u vrijeme raspoređivanja trupa UNPROFOR-a kao i u vrijeme događanja u Srebrenici, Bihaću i Goraždu i uporediti ih s britanskim angažovanjem na terenu. Šta mi možemo otkriti u vezi s komandovanjem? Trebalo bi da ispitamo i ulogu "prijatelja Srbije" i njihov uticaj na britansku vladu. Na primjer, konzervativac Henry Billingham, član Parlamenta, hvalio se o vezama svoje vlade u beogradskom magazinu "Intervju" (februar 1995.). On je bio sekretar od 1992.g. tadašnjem ministru odbrane, a koji je sada ministar vanjskih poslova, Malcolm Rifkind-u (Mark Almond "Nema mira da se čuva", strana 130-131).

3. KANADSKI GENERAL LEWIS MACKENZIE družio se i pio s vojskovođama armije bosanskih Srba. On je ubijedio predsjednika Mitterand-a da se javno susretne s Karadžićem prilikom posjete Sarajevu - u interesu "neutralnosti" ("Smrt Jugoslavije", strana 281-282). Sada je plaćeni agitator srpske vlade (i/ili Republike srpske). Priča se da su MacKenziewe trupe posjećivale srpske logore za silovanje. Premijer bosanske vlade je izjavio da će MacKenzie biti optužen za ratne zločine (BosNet V5+83). Izvori: BosNet i Newsgroup (Dave Lawrence). Treba pribaviti njegove memoare ("Mirotvorac", Douglas McIntyre, Vancouver, 1993.)

4. PONOVLJENI SU PROPUSTI I-FOR-a da pomogne u hvatanju ratnih zločinaca i istraživanju ratnih zločina. Isto tako propustio je da zaštiti, a pokazao je spremnost da pomogne u evakuaciji Srba iz Sarajeva. (Da li ovo pokazuje namjere Anglo-francuske želje da vide raspad Bosne?) Ovo su samo dvije tekuće stvari. Grupa koja se zalaže za podršku Medjunarodnom sudu za ratne zločine treba da se usmjeri i na ovo prethodno.

Bosnia Campaign Solidarity

Nice work if you can get it   1.9.96

Slobodan Milosevic believes he has found just the man he needs to help prop up his cash-strapped regime: Douglas Hurd, Britain's former Foreign Secretary. Since he left the Cabinet, Mr Hurd has become deputy chairman of the National Westminster Bank subsidiary, Nat West Markets. The latter has recently secured lucrative contracts both to advise on Serbia's debt and to help prepare PTT, Serbia's telephone system, for privatisation.

Mr Hurd has recently been in Belgrade, where he met Mr Milosevic for a discreet breakfast on July 24th, arranged by British ambassador Sir Ivor Roberts. According to one well-placed source: "Hurd came to thank Milosevic for the business, and he did this because Nat West wants to scoop up forthcoming privitisations in the electricity and oil sectors which will be worth millions."

Dame Pauline Neville-Jones, until recently Britain's most senior woman diplomat, is also now a senior Nat West employee and was present at the secret Belgrade breakfast. During the Bosnian war she worked closely with Mr Hurd, hammering out Britain's Balkan policy. Both Mr Hurd and Dame Pauline are currently on holiday and were unavailable for comment.

The Sunday Telegraph

BBQ for Workers Aid members organised by Tuzla miners

A plan for steel

" We drive along the road to Zenica that has been open only since the Bosnia army push last September re-took the area from the Chetniks. The drive is through breathtakingly beautiful countryside – covered in snow but basking in spring sun – and through the most truly depressing remnants of barbarism. Mile after mile of road surrounded by uncleared minefields and through 'ethnically cleansed' and deserted villages. One village at the Tuzla end of the journey has a cardboard placard on the outskirts saying 'Srebrenica'. Here refugees are being resettled, but only women, children and old men.

Our driver tells us about Zenica. It has a steel plant and coal mines. During the eighties, the Yugoslav steel industry was in financial crisis. The plants were old and could not compete on the world market. The Yugoslav authorities paid British Steel to draw up a modernisation plan. They recommended closing many of the plants and concentrating new equipment in a few places. Tens of thousands of workers would have to be sacked.

But how could the Federal authorities implement this plan? There were already mass protests in Belgrade over unemployment and falling wages. If the plan was carried out there would be riots.

War has implemented the plan. The steel plants are closed or destroyed. Instead of protesting, steel workers have been pushed into violence against each other. On both sides of the lines they are now unemployed. In Bosnia, the Dayton agreement stipulates that all reconstruction must be on the basis of 'free market' (ie capitalist) terms. In Serbia and occupied Kosova, President Milosevic is pushing through the privatisation of heavy industry. Metal mining and production is being taken over by a Greek company, *Mytilinaeos*. "

BOB MYERS

For a long time the fate of Kosova and its struggle against Serb nationalism had nagged away in Workers Aid. We often talked of trying to make contact with people there, but the pressure of the convoys had never allowed this.

Back in 1989 the Durham miners had been visited by a delegation of miners from Kosova, just at the point when the Serbian regime was annexing the Autonomous Region and trampling on the rights of its Albanian population. The Kosova miners had gone on underground hunger strikes to protest against this discrimination. Durham NUM sent messages of support to their fellow miners but lost all contact with them as massive repression hit Kosova.

So now Workers Aid set about trying to get a message from Durham to the Kosova miners. A refugee in Durham gave us several telephone numbers in Pristina, the Kosovan capital. For several days we tried all the numbers without success. Lines were dead. Then suddenly a ringing tone. The person at the other end answered. We asked if he could get a message to the Kosova miners? Yes, he knew them well, but could we stay on the phone so he could tell us about the situation of education in Kosova? It turned

17. 3. 96

NATO watches as mobs attack Muslims

Bosnian refugees trying to return to their homes, or visit family graves, have been attacked by organised and armed Serb nationalist mobs, while NATO troops and helicopters looked on.

NATO 'peace' Implementation Force (IFOR) troops have had orders to stop families trying to cross the front line without Serb authorities' permission.

At least two Muslims were shot dead, and others injured, when they tried to visit family graves in Serb held territory near Sjenina, west of Tuzla. Some people were chased into a minefield. NATO said seven dead or injured had been evacuated.

out that we were speaking to the President of the teachers' union. He begged us to come immediately to see for ourselves how people were living.

Three weeks later, in December, two Workers Aid members set out for Kosova. We went via Tuzla which we could now reach with a 25 hour, non-stop car drive. In Tuzla we held meetings with the teachers and miners. With the teachers we made firmer plans for the ex-Yugoslav teachers' meeting, agreeing it should be held the following March in Hungary, on neutral territory. The miners reported that they were coming under increasing pressure to agree to the sacking of non-working miners. The problems had been made worse by the return to the pits of miners demobilised from the army. The government were trying to persuade the union that the mines could not carry the costs of all the pre-war labour. The government promised that new, alternative employment would come from various development schemes proposed by the international community. When we heard this we suggested that another delegation should come to Britain specifically to discuss with British miners their experiences of 'new', 'alternative' jobs following the pit closures in Britain.

Both the teachers' and miners' unions wrote letters for us to take to their colleagues in Kosova with whom no contact had been possible since 1990 – no mail or telecommunications channels existed.

We travelled through Serbia whilst daily mass demonstrations were taking place in Belgrade, protesting against Milosevic's annulment of local election results which his 'socialist' party had lost. We reached Kosova and spent several days with the teachers and the miners who showed us the reality of life under Belgrade's military rule.

For four years we had witnessed 'ethnic cleansing' by war. In Kosova we saw a slower, less dramatic, but nevertheless just as determined form of 'ethnic cleansing'.

Kosova miners

We met Mr. Kurti, his wife and six children. Their house was in total decay. In the room we sat in there was a cooking stove. It was unlit although the temperature was near freezing. He explained that a neighbour had given him some wood but he had to ration it. He introduced us to his children and explained that the eldest boy, who was fourteen, was the only person able to try and earn money. He went every day into the town with a wheelbarrow to earn money by acting as a carrier. If the miners were seen by the police trying to earn money in any way they would be beaten up. But clearly it was very distressful to Mr. Kurti to have to see his child go out like this.

Mr & Mrs Kurti's son

He explained that the miners managed to get some aid from Mother Teresa but his children had only one pair of plastic sandals between them so they could only take it in turns to go to school. Mr. Kurti told us that there had always been oppression of Albanians in the mines. Even if a Serb and Albanian did the same job the Albanian would be on a lower rate of pay. Not only were Albanians generally excluded from higher grades of work, they were also given the worst jobs. His mine (a gold mine) had seventeen levels. On his level the men worked up to their waist in water. No Serbs worked on this level. Mr Kurti's wife had TB but could not afford medical treatment.

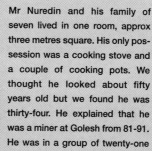

Mr Nuredin and his family of seven lived in one room, approx three metres square. His only possession was a cooking stove and a couple of cooking pots. We thought he looked about fifty years old but we found he was thirty-four. He explained that he was a miner at Golesh from 81-91. He was in a group of twenty-one men who had been the first to be sacked. They were accused of aggressive behaviour but he knew that their sacking was an attempt to intimidate the rest of the miners. Some men were imprisoned. They sent him to trial but he was not sent to prison. He then went to Macedonia to find work but the authorities there destroyed his passport and made it impossible for him to work. He now tried to sell cigarettes in the local area. He apologised for being unable to offer us any hospitality but he had nothing, not even bread for his children. Their health is bad. Two of them have hernias but he had no money for operations.

We sat with Mr Gadrakij, his wife and six children in a room with bare earth floor covered with a plastic sheet and then a rug. He told us that in 1990 he was preparing to go on third shift when the police came and announced the men had 5fiveminutes to evacuate the mine otherwise they would be shot. This was their dismissal. The mines were closed to Albanians. No explanation. Since then he has found some work during the summers, whatever he can find to help the survival of his family. His eldest daughter could not finish secondary school as she had no shoes or clothes. Now some neighbours are trying to teach her to be a hairdresser. His wife told us that life was hard. They only had this one room to live, eat, sleep and wash in. They live day by day hoping that something will get better.

Extract from Workers Aid pamphlet, **Kosova: Apartheid in Europe**

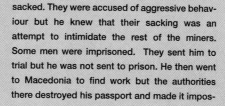

UN hides the evidence

To kill 5,0000 was not a simple affair. Death pits had to be dug, victims captured, bussed, shot, buried; killers radioed, rostered, refreshed, rested. A massacre of 5,000 people is not easy to hide. One important piece of evidence of massacre was film shot by a Serbian cameraman, Zoran Petrovic. His film showed Serbs, sporting the blue berets of the UN's DutchBat, making Nazi-style selections, men to the left (and death), women to the right (and safety).

When the Dutch pulled out, troops inside their armoured personnel carriers heard soft, repeating 'bangs' as people, Muslims, were crushed under their tracks. The Dutch Defence Ministry de-briefing report continued: "Refugees (dead and/or alive) were run over." One senior Dutch officer based in Bosnia at the time told me later: "We don't know how many people were killed. They were hanging on to the tracks and the wheel arches, like Indians on a train."

One soldier had a camera. He took photographs of terrified refugees and of nine corpses. All of them had been shot in the back at heart level. The soldier's film was destroyed when it was wrongly developed by the Dutch Ministry of Defence – "human error," they said.

The Dutch surrendered their weapons and vehicles, against orders, and even their blue UN flak jackets, helmets and berets. Muslims may well have then seen the blue helmets – not realising they were being worn by the enemy – and surrendered.

One soldier used a camcorder to record the shelling of Srebrenica, and the later shelling of Potocari. This tape was also destroyed. The Dutch government destroyed evidence of the massacre; the American government sat on evidence of the massacre, delaying the release of spy satellite or drone photos of the killing until three weeks later; the British government gave prominence to reports that no one had been massacred.

When the women of Srebrenica arrived in Tuzla, they were hysterical. They made the throat-cutting gesture to explain what had happened to their men. But they had no evidence. It is less easy to dismiss the evidence of the Serb cameraman Zoran Petrovic's film. It reveals men prisoners herded into a remote field, as Serbs readied their weapons. What happened next was erased by the Serb cameraman because of his fear of repercussions.

The film goes black.

JOHN SWEENEY (from an article originally published in **The Observer,** Dec 8th, 1996)

During 1990 nearly all Albanians had been sacked from their jobs: all Albanian hospitals, schools and libraries closed and books were pulped. To be an Albanian was to be a non-person. The people who escorted us round likened their situation to apartheid in South Africa, with the difference that in South Africa the blacks at least had some sort of schools and hospitals provided. In Tuzla we had been with people in the midst of siege and war but somehow the atmosphere in Pristina was more oppressive and awful. Tuzla, even in the worst days of deprivation, had been free. Pristina was under occupation.

The Serb nationalists hoped that this persecution would drive the Kosovan Albanians into Albania, but as in Bosnia they met resistance. When all education premises had been placed under military control and closed to Albanian pupils, the 20,000 sacked Kosovan teachers had set up their own schools and universities in basements, garages and spare rooms, all organised by their union. People survived with money sent by family members working abroad. We visited the 'underground' schools and universities. In a technical school the staff explained how hard it was to teach without any access to equipment. As we left a teacher asked us, with desperation in her voice, to tell the world what we had seen. She had pupils who were seriously ill but there was no treatment available. In a secondary school class we talked with the forty or so teenagers packed into a room in a house, all with their coats on in the sub-zero temperature. One girl asked us,

Workers Aid members with members of the miners' union committee of the Stari Trg region, Kosova

"Do people in Britain know what is happening to here?" We shook our heads. "For the last four years we have been in and out of Bosnia, only a few hundred kilometres away, and even we knew little of what is happening here."

Their teacher smiled and added, "But I am sure your gov-. ernment knows."

For the Kosova miners, we were the first people to visit them since the Serbian occupation began – their first contact with the outside world. We visited the homes of sacked miners. For six years they had been without any income and they and their families were without clothes, food or heating. The union committee, however, told us they were not so much interested in 'aid'. They wanted to make contact with trade unions in western Europe, to explain to them what was going on in Kosova, hopefully to gain their support for their demand of independence for Kosova.

On our arrival in Pristina our hosts had parked our car, with its foreign number plates, in a back yard and driven us about in a local car to avoid police attention. When we left they gave us a book with a photographic record of their struggle against Serbian nationalism. They advised us to hide it under the car mats in case we were stopped by police road blocks. Luckily we had missed them on the way in by taking a wrong road and coming via a tiny back route over the mountains. We promised the miners and teachers that we would try to help them visit Britain as soon as possible.

On our way home we went to Slovenia to try and resume contact with the miners. However, at the union head office we found Frank Druks, who had been so supportive of our work in 1993, had been replaced by a man with something of an identity problem. He first handed us his card, giving his title as Director of the Slovenian energy company, then took it back and gave us another one on which he was President of the Energy Union. This schizophrenia was apparently no problem for the British and European trade union federations. Having kept a safe distance from Bosnia throughout the war they had for some time been busy advising the 'new', 'democratic' trade unions in Slovenia and Croatia.

Independent Union of Miners,
Stari Trg/Golesh,
Kosova.   December 24th, 1996

For the last seven years Albanian Miners of Kosova, alongside 130,000 other workers, have been locked out of their workplaces. The pretext for this lock-out was a General Strike in 1990 organised to protest against the discriminative measures and annexation by the Serbian regime against Kosova's Albanian workers. The main reason for this lock-out was the regime's plan to use starvation to force workers to leave their country, and in this way to 'ethnically cleanse' Kosova of its 90% Albanian population. In these repressive circumstances the miners, teachers and other workers organised their independent trade unions to do everything possible to defend their members. For this defiance, trade unionists have been subjected to continuous harassment with many arrests, beatings, and imprisonments.

The situation of miners is getting worse day by day, but despite Serbian state repression, they have not stopped their union activities. Because of our situation of bad health and poverty we appeal to miners internationally to show their solidarity with us. We also need you to demand that various commercial enterprises and governments cease their co-operation with the National Socialist regime in Belgrade in the exploitation of our mines and factories in Kosova.

We extend a warm welcome to trade unionists to visit us, to see for themselves the nature of life under our 'apartheid' system. Please contact us by phone or fax on 00 381 38 26 112 (connection is very difficult but please keep trying). Please send financial assistance to Durham NUM.

Miners greetings,

SKENDER SEJDIU, Vice President

The Husina uprising

On December 21st, 1920, miners throughout Bosnia-Herzegovina, then part of the Kingdom of Yugoslavia, went on strike. The Bosnian Prime Minister told the strike committee that he would use force to break the strike. The government tried to recruit strike breakers but none could be found in the Tuzla basin. They did manage to set up a 'People's Militia' drawn from the dregs of society. They carefully recruited people of Serb origin to use against the mainly Muslim, Slovene and Croat miners of Tuzla region.

The strike was solid and the authorities looked for ways to counter-attack. The press went on an all out war against the miners. Priests in the mining areas preached sermons against the strike to the sisters and wives of the miners. Only the workers' press spoke up in defence of the strike. On December. 24th, the *Voice of Freedom* wrote:

Yugoslavia leads the world in placing the entire burden of Government spending on the backs of the workers while refusing to do anything for their welfare. The living conditions of miners are appalling. Colliery management use a system of fines to reduce wages to below starvation levels. Safety in the mines is ignored and the victims of accidents receive no compensation. In Zenica there are 1,750 miners who barely have clothes or shoes to wear.

The authorities resorted to an old tactic and ordered the eviction of all foreigners from mine-owned housing and banned the local population from sheltering them. This meant that many miners and their families, originally from Slovenia, Hungary and elsewhere, would be thrown out into the harsh Bosnian winter.

The miners had harsh experience of this method of dividing Bosnian and non-Bosnian and took affairs into their own hands. Forty-five families, mostly Slovenes, were moved by the strike committee to houses of miners in Husino. The following day sixty more families were moved to Lipnica and Ljubace.

On the 25th, a general meeting of miners and peasants from all the villages in the Tuzla region resolved that if the authorities tried to use force to evict the non-Bosnian families the miners would reply with force. They set up patrols and lookouts and began to collect whatever guns they could lay their hands on. Miners, non miners, men, women, Bosnian and non-Bosnian stood shoulder to shoulder against the threat of force to victimise the Slovenian miners. There was no turning back now. Years of degradation and suffering had turned to defiance and revolt.

On the 27th, police went to Husino and other villages to try and arrest the Slovene and other foreign miners. In Husino, the anger of the miners finally broke when police began to destroy the few miserable possessions of a Slovene woman. She tried to stop them. Three police began to beat her up but found they were surrounded by miners and tried to shoot their way out. People fired back and one policeman was hit. He was carried, bleeding, into a house. One young miner, Jure Kerosevic, organised for a horse drawn cart to take the injured man to hospital, but he died on the way.

In Tuzla the Chief of Police called for reinforcements and two units of infantry were brought from Sarajevo. During the night of the 27th a force of fifty police, twenty People's Militia thugs and two infantry units, armed with rifles, machine guns and cannons marched on Husino and Lipnica. Before they set out the Chief of Police gave them orders. "There are no rules. You can kill who you like – men, women or children. One of the

WORKERS FIGHT: Workers of Zagreb. Vote for the Workers Peasants Republican block. Leader of the list is the imprisoned miner, Jure Kerosevic.

strikers is going to hang." The attack on Husino began at 11pm and lasted through the night, the town falling to the government forces at sunrise. Lipnica was taken later the same day.

The police, troops and especially the People's Militia inflicted terrible beatings and tortures on everyone they could lay their hands on. Miners' leaders were forced to walk miles through mud and snow to Tuzla. As they passed through outlying villages they were beaten over and over to instil fear in other workers. In Tuzla prison the beatings continued as the police demanded to know the name of the person who shot the policeman. In the course of police beatings seven miners were murdered. A total of twenty seven children were left without fathers.

The miners in the Tuzla region were the most militant and best organised section of the union. With the arrest of their leaders the strike in other places began to collapse after two weeks. Many miners were forced back to work at gunpoint. Even leaderless, the Tuzla miners held out for four weeks. By this time 350 strikers were in prison.

Everyone who feared the growing unity of workers tried to find ways to divide their solidarity. The Serbian nationalist Radical Party paper *Serbs Voice*, applauded the use of force against the strikers, accusing them of being haters of everything Serb and called for the hanging of all 350 men. The Greater Serbian nationalist press claimed that the strike was aimed at overturning the Kingdom of Yugoslavia and restoring Austro-Hungarian rule. They simultaneously claimed that the 'communist' miners were being controlled from Moscow.

As news spread of the repression, workers across Yugoslavia organised protests but the government responded by banning all working class publications.

332 miners were released after over a year in detention. Juro Kerosevic was charged with the murder of the policeman. At his trial only one witness could be found who was prepared to testify against him, but the judge found him guilty. Kerosevic was returned to prison to await sentence. That night he found himself in a cell with a worker who had managed to smuggle in a small knife. Kerosevic took the knife and hid it in his cap with the intention of killing the judge. The following day, when he was taken into court, he found that the trial judge had been replaced with another man. Kerosevic felt too little hatred to kill him. The judge however had no hesitation in sentencing him to be hanged at 4.30 am the next morning. He asked if Kerosevic wanted to see a priest. The twenty year old miner replied, "Why should I want a priest? I'm not a sinner. It's you who need a priest since you have condemned an innocent man to death. I only asked for bread and you gave me a rifle butt. Even this wasn't enough for you. I am completely innocent but you give me death. I will die for the working class, for justice. I am not afraid of death. You want to see me on the gallows to try and scare other workers with my death.

But it wont happen. I'm master of my own life and my own death and you'll see how those who fight for justice die without fear."

Then, pulling out his knife, Kerosevic slashed his own stomach three times and was about to strike again when guards overpowered him. They rushed him to hospital to ensure that he survived long enough for him to be hanged. He spent forty days in hospital. But this delay gave workers time to act

Jure Kerosevic (painting by Ismet Mujezinovic)

Across Yugoslavia and across Europe working class militants organised protests. The Bosnian miners struggle for unity had become a catalyst which led to workers far beyond the borders of Yugoslavia seeing their own fate bound up with the fate of Kerosevic. This international protest, which the Yugoslav government feared would spark off further unrest, led to Kerosevic's sentence being reduced to twenty years in jail.

Kerosevic was twenty years old when he was taken to Zenica prison to begin his sentence. For the first three months he was kept in solitary confinement. Then he was allowed to work in the joinery shop, but even here all conversation between prisoners was forbidden. Not until he was freed in 1939, aged thirty-seven, was he able to read about the international workers' protests which had saved his life.

Prison had not broken Kerosevic's spirit. He returned to Husino on the eve of World War II and soon joined the partisans to fight against fascism. Nor had other miners in the Tuzla basin lost their militancy or their hatred of oppression and division. Miners and other workers in the partisans liberated the Tuzla basin and in 1943 it became the largest 'free territory' in Nazi occupied Europe, a haven to all people.

Edited extract from Workers Aid pamphlet The 1920 Bosnian Miners' Rebellion

Postscript. Every year the Bosnian miners commemorate the Husina uprising with a holiday and festivities. In 1996, mine managers told the miners' union that they would no longer support the commemoration as it related too much to the 'red' past. The miners' union replied that they would organise the festivities themselves. Managers later changed their minds and agreed to support the day. The union told them to get stuffed. They organised things by themselves.

Bihac: the effects of two years of seige by Serb nationalists

Chapter 10

FEBRUARY 1997 In contravention of the Dayton Agreement, Republica Srpska and rump Yugoslavia (Serbia) sign co-operation agreement.
JULY 1997 First middle ranking war criminal arrested. Karadzic and Mladic still move freely.
SEPTEMBER 1997 In municipal elections, Tuzla re-elects a multi-ethnic coalition headed by Selim Beslagic.

The spirit of unity survives

On our journey from Tuzla to Kosova we had entered the Chetniks' Republika Srpska to try and cross the River Sava at Brcko, as we knew that the bridge was still intact. Brcko had seen bitter fighting and its' Muslim population are still unable to return to their homes. On reaching the bridge the local police refused to let us cross as we had come from Tuzla. We only managed to use the bridge after IFOR troops intervened. We had British passports, but Bosnians were queueing for hours for the ferry at Orasje. IFOR troops, meanwhile, have their own pontoon bridges. It is still the case now, in 1998, that in Brcko, an intact bridge remains under Chetnik control and impassable to Bosnians. This is the peace that Dayton has brought.

Fighting for us

" We were stopped in Kresevo by the Croatian nationalists who run a pocket of central Bosnia. Their Oxford trained Captain was clearly a psychopath. He hated Muslims, and mine was the only white British face amongst the crew; I was terrified for our Asian drivers. They took me inside a small Police station and sat me on a chair with an electric heater underneath – it was August. Then they shouted at me for two hours. They wanted our trucks and supplies, and us in jail. We were saved by our tiny, eighteen-year-old interpreter. She argued her way into the room I was in, and then had a nose to nose argument with our psychopath. It turned out that her mother was deputy police chief in Jablanica and would stop all traffic in and out of their enclave if the HVO didn't leave us be. They gave way.

In Kladanj we went to a damaged school with our load, not knowing why. Then we realized the school was jam-packed with women and kids and a few old men, who had all arrived from Srebrenica over the previous twenty-four hours. One woman had walked with her disabled twelve-year-old son over her shoulders. There were no provisions of any kind, the local people being poverty stricken themselves. The local women had brought everything they could spare in half a dozen wheelbarrows, but there were at least a thousand desperate people crammed into the school gym. It was a pitiful scene.

We unloaded everything we had, and helped as much as we could, though many of our younger members were in shock and the problem was clearly beyond us. Not one aid agency knew these people existed. One of our boys dropped a box of biscuits and there was a scrum of children within seconds, literally fighting to eat. I was not in the Bosnia I knew anymore. That was the most depressing day of my entire life. God alone knows how the women and kids felt.

Sometimes it seems that Bosnia just meant fear, paperwork, arguments, breakdowns and hours at the wheel (twenty-two hours was my longest stint – in the dark on a goat track that a Workers Aid truck drove off a few months later. In daylight.) But it was more than that for everyone who went there. I think we all have a massive respect and a lasting gratitude to the people of Bosnia, and even for each other. The Bosnians fought for us, while our politicians deserted them. They asked for nothing except the right to defend themselves, and in so doing stood up for the right of all civilized people to live together, and to reject racial paganism and barbarity. Workers Aid, and the individuals who made it, took sides, but everyone involved knows that it was the Bosnians who were actually defending civilisation and what we believe in. "

PHIL O'CONNELL

The nationalists, with Milosevic at their head, had set out to divide the people of Bosnia and Yugoslavia in an attempt to cling on to power and wealth in the face of a growing economic and social crisis. Their violence was supported by the western powers pursuing their own plan – the restoration of capitalism. In Yugoslavia, where 80 per cent of factories, mines etc were socially owned, that simply meant robbery.

After Dayton, the western powers slowly extended their control of the region. In December 1997, they announced that they were giving NATO troops the power to remove anyone in authority anywhere in Bosnia who did not comply with their demands. They brought some of the extreme nationalists to heel, not out of any moral concern but to advance their own interests. The mass murderers had done their job and were now a costly nuisance. Bosnian people were divided, exhausted and reduced to poverty. In these circumstances resistance to the values of the free market and to the theft of their socially-owned property would be minimal, but to exploit the region successfully there had to be some re-integration. The profitable exploitation of labour and resources would be almost impossible without the restoration of roads, railways and trade between different parts of ex-Yugoslavia.

For western governments the trick was to partially re-integrate the region economically, while keeping its' people divided and powerless. A few of the lesser war criminals could be removed to assist this re-integration of production. After four years of ignoring every desperate plea from Bosnia's defenders, western politicians, including Robin Cook, the new Labour Foreign Minister, began to lecture Bosnians on 'multi-culturalism' and 'tolerance'.

A stream of business advisors flew between Zagreb, Sarajevo, Pale and Belgrade. These advisors included the ex-British Foreign Secretary, Douglas Hurd, now representing the National Westminster Bank and advising Milosevic on privatisation – for a fee of $10million. Hurd was by no means the only British politician with financial links to the Serbian regime.

Amongst them were two Labour MPs, Dr David Clark and Dr John Reid, who spent three days during the war in a luxury Geneva hotel with Radovan Karadzic, who paid their expenses. Their relationship with a mass murderer has not harmed their careers. Clark is now Chancellor of the Duchy of Lancaster and Reid is the armed forces minister!

Robin Cook – human rights will be the cornerstone of Labour foreign policy – developed co-operation with Biljana Plavsic, the Bosnian Serb extremist. She had supported genocide against the Muslims but was quick to see which way the wind was blowing following Dayton and broke ranks with Karadzic, offering herself as the reasonable Bosnian Serb leader the west could do business with.

Under the terms of Dayton, national elections were held in Bosnia and the results replicated those held on the eve of the war. The three ethnic-based parties all won in the areas Dayton had assigned to Serbs, Muslims and Croats. This was hardly surprising. In Republika Srpska and Herceg-Bosna, the extreme nationalists – who had grown rich and powerful on war – remained in control of the media, the police and every aspect of life. Even in the Bosnian areas- the Muslim SDA tried to intimidate any opposition. Haris Silajdzic, who resigned as Prime Minister and broke from the party, was attacked when he tried to hold an election rally in Cazin.

Goddess Biljana

"We are disturbed by the fact that the number of marriages between Serbs and Muslims has increased..........because mixed marriages lead to an exchange of genes between ethnic groups, and thus to a degeneration of Serb nationhood."

BILJANA PLAVSIC

(Oslobodenje, Sarajevo, May, 1994)

Despite the war, and the scheming of the 'victors' to bury all remnants of the Partisan revolution, some people were still not willing to let go of the past.

In January 1996, a conference of the International Trade Union Solidarity Campaign in London was opened by four speakers – Fikret Suljic from the Bosnian miners, Skender Sejdiu from the Kosovan miners, Agim Hyseni from the Kosovan education union and Radoslav Pavlovic from Serbia. Their reports of ongoing efforts by working people to defend their national and workplace rights had an unmistakable echo of past struggles.

Workers Aid had arranged for the four Bosnian and two Kosovan miners to meet local councillors and NUM members in the ex-mining areas of Bolsover and Easington. Bolsover Councillors took them on a tour round the closed collieries. Car repair firms and the like occupied some of the empty pit-head buildings. The council had managed to attract several hundred new jobs, low paid and non-union, to replace the 10,000 jobs lost in local mines. Sacked miners had been offered thirteen week retraining courses in carpentry and other skills, with a free set of tools thrown in. There were no jobs going, even after the 're-training', but the tools could be sold so miners signed up for the courses. The Bosnian and Kosovan miners, who knew about the history of the once powerful British trade unions, were shocked. In Bosnia the miners were being fed the same promise of alternative jobs if they accepted pit closures. They asked the British miners why the 1985 strike had been lost. "Because we didn't get support from other unions," came the immediate reply.

While the miners travelled round the country talking to people, including the Liverpool dockers once again, the President of the Kosova Teachers' Union met with teachers and university lecturers.

At a meeting with Labour MPs in the House of Commons, the Kosovans asked if a future Labour government would support Kosova's demand for independence. One MP replied that the international community had recognised the independence of the republics when Yugoslavia broke up, but they would have problems accepting the break up of the republics themselves, ie Serbia. The Kosovans pointed out that Kosova was not part of Serbia, except

Kosovan, Bosnian, Serbian and British trade unionists at an international conference in London

through illegal military occupation. In Federal Yugoslavia, Kosova's status had been similar to the republics and it therefore had equal rights to independence.

Three months later, on May 1st, Labour was elected. With two million Kosovan Albanians facing a slow death the new Labour government and the US administration indicated that the problems of Kosova could only be dealt with in a Serbian context – diplomatic code for saying Kosova belonged to Serbia.

NUM members in South Wales welcome Resad Husagic

From the Bosnian miners

The Union of Independent Trade Unions of Bosnia-Herzegovina, with unions covering all industries, was formed in 1992. After the invasion of the country only a small number of unions, including the coalminers, continued to function.

During the war, we tried to keep functioning in all the mining communities: Tuzla, Lukavac, Zivinice, Banovici, Kakanj, Zenica, Breza and Gracanica. We worked with all our members in the defence from aggression, spreading the truth about events in Bosnia-Herzegovina, making provision for humanitarian aid for the survival of miners as well as our union organisation.

More then 60 per cent of miners joined the Bosnian army. Many miners were killed trying to defend their right for freedom and a decent life. Other miners worked to produce coal, vital for production of electricity and heating. We regarded our labour and coal as humanitarian help for our people and worked without pay.

We tried to make contacts with trade unions and the workers' movement of Europe so they could inform the public in their countries about the situation in Bosnia-Herzegovina because the governments of most western countries hid the truth. Sadly we had little success.

In 1993 we heard of a convoy of workers' aid to support our struggle against the barbarism of the Chetnik's army. With this we started to receive messages of workers' solidarity from Scandinavia, France, Belgium, Spain, Brazil, Italy and Croatia. The convoy was stopped in Croatia. One small part reached Tuzla on November 13th, 1993. The people who came and brought a small amount of aid would become part of history for their superhuman effort in getting past all obstacles. They broke the blockade at the time of the fiercest attacks on Tuzla.

The Workers' Aid campaign continued and we got more help from workers from Britain, Spain, Sweden, Denmark and Italy. We had great hopes and many disappointments. We had so many miners that the aid that came was never enough but miners saw they were not alone and this was a huge moral support.

Despite the very difficult war circumstances our union did everything it could to assist this growth of solidarity. We had very good co-operation with the Trade Union of Energy, Chemical and non-Metal workers from Croatia. A delegation from our Union visited Croatia in 1995. We also developed co-operation with Workers Aid for Bosnia and especially Bob Myers who organised our many visits to Britain.

I had the honour to lead the delegations which visited Britain in April and July, 1996. We made contacts with a lot of trade unions: Dockers in Liverpool, T&G, CWU, Fire Brigades Union, NUM from Durham, Fords, Scottish TUC and Bill Speirs and many others. It was a special honour to visit the Durham NUM Gala in July. I was with Dave Temple, ex-Durham miner, great friend and great host, who introduced us to the Miners' Trade Union of Australia.

The aim of the visits was to bring together the trade unions of Britain with our union and to ask for support. During the war our trade union was left without any equipment or money. Miners were working without salary and couldn't pay membership fees.

Our trade union has kept its' independence from management, government and political parties. We worked to strengthen our multicultural community. When the war stopped our union pressed management to pay miners a 50DM monthly salary starting from January, 1996. In March we organised strikes and got an increase to 70DM. In May, after several days of negotiations, we achieved another increase, but even then our pay was below subsistence level. We are also demanding that government settle our long term future.These negotiations are continuing and we will use all lawful solutions, from negotiations to strike, to bring the lives and working conditions of miners to a higher standard.

Sretno! (miners' greetings)

FIKRET SULJIC (President, Autonomous Trade Union of Coal Mine Workers of Bosnia Herzegovina)

Stamp collecting

" The power of the stamp! In many countries, especially in Eastern Europe, the rubber stamp has an almost mythological property. Everything in life that needs official approval – from adding a new toilet to your house to burying your dead relative – needs a written permission with a stamp. Without documents you can do nothing and a document without a stamp is worthless, a joke.

The long drive of the convoys are interrupted only by breakdowns, overnight stops and 'stamp collecting' at borders, where large amounts of paper-work must be completed. First on one side of the border and then the same again, twenty metres further on. And every piece of paper must be stamped.

When fifteen lorries arrived at the German Austrian border in March, 1994 the Head of German Customs, a big man with a cap, came out to the lorry park where everyone was busily putting Workers Aid for Bosnia stickers on the trucks.

"Who is in charge?" he asks.

"I am," I reply.

"Can I see your papers please?" I stall.

"My friend has them."

"Please bring them to my office in ten minutes."

We have no papers.

I go and look for Mr. Fazlovic, who has organised most of the lorries. In the Customs chief's office Mr Fazlovic explains we have no papers.

"No papers? But this is impossible!"

Mr. Fazlovic patiently explains our situation. The road to Tuzla is open after a year of blockade. Even two days earlier we had not been sure what we were doing, how many lorries were going etc. Now we are here. Our lorries are full of food. Bosnians are starving. Please let us pass.

Can Mr Fazlovic hope to convey the meaning of the starvation and misery only a few hours drive away to this well fed civil servant? After much discussion the Head of Customs declares, "For German customs it is OK. You can pass. Now we must go and see if it is the same for Austrian customs."

We go over the border and into the office of the Head of Austrian Customs. Head of German Customs explains situation to Head of Austrian Customs. They both have a good laugh at the idea of people turning up at their border with no papers. They both agree how impossible it is to cross without papers. But together they slowly dismantle the huge barrier of bureaucratic obstacles that block our passage from one bit of motorway to another bit one centimetre further on. They finally manage it. They applaud each other for their cleverness at finding a way through the problems that stop us moving that one centimetre.

"Austria and Germany both agree you can pass." We all shake hands. Head of German Customs now takes us to the customs offices to explain the routine for passing the border.

"First you must come here to Window 7 – make a note, Window 7. They will stamp your paper here. We walk on up the corridor. "Then you come here to window 11. You get another stamp. That is the German side finished with. We go on to the Austrian offices. "Now you come to Window 22. Get a stamp. Then up to Window 27. Another stamp. Four stamps and you can go. You must get four stamps." The person in charge of the convoy papers becomes a stamp collector.

Of course at each of these windows getting the stamps is not straightforward. Your lorries must be the right weight, tinned meat must be inspected, your vehicle papers must be in order, etc etc. Often your papers are thrown back by the clerk. He will not tell you what is wrong. You have to work it out yourself or seek help from other lorry drivers, a fraternity of international bureaucrat haters. "

BOB MYERS

One evening during their visit, the people from Bosnia, Kosova and Serbia watched a video of Ken Loach's film about the Spanish Civil War, *Land and Freedom*. In 1936, Yugoslav workers had gone to fight against Franco and we had met many people who likened that war with the war in Bosnia. Whatever similarities there might be, there was clearly a great difference in outcome. The triumph of Franco's fascist forces led to a terrible defeat of the workers' movement in Spain and forty years of dictatorship. It also demoralised the whole European working class. 1n 1996, after four years of fascistic war even more barbaric than that in Spain, it was true that Bosnia lay in ruins, its' working people separated by 60,000

UNITED INDEPENDENT TRADE UNION OF KOSOVA
MINERS TRADE UNION STARI TRG

To Mr. Bob Myers
    Mr. Dave Temple

Dear Friends,

We received Your letter and we are very thankfull for it. We also appreciate Your concern about our miners and about current situation in Kosova.

We are very happy to hear that problem of Kosova and conditions in which are living Kosova miners are more familiar to you and to the British public. As You already know our miners are living in terriabe conditions without job, without any source to survival with their families.

Thatfore Your activity and Durham Miners' Union action to collect money for our miners was very good received, because this remind all as, that in trouble You know who are Your friends.

You also mentioned that You are ready to sent food and clothes for our miners but being that cost of transporting is very high we will investigate possibilities for transportation throught some humanitary organisations as Red Cross or Mother Teresa, about which we'll inform You.

About of collected money, we think that the best way to arrive money to our miners is throught our account in DARDANIA BANK in Tirana, Albania (please take a look to another page).

We thank You very much for Your protest outside the serbian Embassy in London but in same time we bag You to protest in all Trade Unions organisations and communities where You have influence, against agreement between the private company from Greece by the name "Mytilineos SA" and our company "TREPÇA" (from which company serbian regime sacked about 14.000 albanian employees). According to this contract "Mytilineos SA" will invest about 500 mil. $ and in return "TREPÇA" will sent metals of our mines. All this with out agreement of employees to whom belong "TREPÇA" company.

With greate hope that our collaboration will continue with concrete results we sent to You and to all friends in Great Britain best regards,

Xhafer Nuli, 8th May 1997
President of Miners Trade Union Stari Trg

Best regards to Mr. Bob Myers from Mr. Shasivar Begu
Best regards to Mr. Dave Temple from Mr. Nazmi Mikullovci and Mr. Bejram Mustafa.

NATO troops and local nationalist war lords. Yet the Bosnian miners were not cowed. They spoke of their determination to fight against the sacking of miners and to defend the benefits they had enjoyed in the past.

During the visit we began to talk about the idea of an international miners' conference to discuss the problems of miners everywhere. Bosnian workers, especially in Tuzla, were coming out of the war still looking for help, but at the same time beginning to talk about internationalism and trying to find a way to unite working people even beyond the borders of Bosnia. There was no mood of defeat.

Our new link with Kosova continued. Not long after their visit, the miners informed us that Milosevic had done a deal with a Greek company to resume production in Kosova's rich metal mines. This Greek company, *Mytilineos*, had been buying up metal mining and manufacturing companies in Bulgaria, Poland, Hungary and now in Macedonia and Serbia. Even though the sacked Kosovan miners were legally part owners of the mines, they were not consulted about the deals. Production was re-started using Polish labour, with Serbian police guarding the mines to prevent the Kosovans explaining the situation to the Poles. The Kosovans asked us to help stop this robbery of their resources. We organised for another Kosova miner to visit Britain to discuss their problems with MPs and Euro MPs. He met with little sympathy from the politicians except Labour MP, Jeremy Corbyn. The Kosovan miner, who spent over a year in jail following the underground protests, travelled to Brighton for a pre-arranged meeting with Tony Benn, but on arrival Benn refused to talk to him. As always warmth and support did come from working people. He stayed for one week in the ex-mining community of Shirebrook where sacked miners and other people started to collect aid for the Kosova miners. We wrote to the Greek trade unions asking them to meet with a Kosovan delegation. The union leadership in Greece had been very pro-Milosevic, collecting money for the Chetniks to 'defend socialist Yugoslavia'. We were, therefore, not surprised when we initially got no replies, but after more letters were sent we finally received a telephone call from a Greek union newspaper. The door had opened a crack.

You needed guns

I went to Bosnia with a Workers Aid convoy comprising French, Spanish and British food trucks and the *Desert Storm* sound system. Many people, on the convoy and back home, doubted the relevance of a sound system. However, I had been part of the *Demolition* sound system in Manchester and believed strongly in the political and cultural power of music and free parties.

During war life still goes on. People try to get on with their lives as best they can. The bars are still open, people try to get to work, to school. If anything, when your backs are against the wall, the need to party together is greater.

Bosnians were not fighting for gain, glory or patriotism, but for their lives, their towns and the lives of their families. We have seen the fate of the unarmed civilians of Srebrenica. They felt they had been forgotten by the rest of the world.

The youth of Tuzla were aware of the revolution in dance music sweeping Europe but had not been able to experience it because of the war. For a Scottish sound system to drive 2,000 miles in a dodgy old truck, through six borders, Croat bandit territory, UN road blocks and the front line, to play the best bangin' British dance music was appreciated for the act of friendship and solidarity that it was offered as. They didn't ask: "Why are you here?" They asked, "When are you coming back?"

We left Tuzla by 'snipers' alley' – a road along a valley with snipers on the top of the ridge. The convoys had to drive as fast as they could along this valley at night with their lights off in order to avoid being hit. We were at the safe area waiting to go through. There was a delay as the previous convoy had been hit. A Bosnian soldier came up to me. You could always tell the Bosnian soldiers; they wore trainers, had no proper equipment and old police rifles. His eyes looked tired and resigned. Maybe his family had been interned and his friends killed. He said to me: "Thank you for bringing food, but we need guns and bullets. They have tanks and planes. We have nothing. If we could defend ourselves you would not have to bring food. Go and tell that to the people in your country."

Since the Dayton Agreement, things have changed in Bosnia. We wanted to go to celebrate their first Christmas of peace. For the first time it was possible to drive to Sarajevo, previously only accessible through a mile long, four foot wide, man made tunnel. Sarajevo had been without water and electricity been and shelled constantly for three years, but still managed to retain some of its pre-war cosmopolitan atmosphere.

Sarajevans we met were initially sceptical about our reasons for being there. Since the peace accord the city had been swarming with Christians, media types and minor celebs wanting to be filmed/photographed doing something for poor Bosnians. Sarajevans were particularly sick of Americans trying to give them teddy bears.

Any doubts we had about being there evaporated when we saw *Club Obala* throbbing on the Saturday night with hundreds of sweaty Bosnian ravers stomping and screaming for more. Attitudes warmed further after an interview we did with *Radio Zid (Wall Radio)*, Sarajevo's youth and only non-government radio station. The DJs played a damn fine set live on air. Then we explained we were British anti-fascists (I had never defined myself as such before) and, not having access to money, music was the only way we could give something significant to the people of Bosnia.

At the end of the interview the presenter asked: "Is there any message you have for the people of Sarajevo?" That stumped me, then remembering the soldier at snipers' alley, I blurted out: "During the war we brought food, medicines and music, you needed guns. I wish we could have brought guns. I'm so ashamed of my government. I'm so sorry, I wish we could have done more to help." And I still do.

JOE MARSHALL (from SQUALL, Summer, 1996

Thanks to *Club Obala*, Sarajevo, Emir at the Metelkova squat, Ljubijana, Bob at Workers Aid and Keith.

While the joint Kosovan-Bosnian delegation were in Britain, preparations were being made for a meeting of teachers from ex-Yugoslavia. Balazs Nagy, the Hungarian who had joined the first convoy, persuaded the Hungarian teachers' union to host the meeting in their hotel in Budapest.

From different parts of ex-Yugoslavia the teachers came together for the first time. There was an enormous gulf of experience and outlook, but a short resolution was passed welcoming the chance to meet and defending the right of children to an education free from discrimination. Education International, the international union federation, were invited to the meeting but chose not to come. Representatives from their Brussels HQ had made frequent visits to teachers throughout ex-Yugoslavia, but they seemed less enthusiastic about teachers getting together themselves.

Despite its' tensions, the teachers' meeting in Budapest provided a new outlet to the spirit of unity which our convoys had been supporting for three years. Without adequate money, with clapped out lorries, without official bits of paper we should have had, we had kept the convoys going. Even though we had not succeeded in turning the outrage felt by millions into a large movement, we had played a part in the survival of that unity, and we were now finding new ways to help it blossom. The miners had delivered their May Day message from the balcony of Liverpool Town Hall to the crowds below, and now the teachers from Tuzla were passing on their ideas and hopes to colleagues from across ex-Yugoslavia.

In the summer of 1997, the Bosnian government outlined plans to introduce ethnically divided curricula into schools. The Tuzla teachers led an immediate protest alongside parents and children. Together, they refused to allow the SDA politicians to do in peacetime what the Chetniks had failed to achieve in war: divide child from child.

In local government elections Tuzla region repeated its pre-war rejection of all nationalist parties. Selim Beslagic and a list of candidates from all ethnic backgrounds were re-elected, despite the huge influx of tens of thousands of Muslim refugees. This victory was not just a boost for the people of the Tuzla region. It gave heart to many people in areas still dominated by nationalists to speak out and organise for a united Bosnia.

On the Arms Embargo

The arms embargo was imposed by the UN in September, 1991. At that time there were no Bosnian defence forces and raw recruits were left to defend their communities against the 'ethnic cleansers' with little more than hunting rifles. The Serb nationalist forces had at their disposal a large part of what had been Europe's fifth biggest army, the JNA, which, over the preceding nine months, had been purged of non-Serb officers and its red star insignia changed to that of the Serbian white eagle. Even three years later, in November 1994, the effects of the arms embargo can be seen in the massive disparity in military equipment.

State/ Parastate	soldiers/ officers	tanks	APCs	heavy artillery	rocket launchers	anti-tank guns	light arms
BOSNIA/H	210,000	45	30	400	55	35	445,000
REPUBLIKA SRPSKA	135,000	400	250	1800	70	200	250,000
KRAJINA SERBS	38,000	200	150	600	40	80	50,00
SERBIA	185,000	2200	1100	4500	190	480	1,500,000

(Source: Karl Gorinsek, former commander of the Republic of Croatia's armed forces in East Slavonija, *Pecat*, Zagreb, 25/10/94)

Serbia proper contributed only relatively small but key numbers of regular JNA soldiers but irregular forces from Serbia such as Arkan's Tigers and Seselj's White Eagles were supplied and staffed by the JNA, and used to spearhead brutal 'ethnic cleansing' throughout Bosnia. The army in Serbia also functioned as an un-ending source of new arms and equipment for the Bosnian Serb nationalists, and as a conduit for military hardware from Russia.

The justifications given for the continuation of the arms embargo by western politicians were numerous. The memorable soundbite claiming that lifting the arms embargo would only "create a level killing field" came from the Old Etonian pacifist, Mr Douglas Hurd.

The Garden of Rest, Tuzla, where the young people of all backgrounds who were killed in the Tuzla cafe shelling are buried side by side. Rusmir Ponjavic was known to Workers Aid members, having helped us unload in 1994

FOR BOSNIA: a work by British artist Julie Read, incorporating some of the signatures collected outside Downing Street protesting at the handing over of the Srebrenica 'safe haven' and the subsequent massacres

Vic Doggart, stiltwalker; the Art of Freedom Festival, Tuzla, July, 1996

Bottom right and below: The first Srebrenica demonstration, July, 1995

The trade union convoy, August, 1995

Members of
Teeside Bosnia
Solidarity
Campaign with
Women from the
*Hands of
Freedom* organi-
sation, Banovici

Mr Kurti, sacked
Kosova miner,
with his family

Srebrenica refugees in a
Tuzla hostel

Journalist Melanie
MacDonough speaking at
a Bosnia Solidarity
Campaign rally

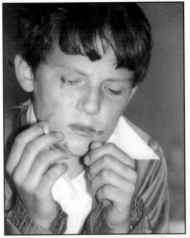

Fish, growing up fast in Tuzla

Nusret, concentration camp survivor and Workers Aid campaigner

Tony, ex-ship-yard worker and Workers Aid campaigner

New Years' Eve, 1994 – the *DESERT STORM* sound system brings revellers out onto the streets of Tuzla

Teachers from ex-Yugoslavia meet in Budapest

Attendance: Presidents of: Union of Pre-school Education Workers of Croatia; both Secondary and Primary School Education Unions from Tuzla Canton; Education Workers' Union of Vojvodina; Independent Union of Education Workers of Serbia accompanied by a union council member; Primary School Section of the Union of Education, Science and Culture of Kosova and a Bosnian teacher working in France who had helped coordinate the meeting through the International Solidarity Section of the French education union, FSU. Visitors: delegate from the Education Section of the Spanish CGT; from Hungary, a representative of the International Trade Union Solidarity Campaign; from Workers Aid, Radoslav Pavlovic and Bob Myers. The Vice President of the Kosova union was stopped en-route by Serbian border police. The Slovenian Education Union discussed sending a delegate but after long arguments decided not to. The Hungarian Teachers' Union provided accommodation, food and a meeting room. The meeting started with reports from each union.

Bosnia – Union rebuilding in Tuzla canton was rapid, but progress was more difficult elsewhere. Tuzla schools faced difficulties as the government diverted resources to other regions. Inside the union there were differences over the future of an undivided country. Some people wanted a union constitution stating the union was for all teachers in Bosnia-Herzegovina while others wanted a constitution only for the area under present Bosnian government control (ie accepting Srpska Republika as permanent)

Croatia – The union was independent of other union federations. After Croatia's independence a new union federation had grown up opposed to the old state controlled unions. The union had been part of this federation but this federation had come under government control and was proving to be acquiescent in the destruction of workers rights and living standards.

Vojvodina – The union had been formed last year as the old state controlled 'union' was only a part of state administration. Teachers had problems with low wages and overcrowding in schools. There had been an influx of refugees from Croatia and Bosnia. The government put the extra children in existing classes with no extra teachers. Classes often had forty children. Teachers recently had a strike (this extended to Serbia as well) and during the strike they had gained many more members but had been unable to win their demands over pay and class sizes etc. The government had used the media to claim the strike was over. The union were unable to counteract this propaganda.

Serbia – The union was growing rapidly as people left the old state union. Both Serbian and Vojvodina unions had taken part in the anti-Milosevic demonstrations but did not support the opposition parties, none of which had policies that would benefit workers.

Kosova – In 1990, all Albanian teachers were sacked and schools closed by police and then used as military barracks or as refugee reception centres for Serbs brought in as colonists from Croatia and Bosnia. The union was organised in 1990 in response to the repression of education. All Albanian teachers in Kosova were members but the union was open to anyone and Serbs had been members until they were forced to leave by the authorities. The union organised education for the 400,000 excluded students from primary to University level. People paid 5DM a month to the fund the schools and Kosovans working abroad gave a percentage of their salaries. He described the apartheid system whereby all Albanians were excluded from health care, education, employment, sport etc by the occupying Serb forces.

The teacher from France reported on union organisation in the west in response to a number of questions relating to privatisation of education, strike pay, union finances and relations with government and political parties etc. These reports led to discussion about what the purpose of the meeting was.

Deep divisions surfaced when the Kosova representative asked why the Kosova teachers had received no help from teachers in Serbia. The Vojvodina representative felt this was a political question. His union was only concerned about education problems in Vojvodina. This led to a discussion about trade unions and politics. Everyone present agreed that Communist Party control of the unions had destroyed them as proper unions and that it was important that unions were kept independent of party control. After some doubts, everyone agreed that the unions had to take political stance on issues – especially education. The Serb and Vojvodina representatives then said that they had no knowledge of events in Kosova, but that they would report the information they had been given to their members.

People were coming from only a few hundred kilometres apart but were worlds apart in terms of experiences. The Serb and Vojvodina representatives hated Milosevic, recognised that the old 'unions' and media had been completely under state control, but they still had not disentangled all the lies they had been fed and had not yet experienced the shocks that might make it possible for them to comprehend information coming from the other people. The Serb representative thought all the ex-Yugoslav politicians had been responsible for destroying Yugoslavia, all equally guilty of waving the flag of nationalism to save their own skins. He did not think that Milosevic and Serbia had played any great role in the Bosnian 'civil war'. He felt that if Bosnian Serbs and Muslims could not live together then maybe it was better they part. But this ignorance of the Serb representatives about events was coupled to something else which must be a parallel to wartime Germans and their 'ignorance' of the concentration camps.

When the Kosovan invited the Serbs to visit Kosova and see things for themselves, the Serb President asked, would the police allow them in? But if nothing was going on in Kosova why would Serb police stop a Serb going there? On the edge of a consciousness that knew nothing was an awareness of something unthinkable.

The Kosovan, Croat and Bosnians tried to explain to the Serb and Vojvodina representatives what had happened to them. The Bosnian teacher from France proposed starting a trade union information bulletin for ex-Yugoslavia.

In proposing this he described the situation in Europe and explained that workers everywhere faced the same problems. The Hungarian representative said that while everyone had common problems what was important in this meeting was the problem that was specific to ex-Yugoslavia: ethnic division. The question for education workers was whether or not to be against multi-cultural education.

This reopened the differences. The Tuzla Primary Union President spoke on the defence of mutli-cultural education against the perspectives of fascism. She thought that the meeting had to produce a statement on how it saw this question. The Tuzla Secondary Union President told how they had struggled for three years, ignored by most of the international trade union movement. She felt bitter that fellow teachers across ex-Yugoslavia had ignored their plight.

But the Croatian President then asked her why no-one in Bosnia had tried to stop JNA troops being moved from bases in Bosnia to attack Croatia, especially Vukovar. In Croatia people had sat in front of JNA tanks to stop their invasion of Slovenia. These exchanges were not made in an angry way, more in thought, sadness and regret, bringing home the truth that the nationalists had attacked an unprepared, unorganised, fragmented working class.

Following the Tuzla proposal for a resolution the following statement was agreed.

Representatives of education unions from BiH, Croatia, Kosova, Serbia and Vojvodina met March 22/23 in Budapest to exchange information and to discuss future cooperation in building unions based on the principles of union democracy, solidarity between all trade unionists and unions free from government control.

All unions represented share a common concern for the future of education for all pupils free from discrimination. We all share a common concern for the proper provision of educational facilities for all pupils and students and for the rights and welfare of all education workers.

It is agreed to start a regional trade union information bulletin to allow exchange of news from all areas of trade union activity in the region.

We appeal to all trade unionists around the world to assist us in our efforts to defend education for the next generation and to defend basic trade union rights.

The Kosova representative wanted a reference to discrimination in Kosova. The Vojvodina representative thought that it was wrong to single out a particular problem as they all had problems.

The FSU member appealed for the Kosovan to accept the statement as it

stood. He thought that to include specific mention of Kosova would make it difficult for the Serbians to introduce the resolution into their unions. The Belgrade regime was doing all it could to discredit the new, independent unions and would use support for Kosova to cause further confusion. The Serbians had agreed to take back the Kosova report. They should be allowed to make their way cautiously. This was accepted.

Sitting in a hotel in Budapest it was easy to forget the war but in the closing speeches all the horrors of the past came spilling out. The Tuzla Primary Union President spoke of the nightmare they had lived through. With tears pouring

From left: Hungary, Spain, France, Serbia, Hungary, Serbia, Serbia, Kosova, Vojvodina and, sitting, Bosnia, Bosnia.

down she begged the Serbian comrades to understand that teachers had seen children die or terrorised, but she and her colleagues had never sunk to the level of the fascists, they had never become 'anti-Serb'. They fought for the unity of all people.

The Croatian President also had to take a long pause soon after she started speaking to try and compose herself. She had witnessed Vukovar. Serbs must see that fascism would come home to Serbia and since there were no ethnic minorities it would pick on people for their ideas – on those who supported democracy, trade unions and freedom. The Serbian President welcomed the chance to meet and discuss. It was clear to him that they must continue this exchange of views.

Finally everyone thanked teachers from Britain, Spain and France who had contributed money to allow the people to get to Budapest.

BOB MYERS, March 25th, 1997

In September 1997, Fikret Suljic visited Britain once again at the invitation of the Scottish TUC and the *Hazards at Work* conference in Bradford. In between these meetings Fikret spent a day talking with Workers Aid about how to continue our collaboration. It was not easy to see where we were going. Listening to Fikret talking about the growing determination of the miners to fight against privatisation it was possible to hear the Bosnian workers reclaiming their past and with it gaining a clearer view of their future. He spoke about the working class, about the legacy of the Partisans, ideas which had hardly been heard in the confusion following the break up of Yugoslavia. The old 'communist' turned nationalist politicians, now hell bent on becoming the new capitalists, had dominated political and cultural life. Just after the war, miners in Banovici had told us they were worried about privatisation but that everything depended on government. The government would decide. The miners could only wait and watch. A year later they were neither waiting nor watching. A letter was sent to the government demanding answers to the miners' demands concerning the future of the industry. The union council agreed that if no reply was forthcoming they would tell the government they no longer recognised its' authority.

Our discussion with Fikret Suljic returned to the idea of an international miners' conference. As a first step, Fikret proposed that Dave Temple, an ex-miner and Workers Aid supporter, should visit Bosnia to inform miners about the experiences of the British miners strike, to help strengthen their resistance to privatisation.

A woman's search for truth

" July 11th, 1997. I was in Tuzla for the second anniversary of the massacre of Srebrenica. The surviving women had planned to visit the mass grave of their menfolk in Djulici, to lay flowers there and to pray. Four of us from England and nine from Spain gathered together with seventy women in an office that Friday morning. We had to cross into a Serbian nationalist area. There was heated talk about what might happen. Just that day a British soldier had shot dead a Serb war criminal. The atmosphere was tense.

The UN then announced that they would provide no protection for the women. They said that the threat of ambush, of the stoning of these women by the Serbs at Djulici, was very real. Finally the march organisers decided not to go. But the flowers were arriving, and so were more women. The buses were waiting.

So despite everything we all decided to go without permission.

We walked first to the memorial to the seventy young people killed in Tuzla in May, 1995. It was there decided that only two from England and one from Spain should accompany the women because of the risks involved.

Un moment de l'actuació d'Adrià Puntí, ahir a la nit a Fontajau. Foto: LLUÍS ROMERO

El concert d'Ajuda Obrera a Bòsnia va reunir un públic nombrós i heterogeni

XAVIER CASTILLÓN
■ Girona.— Unes cinc mil persones van assistir ahir a la nit al concert organitzat per Ajuda Obrera a Bòsnia. El Pavelló de Fontajau es va anar omplint progressivament d'un públic tan heterogeni com el cartell de la nit, format per alguns dels grups més significatius del rock català recent. La presència de Lax'n'Busto, Gossos, Sopa de Cabra, Sui Generis, Kitsch o Adrià Puntí —que hi actuava per primera vegada en solitari en un gran recinte— i el molt raonable preu de l'entrada —500 pessetes— van ser els dos factors que van aconseguir relativitzar el fet que els universitaris es trobin en plena època d'exàmens, de manera que Fontajau presentava una més que bona imatge i Ajuda Obrera a Bòsnia va aconseguir fer una bona caixa per finançar la seva tasca humanitària.
Tal com estava previst, Wonder Fool Baby Dolls va obrir el macroconcert poc després de les 9 de la nit, donant pas d'aquesta manera a gairebé set hores de música en directe. Cada grup va actuar-hi durant gairebé vint minuts i, en general, es va aconseguir un ritme bastant àgil, tot els inevitables lapsus provocats pels canvis d'equip entre grup i grup. La màxima afluència de públic va tenir lloc, aproximadament, entre les 10 de la nit i les 2 de la matinada, hores entre les quals es van concentrar els grups més destacats de la vetllada. El balanç global d'aquesta iniciativa ha estat absolutament satisfactori.

Press coverage of Spanish Workers Aid concert raising money for the Srebrenica campaign

We drove out of Tuzla. It was terribly hot and thundery. There were two helicopters flying overhead. After thirty minutes' drive we were stopped by S-FOR troops. The women climbed out of the buses. They showed photographs of their dead menfolk. They spoke to the security forces and to the press. They cried. They argued. The tears they shed, their strong emotions, affected us all. These women, whose lives until two years ago had centred on their families and their homes, had lost everything. Most of all they had lost all their men; husbands, fathers, all gone. Who knew for sure? Who cared? Finally, we were allowed to move on.

We met a second blockade further on, and again the strong emotional power of these grieving women seemed to influence the forces, and we went forward. The helicopters stayed overhead. The security forces watched from distant hillsides. The heat of the day was oppressive. We were in isolated countryside, narrow roads, few people. ☛

The third time we were stopped, the S-FOR moved in their tanks and blocked our route. All the women got out and stated that they would walk rather than go back. We were apprehensive. We did not understand all that was being said. In a way it would be madness to follow them into this unknown, isolated territory. But here were seventy peaceful women, determined to march, carrying their banners past the tanks, past the local police, past the soldiers. Women who were saying, "You cannot stop us from visiting our menfolks' graves." Now they were quite unprotected as they walked. Despite all the threats, they were now alone. They continued their march undaunted by the voices of authority, undaunted by their own tears.

So we followed them. I felt so strongly that we could not watch them walk away from us. We were with them, and would stay with them. We walked a long way along a dusty country road through a deep-sided valley. The helicopter clattered noisily. All else was still.

Suddenly we met barbed wire across the road. The Russian soldiers of S-FOR stood behind it. Again the women demanded their right to lay their flowers on the graves at Djulici. Again there were arguments and tears. Many of the older women were now tired and sat down, searching for a piece of shade. Finally they were allowed through. The buses were brought forward and were searched thoroughly. Then the women were allowed through two at a time and were also searched by the soldiers. This became another emotional situation. The scene reminded them of what had happened at Srebrenica on July 11th, 1995.

Workers Aid and Ayuda Obrera members at the Women of Srebrenica office, Tuzla

We got on the buses at long last and drove off up the road into the forest. The women pointed out to me a place where six hundred men had been killed. We arrived at Nezuci which has a memorial to twenty Bosnian soldiers buried there. The women sat around it and prayed. They read the Koran and laid flowers on the graves. But these were not the graves of their loved ones. Djulici was forbidden to them that day. People from the village joined us and we stayed for half an hour.

We then drove on to yet another village, where there was a gathering of people including the Mayor of Srebrenica. Here several speeches were made. Although I didn't understand the words, I understood the tears and sadness of these women. Some were sitting, some standing, the banners were held up for all to see. We shared their outpourings of grief, but how

can we even begin to understand the horrendous tragedies that they have been suffering, as they seek to find the truth of what happened to the ten thousand men and boys on that dreadful day two years ago. We can only begin to imagine the horrors that are being suffered still in Bosnia, and we must never forget them.

Finally the villagers served us tea and food. We climbed back into our buses and drove back to Tuzla. The two helicopters flew back to their base. Who had they been protecting? Finally the women accepted that they had not reached Djulici. Not that day anyway. But perhaps one day soon the whole world will get there, and will know the truth of Bosnia. „

NASEEM AKHTAR

During the war, Workers Aid members often stayed with an engineering worker in Tuzla. He and his wife both proudly described themselves as socialists but they asked why Workers Aid delivered most of its' aid to the unions. They knew we got little support from the unions in Europe and in the war the unions in Tuzla were far from being a prominent organisation. The Town Hall, the Tuzla Civic Association, the local army commanders and above all, workers on the front lines seemed to be the centre of organising resistance to the fascists. We were 'Workers Aid', not 'Union Aid', so why didn't we just organise help from workers to workers.

The question was repeated by many of our supporters in Britain who were not trade unionists. Most of our appeals to the unions fell on deaf ears, so why try to flog a dead horse? Support was coming from people outside the unions so why did Workers Aid continue to emphasis the trade unions?

This question began to be answered from Bosnia itself. Following the truce, the alliance within Bosnia that had fought the Croat and Serb nationalists began to split into its' constituent parts. SDA politicians busied themselves with administering their state for Muslims and, like all politicians in the region, with the business of making money by greasing the path of their visitors from western banks and enterprises. Even the anti-nationalist Bosnian social democrats, while still holding out the idea of a united Bosnia, saw no other way forward for society except through the free market, the very force that had driven the destruction of their society.

Bosnian society had a history and the present war was not the first attempt to destroy it. The whole century had been a conflict between unity and division, with the workers' struggles for a better life the driving force for unity. In the recent war they had been the first people at the front and it was they who made the greatest sacrifices. The rich and powerful had helped their families get out of Bosnia and, while workers had starved, a new breed of entrepreneurs had grown rich on war profiteering.

Everyone who sought personal gain tried to bury the real history of Bosnia, above all the fact that without the revolutionary Partisans, multi-ethnic society would not have sur-vived World War II. They tried to hide this past. There were too many experiences there that could threaten the new schemes to enrich the few and impoverish the majority. The thousand and one lessons that previous generations had learned in defeat and victory could assist Bosnian working people to overcome the problems that now confronted them. These experiences of mass action were contained not just in books but within the workers' own organisations. In war the working people of Tuzla and other towns tried to defend the most basic legacy of the partisans – workers' unity. As soon as war stopped they turned their attention to restoring everything that had flowed from this unity: free education and health care, employment rights and a decent life. Inevitably they sought to do it through their own organisations, above all through trade unions which have always been the basic organisation of working people defending their rights. This was happening not just in Tuzla but right across ex-Yugoslavia. In some cases the people's fighting spirit could be expressed through existing organisations, like the Bosnian miners' union. In other cases the old organisations proved to be a barrier and had to be transformed or even discarded. This was already happening in Serbia where people were breaking free from the state controlled unions and organising new unions.

This problem of unions becoming bureaucratic is true both for ex-Yugoslavia and Britain, but despite this, in both places the unions embody a certain history. World-wide it has been through trade unions that people have turned their fighting spirit into collective action. So when Workers Aid continued to direct its' work towards the British unions, it wasn't only that they contained eight million members and were therefore a potentially big source of support, or that the Bosnian unions could help with organising aid distribution more directly. Within union ranks was the collective history of struggles, vital to build an effective movement of solidarity with Bosnia. In the course of our campaign it became clear that the European trade unions and all the workers' political parties, organisations that had their origins in these past battles of working people, were now incapable of articulating this history. The TUC and individual unions appeared to have nothing to do with the Bosnian tragedy. In fact they played an indispensable role during the war in ensuring that the horror felt by people throughout society was never translated into action by the workers' movement. The union and Labour bureaucracy imprisoned this past and strangled every effort to revive it. Seventy years earlier a Bosnian miner sentenced to death had been saved when his plight touched miners across the continent and their unions turned these feelings into organised protest. In the 1990s, the union leaders did the opposite.

Student Aid for Bosnia

Student Aid welcomes support from all students and, apart from the obvious exclusion of racists and fascists, is happy to include any student in our work, regardless of political outlook.

Much of our work has been focussed on the sending of material aid through our convoys. However, Student Aid was not formed to simply send aid. The people of BiH only needed this kind of support because of the actions of the Serbian nationalists and others who sought to destroy Bosnia-Herzegovina to further their goal of 'ethnically' pure states.

For us the purpose of taking aid has been to strengthen those forces fighting for a united, multi-ethnic BiH, both inside and outside the country.

What We Stand For

- An undivided, multi-ethnic BiH within its pre-war boundaries
- The right of all refugees, whatever their nationality, to return to their homes
- The right of all refugees to asylum from 'ethnic cleansing' and political persecution - no forced repatriation
- The prosecution of all war criminals

Gun-running in the NUT

" In Haringey National Union of Teachers (NUT) Association we invited Vaughan Thomas, a local bus driver and TGWU shop steward, to speak about his experiences on an early WAB convoy. Before Vaughan spoke the meeting agreed a donation of £50 to Workers Aid. The only person to vote against it was Pat Turnbull, a member of the Broad Left, a caucus led by the Communist Party (Morning Star) within the NUT. After Vaughan's contribution, the secretary of the Association, Tony Brockman, recently elected to the NUT's National Executive, asked him whether the convoys were purely humanitarian or had a political purpose? Vaughan gave an honest account of Workers Aid aims and added that he believed the Bosnians had a right to defend themselves. Following this meeting I was told there was a rumour circulating in the local Labour Party that Workers Aid was gun-running to Bosnia!!

Workers Aid never received the £50 despite correspondence and the gun-running slander became well known.

When the International Department of the NUT finally agreed to meet a trade union delegation from Tuzla in the spring of 1995, the outcome of the meeting was very positive, despite Broad Left member Malcolm Horne's demands to see photographs proving no guns were transported on the convoys! The NUT agreed to send a circular to all associations inviting financial contributions to a fund which would be used to buy educational equipment for the Trade Union convoy leaving in July 1995.

In July, the trade union convoy delivered this educational aid. On the way back we discussed the problems of raising Bosnia in the British trade unions with fellow convoy member Tony Samphier, from the National Union of Journalists. He submitted an article on the convoy to *The Teacher*, the NUT magazine which every member receives. It was published – an important achievement – but with all reference to Workers Aid taken out. It was printed beside an advertisement for Feed the Children, the organisation supported by the TUC. And who edits *The Teacher*? None other than Tony Brockman, secretary of Haringey Teachers Association. "

PHIL EDWARDS, East London Teachers Association

With the end of the war the role of the union leaders in events became even clearer. Alongside the financial advisors and speculators who descended on Sarajevo were delegations from British and European trade unions. In 1996, the biggest British trade union, UNISON, sent two delegations to Bosnia. During the war they had never even replied to appeal letters sent by Bosnian trade unions, let alone set foot in the country. Now they arrived with fine speeches of support to rebuild Bosnian trade unions. However their offer to the President of the electricity supply union in Sarajevo to advise him over privatisation plans showed their real role; as the new missionaries for a colonial free market invasion. Emilio Gabaglio, European TUC President, made clear to Bosnian union representatives that they had to operate within the framework of the Dayton agreement, within the framework of capitalism.

The British unions worked against a united Bosnia, both during and after the war. But who do these organisations and their history belong to? Without a fight to change their policies we would have been accepting that past experiences would remain forever cut-off from a new generation of people trying to change the world. We would have had to re-invent the wheel. Meanwhile, the union bureaucrats, speaking in the name of those past struggles and utilising all the accumulated resources, would continue their collaboration with the restoration of capitalism in Bosnia. British workers clearly have to transform their present organisations in order to be able to act in defence of their own and others' rights. We tried and are still trying to help that process. After a few visits the Bosnian miners also began to see how things stood. Speaking at a meeting called by the Liverpool Dockers, Fikret Suljic, called upon British workers to do everything possible to win a victory for the dockers and to get rid of the union bureaucrats who refused to support them.

In December 1996, members of Workers Aid and Ayuda Obrera held meetings with women who had been driven from Srebrenica. Their demands for truth and justice, so simple and basic, were a challenge to all the Dayton signatories. Their demand for the truth about the massacre pointed the finger at Milosevic, at the Dutch UN troops and at the UN and the superpowers. The women wanted the mass graves exhumed so that they could know for sure who had died. The NATO troops found excuse after excuse to avoid a thorough uncovering of graves. The women had to live in continuous uncertainty. They knew thousands had been killed, but was their husband or their son one of them, or had they somehow survived? They needed to know.

Women of Srebenica, Tuzla   **September 15th, 1996**

To all the women of the world

July 11th, 1996 was the first anniversary of the suffering in Srebrenica. Many women around the world responded to our appeal to mark that day of sorrow and hopelessness. We are grateful for that support. We must continue searching for the truth about the fate of all our relatives who disappeared.

At our meeting on the July 11th, 1996 we restated our views and our demands.

• Srebrenica was a UN safe haven.

• Srebrenica was betrayed.

• Srebrenica is a place where the conscience of humanity collapsed.

• Many people now live in Srebrenica who never lived there before. Their presence is an attempt to hide the crimes committed by others. Srebrenica is the sin of the whole world.

Because of the genocide of the people of Srebrenica we demand:

1. The Truth – the truth of the fate of our dearest loved ones.

2. Punishment – for all who committed these crimes. Punishment – for all those who did nothing to stop these crimes.

3. We demand – that people who did not live in Srebrenica before July 1995 leave and that all original inhabitants are able to return home.

4. We demand – that Srebrenica and Potocari are designated as monuments, dedicated to the victims, as a warning to the whole world. The town must become a World Anti-War Centre.

5. We demand – that all the victims of genocide be buried in the territory of the UN safe haven of Srebrenica so that the result of this protection can be seen. Then this cemetery can be protected as a monument for innocent victims of genocide in the heart of Europe at the beginning of the 21st Century.

6. We demand and hope that Srebrenica never happens to anyone else, that Srebrenica is never forgotten and that Srebrenica is never repeated.

These are our demands. We will persist in our search for the truth about our loved ones and punishment for the criminals. In this we need your support.

Women of Srebrenica

Similarly, the women's demand to be allowed home to Srebrenica challenged all the politicians who had decided on carving up Bosnia and on which people could live where.

In March 1997, three of the women went on a speaking tour of Spain organised by Ayuda Obrera. In November, four people from Srebrenica came to Britain where meetings had been organised round the country by Workers Aid and Bosnia Solidarity Campaign.

The refusal of these women to be silenced about what happened in Srebrenica highlights the farce surrounding the war crimes tribunal at the Hague. Those responsible for the biggest massacre of the war cannot be brought to trial because they are the Dayton signatories – the governments of Britain, France, the US, Serbia, Croatia and the UN itself.

The women, mostly now refugees in Tuzla, have organised themselves and elected their own committee to pursue their demands. Even from exile they stood candidates in the local elections for Srebrenica and won the majority of the seats on the council. But who is going to oversee their return, to allow them to take control of their town? We will continue to help the women make their voices heard. The most monstrous crime of modern European history must not be swept under the carpet in the interests of reconciliation, reconstruction and profit.

Almasa Alic of the Women of Srebrenica, speaking at the University of London

Former UN Special representative, Yasushi Akashi, and General Sir Michael Rose; both are accused by the Women of Srebrenica of complicity in genocide

Edinburgh public meeting, Women of Srebrenica speaking tour

Justice in The Hague

The first sentence passed by the International Tribunal in the Hague for crimes against humanity was upon the young Bosnian Croat, Drazen Erdemovic. Under orders, he had carried out the massacre of civilians in Srebrenica and was sentenced to ten years in prison. This expresses the hypocrisy of the International Tribunal. Its'' role is to soothe the legitimate feelings of world public opinion over the horrors committed in Bosnia while doing exactly what the leaders of the United Nations tell it to do.

Bosnia is full of Serb or Croat fascist criminals. They go about freely under the noses of the international police. Some of them have become respectable MPs or functionaries of a state which is in tatters and whose very existence depends on the whim of foreigners. But the tribunal has only been able to lay its' hands on a few junior people. None of the big figures who actually ordered the genocide are on trial.

Erdemovic, like so many others, was suddenly mobilised into Karadzic's army. Nobody explained what the war was about or asked his opinion of it. As a Croat in Serb-held territory he was sent to fight against Muslims. Refusal would have exposed him to real danger. In a fascist army, the terror waged against the individual will is absolute.

Ratko Mladic gathered together these non-Serb elements in the chaos of war and organised a special unit to carry out raids behind Bosnian Army lines. Many of these Bosnian Croats must have weighed their words carefully when offered this assignment. What was worse, to risk immediate death or to put off the evil day? But once they were on a mission, the danger was doubled. The Serbs treated them as renegades because they were not Serbs. Sent into enemy territory, they faced immediate execution as saboteurs if caught by the Bosnian Army. Heads you win, tails I lose.

Erdemovic's unit survived. It was then ordered to carry out the butchery in Srebrenica. Ratko Mladic wanted to get rid of the sabotage unit by plunging them up to their necks in crimes. Nobody would escape guilt. To refuse to shoot would simply be to choose a place alongside the Muslims at the bullet-scarred wall.

What saved Erdemovic's life was his testimony given to a British journalist in return for an escape route to The Hague, his only refuge. It is the most terrible account of Serb fascist barbarism. Erdemovic tells of an old Muslim, weeping with fear, who begged him to save his life, 'because he had often helped Serbs'.

Erdemovic gave him a cigarette, sat down next to him. While the old man continued begging, he wondered what on earth to do with the old man and with himself. But his platoon commander was a character steeped in blood whose name isn't even mentioned by the court in The Hague. He brutally took the old man from Erdemovic, took the cigarette off the old man and thrust him into line with the others.

Do these professional servants of justice at The Hague have any human feeling? They had poor Erdemovic in their hands for six months. They have all the factual documentation, all the political, diplomatic and military data on the fall of Srebrenica. They cannot conceive of the tragic dilemma of having to choose between your life and someone else's, someone who has done you no harm but whom you cannot save even by sacrificing your own life, a life caught in a vice between suicide and madness.

The judges did stop for one moment to wax tender about Erdemovic's tragic fate. Morally unable to drag him in front of the court, they stated he was suffering psychic trauma and was unfit to appear. This itself was a cowardly get-out, since Erdemovic was not mad. He decided to go to The Hague precisely to avoid going mad.

Then, several months later, he was declared healthy and fit to be tried as a war criminal. The political telephone lines hummed in the judges chambers and finely-drawn diplomatic appreciations were exchanged. Erdemovic was made out to be a dangerous, premeditated criminal. If the Tribunal showed him too much understanding and clemency it would bring itself into disrepute. So he got ten years in prison – not for war crimes, but to stop him testifying for another ten years. This sentence has the same significance as Mladic's army digging up the mass graves and hiding the bodies in the woods. Its' aim is to hide the truth about Srebrenica.

Erdemovic is sentenced to ten years in prison, half of what Radovan Karadzic and Ratko Mladic could eventually face. Erdemovic gave himself up voluntarily for the sake of his conscience and to live at peace with himself. Karadzic and Mladic are still at large, play chess, thumb their noses insolently at the UN. Erdemovic accepted the sentence, sadly but respectfully. He accepted all the facts and made no attempt to diminish his own responsibility. But what about us citizens, as they like to call us? Do we have the right to remain silent in the face of such a cynical sentence?

Drazen Erdemovic was snatched out of his normal life and made the hostage of a vicious spiral he neither wanted nor clearly understood, which he had no strength to resist and where he was not responsible for any decisions. His fault was that he didn't know whether he was a Yugoslav, a Croat or a Bosnian, because like twenty million Yugoslavs he was confused.

He has been locked up to stop him talking, to stop his accusations being published in book form, to stop a film about it being made and going around the world, in brief, to bury the truth about Srebrenica.

The prosecution says he killed about seventy people as part of a firing squad. But under what conditions? Could he escape doing it? Almost all the current leaders of ex-Yugoslav republics agreed to sending federal troops to Kosova in 1988, the real prelude to the wars that followed. One after the other the political and military leaders of the former Yugoslavia implicitly or openly recognised that they had not realised what was at stake, that they had been tricked by Milosevic, that they were honest but naive. How could a twenty year old Bosnian youth be less naive, better educated and more far-sighted than all these graduates of military colleges or universities? The current Yugoslav chief of staff, General Perisic, decided to go ahead with the destruction of Mostar, and he allowed his well-known colleague, the Croat General Praljak, to finish it off. Neither of them has been prosecuted by the tribunal.

The tribunal in The Hague should have released Erdemovic and made his whole testimony a book of accusation against those who really instigated the war. Erdemovic was a cog in an insane machine.

Class justice is not as complicated as it likes to appear. They decided not to release Drazen Erdemovic since he would continue his struggle for truth, but nor could they give him the maximum twenty years because, horror of horrors, what would they do if they were brought Karadzic and Mladic? So they split the difference. It is as simple as that. They cut a deal on the justice market the way they do in the stock exchange.

If Erdemovic deserves ten years, what do Karadzic and Mladic deserve? A thousand times more at least.

To be true and lasting, the peace in Bosnia needs to deal leniently with the minor actors in the war and to punish ferociously its' instigators and those who gave the orders for the destruction and the massacres. For a start Karadzic and Mladic need to be tried, in Sarajevo itself and in public. Their heads are the minimum price to pay for any justice and peace. And these two are not the only ones.

The justice in The Hague stands on its' head with its' feet in the air, hypocritical to its' very foundations. A banner carried on an anti-war march in Belgrade made me realise that the only people entitled to prosecute and punish Serb criminals were those Serbs who had refused to let their name be besmirched by the crimes committed in Bosnia. The banner read:

'Forget The Hague! We will judge you!'

RADOSLAV PAVLOVIC, December, 1996

Searching for the lost boys

This week the 'Women of Srebrenica' are on a tour of Britain; at the same time, two films focusing on the experiences of children of the Bosnian capital are being released. **Jonathan Steele** on the massacres that will not go away

Horrors are easily forgotten and the war in Bosnia is more easily forgotten than most. So it is an irony that this month's London Film Festival has been treated to two films focusing on true episodes involving children in the Bosnian capital. Michael Winterbottom's Welcome to Sarajevo, a fictional account based on the adoption of a Bosnian child by ITN reporter Michael Nicholson, and Bosnian director Ademir Kenovic's Perfect Circle, turn the trauma of war in the former Yugoslavia into powerful fiction.

Yet neither is as desperate or painful as the memory which the survivors — who call themselves simply the Women of Srebrenica — have brought here on a two-week speaking tour, the first to this country. They have come to Britain with a mission — to persuade the British public and its government to help them find the truth, and will be meeting with a Foreign Office minister to press their case.

Although the killings of civilians in eastern Bosnia have been called "Europe's worst massacre since the second world war", the Women of Srebrenica still refuse to accept the

7,000 missing people are dead. "My two boys said they would go to the mountains, and try to reach the government-held town of Tuzla," says Kada Aljic-Pasic, 45, as she haltingly recalls the day in July 1995 when Srebrenica fell to the Bosnian Serb army after three years of siege. "I

Kada Aljic-Pasic (in front) and Almasa Alic, two 'Women of Srebrenica' who lost their sons
PHOTOGRAPH: GARRY WEASER

The Guardian, 18/11/97. The visit by the women from Srebrenica attracted coverage on CNN, Breakfast News, BBC Radio 4 and several national newspapers

The Edinburgh audience

Women in struggle

Silence has seldom seemed so eloquent. Kada Aljic-Pasic had come across Europe from the south-east to the north-west; from Bosnia-Herzegovina to Scotland. For two weeks she travelled through England, explaining why she, and her colleagues, had come: they needed to know whether or not their menfolk were dead, and if they were – as seemed almost inevitable – to find their graves and mourn. They wanted the British government, and the British people, to help.

But, at the last meeting of the tour, before 100 people or more in the Victorian grandeur of Edinburgh's City Chambers, Kada, aged forty-five, but now seeming older than her years, faced the microphone.......and could only quietly weep.

She had not seen her elderly father nor her two sons since July 1995, when United Nations forces, having lured the citizens of Srebrenica into the false security of being in a 'safe haven', stood back and allowed the Chetniks to round up, and almost certainly to murder, most of the men still in the town. Another mother, Almasa Alic, also in her mid-forties, sat beside Kada. Her two teenage sons had been in the 'safe haven': they "were left under UN protection," she said, "but they just handed them over. Our innocent children were taken away at the

orders of the Serb army....."

While Kada and Almasa, physically and emotionally exhausted, could say little publicly in Edinburgh, their stories did not go untold. Both in the City Chambers, then, late at night in the Cameo cinema where the Michael Winterbottom movie *Welcome to Sarajevo* had just opened, the third member of the Women of Srebrenica delegation, Emira Selimovic, acted as spokesperson.

A student and human rights worker, in her twenties and with near-perfect English, her father had been one of the 10,000 men and boys handed over by the UN to the Chetniks. She had left her studies at Sarajevo University to play her part in seeking justice from 'the international community'. All evening she spoke, handling questions ranging from the simplest to the most sophisticated.

In the City Chambers the meeting – under the title 'Women in Struggle' – had been broadened to include the Women of the Waterfront, the organisation of partners and friends of the Merseyside dockers, over two years into their fight against casualisation and arbitrary dismissal. Some who had come to hear the Bosnians seemed initially shocked by the link, particularly since a last-minute difficulty meant that the Mersey women were represented by a man.

But by the evening's end the idea of common struggle must have entered the consciousness of most people present, including many whose impulse for supporting the Women of Srebrenica was humanitarian or religious rather than political. And the dockers' fight, seen in the overwhelming context of the Bosnian tragedy, seemed heightened rather than diminished in its human significance.

At the cinema there was a different audience: over a hundred movie-goers, already engaged by a story based on the wartime rescue of a Sarajevan orphan by ITN reporter Michael Nicholson. Many were less informed than those at the public meeting: they questioned the Srebrenica women until the next showing of the movie could be postponed no longer.

My memories of watching them leave are of a bewildered young man trying, perhaps for the first time, to understand how to comfort a weeping girl-friend; and of the youthful management's tolerant nervousness as the exit to the foyer was blocked by people determined to donate and sign the mailing-list. Rather than insist that they go outside, the front-of-house man speeded up the process by sending off for extra paper and more pens.

Terry Brotherstone

The Workers Aid banner: Necemo Etnicko Razdvajanje! Dole fasizam!

Disparities within former-Yugoslavia

Some people on the left supported Milosevic because he was trying to hold 'socialist Yugoslavia' together. But the table below shows how 'socialist Yugoslavia' meant different things to different people. The massive disparities between the various republics and regions, disparities which grew during forty-five years of 'socialism', give the lie to those nostalgic for the past without any critical attitude. The most glaringly exploited region in former-Yugoslavia was Kosova which, despite its valuable mineral resources, remained a polluted source of raw materials and its' Albanian population a colonised people. In 1989, Kosovan demonstrators shouted the slogan "Kosova works – Belgrade grows!"

	Population	Per capita social product	Unemployment
Yugoslavia	100	100	16.2
Slovenia	8.1	212	1.7
Croatia	19.8	123	7.7
Serbia	24.6	93	17.7
Kosova	8.3	31	55.9
Vojvodina	8.6	119	15.2
Bosnia-Herzegovina	18.9	74	23.9
Montenegro	2.8	78	24.5
Macedonia	8.9	66	27.0

Compiled from Harold Lydall, *Yugoslavia in Crisis* and *Yugoslavia Annual Statistics for 1991*. All figures percentages.

Tuzla   December 10th, 1997

Dear Friends,

The truth about the enormous tragedy taking place in Bosnia was so slow to reach the outside world. It was Workers Aid who started international solidarity action for Bosnia. By spreading information about our principles of living together in multi-ethnic and multi-cultural BiH you strengthened our fight against nationalism and the division of BiH.

You risked your lives to help us with convoys of food and school equipment. Through our discussions you came to understand our problems and on your return did your best to pass on our messages and appeals in Britain and throughout Europe.

Your campaign of solidarity and moral support through developing trade union links, demonstrations and publications enabled our voice to be heard in Europe. You have the right to be proud of what you did in 1993/94. You chose 'the right side' when the rest of the world didn't know who to support or did not want to take sides.

You have been our best friends. During the war you provided us with aid and moral support but, above all, you let us know we were not completely alone.

With your help we were able to organise the first ex-Yugoslav teachers' trade union conference in Budapest where teachers exchanged their concerns for the future of education in their counties. We were happy to meet like minded teachers, strong personalities who shared our rejection of every kind of nationalism. At the conference our aim was show the example of Tuzla, where people live and work together, and suggest that this model should be accepted and applied in other areas.

Today this model of life exists throughout our Tuzla-Podrinje Canton. We hope it will spread.

Thank you for all your support!

President of Independent
Trade Union of Secondary
Education

Mevlida Altumbabic
tel/fax++38775239541

President of Independent
Trade Union of Primary
Education

Murveta Stevic
tel/fax++38775233607

In 1997, the Bosnian government, speaking on behalf of its US sponsors, advocated the privatisation of parts of the mining industry. 20,000 miners demanded it stay in public hands. In November, two Durham miners went to Tuzla and held a seminar with representatives from most of the Bosnian pits. They went over the history of the British miners, the 1984-85 strike and the war the British ruling class had waged against miners and their union. This report had the same purpose as our convoys. Both were aimed at helping the miners determine their own future. During this visit, definite plans were made for the international miners' conference.

In November, Resad Husagic, from the Tuzla miners, and Murveta Stevic, from the primary school teachers' union, came to Britain to address a conference organised by the Movement for Socialism. At the conference, Resad Husagic spoke about the problems facing the working class in Bosnia, about the growing determination of workers not to be used as cheap labour and he announced that the Bosnian miners would host an international workers' conference in 1998. Finally, on behalf of his union, he thanked Workers Aid for everything they had done, for the aid they had brought in desperate times, but even more for the ideas they had spoken about in Bosnia, the vision of an international working class movement that would help all those in need.

For us, the two things could not be separated. We did not take food and just happen to have these ideas. The convoys and the proposals we made to the miners both came from a conviction that working class action to stop a new rise of fascism was necessary and possible.

Autonomous Union of Coalminers of BiH   November 20th, 1997

An international workers' conference to discuss the defence of social property and the problems of unemployment and casual labour – March 14-15th, 1998, Tuzla, Bosnia.

Dear Friends and Comrades,

On behalf of all Bosnian miners and their families we invite you to a conference to discuss the problems of privatisation, unemployment and casual labour.

Nationalist aggression in Bosnia and ex-Yugoslavia has left the working class with very great problems. Industries are destroyed. Throughout the region there is very high unemployment. Working people are impoverished and their rights are ignored. Once again in war, miners and workers have fought for the unity of the working class, regardless of their national identities and especially against any ethnic division.

Now, in Bosnia, politicians and financiers want to privatise our socially owned coal mines and other industries. With the information our union has from fellow miners in Britain and around the world we are convinced that this privatisation is not in the interests of our miners. We can only see it adding to the unemployment and use of casual labour that is now a worldwide problem. Nor will it lead to a sensible use of our natural resources.

We are aware that as miners in Bosnia we will find it very difficult to stop these privatisation plans by ourselves. We need to plan the future of the mining industry in co-operation with working people across Europe in a way that will benefit people. We also know that it is not only in Bosnia that people are facing these problems. It is for this reason that we hope you will send representatives to this conference, where we as working people can seek solutions to our common problems.

Miners' Greetings!
RESAD HUSAGIC
Secretary, Tuzla Miners

The 1945 Yalta deal struck between Moscow, London and Washington did more than isolate and curb the Partisan revolution in Yugoslavia. A line was drawn between east and west and the people of Europe, above all the working class, were divided and suppressed. During the next four decades, the idea of the working class movement transforming society, of the mass of people taking direct, collective control of their lives, was confined to the outer fringes of the labour movement, excluded by both the Stalinist and Labour bureaucrats who, in different ways, undermined every grassroots, working class initiative. Then, in the 1980s, social upheavals in eastern Europe shattered the tyrannical rule of the 'communists'. The break-up of the regimes that had grown out of Stalin's despotism certainly plunged the world into confusion and chaos, but the demise of regimes which had oppressed the working class meant a new opportunity for people to take events into their own hands.

The response to the proposal for a Workers Aid convoy showed the extent of this opportunity. Thousands of people, with very different ideas, helped turn a vision of working class action into a living movement. Solidarity broke from the confines of empty resolutions or exchange visits of bureaucrats, and became practical support to our fellow people. It was a sign that the barrier between east and west had come down.

Getting convoys through the madness of endless customs' checks and passport controls, seeing the desperate plight of refugees shut out from 'Fortress Europe', only reinforced our desire for a Europe and a world without borders, where people could come and go as they pleased. European leaders speak loudly and at length about their 'united Europe' but when it came to Bosnia every one of them supported division through fascist mass murder. A Tuzla MP was right when he wrote (see page 68), "perhaps a united Europe's last hope is this city in northern Bosnia that continues to resist the attacks of national fascism." At stake in Bosnia is the future of a humanity free from division.

In the midst of the convoy campaign came the news of mass starvation in Somalia. Some Bosnian refugees collecting food for a convoy inside a supermarket said that we should be sending food to Somalia. People there were in an even more wretched state than in Bosnia. Our forces were too small to even reach different towns in Bosnia, let alone Somalia, but this global solidarity amongst people is what is needed.

There is no end to this narrative. As we write this last page we are busy translating the invitation letter for the Tuzla conference into many different languages. News is already coming in of delegations coming from Russia, Hungary, South Africa, Spain, Greece and the UK and we would certainly welcome further support from anyone reading this book. In Bosnia the miners are meeting with other unions to ask them to participate in the conference. It has changed from being simply a discussion amongst miners into a conference for all workers to talk about the problems of privatisation, casual labour and unemployment – one step towards creating the kind of movement in the working class that can begin to seek solutions to these problems of people in Europe, in Somalia, of people everywhere.

The nationalists set out to destroy the Yugoslav working class. The British government gave them assistance and at this moment they probably feel they have done pretty well. Anyone with a feel for history can see they have failed. Far from destroying the Yugoslav working class they have set loose the real spirit of the Partisans, a spirit which over the years became more and more buried under a bureaucratic apparatus. This spirit is not only growing in Bosnia. It is an inspiration to thousands like us around the world who have had enough of a world of national boundaries and ethnic divisions. As Dot Gibson wrote when she first arrived in Tuzla after our nine month battle to get through the siege, "We will show them that there *is* a greater force than the UN with all its high powered equipment, trucks and tanks."

Husinska buna

When fascists aimed the shell which inflicted the massacre in Tuzla's centre it was their recognition that their advance had been stopped; it was the revenge of those who now under-stood that they could not divide the town and would not be able to set foot in it again. Karadzic and Mladic had been obliged to try to settle other things before they could put the lid on Tuzla – force the capitulation of Sarajevo, conquer the capital, even if it was only half of it, and liquidate the three enclaves in the east, which had no real strategic significance but had to be removed because they were a living vexation for the 'ethnically cleansed' Greater Serbia. The courage of Sarajevo and the martyr-dom of Srebrenica brought about the failure of their ignoble blitzkrieg. Tuzla, workers' bastion, symbol of the multi-ethnic future of Bosnia-Herzegovina, was saved. If we made even the smallest contribution to the saving of Tuzla, by taking a modest amount of aid, by focussing interna-tional attention on this town, by helping its voice of resis-tance be heard, we do not take from this any personal reward. It was nothing but a simple duty.

At school in Serbia we were taught a history of the Yugoslav workers' movement that was emptied of workers and filled with Stalinists. Tito alone took up more than half the available space. Thus we heard of the 1920 Husina miners' revolt only very vaguely.

As part of the 1968 student movement in Belgrade that began to criticise the bureaucracy, I heard comrades sing the work-ers' song *Husinska buna* (*Husina uprising*). Deep, tragic strains, inspiring courage. The words are from recent times (the partisan war), but the melody comes from the deep reservoir of the international workers' movement. It is sung alongside the Marseillaise and the Internationale. Having only learned to sing it in my heart, I have lost the words and even the tune, but not the memory. If the working class in this region raises its' head again, this will be its' song.

In 1969 there was another mining dis-aster, at Kakanj, one of a series of such disasters in the 1960s. The bureaucracy flattered the miners in its propaganda, but did very little to improve their atrocious conditions of work or to remunerate them for their pain and sorrow. The miners were reduced to stealing bread from their workmates. They started a strike and took the train to Sarajevo to confront the government. The police stopped the train and made the miners disem-bark in open country. Our paper, STUDENT, wrote about it, and we organised in solidarity. Some comrades started a hunger strike. Our hearts were with the miners, but we did not know how to make any connection with them. The repression which descended on Belgrade in the spring of 1969 broke us up completely.

What we had been unable to do for the Bosnian miners in peace-time, I have tried to do in time of war. A small contri-bution from the working class in Serbia.

RADOSLAV PAVLOVIC

Other Workers Aid publications

The Games the UN play – In 1993 South African doctors put together the world's largest mobile hospital constructed in fifty ocean going containers. It was shipped to Split and from there it was due to go by road to Bosnia. This pamphlet, written by one of the accompanying doctors, details how the UN prevented the hospital leaving the docks and reaching people in desperate need. Price 50p

Bosnia: Solidarity not charity – A report of the 1995 trade union convoy to Tuzla written by National Union of Journalists' representative, Tony Samphier. Price £1

The Bosnian miners' rebellion of 1920 and our struggle for unity – an account of the Husina uprising and the trial of Jure Kerosevic. Price £1

Kosova: Apartheid in Europe – A report of the Workers' Aid visit to Kosova in December, 1996. Price £1

An outline of how the international trade union organisations supported the ethnic division of Bosnia-Herzegovina and the subsequent transfer of its' socially owned property to control by western banks – Following Dayton many delegations arrived in Sarajevo from the offices of the European trade unions, all offering help to Bosnian trade unions. What were they doing there? Why had they been absent throughout the war? Price £1

UNISON and the war in Bosnia. A correspondence – letters between Workers' Aid and Britain's biggest trade union concerning the activities of both organisations during the war. Price 50p

All available by post from Workers Aid for Bosnia, 35 Hilton Road, Leeds LS8 4HA. Cheques payable to 'WAB – Taking Sides'. Please add 50p postage.

We would welcome support from anyone reading this book. Workers Aid for Bosnia continues as a campaigning organisation and is currently fund-raising for a Bosnian edition of this book.